School-Based Curriculum Management and Lesson Study for Teacher Education

Tetsuo KURAMOTO
and Research Group

Publisher: MARUZEN PLANET CO., LTD.
Distributor: MARUZEN PUBLISHING CO., LTD.

School-Based Curriculum Management and Lesson Study for Teacher Education
Tetsuo KURAMOTO and Research Group

©2025 Tetsuo KURAMOTO
All rights reserved. No part of this book may be reproduced or transmitted in any form or by any means, electronic or mechanical, including photocopying, recording or by any information storage retrieval system, without the prior written permission of the copyright owner.

The original English language edition published by Maruzen Planet Co., Ltd., TOKYO.

PRINTED IN JAPAN

Contents

Foreword ·· 3
Mohammad Reza SARKAR ARANI, Nagoya University
1. Reconstruction of instructional design through curriculum management   3
2. Curriculum management from the perspective of transnational lesson study   4
3. Revising curriculum and inspiring student learning process across-cultures   5
   3-1. The English in comparison with the French   5
   3-2. The Japanese in comparison with the French and English   6
4. Exploring appropriate approaches to research on curricular activities   6

Introduction
School-Based Curriculum Management for Teacher Education: The Future Development of
Curriculum Study and Lesson Study ·· 11
Tetsuo KURAMOTO, Shizuoka University of Art and Culture
1. Theory and Practice of School-Based Curriculum Management (SBCM)   11
   1-1. School-Based Curriculum Management—From a theoretical perspective   11
   1-2. School-Based Curriculum Management—a practical and engaging approach   13
2. What is Curriculum Study and Pedagogical Content Knowledge (PCK)?   14
3. School-Based Curriculum Study and Lesson Study—The Perspective of SBCM—   15
4. Pedagogical Research Question—First, Second, and Third Circles—   17
5. The Structure of School-Based Curriculum Management and Lesson Study   18

Part 1.
Illuminating International Research of Curriculum Study and Lesson Study for Teaching Training Development

Chapter 1
The Literature Review: Research on School-Based Curriculum Management Overseas ·········· 27
Tetsuo KURAMOTO, Shizuoka University of Art and Culture
1. Purpose of the School-Based Curriculum Management Research   27
2. Reviewed Previous Research Regarding School-Based Curriculum Management   29
   2-1. School-Based Curriculum Management in Curriculum Development   30
   2-2. School-Based Curriculum Management in the relationship between organizational
      improvement theory and systems theory   30
   2-3. School-Based Curriculum Management in School Improvement   31
   2-4. School-Based Management and Effective Schools   32
   2-5. School-Based Curriculum Management in School Culture and Leadership   33
3. School-Based Curriculum Management Components and School Improvement   34
4. School-Based Curriculum Management for School/Community Improvement from the
   Perspective of Curriculum Leadership   36
5. Conclusion   37

Chapter 2

Exploring Service-Learning SOFAR Model in School-Based Curriculum Management: Inspiring Hope for Community Impact ·······································41

Tetsuo KURAMOTO, Shizuoka University of Art and Culture

1. Introduction   41
   1-1. Service-Learning beginnings   41
2. SOFAR Model from Educational Management and Educational Methodology   44
   2-1. SOFAR model and SBCM   44
   2-2. The significance of the SOFAR model in School-Based Curriculum Management (SBCM)   44
3. School Curriculum Development and the SOFAR Model—School-Based Service-Learning Study—   45
4. The SOFAR Model from SBCM and Transformative Curriculum Leadership (TCL)   47
   4-1. SBCM and Transformative Curriculum Leadership (TCL)   47
   4-2. SBCM & Transformative Curriculum Leadership (TCL) and the SOFAR model: a vision for Transformation   48
5. The 1st, 2nd, and 3rd Circle of SBCM & SOFAR Model   49
   5-1. The 1st circle of the SBCM & SOFAR model   49
   5-2. The 2nd circle of the SBCM & SOFAR model   50
   5-3. The 3rd circle of the SBCM & SOFAR model   51
6. Conclusion—The Structure of School-Based Service-Learning Curriculum Management—   51

Chapter 3

Applying Variation Theory for Instructional Design: Learning Study in Hong Kong ·············57

Eric C. K. CHENG, Yew Chung College of Early Childhood Education, Hong Kong/China

1. Introduction   57
2. Lesson Study   58
3. Learning Study   58
4. The Variation Theory of Learning   59
5. Procedures for Conducting Learning Study   60
6. Design the Pattern of Variation   63
7. A Learning Study Case: Principle of the Lever   64
8. How Does Learning Study Enable Teacher Learning?   64
9. Conclusion   66

Chapter 4

Contemporary Adaptations to Lesson Study in the Age of ICT ·······························69

Bruce LANDER, Matsuyama University

1. Introduction   69
2. The Impact of Technology on LS   69
3. Data Collection Process   69
4. Digital Teacher Collaboration   70
5. Evolving Tech Tools in the LS Classroom   70
6. Technology Assisted LS   71
7. Technology Awareness   72
8. LS Research Communities   73
9. Community of Practice   73
10. The Covid Impact on Education   74
11. A Catalyst for Change   75
12. Lowering the Reliance on Digital Imports   77

13. Knowhow is Crucial　77

14. AI in Education　77

15. Criticism of AI　78

16. Conclusion　78

Chapter 5

Interrelation of Lesson Study and Curriculum in Kazakhstan ··································81

Tavilya AKIMOVA, Center of Excellence, NIS, Kazakhstan

1. Understanding the Curriculum　81

2. State Compulsory Educational Standard (SCES) of Kazakhstan　83

3. Which Components of the Kazakhstani Curriculum Can Be Influenced by Lesson Study?　87

4. Conclusion　91

Chapter 6

On-the-Job-Training (OJT) for Novice Teachers in Aichi Prefecture ·······················93

Anthony RYAN, Nanzan University

1. Introduction　93

2. On-the-Job-Training (OJT) and Off-the-Job-Training (OffJT)　94

3. The Teacher Development System in Aichi Prefecture　96

4. The Novice Teacher OJT system　101

5. Conclusion　106

Chapter 7

Empowering Learners: Cultivating Autonomy in Japanese University English Education ········113

Jack RYAN, Shizuoka University of Art and Culture

1. Introduction　113

2. Learner Autonomy　113

3. Theoretical Frameworks & Learner Autonomy　114

　　3-1. Self-Determination Theory　114

　　3-2. Social Cognitive Theory　115

　　3-3. Other Perspectives　115

4. Challenges and Barriers to Learner Autonomy　116

5. Action Research　118

6. Strategies for Fostering Learner Autonomy　121

7. Discussion　122

Part 2.

Insights of Lesson Study in Teacher Education and Curriculum Development— Showcasing in the Context of Digital Transformation in Vietnam

Chapter 8

Exploring a Cost-Effective Online Teacher Training Model During the COVID-19 Pandemic: Insights from Vietnam ··127

Thanh-Nga NGUYEN, Ho Chi Minh City University of Education, Vietnam

Hoai-Nam NGUYEN, Hanoi National University of Education, Vietnam

Thanh-Trung TA, Ho Chi Minh City University of Education, Vietnam

Viet-Hai PHUNG, The University of Da Nang - University of Science and Education, Vietnam

Thuy-Quynh LE-THI, Ho Chi Minh City University of Education, Vietnam

1. Introduction　127

2. Theoretical Framework　128

2-1. Online continuing professional development　128
2-2. Online continuing professional development in Vietnam　129
2-3. CPD model evaluation　130
3. Aim and Research Questions　131
4. Results and Discussion　133
5. Conclusion and Practical Implications　137

Chapter 9
Curriculum Management in Teacher Education: Visualized in Vietnam with Lens of Digital
Transformation ···143
Nam-Phuong NGUYEN, Hanoi National University of Education, Vietnam
Van-Tu NGUYEN, Northeast Normal University, China
Quoc-Khanh MAI, Hanoi National University of Education, Vietnam
Trung-Kien PHAN, Hanoi Metropolitan University, Vietnam
1. Context of Teacher Education in Vietnam Amidst Digital Transformation　144
2. Teaching Competency and Its Development in Teacher Education in Vietnam within the
   Context of Digital Transformation　147
   2-1. Teaching competency and its development in teacher education　147
   2-2. Structure of teaching competence in teacher education in Vietnam　149
   2-3. The process of developing teaching competencies in teacher education within the context of
        digital transformation　151
   2-4. Recommendations for ensuring the implementation of the teaching competency
        development process in teacher training within the context of digital transformation　154
3. Conclusion　155

Chapter 10
Practice of 'Lesson Study' in Japan and Vietnam within the Contemporary Era ···············159
Dinh Chien TRAN, Hung Vuong University, Vietnam
Nam-Phuong NGUYEN, Hanoi National University of Education, Vietnam
1. Introduction　159
2. Research Results　161
   2-1. Aspects of the educational context contemporarily in Vietnam and the requirements for the
        move of teachers' professional development　161
   2-2. Lesson study in Japan: Lens and the practice　162
   2-3. Lesson study in Vietnam: Insights and the practice　164
   2-4. Designing demonstration lessons　166
3. Reflection　171
4. Recommendations to Lesson Study Delivery in Vietnam as Continuing Professional
   Development for In-Service Teachers　172
5. Conclusion　173

Chapter 11
Classroom Management: A Dimension of Lesson Study Encountered in Vietnam ··············179
Duc Giang NGUYEN, Hanoi National University of Education, Vietnam
Thi Phuong NGUYEN, Vietnam National University, Vietnam
Van Hai TA, National Academy of Educational Management, Vietnam
Minh-Yen NGUYEN, Scholar Vietnam Education System, Vietnam
1. Introduction　179
2. Overview of Classroom Management　181
   2-1. What is classroom management?　181

2-2. Structure of classroom management 182
3. Conclusion 189

Part 3.

School-Based Curriculum Management from the Perspective of Lesson Study and Teacher Education in Japan

Chapter 12
Creating Learning Communities for Home Economics Teachers and Knowledge Management: Under the Times of Rapid Change and Unpredictable Society ·····························193
Kaoru HORIUCHI, Yokohama National University
Sachiko NAKANISHI, Yokohama National University
1. The Social Background and the Improvement Trends of Teachers' Qualifications 193
2. Initiative-Taking Training Opportunities to Support "Teachers Who Continue to Learn" 194
3. Current Situation and Issues Surrounding Home Economics Teachers 195
4. Knowledge Creation Mechanism of Home Economics Teachers 196
5. Case Study: How Teachers Improve Their Competence with Knowledge Management Systems 198
6. Conclusion 199

Chapter 13
Strategizing and Developing Lesson Study through Systems Thinking Using the Curriculum Management Model ···203
Tomoko TAMURA, Osaka Kyoiku University
1. A Theoretical Model for School-Based Curriculum Management 203
   1-1. Examination of the preceding models 203
   1-2. Embracing systems thinking in School-Based Curriculum Management 204
   1-3 Elements and interconnections within the School-Based Curriculum Management 204
2. A Case Study of a High School—The Strategic Implementation Process of Lesson Studies using the CM-Model 207
   2-1. Initiating reform at X High School: Principal Y's strategic approaches and communication Challenges 208
   2-2. Analysis of the actual situation using the CM-Model 208
3. Second Half of the First Year of Reform—External Support Focusing on In-School Training 210
4. Second Year of Reform—Emphasizing the Role of Middle Leaders 213
5. Evolution of Faculty Perspectives 215
6. Implications from the Case Study 216
7. Integrating LS and SBCM 217

Chapter 14
Analysis of the School Improvement Process within the Framework of Curriculum Management ···221
Toshiya CHICHIBU, National Institute for Educational Policy Research
1. Introduction 221
2. School Improvement at T Junior High School 223
3. Dynamic Process of Curriculum Management 227
4. Direction of Training from a Curriculum Management Perspective 227

Chapter 15

A Study on the Future of Lesson Study in Japan— An Individual Lesson Plan Using
"Zaseki-hyo" ···229
Kiyotaka SAKAI, University of Teacher Education Fukuoka

1. Introduction   229
2. Achievements and challenges of Lesson Study in Japan   230
3. Lesson Study using a Seating Chart   231
    3-1. What is a seating chart?   231
    3-2. Today's significance of lesson study using a seating charts   232
    3-3. How to conduct a lesson study session using a seating chart   232
    3-4. Types of seating charts and points to consider in their preparation   233
    3-5. Extracted students and seating chart   235
    3-6. Seating chart and lesson plan   235
4. Practice and Consideration   236
    4-1. Student understanding and student learning   236
    4-2. Involvement, connection, and linkage   237
    4-3. Lesson study system   237
    4-4. Teachers as reflective practitioners   238
    4-5. Raising teachers' awareness for understanding students   239
    4-6. Use of seating chart for student understanding   239
    4-7. Study of the transformation of teachers' awareness   239
5. Conclusion   243

Chapter 16

Student Attitude Shifts within the International Baccalaureate Curriculum: Insights from
Student Narratives ··247
Yuya AKATSUKA, Sagami Women's University

1. Backgrounds   247
2. Learning Transition from Positivism to IB Constructivism   248
3. Methods   249
    3-1. Participants   249
    3-2. Methods   250
    3-3. Results and findings   250
        3-3-1. Embracing freedom in learning   250
        3-3-2. Transitioning to active learning   251
        3-3-3. Fostering a culture of caring   251
        3-3-4. Empowering independent learning   251
4. Conclusion   252

Chapter 17

Transformation of Student Consciousness through Service-Learning Focused on Hip Hop·····255
Takeshi BABA, Baiko Gakuin University

1. Introduction   255
2. What is Hip Hop?   256
    2-1. The background of Hip Hop's emergence and the essence of Hip Hop   256
    2-2. The spread of Hip Hop in Japan   257
3. Hip Hop Based Education   258
    3-1. What is Hip Hop Based Education?   258
    3-2. Theoretical background of Hip Hop Based Education   258
4. Practice   259

5. Analysis 261
   5-1. Data collection 261
   5-2. Analysis method 262
   5-3. Ethical considerations 262
   5-4. Analysis results 262
6. Considerations 265
   6-1. Question 1: How did the impression of "social contribution" change when "Hip Hop elements" were added? (How did it affect the motivation to take the course?) 265
   6-2. Question 2: How did the motivation to engage in the initiative change as a result of addressing local issues under the theme of "social contribution through Hip Hop" rather than just "beach cleaning" or "tourism promotion"? 265
   6-3. Question 3: How did the level of interest and concern regarding the marine litter issue and tourism attractiveness issues in Yamaguchi Prefecture change compared to before the start of the course? Also, do you think Hip Hop influenced this change? 266
   6-4. Question 4: How did your motivation towards the course change after taking classes that incorporated Hip Hop elements? 266
7. Conclusion 267

Chapter 18
Self-Analysis Sheet Methodology for Teacher Training ·······················273
Masataka ISOBE, Aichi University of Education
Toshifumi KAWAMURA, Nisshin Nishi Junior High School
Daisuke ITO, Akita Prefectural University

1. Introduction 273
2. The Need for Self-Regulation 274
   2-1. Educational practice using self-adjustment sheets 274
   2-2. Research subjects and methods 274
   2-3. Results and discussion of the study 275
       2-3-1. Qualitative analysis of teacher training using the "Self-Adjustment Sheets" 275
       2-3-2. Quantitative analysis of trends in self-regulation skills of teachers by age 276
   2-4. Summary and future prospects 277
3. The Coming of Society 5.0 278
   3-1. Proposed evaluation criteria table for information use skills 280

Chapter 19
Mentoring and the State of Teacher Training ··························289
Takehiro WAKIMOTO, Yokohama National University

1. Overview of This Chapter 289
2. History of Mentoring in Japanese School Settings 289
3. Team-Based Mentoring in Japan 290
4. Research on Effective Mentor Teams 293
5. Succession of Mentor Teams 297
6. Conclusion 299

Chapter 20
Reforms and Issues in Developing School Administrators through Administrative
Training in Japan—As a Fundamental Condition for School Curriculum and
Organizational Development— ··························301
Atsuko HOMMA, Doctoral program student, Hyogo University of Teacher Education
Yasuki OHNO, Hyogo University of Teacher Education

1. Introduction   301
2. Framework and Trends in School Administrators Training in Japan   302
   2-1. Basic framework for school administrators training in Japan   302
   2-2. Current trends in school administrators training led by boards of education   303
      2-2-1. Brief history of school administrator training after WWII   303
      2-2-2. Political / practical trends in school administrators training in the 2000s and 2010s   303
3. Current Conditions and Issues of School Administrator Training by Prefectural and Designated City Boards of Education   305
   3-1. Research design and prior literature   305
   3-2. Perspectives and methodology   305
   3-3. Findings from case studies   306
      3-3-1. Case 1: A Prefectural Board of Education (APBE)   306
      3-3-2. Case 2: B Prefectural Board of Education (BPBE)   308
      3-3-3. Case 3: C Prefectural Board of Education (CPBE)   308
      3-3-4. Case 4: D City Board of Education (DCBE)   310
   3-4. Consideration   312
   3-5. Further examination of changes in school administrator training before and after the institutionalization of "indicators" (Case 5)   313
4. Conclusion: Achievements and Issues of School Administrator Training   313
   4-1. Achievements   313
   4-2. Issues   315

Final Chapter
The Future of Research: School-Based Curriculum Management and Lesson Study for
Teacher Education ···319
Tetsuo KURAMOTO, Shizuoka University of Art and Culture
Mam CHANSEAN, National Institute of Education/Cambodia
Masataka ISOBE, Aichi University of Education
1. The Future Research Vision: School-Based Curriculum Study & Lesson Study (1st Circle, 2nd Circle, 3rd Circle)   319
2. Future Research Purpose No.1: School-Based Curriculum Management and Knowledge Management   322
3. The Future Research Purpose No.2: Empowering Educators and Administrators: Managing School-Based Curriculum and Lesson Study to Cultivate Intellectual Capital   324
4. Conclusion: School-Based Curriculum Management and Teacher Training by Using Intellectual Capital: Empowering Educators and Policymakers   325

Contributors ··333

Foreword
Mohammad Reza SARKAR ARANI, Nagoya University

The main research questions addressed in this cross-cultural study are how school-based curriculum management policy can lead to the identification of teachers collegial learning, and how the inter-professional perspective of teachers provides a supportive learning environment to reflect and transform their cultural script of teaching for mindful learning.

The authors of this book have highlighted lesson study as an approach of curriculum management in school to link theory and practice and expand professional development for school improvement through teachers collegial learning and school-university partnerships.

1. Reconstruction of instructional design through curriculum management
This study has been mainly conducted in Asia with more case-based study of cross-cultural approaches in quantitative and qualitative research on teaching, school-based curriculum management, and analyses of classroom practices and lesson analysis. It provides a reasonable way of identifying evidence of promoting critical and cultural discourse analysis in curriculum management, teachers learning, learning study, school improvement and teaching and learning by using case-based study and ethnographic research methods, comparative studies and cross-cultural lesson studies.

Since my early career, I have been fascinated with how to discover perspectives, ways of thinking and behaviors across different school cultures. For instance, a growing body of anthropological research findings were reviewed to identify a hypothesis that cultural notions and language effect the methods of verbal communication (oracy), thought and writing style (literacy). This creates different basic structures and logics of teaching and research traditions on teaching and school curriculum (e.g., Bloom, 1981; Prior & Lunsford, 2008; Miyamoto, 2008; Mason & Washington, 1992; Schwap, 1973). For instance, the author used a case-based study for this examination (e.g., Sarkar Arani, 2016). This case-based study was mainly employed as a qualitative research method for data collection, including cross-cultural lesson study meetings in Iran and Japan and semi-structured interviews with the participants of the meetings. In so doing, the study plans to make apparent the structure of meaning hidden in teaching process/lesson practice and hidden curriculum within schools. The structure is only revealed by comparing in the cultural context, through the eyes of educators having different socio-cultural perspectives.

In this book 'qualitative research' has developed further hypotheses about how the quality of teaching can be raised, and provides co-inquiry, self/group-reflection (technically, practically and critically) and collegial learning of teachers and researchers for generalizing findings in a case-based curriculum management study (Doyle, 1992b;

Manen, 1977; Lortie, 1975; Pinar et al., 1995; Ravitch, 2020). As Gruschka mentioned in his research, "we tried to understand the inner logic of teaching as a pedagogical project, that is, understanding instead of measurement, related to the pedagogical function and meaning of teaching" (2018, p.86). Therefore, the potential of contrasting perspectives in qualitative research in the school and classroom is the opportunity to shape and diversify thinking and viewing the inner logic of a lesson through different theoretical perspectives such as social cognitive theory and variation theory of learning. This means that, if researchers can work with educators of varying nationalities, the quality of research in curriculum studies and instruction in this manner can be further advanced (Marton, 2014; Bandura, 1986; Sarkar Arani et al., 2020; Sarkar Arani, 2022a; Tyler, 1949). Biesta also points out the significance of viewing the inner logic. He said that "[b]y looking through a different theoretical lens, we may also be able to understand problems that we did not understand before, or even see problems where we did not see them before" (Biesta, 2010, p.45). This is one of the reasons why this kind of inter-national, inter-professional, inter-language, inter-communication styles, and cross-cultural study on school-based curriculum management is necessary to develop an effective research method. Viewing the inner logic or theoretical lens "aims to make explicit the beliefs and values that underpin and shape teaching and learning in different cultural contexts, and which teachers are largely unaware of" (Elliott, 2016, p.279).

2. Curriculum management from the perspective of transnational lesson study

Practitioners and researchers living in the same school or academic culture share the culturally built perspectives. They grew up in the same culture and share the same values which shape their ways of thinking, attitudes, art of reasoning and behaviors. The culturally built values also shape the roles of their language involved in communication, social connection system, discourse analysis, service-learning and reasoning styles and way of thought in both verbal and non-verbal behaviors. Now we need to know what those perspectives are, on what values and beliefs they have developed, and how we can clarify those perspectives so that we may see more clearly what is happening in the schooling program, curriculum management, classroom activities and lesson praxis. Responding to them, it is necessary to conduct evidence-based study across different cultures to examine curricular activities and pedagogical phenomena in the school.

In this book curricular activities refers to policymaking; design and development; evaluation and implementation on different levels. Akker (2003) offers the next four distinctions: "system/society/nation/state (or macro) level, school/institution (or meso) level, classroom (or micro) level [and] individual/personal (or nano) level" (p.2). This book aims to help policymakers, practitioners and researchers discover a new theoretical framework for understanding curriculum phenomena and an alternative practical recipe for reconstructing the situation for a curriculum management platform in practice and through the above different four levels (macro, meso, micro and nano) transnationally.

The authors of this book, fortunately having different academic backgrounds, offer traditionally unique perspectives to analyze curriculum forms and typology on different levels. However, the authors in this volume try to focus more on curricular activities and the classroom phenomenon. They also try to expose, explore and establish the paths leading to more effective collaboration and dialogue between policymakers, researchers and practitioners in the various levels of the curriculum. Collaboration is important and effective, because unfortunately, we can't see our perspectives/eyes ourselves. The effectiveness can be observed and improved only in interaction with others. The quality of the perspectives is the so-called "the quality of lens" (Sarkar Arani, 2022a). They can more effectively analyze teachers' pedagogical reasoning and teaching scenarios in the classroom through their lens: perspectives. The educational scenarios, the so-called "teaching script" and "school curriculum," always flow in the socio-cultural situation, like in class, as fed from cultural resources and/or values and vision.

As Akker (2003) mentioned in his reviews, typology of curriculum can be represented as "[v]ision (rational or basic philosophy underlying a curriculum); [i]ntentions as specified in curriculum documents and/or material; [c]urriculum as interpreted by its users (especially teachers); [a]ctual process of teaching and learning (also: curriculum-in-action); [l]earning experiences as perceived by learners; [and] [r]esulting learning outcomes of learners" (p.3). By engaging 'school-based curriculum management,' the authors, having culturally different backgrounds, analyze the classroom phenomenon and curriculum management through their lens and reconstruct curricular activities in the school and the cultural foundation of learning (Doyle, 1992a; Li, 2012). That makes it possible to develop a more authentic theoretical framework suited for a particular curriculum that refers to a course of study or as Taba (1962) stated a "plan for learning" (quoted from Akker, 2003, p.2), which will be renewed by another culturally analytical conduct in practice. The curriculum management discourse also delivers various platforms for discussion and analyses curricular activities through combining a different language of curriculum; "the language of critique with the language of possibility" (Giroux, 1988, p.195).

3. Revising curriculum and inspiring student learning process across-cultures

This book provides cross-cultural studies that have the potential to offer contrasting perspectives for improving the quality of teaching, culturally understanding the meaning of curriculum management policy and the logic of teaching in depth. Therefore, it is crucial to consider the educational basis, research traditions on teaching, school culture and organization, cultural script of teaching and 'curriculum management' in practice. Let's look at an example to get a clearer understanding of this phenomena in detail.

3-1. The English in comparison with the French

Alexander (2005) examines how comparative enquiry reminds us of the language and communication system/style and cultural constructs of education, the so-called 'talk/ write pedagogy.' He concludes that "we have England's traditional and unchanging definition of the educational 'basics' as reading, writing and calculation, but emphatically not speaking. On the other hand, French schools celebrate the primacy of the spoken word. Here, literacy: there, language (p.5)." The England culture, according to Alexander, intentionally focuses more on 'dialogue' rather than 'conversation' based on a

Bakhtinian version of dialogue, in which the critical issue is what follows from answers: "if an answer does not give rise to a new question from itself, then it falls out of the dialogue" (Bakhtin, 1986; quoted from Alexander, 2005, p.8).

3-2. The Japanese in comparison with the French and English
In the case of Japanese culture, as Ishii reported, people tend to be dependent on each other while forming cohesive groups. They are not trained at home or at school to participate actively in various oral communication activities (Ishii, 1984, p.55). Quoting from Kobayashi's research of 1980, Ishii shows that in Japanese society, a person who is good at mind-reading and perceiving intuitively another person's thoughts and feelings is highly appreciated for having what is called sasshi competence (Ishii, 1984, p.55). Therefore, "it is possible that the fear of such magical power of language, internalized in Japanese culture, has established the common belief that silence is a virtue, and speech is a vice" (Ishii, 1984, p.53). That literally means "enryo-sasshi communication as one of the basic principles underlying Japanese interpersonal relations" (Ishii, 1984, p.49).

Consequently, to apply 'learning from comparison' for understanding the meaning of literacy and role of language to improve the quality of teaching, it is crucial to consider the educational basis, curriculum management policy, school organization/culture, learning styles, research traditions on teaching, teachers collegial learning structures and the cultural script of teaching.

4. Exploring appropriate approaches to research on curricular activities
Reading this book is an effective way of promoting the cultural approach to school improvement, research on teaching and learning and curriculum management. This expands critical discourse in the process and methods of teaching, learning and nurturing and providing a language for intercultural understanding of curriculum, dialogue and perception among cultures. Cross-cultural research reveals some of what remains hidden in critiques, and intellectual and internal conflicts (Apple, 1979; Kaplan, 1966) and challenges mental presuppositions as wells as discussion of "the practical," "the quasi-practical," and "the eclectic" (Schwab & Harper, 1970). It helps to review what has been learned and rethink behavior for greater empowerment.

More specifically, researchers can clarify specific decisions made in the curriculum development process and class through evidence-based curriculum management and post-lesson discussion, reflection in and on action, transcript-based lesson analysis and class observations as well as types/styles of learning and learning theories (Lo and Marton, 2011; Marton, 2014; Li, 2012). As Stenhouse (1975) argues, the teacher is not faced with the problem of generalizing beyond their experience. Regarding this point, "the utility and appropriateness of the theoretical framework should be testable; the theory should be rich enough to create new and profitable questions" (Stenhouse, 1975, p.157). This may be a belief that underlines the research lifeworks/projects/styles of the authors of this book. The authors and their international research teams collaborate in expanding cross-cultural studies of curriculum, transnational dialogue and the application of critical lenses to further the examination of lessons, understand and elicit changes in curriculum management, and recognize a crisis of principles in curriculum and generalize the findings (Schwab, 1973). It may also open a dimension of variation towards curriculum studies in theory and practice.

For over a decade, the numerous transnational lesson study research projects have been conducted. I have tried to show that the script produced in each lesson practice is a 'cultural artifact' acquired over time by people within that culture and community (Gruschka, 2018). The authors of this book have also tried to show that policy of each country-case of curriculum management is a 'cultural artifact' acquired over time by people within that culture and community, which I call "craft pedagogy" (Sarkar Arani, 2022b; Doyle, 1992b). This is the main argument as to "why changing teachers will not automatically produce [significant] changes in teaching" (Stigler and Hiebert, 2009, p.12).

It is difficult to identify specific cultural artifacts because they unconsciously underpin and shape teaching and learning in different cultural contexts (Sarkar Arani, 2016, 2017, 2020, 2022a). In the case of Japan, for example, Ishii reported that "[t]ruly, Japanese society is changing speedily, from rural to urban and from agricultural to technological, under the global impact of industrialization and westernization. It is no wonder that the fundamental values in Japanese culture on which enryo-sasshi communication functions will remain unchanged" (Ishii, 1984, p.58).

Finally, you may ask why we do this with the company of others, especially in this book. According to Benedict, "[t]he lenses through which any nation looks at life are not the ones another nation uses. It is hard to be conscious of the eyes through which one looks" (1946, p.14). It means that we cannot see the quality of our lens ourselves. Through interaction with others, we realize the diversity and difference as well as challenging the familiar, the depth or the amount of our foresight and impressions and possessions. We can see everything, but we cannot recognize and accurately know the quality of our lens.

Through the interactive process, we realize the quality of our lens and ways of defining, understanding and solving problems and the quality of solving (Sarkar Arani, et al., 2024). We usually think that we are sure of what to see and talk about. However, we can only make the quality of our lens clearer in interaction with others. Then, perhaps our certainty turns into doubt again, and that is the beginning of questioning why. Then, thinking and learning take place again, and from that, a new proposition emerges. In that alternative proposition and critical pursuit, the authors of this book try to lead the way to more effective dialogue between nations as well as policymakers, researchers and practitioners on research in teaching praxis, curricular activities, teacher education/collegial learning, and the landscape of curriculum inquiry and instructional reconstruction. The quality of our lens is improved only in the interaction with others.

References

Alexander, R. J. (2005). Culture, dialogue, and learning: Notes on an emerging pedagogy. Keynote Speech at 10th International Conference of International Association for Cognitive Education and Psychology, University of Durham, London, July 10–14.

Alexander, R. J. (2012). Improve oracy and classroom talk in English schools: Achievements and challenges. A Presentation Given at the DfE Seminar on Oracy, The National Curriculum and Educational Standards, Durham, Feb. 20.

Akker, J. (2003). Curriculum perspectives and introduction. In J. van den Akker, W. Kuiper and U. Hameyer (Eds.), *Curriculum Landscapes and Trends*, London: Kluwer Academic Publishers.

Apple, M. W. (1979). *Ideology and Curriculum*. Boston, MA: Routledge & Kegan Paul.

Bakhtin, M. (1986). *Speech Genres and Other Essays*. University of Texas Press, Austin, TX.

Bandura, A. (1986). *Social Foundations of Thought and Action: A Social Cognitive Theory*. Englewood Cliffs, N.J.: Prentice-Hall.

Benedict, R. (1946). *The Chrysanthemum and the Sword: Patterns of Japanese Culture*. Boston: Houghton Mifflin Company.

Bloom, A. H. (1981). *The Linguistic Shaping of Thought: A Study in the Impact of Language on Thinking in China and the West*. New Jersey: Lawrence Erlbaum Associates, Publishers.

Doyle, W. (1992a). Constructing curriculum in the classroom. In F. K. Oser, A. Dick, and J.-L. Patry (Eds.), *Effective and Responsible Teaching: The New Syntheses*, 66–79, San Francisco, CA: Jossey-Bass.

Doyle, W. (1992b). Curriculum and pedagogy. In P. W. Jackson (Ed.), *Handbook of Research on Curriculum*, 486–516, New York, NY: Macmillan.

Elliott, J. (2016). Significant themes in developing the theory and practice of lesson study. *International Journal for Lesson and Learning Studies*, 5(4), 274–280.

Giroux, H. A. (1988). *Teachers as intellectuals: Toward a critical pedagogy of learning*. Massachusetts: Bergin & Garvey Publishers, Inc.

Gruschka, A. (2018). How we can and why we have to reconstruct teaching. *Journal for Lesson and Learning Studies*, 7(2), 85–97.

Ishii, S. (1984). Enryo-sushi communication: A key to understanding Japanese interpersonal relations. *Journal of Cross-Currents: Language Teaching and Cross-cultural Communication*, XI(1), 49–58.

Kaplan, R. B. (1966). Cultural thought patterns in intercultural education. *Language Learning*, 16, 1–20.

Kobayashi, K. (1980). Shokuba no ningen kankei [Human relations organizations]. In Hiroshi Minami (Ed.), *Handbook of Japanese Human Relations*, Tokyo: Kodansha.

Kobayashi, V. N. (1984). Rhetorical patterns in English and Japanese, Unpublished Doctoral Dissertation, Teachers College, Department of Applied Linguistics, Columbia University.

Li, J. (2012). *Cultural Foundations of Learning: East and West*. Cambridge: Cambridge University Press.

Lo, M. L., & Marton, F. (2011). Towards a science of the art of teaching: Using variation theory as a guiding principle of pedagogical design. *International Journal for Lesson and Learning Studies*, 1(1), 7–22.

Lortie, D. C. (1977). *Schoolteacher: A Sociological Study*. Chicago: The University of

Chicago Press.

Manen, M. V. (1977). Linking ways of knowing with ways of being practical. *Curriculum Inquiry*, 6(3), 205–228.

Marton, F. (2014). *Necessary conditions of learning*. Routledge.

Mason, J., & Washington, P. (1992). *The Future of Thinking*. London: Routledge.

Miyamoto, E. T. (2008). Processing sentences in Japanese. In S. Miyagawa and M. Saito (Eds.), *The Oxford Handbook of Japanese Linguistics*, 217–249, Oxford: Oxford University Press.

Moore, C. A. (1967). Editor's supplement: The enigmatic Japanese mind. In C. A. Moore (Ed.), *The Japanese Mind: Essential of Japanese Philosophy and Culture*, 288–313, Honolulu: East-West Center Press, The University Press of Hawaii.

Pinar, W. F., Reynolds, W. M., Slattery, P., & Taubman, P. M. (1995). *Understanding Curriculum: An Introduction to The Study of Historical and Contemporary Curriculum Discourses*. New York, NY: Peter Lang.

Prior, P. A., & Lunsford, K. J. (2008). History of reflection, theory, and research on writing. In C. Bazerman (Ed.), *Handbook of Research on Writing: History, Society, School, Individual, Text*, 81–96, New York: Lawrence Erlbaum Associates.

Ravitch, D. (2020). *Slaying Goliath: The Passionate Resistance to Privatization and the Fight to Save America's Public Schools*. New York, NY: Alfred A. Knopf.

Sarkar Arani, M.R., Lander, B., Shibata, Y., Iksan, Z. & Tan, S. (2024). "Doing fractions" and "understanding fairness": Examining the cultural scripts of a mathematics lesson through the eyes of Japanese and Malaysian educators, *Prospects*, 54, 873-890.

Sarkar Arani, M. R. (2022a). Foreword, In M. Hallitzky; C. Kieres; Emi Kinoshita; N. Yoshida (Eds.). *Unterrichtsforschung und Unterrichtspraxis im Gespräch Interkulturelle und interprofessionelle Perspektiven auf eine Unterrichtsstunde*, 7–13, Bad Heilbrunn, Germany: Verlag Julius Klinkhardt.

Sarkar Arani, M. R., Mizuno, M., & Shibata, Y. (2022b). Neriage as Japanese craft pedagogy: Cultural scripts of teaching that promote authentic learning. In J. Zajda & S. Majhanovich (Eds.), *Globalization, Comparative Education and Policy Research*, 113–137, Switzerland: Springer.

Sarkar Arani, M. R., Shibata, Y., Cheon, H. S., Sakamoto, M., & Kuno, H. (2020). Comparison as a lens: Interpretation of the cultural script of a Korean mathematics lesson through the perspective of international lesson study. *Educational Practice, and Theory*, 42(2), 57–78.

Sarkar Arani, M. R., Shibata, Y., Sakamoto, M., Iksan, Z., Haziah Amirullah, A., & Lander, B. (2017a). How teachers respond to students' mistakes in lessons: A cross-cultural analysis of a mathematics lesson. *International Journal for Lesson and Learning Studies*, 6(3), 249–267.

Sarkar Arani, M. R. (2017b). Raising the quality of teaching through Kyouzai Kenkyuu—The study of teaching materials. *International Journal for Lesson and Learning Studies*, 6(1), 10–26.

Sarkar Arani, M. R. (2016). An examination of oral and literal teaching traditions through a comparative analysis of mathematics lessons in Iran and Japan. *International Journal for Lesson and Learning Studies*, 5(3), 196–211.

Sarkar Arani, M. R. (2015). Cross cultural analysis of an Iranian mathematics lesson: A new perspective for raising the quality of teaching. *International Journal for Lesson and Learning Studies*, 4(2), 118–139.

Sarkar Arani, M. R., & Fukaya, K. (2010). Japanese national curriculum standards reform: Integrated study and its challenges. In J. Zajda (Ed.), *Globalization, Ideology and Education Policy Reforms*, 63–77, The Netherlands: Springer.

Schwab, J. J., & Harper, W. R. (1970). *The Practical: A Language for Curriculum*. Washington D.C.: The National Education Association, Center for Study of Instruction.

Schwab, J. J. (1973). The Practical 3: Translation into curriculum. *The School Review*, 81(4), 501–522.

Stigler, J. W., & Hiebert, J. (2009). *The Teaching Gap: Best Ideas from the World's Teachers for Improving Education in the Classroom, Update with a New Preface and Afterword*. New York: The Free Press.

Taba, H. (1962). *Curriculum Development: Theory and Practice*. New York: Harcourt, Brace & World.

Tyler, R. W. (1949). *Basic Principles of Curriculum and Instruction*. Chicago, IL: University of Chicago Press.

Introduction

School-Based Curriculum Management for Teacher Education: The Future Development of Curriculum Study and Lesson Study

Tetsuo KURAMOTO, Shizuoka University of Art and Culture

Abstract

This study, presented at the Japan Society for Curriculum Studies (JSCS) Symposium, underscores our firm commitment to international collaboration. In collaboration with the World Association of Lesson Studies (WALS) and JSCS, the central theme is "School-Based Curriculum Management for Teacher Education: The Future Development of Curriculum Study and Lesson Study" (Kuramoto et al., 2024). WALS and JSCS, as leading organizations in the field of education, play a crucial role in shaping the future of curriculum study and lesson study. The study theme, which we also presented as a keynote symposium at WALS Kazakhstan, not only highlights the global significance of our work but also emphasizes the invaluable role of educators, researchers, and policymakers in this larger educational community, making them feel integral to the research and its outcomes.

https://www.walsnet.org/wals-2024-conference-recorded-sessions/

Therefore, this book, structured around the above research background, is a comprehensive guide to our collaborative research achievement. It provides a detailed account of our findings and their implications, ensuring readers are fully informed and knowledgeable about our work and empowering them with a deep understanding of the research.

1. Theory and Practice of School-Based Curriculum Management (SBCM)

1-1. School-Based Curriculum Management—From a theoretical perspective—

Previous theoretical studies have not clearly defined Curriculum Management in the courses of study in Japan, and related research and literature reviews need further clarification. Given its significant impact on the national school level, it is crucial to re-examine this concept.

As references, from an international and academic perspective, relevant curriculum study can be broadly categorized as follows:

11

1. Curriculum Development:

The curriculum comprises objectives, content, methods, and evaluation theories that embody the educational philosophy.

(Tyler, 1949; Taba, 1962; Goodlad, 1979; Print, 2020).

2. Curriculum Design:

It refers to a learner-centered curriculum, a counter concept to curriculum development theory, which focuses on subjects, and a teacher-centered curriculum.

(Beane, 1997; Wiggins et al., 2005; Pinar, 2012).

3. Curriculum Management:

It is a comprehensive and integrated concept that organizes and manages curriculum development/design and school organizational strategy.

(Saylor et al., 1981; Glanz et al., 2000; Hargreaves et al., 2006; Ylimaki, 2011; Fullan et al., 2015; Bolman et al., 2017; Glatthorn et al., 2017)

Instead of being defined by the Courses of Study in Japan, the most crucial theoretical argument regarding School-Based Curriculum Management (SBCM) comes from international theoretical development (Kuramoto, 2024; Kuramoto et al., 2014, 2021). For instance, the typical argument put forth by the World Association of Lesson Studies (WALS) is highly instructive (Lewis et al., 1998; Lewis, 2002a, 2002b; Cheng & Lander et al., 2024). WALS has a strong presence in the international academic community, positioning it as the international academic version of a teacher education graduate school.

Lesson Study in WALS, teacher education through lesson study, in-school training, and school improvement theory are often seen as partial concepts of SBCM. From the perspective of the fusion and exchange of teacher education theory and practice, SBCM is also a partial concept of Knowledge Management (Nonaka, 1991; Nonaka et al., 1995, 2000, 2001, 2006, 2008, 2009). Furthermore, it is additionally discussed in terms of Intellectual Capital and Action Research. Therefore, SBCM is a concept that integrates two areas: Curriculum and instruction in terms of educational content methods and management in terms of supporting conditions to put the educational goals of school organizations and cooperative community groups into practice. It is based on a dynamic view of curriculum (action research) and the PDCA process theory beyond a static view of curriculum (development and design). This dynamic nature of SBCM, with its requirement for active engagement and continuous improvement, underscores the integral role of educators and researchers in the process, making them feel engaged and integral to the success of the process.

More than just a theoretical concept, SBCM is a powerful tool that empowers educators and researchers to make a tangible difference in their academic institutions. By emphasizing its practical application, educators are empowered to make a real impact, instilling a sense of agency and responsibility. This practical approach to SBCM ensures that educators and researchers feel empowered and responsible for the positive changes they can bring about in their institutions, fostering a sense of ownership and commitment.

In Kuramoto's study, international research on SBCM is being developed based on WALS concepts through the International Scientific Research Program (20KK0050) of

SBCM and Lesson Study for Teaching Training. This research, a collaborative effort with educational institutions in the USA, UK, Finland, Hong Kong, Vietnam, Cambodia, Iran, and others, is yielding results. The collaborative nature of SBCM research is not just a feature but a critical aspect that fosters a sense of belonging to a global educational community. Active participation is encouraged and crucial to this international endeavor for educators and researchers. Engagement in international research collaborations contributes to the global advancement of SBCM, making educators feel part of a larger educational community and fostering a sense of belonging.

The SBCM study has two main components. The first component involves educating and evaluating educational goals through curriculum and instruction. The second component focuses on managing the organization to enhance the conditions that support educational elements, known as school management. Curriculum organization and school management are crucial in promoting academic quality, organizational culture, and school systems, ultimately enhancing student learning effectiveness (Kuramoto Modified, 2024, p.3).

The curriculum studies in SBCM integrate educational management and methodology to address curriculum development and management questions, which are central to school management. They explore how school improvement can impact curriculum development and management and the learning effects it can have on students. SBCM is an integrated field of educational research where educational management and methodology intersect and complement each other (Kuramoto, 2008, p.2).

1-2. School-Based Curriculum Management—a practical and engaging approach—

From a practical and training perspective, it is crucial to comprehend the SBCM, such as the National Institute for Teachers and Staff Support (NITS) and the various local educational centers. Concerning teacher training, it is defined as the overall (first, second, and third circles, hereafter, 1st, 2nd, and 3rd circles) activities of an organization that develops and designs curricula (goals, content, methods, and evaluation theory) and then manages those curricula, which in brief, means the management of a curriculum for teaching practice.

Transformational Curriculum Leadership inspired its practical approach to understanding SBCM in the 1st, 2nd, and 3rd circles and developed for SBCM teacher training. SBCM can thus be understood from the perspectives of the 1st circle (student development), the 2nd circle (teacher and staff development, leadership, organizational development, fostering school culture), and the 3rd circle (collaboration with parents and external organizations, community development). The leader's self-analysis is also essential, focusing on building the curriculum and guiding the school organization with the leader at the center, which is vital for SBCM.

Therefore, to enhance schools through the 1st, 2nd, and 3rd circles, the practical definition of SBCM is to create a school curriculum (pedagogy) systematically driven by leaders of the zero circle (young, middle, and top). The study continuously advocates this, particularly in practical teacher training situations. The 'zero-order circle' refers to the leadership structure within the school, where leaders at different levels (young, middle, and top) collaborate to drive curriculum development and implementation.

The courses of study in Japan call for establishing curriculum management and corresponding theories. However, educational researchers require assistance in comprehending the widespread confusion nationwide concerning the interpretation and implementation of curriculum studies. Our research will be instrumental in advancing SBCM in the global academic community, not just Curriculum Management in the study programs in Japan. Consequently, it will reshape the theoretical and training patterns of SBCM and foster a comprehensive understanding among education researchers and practitioners at both national and international levels (Kuramoto, 2024; Kuramoto et al., 2014, 2021).

2. What is Curriculum Study and Pedagogical Content Knowledge (PCK)?

The significant purpose is firstly to promote theoretical and practical developmental research of School-Based Curriculum Study and Lesson Study (1st, 2nd, and 3rd circles) through a collaborative effort between the World Association of Lesson Studies (WALS) and The Japanese Society for Curriculum Studies (JSCS). This collaboration ensures that international teacher training is developed using the research results and adequate verification is conducted, engaging the educators in a solution-oriented project. Secondly, this research project will summarize the points of contact curriculum and lesson research by adding practical findings, such as improved student performance and teacher satisfaction, obtained from verifying the effectiveness of teacher training and further overseas survey research. In doing so, this study will focus on educational thought and practice of pragmatism (in the U.S. and Asian countries) to overcome the dichotomy of CS and compare it with the relevant theory in Japan. Finally, in collaboration with WALS and JSCS, this developmental research project will establish an international network for research in related fields and enhance global teacher training.

Furthermore, based on the above, the ultimate significance of this research is to build the foundation of a collaborative network of international contributions in pedagogy (educational methodology, curriculum studies, teacher education). Curriculum study (CS) means the research of the 'totality of human learning,' which encompasses all aspects of human knowledge and experience. CS involves studying the overall human learning experience. The study can be understood in terms of the time axis, which represents the accumulation of learning experiences throughout a person's life, and the spatial axis, which can be better understood from the perspective of Pedagogical Content Knowledge (PCK). as shown in Figure 1 (JSCS keynote symposium, WALS keynote symposium, 2024)

In general, PCK, in a narrow concept, often refers to the subject content teaching studies covered by the methodology of subject pedagogy (Shulman, 1986; Stigler et al., 1999; Lewis et al., 2006; Fullan, 2007; Ball et al., 2008; Lewis, 2015). In contrast, PCK, in a broad concept, is an interdisciplinary concept covering various educational methods, management, administration, law, sociology, philosophy, and history, encompassing the

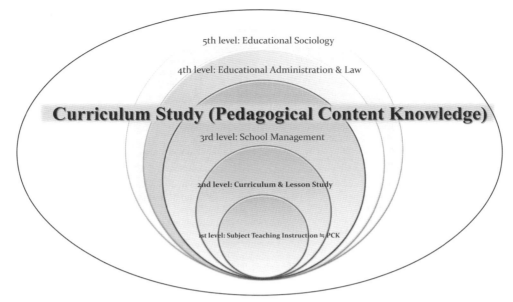

Figure 1: The Structure of Curriculum Study and Pedagogical Content Knowledge

entire CS field. This interdisciplinary nature of PCK makes it an engaging and exciting study area that will capture the interest and involvement of educators, researchers, and individuals interested in pedagogy and educational methods.

The structure of PCK and related content studies can be organized into different levels: subject pedagogy and teaching class theory at the 1st level, school curriculum and Lesson Study at the 2nd level, overall school organization management at the 3rd level, educational administration at the 4th level, and the sociology of education at the 5th level. Based on this understanding, the WALS and JSCS joint project discusses SBCM in the pedagogical content studies structure's 1st, 2nd, and 3rd levels.

3. School-Based Curriculum Study and Lesson Study —The Perspective of SBCM—

The inspiration for this SBCM study came from a paper contributed to The Japanese Society for Curriculum Studies (JSCS) by World Association of Lesson Studies (WALS) President Catherine C. Lewis, Japanese Curriculum Study: Can It Leverage Change Around the World? (Curriculum Studies, Vol. 33, 2024). The Lewis paper targeted the fusion area of Lesson Study (LS: lesson study, teacher training, school improvement) and Curriculum Study (CS: curriculum study, broadly defined: total learning in life, narrowly defined: goals, contents/methods, and evaluation of educational plans), which prompted us to launch this developmental study in collaboration with WALS and JSCS.

LS in Japan is said to have a history of more than 100 years, with the spread of compulsory education in the Meiji Era. Especially in the late 1990s, made-in-Japan LS theories and practices began to be exported and have been closely watched in the international

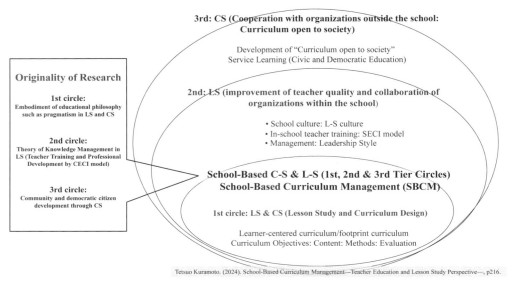

Figure 2: 1st, 2nd, and 3rd Order Circles for School-Based Curriculum Study & Lesson Study

field of pedagogical research (Fernandez & Yoshida, 2004). However, the contemporary significance of LS research, which has been further developed, must be reconsidered as a new stage in 2024. This is because, as is well known, the interpretation of LS is generally that of student learning study. Alternatively, as represented by the Professional Learning Community (PLC), LS can be summarized as an overall teaching practice that implements in-school training with lesson study at its core, measures to improve teacher qualifications and abilities, and ultimately enhances functional school organization in collaboration with the community (WALS conference 2024 Kazakhstan).

In light of the above, when the Lewis paper is reorganized from SBCM (Kuramoto, 2024: Kuramoto et al., 2014), the components of School-Based Curriculum Study & Lesson Study (School-Based CS & LS) are explained in the 1st Circle, 2nd Circle, and 3rd Circle Theories as shown in Figure 2 (JSCS keynote symposium 2024).

The pedagogical significance of the 1st circle is, for example, the embodiment of educational ideas and philosophies, such as pragmatism in lesson research and the construction of evaluation theory (curriculum design and lesson development). In this case, the educational philosophy of pragmatism, such as Dewey's, is used as the goal theory of curriculum development, and the curriculum instruction method and evaluation theory are constructed. More specifically, this category falls under the theory of teaching problem-solving learning, project-based learning, footprint curriculum, and child-oriented pedagogy. (JSCS keynote symposium 2024).

The 2nd circle is a school management activity related to improving teacher quality and collaboration within the school organization. It is the area of school organizational management that interprets LS as in-school teacher training. For instance, the SECI model consists of four stages: socialization, externalization, combination, and internalization. It can be a central concept for improving school organizations through teacher quality improvement and organizational development (Dudley 2012, 2019).

The 3rd circle, which is discussed as a curriculum open to society in the current Courses of Study in Japan, is an area that emphasizes the relationship between school and community and the building of a system of cooperation with organizations outside the school and community members (citizenship education theory). The typical studies of pedagogical significance in the 3rd circle include, for example, Citizenship Education (education of active citizenship and democracy) through Service-Learning, located in the educational thought and practice of pragmatism (Kuramoto et al., 2021). Ultimately, this will structure theoretical and practical development research on School-Based CS & LS (1st, 2nd, and 3rd circles).

4. Pedagogical Research Question—First, Second, and Third Circles—

The first pedagogical Research Question (RQ), a cornerstone of this SBCM study, is to theoretically and practically reorganize the factors of Table 1, 1st, 2nd, and 3rd circles. This project was developed through the collaboration between WALS and JSCS to promote the development of School-Based CS & LS teacher training. This pedagogical project aims to theoretically and practically rearrange the factors in Table 1 and construct an empirical hypothesis model regarding their influence process (See Figure 2).

The second pedagogical RQ will use the results of this research to implement international teacher training (Teacher Training) and verify its effectiveness. The objectives, content (what), and methods and evaluation (how) of LS & CS will be quantitatively and qualitatively examined by the teachers who took these training programs at their schools, school districts, and school boards based on the knowledge management/leadership and SECI model theory (Nonaka, 1991; Nonaka et al., 1995, 2000).

The third pedagogical RQ aims to theoretically consolidate the intersection between curriculum and lesson study research, drawing on the findings from the effectiveness evaluation by international research studies. This project will specialize in the educational thought and practice of pragmatism (USA and Asian countries) with a view to civic education theory, thereby emphasizing the global perspective and the significance

Table 1: Empirical Hypothesis Model: Development of School-Based Curriculum Study and Lesson Study—1st, 2nd, and 3rd Circles

School-Based C.S. & L.S.	A Look at Theoretical Studies Teacher Training and Development (C.S. & L.S.)	A Practical Research Perspective Teacher Training and Development (C.S. & L.S.)
1st circle	Pragmatism (Dewey et al.)	Classroom Theory of Problem-Based Learning (Footprint Curriculum and Educational Theory with Children)
2nd circle	Knowledge management (Knowledge Leadership)	SECI Model
3rd circle	Civic Education (Proactive Citizenship and Democracy)	Service Learning Curriculum Development
Comprehensive perspectives	Curriculum Evaluation (Interpretation of curriculum design)	School-Based Curriculum Management and (C. S. & L. S.)

of cross-cultural research.

5. The Structure of School-Based Curriculum Management and Lesson Study

Lesson Study (LS) has gained significant international recognition and is being implemented in school management development in numerous countries, including specific countries. This global adoption of LS offers a practical and systematic method for enhancing teacher learning and creates a sense of unity among educators and policymakers. The practical benefits of LS, such as enhancing teacher skills, improving student learning, and inspiring and motivating educators and policymakers, underscore its value in education. Teachers engage in collaborative learning, analyzing student progress and teaching methods to enhance their skills. The roots of LS can be traced back to traditional Japanese teacher professional practices, where teaching knowledge and skills were developed through the diagnosis of student learning with the support of school management (Japanese Association for the Study of Educational Administration, JASEA, 2009).

The Ministry of Education, Culture, Sports, Science, and Technology (MEXT) in Japan has recently recognized LS as an excellent approach to teacher education. This official endorsement is a significant step in promoting LS, as it acknowledges the following:

Teachers in Japan are highly evaluated internationally. In particular, the diverse research activities performed to improve classroom teaching in each subject attract incredibly high interest from abroad. Research on classroom teaching based on teachers at each school learning from each other is a system uniquely developed in Japan, which is recently expanding internationally as a 'lesson study' (MEXT /Central Council for Education, 2016).

Kuramoto also suggested applying LS to SBCM to achieve educational goals and sustain school improvement. This application of LS to SBCM offers a promising approach to continuous school improvement, instilling a sense of hope and optimism in the educators. For instance, Nonaka's SECI model, which describes the process of knowledge creation in organizations (Nonaka et al., 1995), can be adopted as an analytical lens to analyze how lesson study could be applied to SBCM in Japanese schools (Kuramoto, 2024). For example, in 2019, Eric Cheng articulated how the SECI model could explain knowledge creation through LS in Transposition of Lesson Study: A Knowledge Management Perspective.

Consequently, Kuramoto's structure of SBCM with LS is shown in Figure 3 (Kuramoto et al., 2014, p.12).

Teachers play a pivotal role in the collaborative process of lesson study. They can learn from each other by sharing their experiences, such as preparing lesson plans, conducting open lessons, and reflecting on other teachers' results. This collaborative approach, often facilitated by the PDCA cycle of LS, fosters a sense of value and importance among educators as they contribute to improving various school functions. (Dudley, 2016; Kuramoto et al., 2012a, 2012b). Lesson study, in this context, can be seen as a knowledge

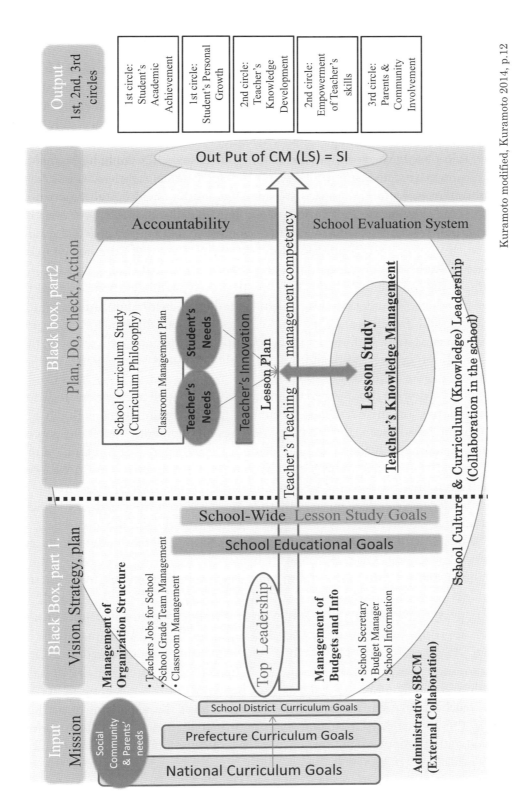

Figure 3: The Structure of School-Based Curriculum Management and Lesson Study

Introduction
School-Based Curriculum Management for Teacher Education:
The Future Development of Curriculum Study and Lesson Study

19

management approach for creating effective pedagogies (Cheng, 2019; Cheng et al., 2022; Kuramoto, 2022).

A culture of teacher collaboration within the school organization is crucial for the successful implementation of lesson study. In Japan, the cultural aspect of Ba is a crucial element in this process, underscoring the significance of cultural factors in educational practices. This emphasis on cultural factors helps educators become more culturally aware and sensitive in their teaching practices. Another critical condition for compelling lesson study is knowledge leadership. The operation of lesson study could be explained by the four knowledge conversion processes of the SECI model (teachers' knowledge creation process in this study); knowledge leadership and Ba could be the supporting factors for compelling lesson study. The study argues that the Ba/school culture, the values/morals of teachers, the leadership of the principal, and other personal factors are positive predictors of teachers' professional development (Cheng & Kuramoto, WALS webinar, Lesson Study: A Knowledge Management Perspective, 2019).

Given the above considerations, this book is structured as follows. It is designed to provide a comprehensive understanding of lesson study and curriculum study, including the 1st, 2nd, and 3rd circles theory. These circles represent different research and practice levels in education, with the 1st circle focusing on classroom-level research, the 2nd circle on school-level research, and the 3rd circle on system-level research and its implementation in education.

The title of this book is School-Based Curriculum Management and Lesson Study for Teacher Education which includes "Part 1: Illuminating International Research of Curriculum Study and Lesson Study for Teaching Training Development," "Part 2: Insights of Lesson Study in Teacher Education and Curriculum Development—Showcasing in the Context of Digital Transformation in Vietnam," and "Part 3: School-Based Curriculum Management from the Perspective of Lesson Study and Teacher Education in Japan."

This comprehensive coverage ensures that the reader is well-informed and knowledgeable about the subject matter, providing a deep understanding of the topics.

Part 1 begins with "Chapter 1, The Literature Review: Research on School-Based Curriculum Management Overseas" and "Chapter 2, Exploring Service-Learning SOFRA Model in School-Based Curriculum Management: Inspiring Hope for Community Impact."

From the perspective of 1st circle lesson research and educational methodology, "Chapter 3, Applying Variation Theory for Instructional Design: Learning Study in Hong Kong," "Chapter 4, Directions for ICT Education and Contemporary Issues for ICT Education and Contemporary Issues, and "Chapter 5 The Interrelation between Lesson Study and Curriculum in Kazakhstan." "Chapter 6, On-the-Job-Training (OJT) for Novice Teachers in Aichi Prefecture" is discussed from the viewpoint of teacher education in the 2nd circle. Furthermore, in the 3rd circle, "Chapter 7, Empowering Learners Cultivating Empowering Learners: Cultivating Autonomy in Japanese University English Education" is discussed.

Specializing in "Showcasing in the Context of Digital Transformation in Vietnam." Chapter 8, Exploring a Cost-Effective Online Teacher Training Model During the

COVID-19 Pandemic: Insights from Vietnam," is concluded **in Part 2**. Especially from the 1st circle of educational technology development standpoint, "Chapter 9, Curriculum management in teacher education: visualized in Vietnam with the lens of digital transformation" is analyzed from the SBCM perspective. Moreover, "Chapter 10, Cross-Cultural Perspectives on Lesson Study: Japan and Vietnam Comparisons," presented the comparative lesson study perspective. Moreover, "Chapter 11, Classroom Management: A Dimension of the Digital Transformation Lesson in Vietnam" was argued.

In Part 3, we delve into unique curriculum and lesson study perspectives. "Chapter 12, Creating Learning Communities for Home Economics Teachers and Knowledge Management: Under the Times of Rapid Change and Unpredictable Society," "Chapter 13, Strategizing and Developing Lesson Study through Systems Thinking Using the Curriculum Management Model," and "Chapter 14, Analysis of the School Improvement Process within the Framework of Curriculum Management," discuss <u>the keywords of this book: SBCM, Knowledge Management, Curriculum Study, and Lesson Study</u>. It offers unique perspectives on these topics, providing a fresh and engaging approach to the subject matter.

These chapters explore significant research in the 1st circle studies. In "Chapter 15, A Study on the Future of Lesson Study in Japan—An Individual Lesson Plan Using 'Zaseki-Hyo,'" the discussion on the "Individual Lesson Plan" as a specific lesson study methodology for student-centered curriculum development is equally significant. Particularly, "Chapter 16, Student Attitude Shifts within the International Baccalaureate Curriculum: Insights from Student Narratives" and "Chapter 17, Transformation of Student Consciousness through Service-Learning Focused on Hip Hop" provide valuable insights into curriculum development and design.

The 2nd circle studies, from the viewpoint of improving teachers' abilities, consisted of "Chapter 18, Self-Analysis Sheet Methodology for Teacher Training" and "Chapter 19, Mentoring and the State of Teacher Training. Furthermore. As a conclusion to part 3, "Chapter 20, Reforms and Issues in Developing School Administrators through Administrative Training in Japan—As a Fundamental Condition for Teacher Training" was presented from the standpoint of the 3rd circle study.

This book is organized to summarize the chapters of part 1, 2, and 3 above and consequently propose the "Final Chapter, The Future of Research: School-Based Curriculum Management and Lesson Study for Teacher Education." This final chapter is a culmination of the insights gained from the previous chapters. It guides future research and practice directions in school-based curriculum management and lesson study for Teacher Education.

References

Ball, D. L., Thames, M. H., & Phelps, G. (2008). Content knowledge for teaching: What makes it special? *Journal of Teacher Education*, 59(5), 389–407.

Cheng, E. C. K. (2019). *Successful transposition of lesson study: A knowledge management perspective*. Singapore, London: Springer.

Cheng, E. C. K. (Ed.). (2022). *Managing school intellectual capital for strategic development: Lessons from Asia and Europe*. New York, NY: Routledge.

Cheng, E. C. K., & Kuramoto, T. (2019, Oct. 28). World Association of Lesson Studies webinar: Lesson study: A knowledge management perspective. Retrieved Aug. 16, 2024, from https://www.walsnet.org/blog/2019/10/28/lesson-study-a-knowledge-management-perspective/

Cheng, E. C. K., & Lander, B. (Eds.). (2024). *WALS-Routledge lesson study series: Implementing a 21st century competency-based curriculum through lesson study: Teacher learning about cross-curricular and online pedagogy*. New York, NY: Routledge.

Dudley, P. (2012). Lesson study development in England: From school networks to national policy. *International Journal for Lesson and Learning Studies*, 1(1), 85–100.

Dudley, P. (2016). *Lesson study: Professional learning for our time*. London: Routledge.

English, F. W. (2000a). *The curriculum management audit: Improving school quality*. Lanham, MD: The Scarecrow Press.

English, F. W. (2000b). *Deciding what to teach and test*. Thousand Oaks, CA: Corwin Press.

English, F. W., & Steffy, B. E. (2001a). *Deep curriculum alignment*. Lanham, MD: The Scarecrow Press.

English, F. W., & Steffy, B. E. (2001b). *Curriculum and assessment for world-class schools*. Lanham, MD: The Scarecrow Press.

Fernandez, C., & Yoshida, M. (2004). *Lesson study: A Japanese approach to improving mathematics teaching and learning*. Mahwah, NJ: Lawrence Erlbaum Associates.

Fullan, M. (2007). *The new meaning of educational change* (4th ed.). New York, NY: Teachers College Press.

Japanese Association for the Study of Educational Administration. (2009). Professional standards for principals: Desired principal image and competencies (2009 ed.). Retrieved Aug. 16, 2024, from http://jasea.jp/wp-content/uploads/2016/12/e-teigen2012.6.pdf

Kuramoto, T. (2008). *A study of curriculum management in the USA: From the service-learning perspective* (アメリカにおけるカリキュラムマネジメントの研究──Service-Learningの視点から). Japan: Fukuro Publishing.

Kuramoto, T., & Shi, H. (2012a). Action research of lesson study in Japan: From the view of student's achievement and teacher's professional development. *Journal of the Faculty of Culture and Education, Saga-University*, 17(1), 119–132.

Kuramoto, T., & Shi, H. (2012b). Summary of lesson study and curriculum management in Japan. *Journal of the Faculty of Culture and Education, Saga-University*, 17(1), 133–147.

Kuramoto, T., & Associates. (2014). *Lesson study & curriculum management in Japan: Focusing on action research*. Japan: Fukuro Publishing.

Kuramoto, T., & Associates. (2021). *Lesson study & curriculum management in Japan: Focusing on action research*. Japan: Fukuro Publishing.

Kuramoto, T. (2022). Developing intellectual capital in Japanese schools through lesson study: A perspective from curriculum management. In E. C. K. Cheng (Ed.),

Managing school intellectual capital for strategic development: Lessons from Asia and Europe, 69–79. New York, NY: Routledge.

Kuramoto, T. (2024). Curriculum study and lesson study development at the Japan Society for Curriculum Studies (JSCS) symposium. Retrieved Aug. 18, 2024, from https://jscs-info.jp/index.html

Kuramoto, T. (2024). *School-based curriculum management: Teacher education and lesson study perspective*. Japan: Fukuro Publishing.

Lewis, C., & Tsuchida, I. (1998). A lesson is like a swiftly flowing river: Research lessons and the improvement of Japanese education. *American Educator*, Winter, 14–17, 50.

Lewis, C. (2002a). *Lesson study: A handbook of teacher-led instructional improvement*. Philadelphia, PA: Research for Better Schools.

Lewis, C. (2002b). Does lesson study have a future in the United States? *Nagoya Journal of Education and Human Development*, 1(1), 1–23.

Lewis, C., Perry, R., & Murata, A. (2006). How should research contribute to instructional improvement? *The case of lesson study, Educational Researcher*, 35(3), 3–14.

Lewis, C. (2015). What is improvement science? Do we need it in education? *Educational Researcher*, 44(1), 54–61.

Lewis, C. (2024). Japanese curriculum study: Can it leverage change around the world? *Japan Society of Curriculum Studies (JSCS), Curriculum Studies*, 33, 99–108.

Lewis, C. (2024). Curriculum study and lesson study development at the World Association of Lesson Studies (WALS) symposium. Retrieved Aug. 18, 2024, from https://www.walsnet.org/2024/

Ministry of Education, Culture, Sports, Science, and Technology in Japan (MEXT). (2016). The Central Council for Education, a working group on higher education, and a teacher training committee regarding improving teachers' quality and ability in charge of school education. Retrieved Aug. 16, 2024, from https://www.mext.go.jp/b_menu/shingi/chukyo/chukyo3/

Nonaka, I. (1991). The knowledge-creating company, *Harvard Business Review*, 69(6), 96–104.

Nonaka, I., & Takeuchi, H. (1995). *The knowledge-creating company*. New York, NY: Oxford University Press.

Nonaka, I., Krogh, G., & Ichijo, K. (2000). E*nabling knowledge creation: How to unlock the mystery of tacit knowledge and release the power of innovation*. New York, NY: Oxford University Press.

Nonaka, I., & Krogh, G. (2009). Tacit knowledge and knowledge conversion: Controversy and advancement in organizational knowledge creation theory. *Organization Science*, 20(3), 635–652.

Nonaka, I., & Hirata, T. (2008). *Managing flow: A process theory of the knowledge-based firm*. London, England & New York, NY: Palgrave Macmillan.

Nonaka, I., & Ichijo, K. (2006). *Knowledge creation and management: New challenges for managers*. New York, NY: Oxford University Press.

Nonaka, I., & Nishiguchi, T. (Eds.). (2001). *Knowledge emergence: Social, technical, and evolutionary dimensions of knowledge creation*. New York, NY: Oxford University

Press.

Shulman, L. S. (1986). Those who understand: Knowledge growth in teaching. *Educational Researcher*, 15(2), 4–14.

Stigler, J. W., & Hiebert, J. (1999). *The teaching gap: Best ideas from the world's teachers for improving education in the classroom*. New York, NY: Free Press.

https://www.walsnet.org/blog/2024/11/29/symposium-an-integrated-research-of-lesson-study-and-curriculum-study-perspectives-from-the-united-states-japan-and-kazakhstan/ (2024.12.31)

https://www.walsnet.org/blog/2019/10/28/lesson-study-a-knowledge-management-perspective/ (2025.02.22)

Curriculum Development

Goodlad, J. I. (1979). *Curriculum inquiry: The study of curriculum practice*. New York, NY: McGraw-Hill.

Print, M. (2020). *Curriculum development and design* (3rd ed.). New York, NY: Routledge.

Taba, H. (1962). *Curriculum development: Theory and practice*. New York, NY: Harcourt, Brace & World.

Tyler, R. W. (1949). B*asic principles of curriculum and instruction*. Chicago, IL: University of Chicago Press.

Curriculum Design

Beane, J. A. (1997). *Curriculum integration: Designing the core of democratic education*. New York, NY: Teachers College Press.

Pinar, W. F. (2012). *What is curriculum theory?* (2nd ed.). New York, NY: Routledge.

Wiggins, G., & McTighe, J. (2005). *Understanding by design*. Alexandria, VA: Association for Supervision and Curriculum Development (ASCD).

Curriculum Management

Bolman, L. G., & Deal, T. E. (2017). *Reframing organizations: Artistry, choice, and leadership* (6th ed.). Hoboken, NJ: John Wiley & Sons.

Fullan, M., & Quinn, J. (2015). *Coherence: The right drivers in action for schools, districts, and systems*. Thousand Oaks, CA: Corwin Press

Glanz, J., & Behar, H. L. (2000). P*aradigm debates in curriculum and supervision: Modern and postmodern perspectives*. Westport, CT: Bergin & Garvey.

Glatthorn, A. A., Jailall, J. M., & Jailall, J. M. (2017). *The principal as curriculum leader: Shaping what is taught and tested* (4th ed.). Thousand Oaks, CA: Corwin Press.

Hargreaves, A., & Fink, D. (2006). *Sustainable leadership*. San Francisco, CA: Jossey-Bass.

Saylor, J. G., Alexander, W. M., & Lewis, A. J. (1981). *Curriculum planning: For better teaching and learning*. New York, NY: Holt, Rinehart, and Winston.

Ylimaki, R. M. (2011). *Critical curriculum leadership: A framework for progressive education*. New York, NY: Routledge

Part 1.

Illuminating International Research of
Curriculum Study and Lesson Study for
Teaching Training Development

Chapter 1

The Literature Review: Research on School-Based Curriculum Management Overseas

Tetsuo KURAMOTO, Shizuoka University of Art and Culture

Abstract

Chapter 1 presents a unique viewpoint: the updated overview of Tetsuo Kuramoto's (2008) doctoral dissertation, "A Study of School-Based Curriculum Management in the United States: A Service-Learning Perspective." This chapter discusses a Ph.D. dissertation that was a crucial reference for ongoing SBCM (School-Based Curriculum Management) research helping to provide a new and insightful perspective at the time of writing.

1. Purpose of the School-Based Curriculum Management Research

The research conducted was a deep dive into the strategies for organizing and managing the curriculum, the cornerstone of school management. It explored the potential effects of school improvement resulting from organizational and management changes and the impact on students' learning outcomes. The focus is on the "integrated field of educational research," where educational management and methodology intersect and complement each other. This book emphasizes the 'integrative research' area of School-Based Curriculum Management (SBCM), which unites educational management and methodology studies. In recent years, school education curriculum research has shifted toward examining educational methodology aspects, such as the effects of curriculum content and methodology on student learning under specific academic goals. Moreover, it considers the crucial role of educators and administrators in creating conditions and managing the organizational aspects. This highlights the significant and relevant research encompassing both the creators and implementers of the curriculum and related organizational management aspects from their perspective (Hunkins, 1980; Saylor, 1981; Unruh, 1984; Marsh & Willis, 1995).

The prevailing international research trends in curriculum development have emphasized methodological teaching and learning theories around educators and students. In terms of the curriculum system operation, the planning phase (Plan) of curriculum development is entrenched within the school system, and its execution phase (Do) is also developed by the organizational system and enhanced through evaluation feedback (Check). The PDCA process of curriculum development and management, which is refined (Action) through evaluation feedback (Check), must align with the organizational system, encompassing the school (Wolfinger, 1997; Wraga, 1996). Consequently, SBCM is positioned at the core of school improvement theory. It offers pragmatic recommendations for a more thorough and integrated school improvement theory, providing educators and administrators with practical insights, equipping them with the necessary tools for effective school management, and empowering them in their roles. These insights can be directly applied to improve their institutions' education quality.

Hence, through a research approach that intersects educational management research on curriculum condition development and educational methodology research on curriculum development, the concept of 'integrative research' is delineated as 'teaching and learning activities related to the educational content and methods of the curriculum that correspond to the educational objectives of the school and the curriculum development that bolsters this educational domain' (Unruh, 1984; Marsh & Willis, 1995). This encompasses curriculum and instruction, a collection of instructional activities tied to educational content and methods, and management, a suite of administrative activities supporting these undertakings to actualize the educational goals of the school and the collaborating community organizations (Wills, 1995). Management constitutes the suite of administrative activities that facilitate these efforts to realize the educational objectives of the school organization and its collaborating community groups (Wiles & Bondi, 1995; Martinello & Cook, 2000).

In other words, it can be defined as a domain that integrates two series of educational activities: teaching and learning activities related to curriculum content and methods that correspond to the educational goals of the school, and management activities as the maintenance of conditions that support curriculum development and is related to all educational activities that produce educational results through curriculum development and management (Kuramoto, 2008). Furthermore, to enhance the quality of curriculum development, it is essential not only to develop curriculum contents and methods but also to have a viewpoint of managing them systematically. Thus, the research area that integrates educational methodology and educational management through curriculum research is the subject of this study.

Given the profound significance of the research above, this study is poised to provide a comprehensive exploration of the international perspective of SBCM, ensuring that educators feel informed and knowledgeable. SBCM, a conceptual category within curriculum development theory, spans from educational methodology to the organizational system. It encompasses curriculum theory in a broad concept, extending the conceptual categories covered by curriculum development theory to the level of conditioning and management of organizational systems. Therefore, using the relevant definitions, the concept of SBCM is as follows). This study equips educators with practical insights and tools, ensuring they are well-informed and knowledgeable.

The SBCM study has two main components. The first component involves educating and evaluating educational goals through curriculum and instruction. The second component focuses on managing the organization to enhance the conditions that support educational elements, known as school management. Curriculum organization and school management are crucial in promoting academic quality, organizational culture, and school systems, ultimately enhancing student learning effectiveness (Kuramoto Modified, 2024, p.3).

The curriculum studies in SBCM integrate educational management and methodology to address curriculum development and management-based questions central to school management. They explore how school improvement can impact curriculum development and management and highlight its effects on students. SBCM is "an integrated field of educational research" where educational management and methodology intersect and complement each other (Kuramoto, 2008, p.2).

Therefore, the discussion of SBCM serves as a touchstone for understanding the current situation and shaping the future of educational practices in Japan. The proposal of 'curriculum management' in the Japanese Courses of Study without sufficient theoretical research has led to confusion at the national level. However, SBCM holds the potential to guide the development of future educational practices, offering a beacon of hope and inspiration. The following is a discussion of previous international research on the effects of SBCM curriculum development and management theory, which is at the core of school system improvement, on enhancing school education. This emphasis on the potential of SBCM to guide the future of education should leave educators feeling hopeful and inspired.

2. Reviewed Previous Research Regarding School-Based Curriculum Management

This study aspires to pioneer a 'fusion' research field between curriculum conditioning theory and content methodology, akin to Japan's integrated learning concept. By delving into School-Based Curriculum Management (SBCM) theory in the United States, the aim is to open new avenues of understanding and potentially revolutionize curriculum development and management. The potential for this 'fusion' to revolutionize the field is exciting and should pique the interest of all those involved in curriculum study.

First, in discussing SBCM in the U.S., the study reviewed previous research in related fields, including (1) Curriculum Development, (2) the relationship between organizational improvement theory and systems theory, (3) School Improvement, (4) School Based Management (SBM)/Effective Schools, and (5) School Culture and Leadership Theory.

The SBCM integrates both aspects of organizational management/condition development and educational content/methodology in a unit school and is understood as a curriculum theory of unity and development of the entire management process that feeds back from the curriculum PDCA process to the improvement and planning process. At the same time, it is argued that placing SBCM at the core of school improvement theory has a certain validity in terms of management activities to improve the organization by developing various conditions related to the curriculum inside and outside the school to increase the educational outcomes of students.

Suppose SBCM is a central part of school improvement theory. In that case, it is possible to construct a cross-section of systematic SBCM only when the perspectives of the curriculum provider and the learning subject are organically integrated. However, although international SBCM has partially discussed the conditioning elements of curriculum research, very few studies have attempted to show its overall structure. Therefore, the research has organized previous studies in various fields that could serve as a partial base for SBCM from the following five perspectives.

2-1. School-Based Curriculum Management in Curriculum Development

In the theory of SBCM in Curriculum Development, the study discussed the "Managerial Aspects of Curriculum Development." This concept focuses on the management activities, which are the conditioning aspects of the curriculum. These activities include planning, organizing, and evaluating the curriculum development process. The study assumed the curriculum development theory regarding goals, contents, and methods and discussed how managerial activities influence these aspects. Managerial Aspects of Curriculum Development focus on the management activities, which are the organizational aspects of the curriculum (Wiles & Bondi, 1995; Martinello & Cook, 2000).

After outlining the historical development of the integrated curriculum, the study discussed the managerial aspects of curriculum development theory. For example, the "Eight-Year Study" was taken up as the subject of analysis, and the managerial issues were extracted at that time. They could be summarized in the following five points (Aikin, 1942):

1) The school's educational philosophy, vision, and goals are clearly defined.
2) There must be a strategic problem with the principal's leadership.
3) The report states that measures were strategically needed to transform teacher collaboration (Collaboration) from a differentiated subject-centered curriculum to an integrated curriculum.
4) Supportive conditions for parents/community are provided.
5) The importance of evaluating learning outcomes and relating them to curriculum evaluation theory.

While still open for discussion, SBCM's managerial strategies hold significant theoretical value (Saylor, 1981).

2-2. School-Based Curriculum Management in the relationship between organizational improvement theory and systems theory

SBCM was constructed from the relationship between organizational improvement theory and systems theory. The fundamental perspective of organizational improvement can be summarized (Katz, 1955; Hunkins, 1980). Organizations generally have well-established behaviors and inherent states, and it is necessary to be innovative and open to flexible change. In organizational improvement, tension among organizational members is essential, and conservative complacency is a disincentive for improvement orientation. Therefore, the key to making organizational improvement possible is for organizational leaders to engage in improvement orientation, clarify strategies regarding vision, goals, and concrete plans, and exercise leadership within the scope of collegial culture. Based on the above points, the studies have concluded that implementing organizational improvement strategies is vital.

This organizational improvement orientation was applied to school education, with a particular focus on the process of improving school organization. The intention here was to foster a sense of unity and alignment by reflecting democracy in the school management process and encouraging "democratic participation in management and democratic organizational development." This strategy was also understood as a means to increase the degree of shared educational goals and lubricate the collaborative system through the collaborative involvement and participation of teachers, parents, students, and the community in the management cycle of the school organization. For example, the study understood that a typical management process theory includes a management process theory of curriculum (Lipitt, 1958; Harvey, 1996).

The relationship between systems theory and school improvement theory could also contribute to creating a theoretical framework for developing SBCM. Biologists' "General System Theory" (GST) has proposed and promoted systems theory. From a biological perspective, a system is open to its environment and interacts with it. Therefore, the study suggested that problem-solving through continuous evolution in new aspects can qualitatively improve a system. This emphasis on constant evolution is intended to make educators feel optimistic and forward-thinking (Jurrow, 1999; Goodlad, 1975; Sears, 1950).

In addition to the above argument, from the standpoint of systems theory, focusing on the boundary between the organization and the environment, an *open system* is defined as one where there is a permeable boundary, that is, a system in which a cooperative relationship is established between the system inside the boundary and the external environment. In addition, ecology is based on the idea that an organization, as a living organism, constantly improves itself while responding to social changes (environment) toward maturity (openness).

Therefore, when an organization's improvement process is clarified, its members' goal orientation is at the center of organizational ecology, and this becomes the theoretical base of organizational management theory, in which the members of an organization collaborate in their respective tasks in connection with these goals.

2-3. School-Based Curriculum Management in School Improvement
The study examined the SBCM in School Improvement (Darling-Hammond, 1995) from the perspectives of school management and school improvement process theory, school improvement theory through receptive capacity and professional development. The points to be noted are as follows (Senge, 1990; Wendell, 1995; Steagall, 2004).

1) Managing the curriculum developed under the school's educational goals is crucial. A robust internal and external organization is essential to ensure its smooth operation and conformity with the goals. This will enable the implementation of educational practices that function accordingly, underscoring the significance of aligning educational practices with the school's mission.

2) The school organization is pivotal in managing the total efforts. It supports and guides the process of proactive personality unification, recognizing each student as a social community member and human resource. The organization of a curriculum for this purpose and collaborative work centered around a group of teachers are integral to this process. Underscoring the crucial role of the school organization in the educational system is also important.

3) A flexible organizational response is crucial, considering the balance of management actors in the curriculum, including the educational issues of the community and the involvement of organizations outside the school in the school organization. This highlights the importance of adaptability in managing the curriculum, making the audience feel the need for a flexible approach.

4) The organization's construction of "receptive capacity" is crucial. It involves an organizational management focus on enhancing external human resources, various educational resources, and financial support. This concept implies the so-called "Manpower, Money, Material, and Management, 4Ms" of SBCM.

The passage explains how to manage the organizational structure in schools that prioritize improvement. It considers curriculum development and management to be critical components of School-Based Curriculum Management (SBCM), which is central to the school improvement approach (Snyder, 1986; Senge, 2000; Elmore, 2002).

2-4. School-Based Management and Effective Schools

The Concept of 'Effective Schools' (ES) is a significant educational reform in a unit school. As the research identified, ES is characterized by three key factors contributing to successful school improvement (Lindelow, 1981; Malen, 1990).

First, in "effective schools," school management focuses on classroom and school management, with high expectations on all students' critical thinking and problem-solving skills. Second, the faculty and staff of the school organization collaborate, and there is an atmosphere of active and direct involvement in making important decisions regarding improving school and classroom management. Finally, these "effective schools" are seen to have a clear educational vision and strategy and are systemically responsive over the long term. It is clear that each teacher, as a member of the organization, is also an active decision-maker in their own "professional development" and that teachers and administrators build professional "receptivity" through a state of organizational participation in democratic organizational management.

Thus, "effective schools" was one educational reform trend. Next, the study took this one step further from an educational management perspective. The study examined SBM, where the unit school was an independent and self-reliant organizational management and developed its own SBCM. In the late 1980s, in the USA, a series of trends in educational reforms were formulated to shift education toward centralization and standardization. At the same time, other reform directions progressed toward decentralization that were different. One of these was SBM. (Lindelow, 1981; Malen, 1990).

SBM is a concept that has emerged in the context of centralization and decentralization. It is a new form of school improvement theory that allows each school unit to manage its personnel, budget, and curriculum development as independently and autonomously as possible from the school district.

Therefore, in this relationship between SBM and school improvement theory, guidance can be found in the famous "school-based curriculum development" (Skilbeck, 1984; 1987), primarily when focusing on its curriculum development and management.

Skilbeck advocates for a more school-side right of independent curriculum development in the trend of decentralization, as opposed to centralized and uniform curriculum guidelines by the central government. Curriculum development is a multi-faceted procedure. It directly leads to the improvement of the unit school located in the educational administration. It also encompasses the stages in curriculum development based on the school analysis of the school environment and situation, determination of curriculum goals, curriculum implementation through designing a curriculum that meets those goals, and evaluation. The curriculum development stage, which is the school's foundation, begins with an analysis of the school environment and conditions, followed by determining curriculum goals, designing a curriculum that meets those goals, and implementing and evaluating that curriculum.

2-5. School-Based Curriculum Management in School Culture and Leadership

The study organized SBCM in relation to School Culture and Leadership. Primarily, the relationship between leadership theory and SBCM is of utmost importance. The study has discussed various leadership typology theories, and international leadership research is flourishing in national studies. Deal and Petrson's study (1994) of principal leadership in the United States is one of the most prominent studies of principal leadership in the United States. It has been introduced and has a huge following in Japan. In their study, Deal and Peterson classify principals' leadership styles into "Technical Leadership" and "Symbolic Leadership," which take into consideration the organizational structure of the school and identify the issue of balancing these two leadership styles (Deal & Peterson, 1994, 1999; Leithwood, 1999; Foster, 1986; Hallinger & Heck; 1996; Foriska, 1994; Leithwood, 1994).

Regarding school culture and SBCM, the Deal and Peterson study (1994) integrates several theories combining leadership, school culture, and school improvement theories.

The school culture theory is composed of the norms, values, and beliefs shared by faculty, staff, parents, and community members, both inside and outside the school unit, and that, over time, gives rise to unique traditions and mainstream organizational behaviors unique to the school. When significant norms and values exist within that organization, and when different beliefs are mixed in, they are shared in new ways, which is reflected in the teaching philosophy for teachers. The components of each specific school culture include the shared models, values, and beliefs that Deal and Peterson mention (1994, 1999). This also includes organizational atmosphere, the structural nature of labor, authority and management structures, small group practice methods, evaluation practices, and time settings specific to each school.

As is evident from these previous studies, the significant remainder of the research on SBCM can be summarized with the following four points. Firstly, although the "School-Based Curriculum Development" theory has been discussed in parts in each item, almost no theory fully grasps its overall structure. There is little awareness of the problem of targeting it as an integrated research area of condition development and content-method series. Second, there is an urgent need for a more specific analysis of curriculum contents/areas, as no research trend attempts to construct a more concrete and specific form of SBCM's overall structure, a crucial aspect in SBCM research (Skilbeck, 1984; 1987). Thirdly, the importance of demonstrating the educational effects on students and learners cannot be overstated in addition to these issues. This is a crucial aspect that needs to be included in SBCM research. The output element of SBCM, which is supposed to be the core of school improvement theory, must also be clarified. Fourth, although the 'boundary theory' has appeared in previous studies of SBCM from the viewpoint of systems theory. Several academics (Goodlad, 1975; Fullan, 1991; Senge, 2000; Elmore, 2002) state that it focuses more on the boundaries of the unit school and how they interact with the more extensive educational system overall. Considering this, understanding these four points on SBCM research is crucial to providing insights into the leadership roles that drive school and community improvement.

3. School-Based Curriculum Management Components and School Improvement

The SBCM is a theory of school improvement that holds great promise. It envisions each school developing a curriculum that provides developmentally appropriate educational content for students to achieve their academic goals. This curriculum is blended with the organizational conditions that allow it to function from a managerial perspective. It is a theory that not only organizes and dynamizes curriculum development and management but also has the potential to improve school and community conditions significantly. This potential instills a sense of hope and optimism in educators, curriculum developers, and researchers.

Hinojosa, influenced by English's theory of SBCM (English, 2000a, 2000b, 2001a, 2001b) and conducting a research study from the perspective of his evaluation theory, organized the components of SBCM and their relationships from his data as shown in Figure 1 below (Hinojosa, 2001, p.76).

When SBCM is viewed as a systems theory, as above, the first significant condition of operation is data focus, utilizing SBCM research. It clarifies the goal setting (objectivity) and starts implementing "management by objectives." The secondary condition

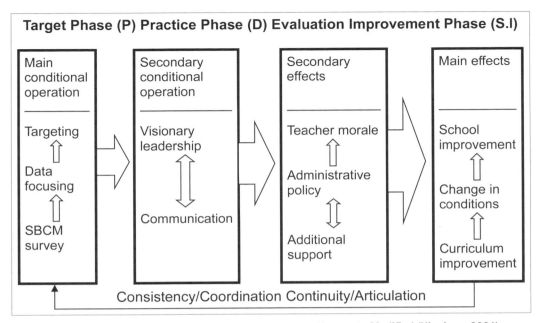

Figure 1: The Overall Structure of SBCM Components, Kuramoto Modified (Hinojosa, 2001)

operation is the planning phase, where proactive leadership and communication among staff members lead to collaboration within the school, which is a secondary input element of the systems theory. Focusing on the implementation phase, the outputs of the SBCM system are staff morale, governance and politics, and additional support, with support fulfilling a secondary effectiveness factor (English, 1975, 1987, 1996). Extra support and administrative policy are theorized as collaborative outside the school. Furthermore, the primary output of the system is the reform of the school organization and system through an improved change in the curriculum. The SBCM is a framework that considers the integrity of the systemic components of the curriculum and structures it.

It is crucial to understand what kind of curriculum the school's organizational structure can construct and implement the curriculum design through collaboration. This collaborative approach addresses conflicts and contradictions in the school's organizational structure. It is also necessary to collaborate with people outside the school community. Curriculum design is the key to understanding and addressing the community's educational needs, fostering empathy and consideration. This emphasis on collaboration makes everyone feel included and part of a collective effort.

SBCM's transformative potential is evident in its systemic output, which reforms the unit school organization and school system through remedial changes in the curriculum. When harnessed, this potential can inspire and motivate educators in their curriculum development efforts. The study has organized SBCM as a framework that considers the consistency of the systemic components of this curriculum and the overall structuring of the curriculum, inspiring hope for significant improvement.

4. School-Based Curriculum Management for School/Community Improvement from the Perspective of Curriculum Leadership

As mentioned, Hinojosa organizes its components as an interaction between developing the organizational system condition, curriculum content, and methodology and builds an SBCM. This section will also explore Henderson's (2000) Transformative Curriculum Leadership (TCL) from these perspectives.

The TCL will start with Service-Learning, which has spread in the U.S. It will organize the overall theoretical picture of SBCM in the school-based curriculum to highlight its practicality of international SBCM in school improvement and community improvement theory. This discussion will clarify how international SBCM can be a practical and impactful tool in these areas, instilling a sense of hope and optimism in all involved. TCL is an expansion of the school-level curriculum development theory. It is organized as a management theory of school and community improvement centered on the curriculum PDCA process, including the TLC components, which refer to Table 1.

Henderson positions school-based curriculum as a strategy for shaping the character of learners (students) through their contributions to the community (2000), with the realization of civic qualities in the community, especially democratic society, as its goal theory. Therefore, this study is positioned to organize a cross-section of SBCM using Henderson's transformational curriculum leadership theory as a framework, especially the TCL concentric circles. Additionally, the study took a more systemic perspective on SBCM for school and community improvement. As a methodology, the study examined SBCM from the perspective of Henderson's curriculum leadership and "Transformative School Culture" and organized it theoretically, particularly within the framework of TCL concentric circles. The research methodology was then applied to the study of SBCM from the perspective of transformative school culture and curriculum leadership. The paper also clarified the appropriateness of setting the school-based curriculum as the analytical perspective, as this research methodology contributes to organizing a cross-section of the SBCM discussed by English (1975, 1987, 1996, 2000a, 2000b, 2001a, 2001b). This transformative potential of SBCM can inspire and motivate educators in their curriculum development efforts, showing them the significant impact they can have on their students and communities.

For example, Henderson positions a school-based curriculum as a strategy for building the character of learners (students) through their contributions to the community, intending to realize civic qualities in the community, especially realizing a democratic society. The goals of SL education can be understood as consistent with the goals of Transformative Education. This concept aligns with Henderson's perspective and aims

Table 1: Transformative Curriculum Leadership Components (Henderson, 2000)

1. Progressive Learning	5. Authentic Evaluation
2. Teaching Artistry	6. Organization Development
3. Program Design	7. School-Community Relations
4. Instructional Planning	8. Leadership Development

at a specific goal or principle of Transformative Education.

However, in constructing the structural nature of SBCM, the five works of literature mentioned in earlier reviews are only partially discussed, and it is necessary to systematize each of these elements to organize the theory of the wholeness of SBCM. The SBCM that structures these partial elements can then be broadly classified into the theory of "collaboration" within the school and "collaboration" between the school organization and the school's external organization. Since this is the perspective from which the managerial aspect of SBCM is analyzed, the study has organized "collaboration" as a practical school improvement theory. Therefore, the study first examined English's cycle theory of SBCM (2000a, 2000b, 2001a, 2001b), which is the most systematic discussion of the theoretical construction of SBCM. Then, the relationship between the components of SBCM, a developed form of this theory, and the theory of school improvement were summarized. It is a potential development of SBCM in Japan, focusing in particular on the management cycle theory of the curriculum that integrates two series of curricula, and it is an attempt to obtain a particular suggestion for the research question of its effectiveness in the process of school system improvement. This potential development can make educators feel intrigued and engaged in the future of SBCM, showing them exciting possibilities for the evolution of curriculum management.

5. Conclusion

This approach to SBCM for school and community improvement (Fullan, 1991; Wade, 1997) is systemic and forward-thinking. The study examined SBCM from the perspective of Henderson's Curriculum Leadership and Transformative School Culture and organized it theoretically, particularly within the framework of TCL concentric circles. The research methodology was then applied to the study of SBCM from the perspective of transformative school culture and curriculum leadership. The paper also clarified the appropriateness of setting the school-based curriculum as the analytical perspective, as this research methodology contributes to organizing a cross-section of the SBCM discussed by English. This stress on the potential impact of SBCM can instill a sense of hope and optimism in educators about the future of education, inspiring them to continue their efforts in curriculum development and school management.

Considering the above, this chapter examines SBCM from the perspective of 'collaboration.' In doing so, the study focused on the cycle theory of SBCM and curriculum leadership theory, based on a summary of previous studies, and the internal and external "collaboration theory" of school organizations (O'Neill & Kitson, 1996). In addition to the methodology of theoretical organization of SBCM research, the study organized a cross-section of the overall structure of curriculum development and management theory based on the school-based curriculum's relevance as this study's analytical perspective. This emphasis on collaboration enhances the effectiveness of SBCM and makes educators feel included and part of a larger educational community, fostering a sense of belonging and shared purpose.

Consequently, the SBCM study has two main components (Kuramoto, 2008, 2024; Kuramoto et al., 2014, 2021). The first involves educating and evaluating educational goals through curriculum and instruction. Whereas, the second focuses on managing the organization to enhance the conditions that support educational elements, known as school management. Curriculum organization and school management are crucial and pivotal in promoting academic quality, organizational culture, and school systems, enhancing student learning effectiveness. This emphasis on the importance of curriculum organization and school management is a testament to the quality of education, instilling confidence in the system and reassuring educators.

References

Aikin, W. N. (1942). *The story of an eight-year study*. New York, NY: Harper & Brothers.

Deal, T. E., & Peterson, K. D. (1994). *The leadership paradox: Balancing logic and artistry in schools*. San Francisco, CA: Jossey-Bass Publishers.

Deal, T. E., & Peterson, K. D. (1999). *Shaping school culture: The heart of leadership*. San Francisco, CA: Jossey-Bass Publishers.

Elmore, R. F. (2002). *Bridging the gap between standards and achievement: The imperative for professional development in education*. Washington, D.C.: Albert Shanker Institute.

English, F. W. (1975). *School organization and management*. Worthington, OH: Charles A. Jones Publishing.

English, F. W. (1987). *Curriculum management for schools/colleges/businesses*. Springfield, IL: Charles C. Thomas Publisher.

English, F. W., & Robert, L. L. (1996). *Curriculum management for educational and social service organizations*. Springfield, IL: Charles C. Thomas Publisher.

English, F. W. (2000a). *The curriculum management audit: Improving school quality*. Lanham, MD: The Scarecrow Press.

English, F. W. (2000b). *Deciding what to teach and test*. Thousand Oaks, CA: Corwin Press.

English, F. W., & Betty, E. S. (2001a). *Deep curriculum alignment*. Lanham, MD: The Scarecrow Press.

English, F. W., & Betty, E. S. (2001b). *Curriculum and assessment for world-class schools*. Lanham, MD: The Scarecrow Press.

Foriska, T. (1994). The principal as instructional leader: Teaming with teachers for student success. *Schools in the Middle*, 3(3), 31–34.

Foster, W. (1986). *The reconstruction of leadership*. Victoria, Australia: Deakin University Press.

Fullan, M. (1991). *The new meaning of educational change*. New York, NY: Columbia University Teachers College Press.

Goodlad, J. (1975). *The dynamics of educational change: Toward responsive schools*. New York, NY: McGraw-Hill.

Hallinger, P., & Heck, R. (1996). Reassessing the principal's role in school effectiveness. *Educational Administration Quarterly*, 32(1), 5–44.

Harvey, T. R. (1996). *Checklist for change: A pragmatic approach to creating and controlling change*. Lancaster, PA: Technomic Publishing Company.

Henderson, J., & Kesson, K. (Eds.). (1999). *Understanding democratic curriculum leadership*. New York, NY: Teachers College Press.

Henderson, J. (2000). *Transformative curriculum leadership*. Englewood Cliffs, NJ: Merrill Prentice Hall.

Hinojosa, E. M. (2001). Superintendents' perceptions of curriculum management audits (Doctoral dissertation). The University of Texas at Austin.

Hunkins, F. P. (1980). *Curriculum development: Program improvement*. Columbus, OH: Bell & Howell Company.

Katz, R. L. (1995). The skill of an effective administrator. *Harvard Business Review*. https://hbsp.harvard.edu/product/12049-PDF-ENG

Kuramoto, T. (2008). *A study of curriculum management in the USA: From the service-learning perspective* (アメリカにおけるカリキュラムマネジメントの研究——Service-Learningの視点から). Japan: Fukuro Publishing.

Kuramoto, T., & Associates. (2014). *Lesson study & curriculum management in Japan: Focusing on action research*. Japan: Fukuro Publishing.

Kuramoto, T., & Associates. (2021). *Lesson study & curriculum management in Japan: Focusing on action research*. Japan: Fukuro Publishing.

Kuramoto, T. (2024). *School-based curriculum management: Teacher education and lesson study perspective*. Japan: Fukuro Publishing.

Leithwood, K., Jantzi, D., & Steinbach, R. (1999). *Changing leadership for changing times*. Buckingham, PA: Open University Press.

Leithwood, K. (1994). Leadership for school restructuring. *Educational Administration Quarterly*, 30(4), 498–518.

Lindelow, J. (1981). School-based management. In S. C. Smith, J. A. Mazerella, & P. K. Piele (Eds.), *School leadership: Handbook for survival* (115–138). Eugene, OR: ERIC Clearing House on Educational Management, University of Oregon.

Lipitt, R., Watson, J., & Westley, B. (1958). *Dynamics of planned change*. New York, NY: Harcourt and Brace.

Malen, B., Ogawa, R. T., & Kranz, J. (1990). What do we know about school-based management? A case study of the literature—A call for research. In W. H. Clune & J. F. White (Eds.), *The practice of choice, decentralization, and restructuring* (115–138). New York, NY: Pearson Education.

Marsh, C., & Willis, G. (1995). *Curriculum: Alternative approaches, ongoing issues*. Englewood Cliffs, NJ: Merrill Prentice Hall.

Martinello, M. L., & Cook, G. E. (2000). *Interdisciplinary inquiry in teaching and learning*. Englewood Cliffs, NJ: Merrill Prentice Hall.

O'Neill, J., & Kitson, N. (Eds.). (1996). *Effective curriculum management: Coordinating learning in the primary school*. New York, NY: Routledge.

Saylor, J. G., Alexander, W. M., & Lewis, A. J. (1981). *Curriculum planning for better teaching and learning*. New York, NY: Holt, Rinehart, and Winston.

Sears, J. B. (1950). *The nature of the administrative process*. New York, NY: McGraw-Hill.

Senge, P. M. (1990). *The fifth discipline: The art and practice of the learning organization.* New York, NY: Bantam Books.

Senge, P. M. (Eds.). (2000). *Schools that learn: A fifth discipline field book for educators, parents, and everyone who cares about education.* New York, NY: Doubleday.

Skilbeck, M. (1984). *School-based curriculum development.* London: Paul Chapman Publishing.

Skilbeck, M. (1987). School-based management and central curriculum policies in England and Wales: A paradox in three acts. In N. Sabar, J. Rudduck, & W. Reid (Eds.), *Partnership and autonomy in school-based curriculum development: Policies and practices in Israel and England* (115–138). Sales: Division of Education, University of Sheffield.

Snyder, K. J., & Anderson, R. H. (1986). *Managing productive schools: Toward an ecology.* New York, NY: Harvest HBJ Book.

Steagall, M. (2004). Perceptions of California superintendents, district-level administrators, principals, and teachers regarding the curriculum management audit as a catalyst for instructional change and improved student achievement (Doctoral dissertation). University of La Verne, California.

Unruh, G. G., & Unruh, A. (1984). *Curriculum development: Problems, processes, and progress.* Berkeley, CA: McCutchan Publishing.

Wade, R. C. (1997). *Community service-learning: A guide to including service in the public school curriculum.* New York, NY: State University of New York Press.

Wendell, F., & Bell, C. H. (1995). *Organization development: Behavioral science interventions for organization improvement.* Englewood Cliffs, NJ: Merrill Prentice Hall.

Wiles, J., & Bondi, Jr. J. (1995). *Curriculum development: A guide to practice* (9th ed.). Columbus, OH: Bell & Howell Company.

Wolfinger, D. M., & Stockard, J. W., Jr. (1997). *Elementary methods: An integrated curriculum.* New York, NY: Wesley Longman.

Wraga, W. G. (1996). A century of interdisciplinary curriculum in American schools. In P. S. Hlebowitsch & G. W. Wrage (Eds.), *Annual review of research for school leaders* (117–145). New York, NY: Scholastic (NASSP).

Chapter 2

Exploring Service-Learning SOFAR Model in School-Based Curriculum Management: Inspiring Hope for Community Impact

Tetsuo KURAMOTO, Shizuoka University of Art and Culture

Abstract

The exploration of the Significance of the Service-Learning (SL) SOFAR model in School-Based Curriculum Management (SBCM) is a dynamic concept that refers to 'the curriculum PDS process that produces results corresponding to the goals in two series: educational activities as a series of Curriculum & Instruction in terms of educational content and methods to achieve the educational goals, and organizational management activities (Management) to establish the conditions to support these activities. Theoretical and Practical research is developed by setting SL as an analytical perspective in the research methodology and examining SL's goals, contents, methods, evaluation theory, and the various conditions for SL-related school organizational management. The urgency and importance of this research is underscored by the role of the SL SOFAR model in SBCM.

1. Introduction

1-1. Service-Learning beginnings

When discussing citizenship education in recent years from the school education perspective, it is essential to consider the spread of curriculum development initiatives throughout the United States following the educational reforms of the 1990s. Service-learning (SL), a contemporary curriculum development theory that integrates academic learning with activities that contribute to others in the community, with the overarching educational goal of improving citizenship in the community, will be a crucial focus of this chapter. Henceforth, in this context, SL will refer to this educational approach. The definition of SL can be summarized as follows (Wade, 1997; Kuramoto, 2008).

Service learning is a transformative process that empowers students to understand the profound connection between living and learning. It instills the essence of being an adult, a free and responsible citizen, and living a compassionate life. This process benefits the individual and improves the community, inspiring hope and optimism.

Before proceeding to discussions concerning SL, it is essential to consider how curriculum development should be considered. Skilbeck (1984, 1987) argues for greater independence in curriculum development at the school level, favoring a decentralized approach over centralized and uniform curriculum guidelines set by the government. Curriculum development directly impacts the improvement of individual schools within educational administration. The stages in curriculum development based on the school include analysis of the school environment and situation, determining curriculum goals, curriculum design, implementation, and evaluation. The first stage of curriculum development, which is foundational to the school, begins with analyzing the school environment and conditions, followed by determining curriculum goals, designing a curriculum that meets those goals, and implementing and evaluating that curriculum.

A critical perspective in this concept is the recognition of the integrity between learning and real life. This perspective, which underpins the growing educational trend to promote the SL curriculum nationally, particularly in the late 1980s, acknowledges that education should not be divorced from the realities of the world. It exists to improve the traditional notion of community in today's society, facing challenges such as the diversification and urbanization of the social structure.

The "National and Community Service Act" (NSCA) of 1990 was enacted in response to the growing need for community service and civic engagement in the US. It provides financial assistance to K-12 and higher education institutions with advanced SL initiatives, as well as service-related organizations and nonprofit organizations, with the legal purpose of further promoting service activities. The legal definition of SL is as follows (NSCA, 1990).

1. Service Learning (SL) systematically coordinates the school and community so students learn and grow through active participation in service activities that address practical community needs.
2. Service Learning (SL) allows students to apply their existing knowledge and skills to real-life situations in the community. This practical application of learning enhances their understanding and fosters a sense of engagement and interest in their studies, making the learning process more meaningful and relevant.
3. Service Learning (SL) is a catalyst for school improvement, extending learning activities beyond the classroom walls to the community. This emphasis on school improvement through service learning can instill a sense of hope and optimism in educators about the potential of this approach to foster a caring and empathetic learning environment.

Following these specifications, this chapter employs SL's theory of educational goals as the analytical framework and aims to discuss the current state of civic education theory in the Japanese community.

Based on the perspective presented by Langten and Miller (1988), SL is associated with specific educational goals. One of these goals is the development of citizenship, which entails transitioning from dependence to independence and interdependence. It involves shifting from a self-centered perspective of the world to recognizing oneself as a member of society. In this context, SL is structured as a form of civic education theory that provides educational opportunities for students to grow from dependency and self-centeredness to mature interdependence and a sense of social responsibility and citizenship through service activities in the school and community (Langten, 1988; Taylor, 1989).

Kinsley and McPherson (1995) explicitly discuss SL from a practical standpoint: When the SL curriculum addresses significant community issues, it allows students to become aware of their significance and learn the responsibility of being part of a community.

On the other hand, Kielsmeier's work (1991) focuses on the leadership theory of community improvement in developing the qualities associated with citizenship within the student. He considers the community, which serves as SL's learning space, a leadership laboratory. He organizes leadership and espouses it as a theory of qualities and abilities that empower students to make a significant difference by pursuing common goals for community improvement and voluntary activities to assist others.

The theory is structurally envisioned as a theory of competence in which students realize significant differences through voluntary activities to help others by sharing a common goal of community improvement. Students emerge as human resources and leaders who contribute to enhancing and creating thriving communities by engaging in activities that recognize the need for community improvement, formulate change agendas, and actively pursue services to solve those agendas (Caposey, 2013).

In addition to the aforementioned civic education theory, into which the above theories can be subsumed, Lickona (1991) emphasizes the importance of character education in enhancing mature and independent personalities while discouraging self-centeredness and dependency.

As Lickona advocates, one key aspect of character education is cultivating a sense of care for others. This method involves examining ethical and social issues such as drugs, homelessness, cancer control, and environmental problems as part of the developmental study of academic subjects and cultivating practical moral skills through solving moral conflicts. Based on the context mentioned earlier, this chapter analyzes the educational goal theory of SL through the lens of civic education theory. It examines the intersection between SL curriculum development theory and practice.

As described later, the study is confident that exploring the Service-Learning SOFAR model (Bringle, 2009), which emphasizes the importance of reflection in service-learning and its implications for curriculum and lesson theory, will illuminate curriculum and lesson theory, offering valuable insights that align with the national educational philosophy and school management.

2. SOFAR Model from Educational Management and Educational Methodology

2-1. SOFAR model and SBCM

Unlike "Curriculum Management in the Courses of Study," SBCM is a central concept in school management theorized by the Japanese Association for the Study of Educational Administration (JASEA) and the Japan Society for Curriculum Studies (JSCS). It has gained widespread acceptance through its practical application in education, providing tangible solutions to school management challenges. SBCM, consisting of 1st, 2nd, and 3rd circles, is a theory that focuses on the development of a curriculum at the core of school management, the management of partnerships within and outside the organization, and the impact of that curriculum on school improvement (Kuramoto et al., 2021).

Therefore, the theory of school improvement shares significant similarities with the Service-Learning SOFAR model in this chapter. It emphasizes problem-solving, educational management activation, positive school culture formation, independent organizational bodies, open collaboration, and partnership theory within and outside the organization. This alignment underscores the shared goals and principles of these two models, providing reassurance about the effectiveness of the SOFAR model in school improvement. On the other hand, while the school organization is an educational system for students' intellectual and human growth, based on the theory of organizational rationalization and democratization, the reason a school organization is an educational system for students' intellectual and human development.

2-2. The significance of the SOFAR model in School-Based Curriculum Management (SBCM)

This model plays a crucial role in shaping the curriculum and managing partnerships within and outside the school, underscoring its importance in education. When reviewing overseas studies of similar research contexts, especially SBCM, it is essential to review relevant previous studies on (1) Curriculum Development, (2) the relationship between organizational improvement theory and systems theory, and internal and external partnership theory, (3) School Improvement, (4) School-Based Management, and (5) SBCM in the USA Development (Kuramoto, 2008; Kuramoto, 2024a).

English (1996), a prominent figure in the SBCM theory, has structured the components of the SBCM system, as depicted in Figure 1. The SBCM system incorporates the SBCM cycle theory and other curriculum development methodologies and can be seen as a 'fusion of two research series.' This fusion combines the school management theory based on internal and external partnership theory with the content method series development, similar to the SOFAR model.

English (2000) discusses Quality Control in Schools, the components of SBCM, and school improvement. It categorizes curriculum development and management theory as a concept of SBCM and its management structure into Curriculum Design and Curriculum Delivery. In other words, this can be interpreted as a theoretical structure that integrates educational management and methodology in curriculum studies (Hinojosa,

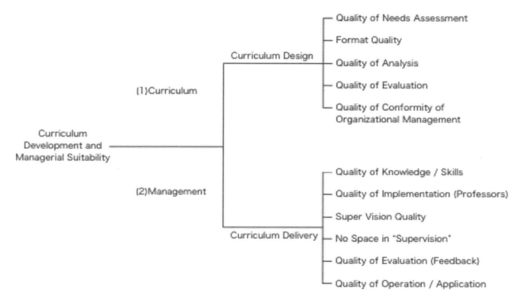

Figure 1: School Quality Control & School-Based Curriculum Management
(Kuramoto modified English, 1996, p.14)

2001).

When discussing school management from the viewpoint of internal and external partnerships within and outside the organization, the SOFAR model from the perspective of educational management and educational methodology is a model that considers how to develop and manage the SL curriculum, which is positioned at the center of school management, and how to create and manage the SL curriculum, which is positioned at the center of school management, and how to develop and manage the SL curriculum, which is positioned at the center of school management. The SOFAR model, from the perspective of educational management and educational methodology, can be summarized as a research field that connects the complementary and mutually overlapping fusion of educational management and educational methodology through curriculum studies based on the propositions of how the development and management of curriculum can improve school organization and what kind of learning effects it will have on students.

3. School Curriculum Development and the SOFAR Model—School-Based Service-Learning Study—

Based on the previous studies above, school improvement theory is essential for setting up the desired image of students through the school's educational goals. For example, when discussing SBCM in SL, the output of SBCM is the achievement of the SL curriculum goals. Specifically, these include the development of citizenship, enhancement of character education, mastery of academic content, and the development of various

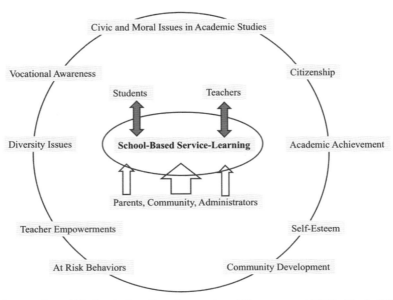

Figure 2: School-Based SL Curriculum Development and Management/SBSL (Nash, 2001, p.55)

abilities such as problem-solving (Kuramoto, 2008; Kuramoto, 2024a).

Nash (2001), who straightforwardly discussed the above at the doctoral dissertation level, has developed a theory of School-Based Service-Learning (SBSL) with the help of SBCM, as shown in Figure 2. First, from the perspective of SBSL curriculum development in the first order circle, the SL curriculum goal theory of Aiming Students includes Civics/Morality in Academic Subjects, Civic Qualities, Learning Achievement, Self-Esteem, Community Development, Problem Behavior Improvement, Responding to Diversity, and Enhancing Professionalism, among others, while advocating for the integration of the SL curriculum.

From the perspective of partnership within the school organization, which is the secondary circle of SBSL, the school organization is considered to be the organizational unit for SL curriculum development and management and is required to be managed through internal and external partnership and collaboration with the teacher group, students, parents, community, and educational administration. The school is considered the organizational unit for SL curriculum development and management. Furthermore, the role of the teacher group, parents, community, and administration (the nature of partnership) cannot be overlooked as a factor in developing management conditions that affect SBSL management, which falls under the tertiary circle. Theoretical similarities between the SBCM and the Service-Learning SOFAR model, which consists of primary, secondary, and tertiary circles to improve organizational capacity by placing curriculum development and management at the core of school improvement, are highly interpretable, and Nash's SBSL is a typical example of such a study.

From the above discussion, it can be concluded that the SBCM of SBSL is a fusion of two series of activities: curriculum and instruction as a series of educational content and methods to achieve educational goals, and Management as a series of organizational

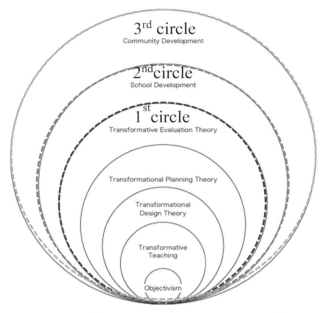

Figure 3: Curriculum Leadership and School Management (Kuramoto modified, Henderson, 2000, p.113)

management activities to support these activities and that the curriculum PDCA process that produces results corresponding to these goals is one of the compelling analytical perspectives for the future re-examination of the SOFAR model.

4 The SOFAR Model from SBCM and Transformative Curriculum Leadership (TCL)

4-1. SBCM and Transformative Curriculum Leadership (TCL)

Re-examining the SOFAR model, it is necessary to examine further the proposition that SBSL can be effective in school organization and community improvement. Therefore, with the SBCM component theory in mind, the study must consider when discussing the perspectives of internal school improvement (internal collaboration/internal partnership theory) and external school community improvement (external collaboration/external partnership theory), Henderson's Transformative Curriculum Leadership (1999, 2000), hereafter TCL, is instructive. The transformative potential of SBCM and TCL offers a hopeful vision for the future of educational management.

As shown in Figure 3 (Henderson, 2000), the TCL is a theoretical framework that structurally supports the SBCM for school organization and community improvement. It is based on the curriculum PDCA process and describes specific curriculum development and management practices in SL and the primary, secondary, and tertiary circles. The components of these circles, which construct them, are outlined below (Kuramoto, 2008; Kuramoto, 2024a). TCL plays a crucial role in SBCM, guiding and shaping its application.

- 1st circle (student development)
  - Progressive Learning
  - Teaching Artistry, Program Design/Instructional, Planning
  - Authentic Evaluation
- 2nd circle (teacher professional development, organizational development, internal partnerships.)
  - Organization Development
  - Leadership Development
- 3rd circle (collaboration with organizations outside the school, external partnerships)
  - School-Community Relations

Henderson's discussion on the TCL's structure is pivotal. It illustrates how the TCL fosters a collaborative school culture by organizing lessons, curriculum planning, and evaluation theory in the 1st circle. This culture, in turn, builds partnerships and collaboration with the internal and external parts of the school in the 2nd and 3rd circles. The TCL, a cross-section of the alignment of the SOFAR model with the SBCM, is a powerful tool for improving school organization and creating a sense of community around curriculum development.

4-2. SBCM & Transformative Curriculum Leadership (TCL) and the SOFAR model: a vision for transformation

Commonly known as the SL and SOFAR model (Bringle, 2009), this model emphasizes the importance of 'Students,' 'Community Organizations,' 'Faculty,' 'Administrators (administrators, principals, school boards),' and 'Community Residents (parents, community residents).' It is a critical framework in our discussion, providing crucial insights into the educational process. SL will further discuss the structure of the SBCM's first, second, and third circles, which can be understood as the layered nature of Henderson's TCL and the SOFAR model. This collaborative effort, which involves all stakeholders in the educational process, particularly values the community's role and recognizes its significant contribution.

TCL develops the educational philosophy of citizenship education and places SL in concrete practice, with a research perspective on school and community improvement through curriculum development. Therefore, SBCM & TCL, which specializes in SL, is a measure (1st circle) to form the character of learners through their contribution to the community, with the realization of civic qualities in the community, especially democratic society, as the curriculum goal theory. Furthermore, the SOFAR model plays a crucial role in emphasizing learning activities that lead to the recognition process of the school organization as a social organization that creates a sense of community (internal 2nd circle and external 3rd circle) as a cognitive process, fostering a strong sense of community among all stakeholders in the educational process.

As discussed in the SBCM & TCL model, three main focus areas exist. The 1st circle involves developing curriculum objectives, content, methods, and evaluation theories

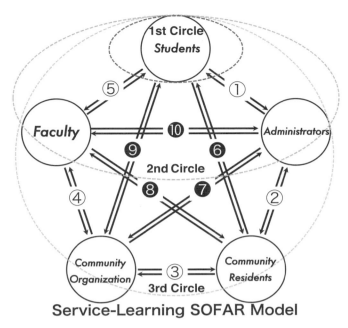

Figure 4: Structure of 1st, 2nd, and 3rd Circles in SBCM & TCL and SOFAR Model (Bringle, 2009)

to promote independent, interactive, and deep learning for students. The 2nd circle, the internal partnership, focuses on collaboration between administrators (such as principals and school boards) and faculty (teachers) to support student development. This includes enhancing teacher and staff professional development, reorganizing school responsibilities, and building a positive school culture. The 3rd, termed external partnerships, underscores the collaborative nature of the model. It involves collaborating with community residents (such as parents) and community organizations (local groups) to foster trust and cooperation with organizations outside the school, including parent groups, community members, non-profit organizations, businesses, and various levels of government. This collaboration creates a sense of connection and belonging, making educators part of a larger educational community (Kuramoto, 2024b).

Though there may be some overlap between these 1st, 2nd, and 3rd circles, the key drivers for advancing lesson study, curriculum development, and school organization come from top management (principals, vice principals) and middle management (department heads). These leaders play a crucial role in steering the direction of the school organization, empowering them to influence and shape the educational process.

5. The 1st, 2nd, and 3rd Circle of SBCM & SOFAR Model

5-1. The 1st circle of the SBCM & SOFAR model

In the 1st circle (Students' Development) in Figure 4, Langten (1998), in a highly similar model to the SBCM and SOFAR model specific to SL, defines that the growth of citizenship is independence from dependence, from self-awareness that one is the center of the world to an awareness that one is one of the members of the social fabric. Therefore, they organize SL as a form of social and civic education theory that provides educational opportunities for students to grow from dependency and self-centeredness to mature interdependence and a sense of social responsibility and citizenship through service activities in schools and communities (Barber, 1984, 1992). Kielsmeier (1991), highly similar to the SBCM & SOFAR model specific to SL, defines the community in which SL is studied as a laboratory of leadership, where students' leadership is defined as the ability to share common goals in a community, assist others, to the idea that Students' leadership is a voluntary self-enlightenment activity in which they share common goals, are dedicated to helping others, and can make a significant social difference.

The above theories of SL curriculum goals are consistent with the 1st circle TCL theory of transformative educational goals. These theories emphasize learning activities in which students recognize the need for community change apart from their agendas and pursue the idea that the school organization becomes part of a social organization that creates a sense of community. It allows the school organization to become part of the social organization that creates the community (Taba, 1962; Boyte, 1989; Lieberman, 1995; Steven, 1998).

5-2. The 2nd circle of the SBCM & SOFAR model
The secondary circle in Figure 4 (Teachers' Professional and Organizational Development.) underscores the crucial role of Administrators and Faculty in the SOFAR model. Their task is to establish internal partnerships and foster school culture to nurture the development of 'Students' in the 2nd circle. This emphasis on internal partnerships and fostering school culture is not just a task but a collective mission that involves everyone in the educational community. Henderson defines school culture as follows (Henderson, 2000).

"School culture is the organizational nature and tendencies of the school, including items such as the following: interrelationships among school members, expectations in classroom life, school rituals, organizational atmosphere, how issues are defined and clarified in terms of methodology, what is evaluated and disciplined, and who provides codes of conduct and authority" (p.160).

The 2nd circle, the TCL theory of school culture, is influenced by the open-mindedness of the organization, participation, responsibility, reflection, caring, and division of roles, which can be essential factors in curriculum development. School culture is also greatly influenced by the culture and value standards of the community that encompasses the school in the tertiary circle, including religious, racial, political, and social factors. There are two perspectives to analyzing school culture: First, content refers to the behaviors and modes of thinking shared by a particular group of teachers and the broader community of teachers related to essential attitudes, values, beliefs, customs, and hypotheses. Secondly, formality refers to the characteristic culture-building patterns among organizational members.

The latter is defined as management culture. It grows from an individualist Culture of Separation to a Culture of Connection and finally to a Culture of Integration. The catalytic element of the transition process of the school's organizational culture is the culture of integration (see Figure 1). The catalytic factors in the transition process of school organizational culture include unique cultural conditions, such as Contrived Collegiality, Comfortable Collaboration, and Balkanization (Henderson, 2000; Caposey, 2013).

5-3. The 3rd circle of the SBCM & SOFAR model

This model outlines the relationships between school organizations, community agencies, and other external entities in the context of curriculum management. This circle is particularly significant as it represents the crucial role of external entities, such as community agencies, in shaping and implementing the curriculum.

SBCM in Japan and Curriculum Management in the Courses of Study traditionally confine the curriculum management entity to school organizations. However, a new perspective emerges when we focus on the 3rd circle in Figure 4 (collaboration with organizations outside the school).

The perspective, which emphasizes the role of community agencies such as nonprofit organizations (NPOs) in SL, opens up a world of possibilities. In fact, in the realm of SBCM, particularly in the context of SL, we have seen numerous instances where community agencies (CAs) like NPOs have taken the lead, demonstrating the transformative power of internal and external partnerships with school organizations, engaging us in their potential and involving us in their exploration. Particularly concerning SL, it is a CA-driven curriculum development and management in which students learn citizenship as members of the community by adapting their learning experiences to the needs of the community through internal and external (2nd and 3rd) partnerships between the CA and the school organization (Kuramoto, 2008). In Japan, curriculum management is conducted by the school organization. However, there are many typical cases in which SBCM is undertaken by CAs, which are social and educational institutions and organizations outside of the school. In developing the SL curriculum, the management cycle is discussed from the viewpoint of creating the conditions for the SL curriculum.

6. Conclusion—The Structure of School-Based Service-Learning Curriculum Management—

Figure 5 shows the SBCM's structural diagram in the SL SOFAR model according to the 1st, 2nd, and 3rd circles of TLS. Three points explain its significance in pedagogical research.

First, from the perspective of 'integrative research,' our study constructs a theoretical structure of SBCM as an activity that organizes and energizes educational content, methodology, and managerial conditions to align with students' development. This approach presents an overall view of the intricate theoretical structure of SBCM, a novel and internationally unexplored area. Therefore, the study explores the structure of SBCM, explicitly focusing on the SL curriculum. This research methodology fosters integrative research' that combines curriculum research theory from the educational content-methodology perspective and management theory from the educational management perspective. The study's significant contribution lies in establishing an integrative research method that elucidates the actual enhancement of schools and communities by creating and implementing the SL curriculum.

Second, organizing the goals, contents, methods, and evaluation theory of SL curriculum development in the 1st circle is crucial. In Japan, the issue of an Integrated Curriculum (IC) with the fundamentals of the subject and curriculum development that integrates experiential activities with the subject content and skills is a topic of discussion in the national educational standard (Taylor, 1989).To shed light on these practical educational issues, the SL curriculum, which is based on a core of service experience activities and develops ICs with the fundamentals of the subject content, is a reliable and inspiring solution (Walker, 1997). The SL curriculum comprises three factors: subject content and skills, community needs, and students' interests (Plan). The relationship between SL lessons (Do) and reflection (Check & Action) is crucial. Developing and implementing the SL curriculum and placing it at the core of school management is an effective strategy for school improvement, and this is the Structure of School-Based Service-Learning Curriculum Management.

Third, the study undertook a comprehensive examination of prior SBCM research in the following five areas, providing a thorough understanding of the subject:

1. The managerial factors are analyzed using curriculum development theory.
2. The relationship between organizational improvement theory and systems theory
3. School improvement theory applies ecological external environment adaptation to organizational management theory.
4. The autonomy of unit schools in SBM/effective schools
5. Principals' and curriculum coordinators' school culture and leadership theories include organizational members' significant behavioral norms/values.

The SOFAR model effectively structures the organizational theory of curriculum management with its partial elements. This model categorizes the elements into the 2nd circle, internal collaboration, which pertains to the school's internal organization. The 3rd circle, external collaboration, can be broadly classified into two categories: internal collaboration, which is internal to the school, and external collaboration, which is external to the school. In the US, SL programs are promoted in school and social education through 3rd circle external collaboration with the federal government, states, local governments, and community agencies (CA). (Kuramoto, C., & Kuramoto, T., 2015). The methodology in which students and youth are actively involved in the community and learn their role as citizens is noted as a form of SL curriculum (Lisman, 1998; Kahne, 1999).

To summarize, School-Based (Service-Learning) Curriculum Management is a theory and practice related to school improvement. It can include problem-solving, educational management activation, positive school culture formation, independent or

Service-Learning Educational Goal: Citizenship Education/Character Education
(Growth of Citizenship, Caring Education of Character, Awareness of Community Members)
(Problem-Solving Method, Critical Thinking, Decision Making Abilities)

School Improvement
1) Relationship between organizational improvement theory and systems theory, 2) School-Based Management (SBM),
3) Effective School, 4) Collaboration of SBCM in School Culture and Leadership

School-Based Service-Learning Curriculum Management

2nd Circle: Curriculum Managerial Aspect
(Curriculum Internal Collaboration)

1) **Lesson Study**
   (Professional Learning Community, PLC)
2) **Knowledge Management Leadership, SECI Model**
   Knowledge Asset, Explicit and Tacit Knowledge, Ba
3) **School Culture**
   1. Organization Development
   2. School- Community relations
   3. Leadership Development
   4. School Culture of Separation, connection, and Integration
4) **Single-Loop Reflection & Double-Loop Reflection**
5) **Visionary Leadership & Communication**
   • Teacher Morale, Administrative Policy, Additional Support
   • Change in Conditions, Curriculum Improvement
6) **Building School Vision and Mission**
7) **Teachers Morale Improvement**

1st Circle: Curriculum Development & Design
(Curriculum Integration)

1) **Curriculum Development Goals:**
   (Citizenship Education & Character Education)
2) **Curriculum Development Contents:**
   (ex, EDGs, Others)
3) **Curriculum Development Methodology:**
   (Students, subjects, & Community's Integrated Needs)
4) **Curriculum Development Goal:**
   (Reflection regarding Self-Esteem, Social Contribution)
5) **Curriculum Design**
   (Student-Centered Education, Bottom-Up Curriculum)
6) **Transformative Curriculum Leadership**
   1. Progressive Learning   2. Authentic Evaluation
   3. Teaching Artistry   4. Program Design
                              5. Instructional Planning

Integrated Field of Educational Research

3rd Circle: Curriculum External Collaboration
(Community Improvement with Partnership)

1) **Community Organization, Industry, and Residence**
2) **Local University, Church, and NPO agencies**
3) **Governmental organization, Board of Education**
4) **Parents, Alumni**

Figure 5: The Structure of School-Based Service-Learning Curriculum Management
(Kuramoto modified, 2018, p.12)

self-supporting organizational structure, and openness and collaboration. Additionally, the ultimate significance of the school organization is to be an educational institution for students' intellectual and personal development. Our research, which underscores the crucial role of school organization in students' intellectual and personal development, can contribute significantly to school improvement. (Kuramoto, 2008; Kuramoto, 2024a).

This study provides practical insights into how curriculum management can improve school organizational systems and increase students' educational effectiveness when placed at the core of curriculum development and management theory. The exploration of the Significance of the Service-Learning SOFAR model in SBCM is a dynamic concept that refers to 'the curriculum PDS process that produces results corresponding to the goals in two series: educational activities as a series of Curriculum & Instruction in terms of educational content and methods to achieve the educational goals, and organizational management activities (Management) to establish the conditions to support these activities. Theoretical and empirical research is developed by setting SL as an analytical perspective in the research methodology and examining SL's goals, contents, methods, evaluation theory, and the various conditions for SL-related school organizational management. This research equips educators, curriculum developers, and researchers with the knowledge to enhance their school systems and student learning outcomes.

Footnote
The research focused on "21K18479 Implementing Partnership-Based Service-Learning in Elementary and Secondary Higher Education, Karaki, K." Chapter 2 is collaborative Karaki research from the perspectives of SBCM (1st, 2nd, and 3rd circles) and TLS.

References
Barber, B. (1984). *Strong democracy*. University of California Press.

Barber, B. (1992). *An aristocracy of everyone: The politics of education and the future of America*. Ballantine Books.

Boyte, H. (1989). *Commonwealth: A return to politics*. The Free Press.

Bringle, G., Clayton, H., & Price, F. (2009). Partnerships in service learning and civic engagement. *Partnerships: A Journal of Service Learning & Civic Engagement*, 1(1), 1–20.

Caposey, P. J. (2013). *Building a culture of support: Strategies for school leaders*. Eye on Education.

English, F. W., & Robert, L. L. (1996). *Curriculum management for educational and social service organizations*. Charles C. Thomas Publisher.

English, F. W. (2000). *The curriculum management audit: Improving school quality*. The Scarecrow Press.

Henderson, J., & Kesson, K. (Eds.). (1999). *Understanding democratic curriculum leadership*. Teachers College Press.

Henderson, J. (2000). *Transformative curriculum leadership*. Merrill Prentice Hall.

Hinojosa, E. M. (2001). Superintendents' perceptions of curriculum management audits. (Doctoral dissertation, The University of Texas at Austin).

Japanese Association for the Study of Educational Administration. (2009). Professional standards for principal: Desired principal image and competencies, 2009 edition. Retrieved from http://jasea.jp/wp-content/uploads/2016/12/e-teigen2012.6.pdf

Kahne, J., & Westheimer, J. (1999). In the service of what? The politics of service learning. In Claus, J., & Ogden, C. (Eds.), *Service learning for youth empowerment and social change* (p.29). Peter Lang Publishing.

Kielsmeier, J. (1991). The nation not at risk: Service-learning in educational reform. In *Growing Hope: A sourcebook on integrating youth service into the curriculum* (1–5). National Youth Leadership Council.

Kinsley, C. W., & McPherson, K. (1995). *Enriching the curriculum through service learning*. Association for Supervision and Curriculum Development.

Kuramoto, C., & Kuramoto, T. (2015). International service-learning in Nicaragua. *Journal of Medical English Education*, 14(3), 99–102.

Kuramoto, T. (2008). *A study of curriculum management in the USA: From the service-learning perspective* (アメリカにおけるカリキュラムマネジメントの研究――Service-Learningの視点から). Japan: Fukuro Publishing.

Kuramoto, T., & Associates. (2014). *Lesson study & curriculum management in Japan—Focusing on action research*. Fukuro Publishing.

Kuramoto, T., & Associates. (2021). *Lesson study & curriculum management in Japan—Focusing on action research*. Fukuro Publishing.

Kuramoto, T. (2024). *School-based curriculum management: Teacher education and lesson study perspective*. Fukuro Publishing.

Langten, S., & Miller, F. (1988). Youth community service. *Equity & Choice*, 15(1), 25–36.

Lickona, T. (1991). *Educating for character*. Bantam Books.

Lieberman, A. (1995). *The work of restructuring schools: Building from the ground up*. Teachers College Press.

Lisman, D. (1998). *Toward a civil society: Civic literacy and service learning*. Bergin & Garvey.

Nash, K. G. (2001). Examining teacher's beliefs about school-based service-learning programs. (Doctoral dissertation, University of Massachusetts Lowell).

National and Community Service Act of 1990, Public Law 101–610, Nov. 16, 1990, 104 Stat. 3127 (42 USC. 12501 et seq.).

Skilbeck, M. (1984). *School-based curriculum development*. Paul Chapman Publishing.

Skilbeck, M. (1987). School-based management and central curriculum policies in England and Wales: A paradox in three acts. In Sabar, N., Rudduck, J., & Reid, W. (Eds.), *Partnership and autonomy in school-based curriculum development, policies, and practices in Israel and England* (115–138). University of Sheffield, Sales, Division of Education.

Steven, G. J. (1998). *Staying centered: Curriculum leadership in a turbulent era*. Association for Supervision and Curriculum Development.

Taba, H. (1962). *Curriculum development, theory, and practice*. Harcourt Publisher.

Taylor, C. (1989). *Sources of the self: Making a modern identity*. Harvard University Press.

Wade, R. (1997). *Community service-learning: A guide to including service in the public-school curriculum*. State University of New York Press.

Walker, D. F., & Soltis, J. F. (1997). *Curriculum and aims, thinking about education series*. Teachers College Press.

Chapter 3

Applying Variation Theory for Instructional Design: Learning Study in Hong Kong

Eric C. K. CHENG, Yew Chung College of Early Childhood Education, Hong Kong/China

Abstract

This paper delves into the application of Learning Study, enriched by Ference Marton's Variation Theory, in instructional design, focusing on Hong Kong. Guided by three levels of variation, Learning Study is explored as a dynamic methodology that enhances student and teacher learning. The paper examines its integration with Lesson Study, outlines the core principles of the Variation Theory of Learning, and details systematic procedures for conducting Learning Study. Emphasis is placed on the role of variation patterns—contrast, generalization, separation, and fusion—in teaching. The paper underscores how Learning Study, deeply rooted in Variation Theory, provides a structured and collaborative approach to instructional design, transforming implicit knowledge into shared pedagogical excellence.

1. Introduction

In the landscape of educational methodologies, the Learning Study model emerges as a dynamic force, deeply intertwined with the groundbreaking Variation Theory of Learning by Ference Marton (2014). Educators from Sweden and Hong Kong are increasingly adopting this model, necessitating a nuanced understanding of applying the Variation Theory to instructional design. The "object of learning" concept within Learning Study extends beyond mere subject knowledge, encompassing skills, attitudes, and values. This paper navigates the intricate relationship between the Variation Theory and Learning Study, exploring how educators can leverage these principles to enhance instructional design.

Guided by three levels of variation (V1, V2, V3), the Learning Study investigates diverse student understandings, teacher approaches, and the strategic use of variation as a teaching tool. We delve into identifying critical aspects of learning content and incorporating four vital variation patterns—contrast, generalization, separation, and fusion—to provide diverse entry points for students. This exploration sheds light on the transformative potential of the Learning Study model, offering educators insights into improving teaching practices and elevating student learning outcomes.

2. Lesson Study

Exploring the relationship between Lesson Study and Learning Study becomes pivotal in understanding the trajectory of educational methodologies and their impact on teaching practices. Lesson Study, stemming from Japan, is a collaborative educational approach aimed at refining teaching strategies and elevating student learning outcomes (Cheng, 2019). Evolving since the Meiji era and gaining prominence in the 1980s and 1990s, Lesson Study involves teachers collectively designing and enhancing lesson plans through innovative teaching methods (Cheng & Chan, 2021). This method follows a PDCA (Plan-Do-Check-Act) cycle, where teachers collaboratively plan a lesson, deliberately introducing variations. One teacher delivers the lesson while others observe student responses, leading to adjustments based on the subsequent analysis. This iterative process drives continual improvement in teaching practices and positively impacts student learning outcomes.

Post-lessons, a reflective phase unfolds, engaging teachers in comprehensive discussions to evaluate the effectiveness of the lesson and pinpoint areas for improvement. This reflective element sets the stage for an ongoing cycle of refining lessons. Beyond its immediate impact on individual teaching approaches, Lesson Study is crucial in teachers' professional development. It creates a collaborative space for educators to collectively enhance their pedagogical knowledge and teaching skills (Cheng, 2009; Cheng & Chan, 2021). As educators and researchers explore the educational landscape, it becomes imperative to consider the evolution of Lesson Study and its impact. In this context, we delve into a related and distinct methodology, Learning Study, which also emerges as a potent force for advancing teaching practices and student learning outcomes.

3. Learning Study

Learning Study, rooted in action research principles, is a dynamic method to enhance teaching and learning while nurturing teachers' professional growth (Cheng, 2009; Cheng & Lo, 2013). Drawing inspiration from design experiments and incorporating elements from Lesson Study and teaching research initiatives, Learning Study emphasizes the theory of variation for pedagogical design within lesson plans (Cheng, 2014). In various settings, from Hong Kong to Sweden, Learning Study, unlike traditional Lesson Study, introduces distinctive elements into the educational landscape (Cheng, 2014).

Similar to Lesson Study, Learning Study views teaching as a sophisticated professional activity, providing teachers with a unique platform to explore student comprehension intricacies collaboratively (Lo, 2005; Cheng, 2014). Through collaborative reflection, teachers engage as reflective participants, implementing theories proposed by others in learning communities (Cheng, 2009). This approach integrates theory into practice, enhancing teachers' educational capabilities and fostering ongoing professional development (Pang, 2006).

Collaborative planning among teachers is central to the Learning Study process, where lessons are designed to induce specific variations in student thinking. Teachers observe and document student responses during the lesson, seeking to understand critical aspects' perceptions or misunderstandings. Post-lesson discussions serve as forums for analyzing variations, refining teaching methods, and planning subsequent lesson iterations (Cheng & Lee, 2019).

In essence, Learning Study seamlessly integrates the variation theory into lesson planning and reflection, enhancing students' grasp of critical aspects. Aligned with the broader Lesson Study philosophy, Learning Study stands out as a dynamic and practical approach to advancing education through collaboration, respect for teachers, and the deliberate introduction of variations in diverse classroom settings.

4. The Variation Theory of Learning

At the core of Learning Study's teaching approach is the Variation Theory of Learning, a framework credited to the Swedish educator Ference Marton (Lo, 2012; Fung-Lo & Marton, 2012). This theory asserts that learning is closely tied to students' ability to discern Critical Aspects of the Object of Learning. Learning Study translates this theory into actionable steps by systematically identifying these critical aspects through variations in student responses. The aim is to craft teaching activities that intentionally introduce variations in student understanding.

The theory posits that learning inherently directs itself towards a specific object and is tied to individuals' perceptions. Learning Study's theoretical assumptions revolve around three key factors: a focus on learning content, the idea that "knowing" involves a particular problem-solving approach, and reliance on three types of variations (Marton & Booth, 1997). These variations involve changes in students' and teachers' understanding of learning content and the intentional design of the research class.

By incorporating these variations, Learning Study emerges as a dynamic and effective approach to advancing education, fostering nuanced student understanding, and promoting continuous improvement in teaching practices among educators. The Variation Theory of Learning, a significant pedagogical framework, places variation at the core of the learning process. It suggests that effective learning occurs when individuals discern variations in critical aspects, identifying key features integral to understanding a concept or phenomenon. Variation, a key facilitator of learning in this theory, is deliberately incorporated into teaching methodologies to expose students to diverse instances related to critical aspects.

The theory emphasizes the importance of contrast, encouraging students to recognize variations and discern and appreciate elements that remain constant. It promotes a holistic view of concepts, aiming to instill in students an understanding of relationships and patterns rather than focusing solely on isolated facts. The theory cultivates discernment as a critical skill, encouraging active engagement, reflection on differences and commonalities, and connecting new knowledge with existing understanding.

In practical teaching, leveraging the theory involves designing learning experiences that introduce variations while guiding students in actively discerning critical aspects. This learner-centered approach recognizes the importance of active cognitive engagement and the constructive role of variation in shaping meaningful learning experiences.

5. Procedures for Conducting Learning Study

Learning Studies follow a systematic research methodology encompassing instructional design, implementation, and evaluation. In terms of method, Learning Studies follow a systematic process that involves planning, implementing, and evaluating a research lesson. These stages are like guidelines for conducting Learning Studies in schools (Cheng, 2009; Cheng & Lo, 2013).

Planning Stage: This is where teachers choose a topic, define what they want students to learn (object of learning), and identify the critical aspects of that learning object. They collect ideas from teachers and students about their understanding of the learning object, which helps identify the variation pattern for designing the research lesson. Teachers then choose suitable approaches and teaching strategies and create a lesson plan.

Implementation Stage: One teacher teaches the planned research lesson, which others in the group observe. The lesson is recorded for detailed analysis. After the lesson, there is a conference where teachers reflect on it, share views, and suggest improvements. Another teacher then teaches the revised lesson to another class, which is repeated until all teachers have taught the lesson.

Evaluation Stage: This stage involves teachers' reflective practices and happens simultaneously with the implementation. Reflective evaluation is ongoing and involves data from test scores, student interviews, and analysis of teaching enactment from video clips. By comparing how teachers taught and student performance, teachers suggest improvements, revise the lesson, and implement it again.

After the inquiry process, the details of the Learning Study are shared through seminars or booklets. Teachers reflect on what they have learned and externalize personal knowledge in presentations, turning tacit knowledge into explicit knowledge. The entire experience is documented, including video clips of research lessons, and each Learning Study is written as a case report, becoming part of the school's shared knowledge. Finally, teachers present the case to the research team and the public. Figure 1 illustrates the steps in conducting a Learning Study. It is crucial to note that "V1" focuses on "student learning," "V2" focuses on "teacher learning," and "V3" is an effective tool and approach to implement the first two.

The initial step in implementing a learning study involves selecting a topic and recognizing teachers' diverse methods of handling that topic (V2). This recognition addresses the adaptive nature of teaching practices, acknowledging various valid approaches to conveying a specific subject.

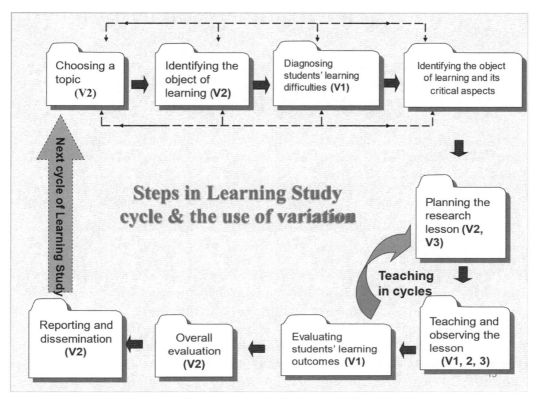

Figure 1: Steps in Learning Study Cycle and the Use of Variation

The second step is to identify the Object of Learning. The "object of learning" is a pivotal concept in Learning Study, encompassing understanding concepts or theories and mastering skills, attitudes, or values. Learning is asserted to be connected to this object, requiring identification of the learning activities. Learning content has two attributes: subject knowledge, a short-term goal, and specific abilities, a long-term goal. When selecting learning content, teachers must consider its position in the subject structure and how students understand it. Questions to ponder include its relevance to educational objectives, cultivating desired abilities, difficulties students might face, and its relation to future subjects.

Developing the Object of Learning (OL) involves meticulously considering key attributes essential for mastery. The relationship with OL is absolute and encompasses the logical and sequential progression of learning, the precise terminology employed in conveying subject knowledge, and the intricate interplay between subject knowledge and the construction of concepts. Identifying key attributes often challenging the learning process is integral to shaping effective teaching strategies. The classroom teaching activities embedded in pre-test papers are meticulously designed, leveraging OL and its Critical Features (CF). Guiding principles for selecting key OL involve expressing learning content systematically and hierarchically, ensuring a comprehensive yet concise presentation within time constraints. In this process, critical considerations include

Table 1: Examples of Object of Learning and Its Critical Aspects

Object of Learning	Critical Aspects
Influence of the ratio of effort arm to resistance arm on effort saving	• The effort point is where force is applied; the fulcrum is the fixed axis of the lever; the load point is where the object receives force. • The distance between the fulcrum and Load is the resistance arm; the distance between the fulcrum and effort is the effort arm. • Longer effort arms result in more effort saving, and vice versa. • Shorter effort arms result in more effort, and vice versa.
Relationship between plate movement and earthquakes	• Plate movement forces result from the flow of magma inside the Earth. • Fractures occur when pressure exceeds what rock layers can bear. • Energy release during rock breakage causes earthquakes.
Surface characteristics of the thermal expansion and contraction phenomenon	• Particles vibrate. • Heat is energy; a higher temperature means more particle energy and considerable vibration. • A cooler temperature means less particle energy and more minor vibration. • Explaining real-life applications of thermal expansion and contraction.

establishing the relevance of OL to students' lives and experiences, defining the desired knowledge and abilities for students, aligning OL with the subject curriculum, gauging OL based on existing student knowledge, and understanding the subsequent knowledge or abilities to be constructed upon this foundational OL. This holistic approach ensures a strategic and comprehensive development of the Object of Learning, fostering a robust foundation for students' educational journey. Table 1 illustrates examples of the Object of Learning and its Critical Aspects.

The third step is to dialogue about diverse student understanding (V1). In this phase, the Learning Study recognizes distinct student perspectives on the same Object of Learning. It acknowledges that students bring diverse backgrounds and perspectives to their learning, and understanding shifts signify meaningful learning experiences.

Once the learning goals are set, the third step involves identifying the critical aspects of the content, aiding students in grasping essential points for developing expected abilities. Teachers need a deep understanding of subject knowledge and recognizing these critical aspects. Consciousness structure limitations necessitate focusing on specific aspects. Once learning content is confirmed, core attributes are selected to explain how students can master it. Each critical aspect contributes to understanding the whole, emphasizing the importance of recognizing how different attributes relate to each other.

The fourth step is to confirm the object of learning and critical aspects to design the pattern of variation (V3). In this step, the focus is on intentional design to induce variations in student understanding. Post-lesson discussions refine teaching strategies based on observed variations, creating a dynamic feedback loop for continuous improvement in the teaching-learning process.

For recognition to occur, some features of something must change while others remain constant. "Variation" is pivotal in the Learning Study, challenging students to identify critical features amid changing or unchanging backgrounds. Students need to experience "variation," where attributes change against a constant background or remain unchanged amid a changing background.

6. Design the Pattern of Variation

The commonly used patterns of variation include contrast, generalization, separation, and fusion. These four variation patterns serve different functions by designing teaching activities to help students identify critical features of the expected learning content. Let us briefly explain the implementation of these four functions through examples:

Contrast: If we want students to grasp the concept of "tall," presenting just one example of something "tall" (like a picture of a taller person) is not sufficient. As things are relative, without something "short," there cannot be anything "tall." So, we need to present both "short" and "tall" things simultaneously (for example, showing a picture of a taller person and a shorter person) for students to discern the concept of "tall" through comparison.

Generalization: When we want students to induce the regularity of certain aspect features of a series of related things, we can use the generalization variation pattern. For instance, to make students understand "red," we need them to experience "red" in different cases, like red socks, red clothes, a red stool, and a red apple. This way, students can "generalize" the concept of "red" and distinguish it from other unrelated attributes (like socks, clothes, stool, and apples). In other words, if a particular feature of something remains constant in a series of consecutive cases, students can easily recognize this feature.

Separation: Taking an example from a common science class where students learn about the color of sunlight, teachers often use a prism to show students the colors dispersed from sunlight. However, if only a prism is used, students might mistakenly think the colors come from the prism. So, teachers can use tools like soap bubbles, CDs, or oil floating on water to show students that a rainbow still appears despite the different tools. This helps students recognize that color does not come from these tools but has another source. To make students thoroughly understand the origin of color, we can combine the "contrast" variation pattern, allowing students to experience that without sunlight, there is no rainbow phenomenon, making them aware of the relationship between sunlight and a rainbow (Lo et al., 2006).

Fusion: Apart from maintaining a certain attribute of something unchanged while changing other attributes or changing a certain attribute while keeping other attributes constant, we can simultaneously change multiple related attributes of something. This explains to students' multiple key attributes of something, the relationships between these attributes, and the relationships between all attributes and the whole. For example, to help students understand what "price" is, we can design the simultaneous variation of the "supply" and "demand" of the same product. This lets students know that the price of a product is influenced simultaneously by the supply and demand for the product.

7. A Learning Study Case: Principle of the Lever

In a Learning Study focused on the "Principle of the Lever," the class begins with an engaging introduction. The teacher presents three images illustrating the critical components of levers—fulcrum, effort point, load point, effort arm, and load arm. The students actively participate, identifying and understanding the positions and definitions of each element. Once this foundation is established, the teacher stimulates critical thinking by prompting students to consider the efficiency of different transportation methods.

Moving into the first activity, students are guided to conduct experiments using tools, with the specific aim of understanding how altering the effort arm impacts the efficiency of the lever while keeping the load arm and load constant. This hands-on exploration not only reinforces theoretical knowledge but also encourages practical application.

Building on this, the second activity maintains engagement and curiosity. Students, using the same set of tools, explore how changing the load arm influences the lever's efficiency while keeping the effort arm and load constant. These experiments provide tangible experiences, fostering a deeper comprehension of the lever's principles.

The Learning Study culminates in a collaborative discussion in the third activity. Students are encouraged to share their findings and insights, contemplating how to design the most efficient lever. This synthesis of experiences from the previous activities prompts students to articulate the effects of changing the fulcrum and the ratio of the load arm to the effort arm on the lever's efficiency. Throughout the study, the teacher acts as a facilitator, guiding the process and encouraging a dynamic exchange of ideas among students. This approach deepens the student's understanding of the Principle of the Lever and cultivates essential skills in observation, experimentation, and collaborative learning.

Topic: Principle of the Lever

Object of Learning: The impact of the ratio of the load arm to the effort arm on efficiency.

Critical Aspects:

1. When the load arm remains constant, a longer effort arm leads to greater efficiency, and vice versa.
2. When the effort arm remains constant, a shorter load arm leads to greater efficiency, and vice versa.
3. The most efficient configuration is achieved when the load arm is the shortest and the effort arm is the longest.

Table 2 illustrates the pattern of variations of the above three critical aspects.

8. How Does Learning Study Enable Teacher Learning?

Learning Study empowers teacher learning through a structured process based on the

Table 2: The Pattern of Variations for the Three Critical Aspects of the Principle of the Lever

Teaching Segment	Discernment Critical Features	Varied	Invaried/Constant
Activity One Weighing (Generalisation)	The length of the load arm remains constant; a longer effort arm leads to greater efficiency Length of the effort arm.	Length of the load arm Amount of force applied	• Load • Fulcrum • Length of the Load arm
	The height of the force point is irrelevant to the efficiency	Height of the force point Height of the fulcrum	All configurations in the experiments above, including settings and levels of efficiency, remain constant.
Activity Two Weighing (Generalisation)	The length of the effort arm remains constant; a shorter load arm leads to greater efficiency. Length of the load arm	Length of the load arm Amount of force applied Load	Load Fulcrum Length of the effort arm
Activity Three Which point is the most efficient for the fulcrum position? (Fusion)	When the load arm is the shortest and the effort arm is the most extended, efficiency is maximized. Fulcrum position	Fulcrum position Length of the load arm Length of the effort arm Amount of force applied	Load

theory of variation, encompassing three key levels—V1, V2, and V3.

V1, centering on students' diverse understandings, recognizes that students approach the same content with distinct perspectives. Teachers identify existing knowledge and learning difficulties through techniques like pre-tests and pre-interviews, offering valuable insights into students' understanding.

V2 delves into teachers' varied approaches to the same content. Recognizing the diversity of teachers' perspectives is crucial, as it helps systematize and externalize valuable practical knowledge. Learning Study provides a platform for mutual observation and reflection, breaking the isolated state among teachers and fostering a professional learning community.

The continuous exploration of V1 and V2 diversity enables teachers to identify learning content and critical features. V3, utilizing the theory of variation, becomes a teaching tool, explaining how teachers organize and design classroom teaching. This step involves consciously designing variation schemes to achieve evident learning effects.

Variation theory, emphasizing diverse perceptions, aids teachers in developing their ways of presenting the object of learning. The theory promotes "powerful ways of acting" derived from "powerful ways of seeing," enhancing teachers' approaches to dealing with future challenges.

Certain critical aspects of the learning object must vary while others remain constant for effective learning. Teachers present a specific object depending on the pattern of variation provided. Different patterns, such as contrast, generalization, separation, and fusion, lead to diverse types of teacher learning.

In the Learning Study approach, teachers are central in constructing learning instructions and activities. They help their colleagues experience and discern specific patterns of variation, thereby strengthening the collective understanding of the object of study. Overall, Learning Study's systematic and collaborative methodology, rooted in variation theory, creates an environment that actively engages teachers, promotes diverse perspectives, and enhances overall professional development.

With "V2," we gain an additional perspective to scrutinize teachers' teaching, research, and collaboration among teachers, prompting teachers to reflect on themselves, their relationships with others, and their interaction with the learning community.

9. Conclusion

In conclusion, Learning Study, guided by Variation Theory, empowers teachers in instructional design. Through a systematic process, it encourages collaboration, reflective practices, and a nuanced understanding of student and teacher perspectives. The deliberate use of variations in teaching methodologies enhances discernment and promotes continuous improvement. Learning Study provides a structured approach and fosters a collaborative learning community, transforming implicit knowledge into shared pedagogical excellence.

References

Cheng, C. K. (2009). Cultivating communities of practice via learning study to enhance teacher learning. *KEDI Journal of Educational Policy*, 6(1), 81–104.

Cheng, E. C. K., & Lo, M. L. (2013). Learning Study: Its Origin, Operationalisations, and Implications. Paris: OECD Education Working Papers, No. 94, OECD Publishing.

Cheng, E. C. K. (2014). Learning Study—Nurturing pre-service teachers' instructional design and teaching competency. *Asia-Pacific Journal of Teacher Education*, 42(1), 1–16.

Cheng E. C. K., & Lee J. C. K. (2019). Lesson Study: Curriculum Management for 21st Century Skills. In Connolly, M., Eddy-Spicer, D. H., James, C., & Kruse, S. D. (Ed.), *The SAGE Handbook of School Organization* (447–464). U.K.: SAGE.

Cheng, E. C. K. (2019). *Successful Transposition of Lesson Study: A Knowledge Management Perspective*. London: Springer.

Cheng, E. C. K., & Chan, J. C. K. (2021). *Developing Metacognitive Teaching Strategies through Lesson Study*. London: Springer.

Fung-Lo, M. L., & Marton, F. (2012). Towards a science of the art of teaching: Using variation theory as a guiding principle of pedagogical design.

Marton, F., & Booth, S. (1997). *Learning and awareness*. Mahwah, NJ: Lawrence Erlbaum.

Marton, F. (2014). *Necessary conditions of learning*. Routledge.

Pang, M. F. (2006). The Use of Learning Study to Enhance Teacher Professional Learning in Hong Kong. *Teaching Education*, 1, 27–42.

Lo, M. L. (2005). Learning Study—the Hong Kong Version of Lesson Study: Development

Impact and Challenges. Matoba, M., Crawford, K. A., Mohammad R. Sarker Arani (Eds.). *Lesson Study: International Perspective on Policy and Practice.* Beijing: Educational Science Publishing House. 133–157.

Lo, M. L., Chik, P., & Pang, M. K. (2006). Pattern of Variation in Teaching the Color of Light to Primary 3 Students. *Instruction science*, 34, 1–9.

Lo, M. L. (2012). Variation theory and the improvement of teaching and learning. Göteborgs Universitet, Acta Universitatis Gothoburgensis, Göteborg.

Chapter 4

Contemporary Adaptations to Lesson Study in the Age of ICT

Bruce LANDER, Matsuyama University

1. Introduction

To say that technology has had an impact on education is an understatement. The digitalization trend is fast upon us. These days, there seem to be very few areas where technology has not penetrated and released an 'app for that,' a login, or a digital ID. The field of lesson study, the now widespread and worldwide educational practice for professional development and pedagogical advancement, is no exception. Lesson studies and how they are conducted have changed with the times. This chapter will introduce some of the ways that lesson study, LS from herein, has adapted to these changes by attempting to answer the following research questions: What changes are being made to adopt ICT to LS, and how are teachers using tech in LS?

2. The Impact of Technology on LS

Technology has impacted the Lesson Study field in two main influential ways. The first involves observation of the research lesson, while the second consists of disseminating data to researchers. With any lesson study, researchers and practitioners collaborate to decide on a research lesson, or RL. Such discussions are usually done in person, usually at the venue where the lesson will be held. This decision is a painstaking process of choosing a suitable class, with the correct contents and, of course, permission from the school and the teacher to have several if not many, researchers enter the classroom to observe the class. Once this step has been reached, researchers are invited to the school to observe the lesson in a somewhat imposing manner that can be nerve-wracking for both the teacher and the students. However, that step now, with widely available tech tools, can be bypassed.

3. Data Collection Process

The most prevalent way of data collection with lesson study research is the material obtained from the RL by means of class observations. After receiving permission to

69

observe the RL educators and researchers would enter the class, taking notes on points raised, pedagogical decisions made, and any other discussions noted between either teacher to student or student to student. This is often done with video cameras placed around the room and voice recorders at the front and on random student desks, picking up conversations between students. Although video recorders may be less intrusive than having strangers in your class, cameras alone can be just as bad, if not worse. Students and teachers may prefer not to be recorded in many cases. As many educational institutions aim to preserve the identity of their students regarding the use of recording devices in the classroom, it seems there is now a practical alternative.

4. Digital Teacher Collaboration

The theme of digital teacher collaboration involves using online tools to facilitate cooperation among geographically dispersed educators. Koutsouris et al. (2017) studied video conferencing and sharing platforms to support lesson study between teachers from different schools and universities. Two teams of mathematics educators, including teachers, a lecturer, and a psychologist, conducted research lessons. Lessons were recorded and uploaded for university members' review before virtual meetings. Despite technical challenges, Koutsouris et al. state that involving university lecturers was beneficial, easing the practical barriers of external involvement. Sharma and Pang (2015) examined elementary teachers' pedagogical shifts in online literacy tutoring via shared documents, video recordings, and reflective practices, fostering improvements in assessment knowledge and instructional strategies.

Various ways of adopting technology to the research lesson in an LS case study are emerging. Hudson et al. (2024) refer to a contemporary lesson study style as technology-mediated lesson study (TMLS), which refers to converting the observation step of the RL to a completely digital means. This new way of class observation does not require the class to be observed by any number of researchers unknown to the lesson's teacher. However, it uses either a series of video cameras and voice recorders strategically placed around the room or an even less imposing method described by Hudson et al. (2024) using the tool Swivl (swivl.com).

5. Evolving Tech Tools in the LS Classroom

One such service that can support LS is a device called Swivl (swivl.com). Swivl is a fee-paying service that provides a robotic platform stand for a camera in the form of a tablet or smartphone placed on a desk at the front or back of the classroom. The robot, equipped with a microphone, is connected by Bluetooth to the device and worn by the teacher, and swivels to track the teacher's movements and record video footage using the device on the platform. Additional microphones in the room can capture student conversations. Videos are uploaded to the Swivl website, where users can distribute the

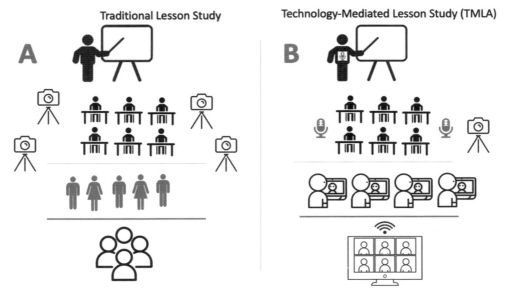

Figure 1: Traditional Lesson Study and Technology-Mediated Lesson Study

footage to LS researchers via links or file-sharing tools. Viewers of the footage can then add time-stamped comments and distribute the footage to researchers and educators elsewhere without needing them to visit the school or observe the class in person. Swivl technology was used in an RL conducted by Hudson et al. (2024) to record teachers' lessons, with a robot capturing video and audio in the classroom. With the relatively cheap service that Swivl provides, there is now no need for multiple video recorders in an RL.

Another good thing about this service is that it minimizes the chances of student identification by focusing primarily on the teacher. Any footage identifying students can be edited by deleting that portion or switching to audio recording only. Swivl's service of having just one camera in the room, pointed away from students, is far less invasive than having observers or several cameras in the classroom.

The traditional format of a research lesson on the left shows that the lesson is attended by the teacher and students and 3 or 4 external researchers. There are usually several cameras placed in the room, often with voice recorders and the addition of several researchers or representatives from educational governing bodies. However, the technology-mediated lesson study (TMLS) bypasses the need for observers, replacing several imposing video cameras with just one that follows the teacher around the room. External researchers or invitees could join the class synchronously through the video stream or view the footage asynchronously. This TMLS is just one way LS has adapted to the influx of educational technology in recent times.

6. Technology Assisted LS

Plenty of other forms of technology-assisted LS projects are being conducted worldwide.

Huang et al. (2021) suggest that there are four different models of technology-assisted LS emerging:

1. A partly assisted model
2. Mixed model including a combination of LS in-person and tech
3. A fully online model consisting of researchers viewing video footage synchronously or asynchronously
4. A hybrid model whereby tech tools (such as Swivl) are used that "supports planning, storing and reviewing of the RL" (2021, p.107).

7. Technology Awareness

One significant outcome of the COVID-19 impact on education is the increased prominence of technology in learning. Japanese universities, for instance, promoted using learning management system (LMS) tools like Moodle, Google Classroom, Blackboard, Edmodo, and Schoology. This shift likely led to lucrative contracts for major foreign IT companies. Consequently, it facilitated the implementation of the Ministry of Education, Culture, Sports, Science and Technology (MEXT) requests to integrate more information and communication technology (ICT) into education, addressing issues of poor digital literacy and enhancing digital skills proficiency. A key objective of the 2018 curriculum changes was to enhance self-regulated learning (SRL) through ICT-driven formative assessment methods, aiming to encourage a shift in learning approaches and promote the development of independent learning skills, as Yamanaka and Suzuki (2020) noted. This strategic shift may also serve to cultivate future IT professionals within Japan, reducing reliance on foreign software and hardware and retaining more IT talent domestically. This ambition was evident in the GIGA project, a substantial investment initiative to provide every student in Japan with a personal computing device, ensuring access to up-to-date hardware, software, and high-speed internet in urban and rural areas (Ishizaki, 2021).

Calleja and Camilleri (2021) propose that the Internet and online media technologies offer diverse applications for use beyond just lesson study, including lesson sharing. Hird et al. (2014) describe lesson sharing as teachers sharing their lessons online for others to use, which can transform how teachers plan, use, and deliver lessons (Hird et al., 2014, as cited in Calleja & Camilleri, 2020). According to Calleja and Camilleri (2021), practitioners can then use the Internet and online platforms to share materials within lesson study communities and enhance the exchange of participants' insights and experiences. The Internet has played a crucial role in recent changes in lesson study.

In Lesson Study, technology encourages teachers to have deeper discussions about student comprehension and education. It fosters a collaborative environment and allows teachers to reflect on their actions, leading to improved classroom practices (Calleja & Camilleri, 2020). While the specific tools used in these cases are not mentioned, it is likely that computer-mediated communication (CMC) tools, such as computer conferencing, email, discussion forums, and social media platforms, are being referred to.

The term CMC may seem somewhat outdated as technology becomes more ubiquitous in education and society. This trend has been particularly pronounced in the past three years, with the rise of online classes and learning with technology becoming the norm. Sharma and Pang (2015), Skultety et al. (2017), and Songül et al. (2018) similarly note that using online technologies in lesson study facilitates deeper conversations about student learning, fosters collegial engagement, and enhances teachers' opportunities for self-reflection and improvement in classroom practices (Calleja & Camilleri, 2021). Although specific tools are not mentioned, they may include CMC-based tools such as Skype, Viber, and the now widely recognized video conferencing tool Zoom, which gained prominence during the pandemic as a popular platform for online lessons.

8. LS Research Communities

Research in lesson study has reiterated the importance of a community of research for practitioners and researchers (Wenger, 1998; Wake, 2022). In Wenger's terms, "teachers who regularly engage in cycles of LS form a community of practice, so the professional learning is central to what it means to be a teacher" (Wenger, 1998 in Wake, 2021, p.15). Wake (2022) further discusses the importance of an LS community of researchers when conducting collaborative lesson study research on an RL or other related discussions. Wake claims that the Community of Practice, or CoP, whereby teachers meet regularly for LS research, helping them form a researcher identity and a sense of community, is a crucial element of the process.

9. Community of Practice

The topic of community of practice has long been discussed in LS research (Chang, 2009; Lewis, 2002; Lewis & Perry, 2015; Stokes et al., 2019). Weaver et al. (2021) continue by stating that CoP plays a key role in the prime objective of improving pedagogy and student outcomes and, most crucially, reduces teacher isolation. Uchiyama and Radin (2009) state that LS can help increase instructional motivation among teacher educators and maintain interest in research, a vital component in itself. Traditionally, though this learning process has been conducted in person.

> *"In LS communities, professional modes of operation prioritize collaborative professional learning focused on the day-to-day classroom practice of teaching and student learning. During such meetings, teachers agree upon and explore questions about teaching and learning in ways that involve them in close-to-practice classroom research. New identities are negotiated and forged which re-position teachers as learners."*

> (Wake, 2022, p.12)

By forming this new bond with fellow colleagues or teachers, further research on practice and pedagogy can be conducted. Having teachers and researchers in the same room simultaneously is critical. Wake continues claiming the need for communities of practice in research, which helps support the notion of collaborative research to improve pedagogy. If this CoP were switched to an online format, it would be less of a burden on teachers, but Wake (2022) continues the physical relationship that result from regular CoP meetings, are crucial to success.

10. The Covid Impact on Education

Weaver et al. (2021) talk about the panic among teaching staff that ensued from the initial switch to online pedagogy for teachers in their working environment in the US in early 2020. The COVID-19 pandemic began worldwide from 2020 to late 2021 but continued in Japan to early 2023 and, some may argue, continues to this day, significantly impacting education. Almost overnight, classrooms, school teachers, and university professors were told to switch their pedagogy to digital format. This, at first, caused panic, confusion, and distress. During that period, I was invited to give a tutorial on conducting lessons with Zoom and integrating classes with other online tools. The tutorial was well attended as many teachers had never used computers in face-to-face classes, never mind online. They needed as much help as they could get. I have never seen such panic in teacher expressions as I did that day. However, with time, educators and students have adapted to this change. Although initially reluctant, many became more proficient users of digital tools available then and raised digital literacy to adapt to sudden changes and learn new digital skills.

The Covid pandemic brought technology in education to the forefront. This period brought about a huge change in how teachers conducted their classes, which helped to highlight the importance of technology in learning. Universities across Japan, for instance, promoted the use of Learning Management System (LMS) tools during this time. Consequently, requests from the Ministry of Education, Culture, Sports, Science, and Technology (MEXT) to integrate more Information and Communication Technology (ICT) into education were addressed, helping to improve digital literacy levels and proficiency in digital skills, which, according to Cote & Milliner, (2017) and Funamori (2017) were ranked consistently low on a global scale. The pandemic helped address these issues.

One major objective of the curriculum changes introduced in 2018 was to enhance Self-Regulated Learning (SRL) through formative assessment techniques with ICT. The intention was to encourage a shift in learning styles, teaching students how to learn independently (LHL) (Lander, 2023), thereby helping them to "acquire the ability to learn and think independently" (Yamanaka & Suzuki, 2020, p.81). Ultimately, the goal might be to cultivate future coders and programmers, reduce Japan's reliance on foreign software and hardware imports, and increase the number of IT professionals within the country. This goal was prominently supported by the GIGA project, which sought to provide every student in Japan with up-to-date computer hardware, software, and high-speed internet, both in urban and rural areas (Ishizaki, 2021). The GIGA project seems to be gradually impacting the digital literacy level of students and teachers.

11. A Catalyst for Change

It could be argued that the sudden increase in the use of technology in schools and educational institutions throughout Japan has an ultimate goal at the macro level. In the classroom, students and teachers alike are becoming more aware of and proficient users of tech tools, helping to adopt formative assessment pedagogy and nurturing self-regulated learners who are becoming better at self-management and, in effect, becoming better independent learners. The following diagram outlines the impact that technology is having on the micro, meso and macro-level.

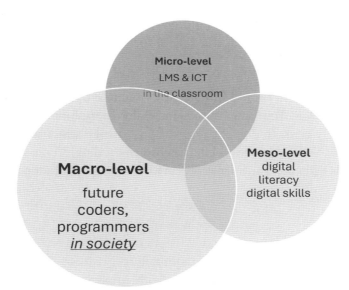

Figure 2: The Impact of Technology at the Micro, Meso, and Macro-Level

Micro-Level
In the classroom
- Improved digital skill set through adopting LMS
- Raising awareness of technology
- Improving digital literacy through ICT tools used in class
- Improving cognitive skills: attention, logic, and reasoning
- Non-cognitive skills: pair work, teamwork, communication ability

Figure 2 above refers to the impact that technology is currently having on education and further afield. At the micro-level, more digital tools are being adopted in the classroom. This helps raise awareness of technology and understanding its power to enhance collaborative learning. With various formative assessment techniques the teacher adopts, students can also foster cognitive skills including literacy, self-reflection, and critical thinking, while at the same time develop non-cognitive skills like teamwork, communication ability, and creativity. These skills are developed in the classroom and can be further adapted in other classes, school-wide and within the community.

Meso-Level
At the school and community level
- Improved digital skill set that can be adapted in other classes
- Digital skill set for use in an increasingly digital world
- Digital literacy improvement for use outside of class
- Raising awareness of technology in society
- An improved understanding of digitalization in society

If conducted successfully and effectively, students can use this new digital skill set in other education-based settings at the school level. New digital skills, memorizing word-processing shortcuts like Ctrl+f for find and Ctrl+A for 'select all,' for example, can be adopted in any subject area and any classroom at the compulsory and tertiary levels of education. The Internet of Things (IoT) (Ganesan, 2014) is gaining pace in many nations worldwide. Ten years later, practically everything is switching online, from national identity cards to digital payments on the high street and applications for a long list of things. Using these tools effectively and productively is standard practice in today's age. Skills gained at the micro-level are then passed on to the meso-level. This trend, it seems, will only advance.

Macro-Level
At the community and nationwide level
- Nurturing of future coders and programmers
- Lowering the current heavy reliance on digital imports
- Expanding the number of domestic digital workers
- Increase domestic digital sufficiency
- Boosting local economy

The ultimate goal in this cycle is to nurture future coders and programmers who can help design and produce locally-made digital products. Japan is a nation that currently relies heavily on digital imports for usage in schools, universities, and businesses nation-wide. If the current trend in raising the digital literacy levels of its students through operatives including one device per child at the school level and introducing basic coding classes from grade 5 of primary school is met, there is a chance, whether minimal or not, that such students may become future coders and programmers. Several universities nationwide are making the huge decision to open IT departments. The university where I am employed has taken this very step. Construction for the first Faculty of Information

Technology on the island of Shikoku began in April 2024 and is due for completion in March 2026. Steps like this, although risky, could, in turn, help Japan to lower its reliance on foreign digital imports and, in effect, boost the economy by producing and exporting domestic digital products of its own.

12. Lowering the Reliance on Digital Imports

Despite the continued reliance on foreign software companies, several domestic firms in Japan have begun releasing similar tools tailored to the Japanese market, such as Cloud-Campus, LearningBox, and LoiLo Note. CloudCampus and LearningBox are emerging Japan-based learning management systems targeting both the education and business sectors, located in Tokyo and Tatsuno, Hyogo prefecture, respectively (cc.cyber-u.ac.jp, nd; learningbox.online, nd). LoiLo Note, a tablet-based platform established in 2007, primarily serves the primary education sector in Japan, promoting active learning in elementary schools (Kurokami & Kojima, 2018). If this trend of domestically produced software continues, Japan will be better positioned to cater to future digital education markets than it currently is.

13. Knowhow is Crucial

Introducing new hardware or software into education or any other sector requires more than just providing the tools; knowing how to use them is crucial. Future researchers in Lesson Study or teacher education must stay updated on the latest tools and technologies, invest time mastering their functionality, and provide training opportunities for pre-service and in-service teachers before incorporating them into classrooms. Additionally, students and teachers also need to be warned of the limitations of each tool and informed about best practices to maintain a safe and secure learning environment. This is increasingly important as cyber security issues continue to rise each year.

14. AI in Education

Artificial intelligence, more commonly known as AI, is a hot topic these days. From social media to chatbots and algorithm-based search engines that remember and log your searches online, AI seems to be everywhere. AI has brought about revolutionary changes, both good and bad. This chapter would not be complete without a mention of the pros and cons of what AI has contributed to the field of education over the past few years.

To begin with, let me provide a short introduction of the benefits of Artificial Intelligence (AI) in recent times. AI has fundamentally reshaped education by offering personalized learning experiences, automating administrative tasks, and improving educational outcomes. AI-powered adaptive learning systems analyse vast amounts of student data to tailor educational content and pacing to individual needs, optimizing learning efficiency and engagement (Taylor et al., 2021). These systems help to provide real-time feedback and adaptive tutoring, enhancing student understanding and retention through personalized interventions (Long & Siemens, 2011). Of course, many drawbacks though in the sudden use of AI have been gaining a huge amount of criticism.

15. Criticism of AI

The first of these is that AI is making us lazy. What used to take several hours, days, or even weeks can now be done instantly with AI. While AI promises educational advancements, it also presents significant challenges and concerns. One critical issue is the potential realization of existing inequalities whereby some students may have regular access to high-spec, modern devices, indicating a heavy reliance on AI tools for their learning. Alternatively, other students may not have this equal opportunity and a general understanding of instructing prompts. This would show a disparity in the usage of such tools. AI-driven personalized learning systems heavily rely on data analytics, which may inadvertently produce biases embedded in historical data, thus disadvantaging some learning groups (Bulger, 2016). Moreover, the emphasis on AI efficiency through automation raises questions about the role of human educators and the quality of interpersonal interactions crucial for effective learning (Williamson et al., 2023). Although it is still in its infancy at the time of writing, AI remains a concern for education and the over-dependency of students who use it.

16. Conclusion

This chapter has attempted to highlight some of the pros and cons of how LS has recently adapted to the integration of ICT in education. LS is adapting to the influx of tech in several ways, helping to make footage for research lessons, traditionally conducted in person, available to a broader audience through digital means, as explained by Hudson et al. (2023) with the term TMLS. Through the literature referred to herein, it can be concluded that the field of lesson study is gradually adapting to the digital trend and further developing from its original setting. Digital tools can open up new ways to conduct lesson studies. However, there remains a conflict. As Wake suggests, the concept of community of practice (CoP), whereby teachers get together regularly, is a critical element of the cycle of LS. The physical relationship that teachers and researchers develop through visiting schools, observing lessons, and meeting regularly also helps maintain levels of motivation. Despite this, Lesson Study is adapting and changing with the times notwithstanding, one thing remains at the core: student improvement and *jugyou kaizen* (class improvement). LS remains an active field of educational research worldwide, and I am sure it will continue to adapt with the times.

References

Calleja, J., & Camilleri, P. (2021). Teachers' learning in extraordinary times: shifting to a digitally facilitated approach to lesson study. *International Journal for Lesson and Learning Studies*, 10(2), 118–137. https://doi.org/10.1108/IJLLS-09-2020-0058

Chang, M. L. (2009). An appraisal perspective of teacher burnout: Examining the emotional work of teachers. *Educational Psychology Review*, 21(3), 193–218.

Cote, T. J., & Milliner, B. (2017). Preparing Japanese students' digital literacy for study abroad: Is more training needed? *The JALT CALL Journal*, 13(3), 187–197. https://doi.org/10.29140/jaltcall.v13n3.218

Fishman, B., Konstantopoulos, S., Kubitskey, B. W., Vath, R., Park, G., Johnson, H., & Edelson, D. C. (2013). Comparing the impact of online and face-to-face professional development in the context of curriculum implementation. *Journal of Teacher Education*, 64(5), 426–438.

Funamori, M. (2017). The issues Japanese higher education faces in the digital age—Are Japanese universities to blame for the slow progress towards an information-based society? *International Journal of Institutional Research and Management*, 1(1), 37–51.

Ganesan, G. (2014). Accessed on Nov. 25th, 2023 in https://cio.economictimes.indiatimes.com/news/internet-of-things/this-is-how-internet-of-things-is-gaining-pace/36299090

Hernández-Rodríguez, O., González, G., & Villafañe-Cepeda, W. (2021). Planning a research lesson online: pre-service teachers' documentation work. *International Journal for Lesson and Learning Studies*, 10(2), 168–186. https://doi.org/10.1108/IJLLS-09-2020-0068

Hird, M., Larson, R., Okubo, Y., & Uchino, K. (2014). Lesson study and lesson sharing: an appealing marriage. *Creative Education*, 5(10), 769–779.

Hrastinski, S. (2021). Digital tools to support teacher professional development in lesson studies: a systematic literature review. *International Journal for Lesson & Learning Studies*, 10(2), 138–149.

Huang, R., Helgevold, N., & Lang, J. (2021a). Digital technologies, online learning, and lesson study. *International Journal for Lesson and Learning Studies*, 10(2), 105–117, doi: 10.1108/ ijlls-03-2021-0018.

Hudson, M., Leary, H., Longhurst, M., Stowers, J., Poulsen, T., Smith, C., & Sansom, R. L. (2024). Technology-mediated lesson study: a step-by-step guide. *International Journal for Lesson & Learning Studies*, 13(5), 1–14.

Ishizaki, A. (2021, May 28). GIGA School Program is finally accelerating Japan's digitalization in education systems. https://edujump.net/news/2856/

Koutsouris, G., Norwich, B., Fujita, T., Ralph, T., Adlam, A., & Milton, F. (2017). Piloting a dispersed and inter-professional Lesson Study using Technology to link team members at a Distance. *Technology, Pedagogy, and Education*, 26(5), 587–599.

Kurokami, H., & Kojima, A. (2018). Development and effectiveness of digital graphic organizers. *International Journal for Educational Media and Technology*, 12(1), 57–64.

Lander, B. (2024). Promoting student-based self-regulated learning with ICT through Lesson Study, Implementing a 21st Century Competency-Based Curriculum Through

Lesson Study. 159–175. Routledge.

Lewis, C. (2002). *Lesson study: A Handbook of Teacher-Led Instructional Change*. Philadelphia: Research for Better Schools.

Lewis, C. C., & Perry, R. R. (2015). A randomized trial of lesson study with mathematical resource kits: Analysis of impact on teachers' beliefs and learning community. *Large-Scale Studies in Mathematics Education*, 133-158.

Long, P., & Siemens, G. (2011). Penetrating the fog: analytics in learning and education. *EDUCAUSE Rev*, 48(5), 31–40

Mitomo, H. (2020). Utilization of ICT in elementary and secondary education in Japan: Its policies and effects, Telecommunications policies of Japan, 239–266. Springer.

Sharma, S. A., & Pang, S. (2015). Creating new opportunities for lesson study in an online reading clinic. *Literacy Research: Theory, Method, and Practice*, 64(1), 415–428.

Skultety, L., Gonzalez, G., & Vargas, G. (2017). Using technology to support teachers' lesson adaptations during lesson study. *Journal of Technology and Teacher Education*, 25(2), 185–213.

Songül, B. C., Delialioğlu, Ö., & Özköse Bıyık, Ç. (2018, November). An investigation of Turkish EFL teachers' development through an online professional development program. In Proceedings of the 26th International Conference on Computers in Education, 647–656.

Stokes, L. R. E., Suh, J. M., & Curby, T. W. (2019). Examining the Nature of Teacher Support during Different Iterations and Modalities of Lesson Study Implementation. *Professional Development in Education and Techniques*, 3rd ed., Sage, doi: 10.1080/19415257.2019.1634623.

Taylor, D. L., Yeung, M., & Bashet, A. Z. (2021). Personalized and adaptive learning. *Innovative learning environments in STEM higher education: Opportunities, Challenges, and Looking Forward*, 17–34.

Uchiyama, K. P., & Radin, J. L. (2009). Curriculum mapping in higher education: a vehicle for collaboration. *Innovative Higher Education*, 33(4), 271–280.

Wake, G. (2022). Designing lesson study for individual and collective learning: networking theoretical perspectives. *International Journal for Lesson & Learning Studies*, 12(1), 7–20.

Weaver, J. C., Matney, G., Goedde, A. M., Nadler, J. R., & Patterson, N. (2021). Digital tools to promote remote lesson study. *International Journal for Lesson & Learning Studies*, 10(2), 187–201.

Wenger, E. (1998). *Communities of Practice: Learning, Meaning, and Identity*. New York, NY: Cambridge University Press.

Williamson, B., Macgilchrist, F., & Potter, J. (2023). Re-examining A.I., automation, and datafication in education. *Learning, media and technology*, 48(1), 1–5.

Yamanaka, S., & Suzuki, K. H. (2020). Japanese Education Reform Towards Twenty-First Century Education. In *Audacious Education Purposes*, 81–103. Springer. https://doi.org/10.1007/978-3-030-41882-3_4

Yursa, H., & Silverman, J. (2011). Developing online lesson study community [Paper Presentation]. NCTM Regional Conference, Atlantic City, NJ, United States.

Chapter 5

Interrelation of Lesson Study and Curriculum in Kazakhstan

Tavilya AKIMOVA, Center of Excellence, NIS, Kazakhstan

Lesson study and curriculum development are intertwined. This approach combines collaborative teacher planning with curriculum implementation to enhance teaching practices and student learning outcomes. Several authors have explored the synergy between lesson study and curriculum development, emphasizing continuous improvement in teaching strategies and content delivery. Lewis, C., & Tsuchida, I. (1998) in the article 'A lesson is like a swiftly flowing river: Research lessons and the improvement of Japanese education' write that '...research lessons are influenced by the national educational policy, but on occasion the influence goes in the other direction'. Lewis, C. and Takahashi, A. (2013) contributed significantly to the understanding of lesson study as a means of fostering teacher learning and improving curriculum. Kuramoto, T. (2014) has contributed to the discourse on lesson study and curriculum development, emphasizing how these practices can enhance teacher collaboration and improve instructional quality. In his work, he highlights the importance of iterative processes in lesson study that allow educators to refine their teaching strategies based on collective insights. Their research often underscores how collaborative practices in lesson study can lead to more effective curriculum development and better educational outcomes.

1. Understanding the Curriculum

A curriculum is a structured set of educational experiences and learning objectives designed to guide teaching and learning in an educational institution. It outlines what students are expected to learn, the subjects or courses offered, the skills to be developed, and the assessment methods to evaluate student progress. Curricula can vary widely between different educational levels (like elementary, secondary, or higher education) and can also be tailored to specific subjects or programs. The main purpose of a curriculum is to ensure that education is systematic, coherent, and aligned with desired outcomes for student learning.

Overall, the curriculum in all countries aims to ensure quality education but approaches to its development and implementation may vary depending on educational traditions and societal needs. In some countries, such as Kazakhstan, the educational curriculum is strictly regulated at the national level, whereas in others, such as the USA, more emphasis is placed on local development of the curriculum. Some countries have greater flexibility in adapting the curriculum to students' needs, while others have a more standardized curriculum. Methods of assessment and testing can vary widely, from extensive use of standardized tests to an integrated approach to assessment.

In the USA, the curriculum can vary significantly from state to state and from one school district to another. Local school districts and schools often develop their own curricula based on general educational standards. Standardized tests are widely used to assess curriculum implementation and student performance.

In the United Kingdom the curriculum for schools is regulated by the National Curriculum, which sets requirements for core subjects and key stages of education. The UK also differentiates between academic courses (e.g., A-levels) and vocational qualifications (e.g., BTECs).

Finland is known for its flexibility in the educational system. The curriculum is developed at the local level with consideration of national goals and recommendations, allowing for adaptation to students' specific needs. The Finnish system places a strong emphasis on individual students' interests and needs, as well as the integration of various subjects.

In Japan, the curriculum is highly centralized and strictly controlled by the Ministry of Education, Science, and Culture. Curricula and programs have a clear structure, with a significant focus on exam preparation. Education is focused on academic achievement and includes traditional subjects such as mathematics and Japanese.

In Kazakhstan the curriculum is strictly regulated by the state educational standards developed by the Ministry of Education and Science. This ensures a uniform approach to the educational process at all levels. The main focus is on compliance with state standards and requirements.

In Kazakhstan, as in other countries, the curriculum plays a key role in organizing the educational process. By integrating lesson study into the curriculum process, Kazakhstani educators can systematically examine and refine their instructional methods while ensuring alignment with national educational standards.

The synergy between lesson study and curriculum development allows for continuous improvement in teaching strategies and content delivery. Teachers work together to plan, observe, and reflect on lessons, using insights gained to inform curriculum adjustments. This iterative process helps bridge the gap between theory and practice, ensuring that the curriculum remains relevant and effective in meeting students' needs.

In order to analyze the mechanism how the Lesson Study and curriculum are interrelated we need to know that the understanding and use of the **term** "Curriculum" may vary depending on the country and its educational system. In Kazakhstan, the term "Curriculum" encompasses both a broad and a narrow meaning. Broadly, it refers to the overall educational framework, including goals, content, and learning experiences across various subjects. Narrowly, it pertains to specific courses or subject matter taught in a particular context, detailing objectives, materials, and assessments for that course. Understanding both aspects is crucial for effective educational planning and implementation of Lesson Study.

2. State Compulsory Educational Standard (SCES) of Kazakhstan

In the broad meaning of the Curriculum in Kazakhstan we talk about State Compulsory Educational Standard (SCES). It is a system of standards regulating education at various levels in the country. The main goal of SCES is to ensure uniform requirements for the quality of the educational process and graduates, which contributes to the harmonization of educational programs and overall improvement in the quality of education.

The SCES establishes the goals and objectives of education, defining the fundamental aims that the system seeks to achieve. It also specifies the main directions and expected outcomes of the educational process, ensuring clarity on the primary focus areas and results.

The content component details the specific educational content that must be covered. Additionally, it includes curriculum plans, programs, and subjects, outlining the requirements for educational content within these frameworks.

Standards of learning outcomes are set to establish benchmarks for what students should achieve. These expected learning outcomes encompass the knowledge, skills, and competencies that students are anticipated to attain throughout their education.

The standard also addresses methods and forms of teaching, providing recommendations for pedagogical methods and approaches, including innovative technologies. Quality assessment of education is another critical aspect, with established criteria and procedures for evaluating student performance and the effectiveness of educational institutions.

Furthermore, the standard outlines requirements for infrastructure and resources, emphasizing the need for adequate material and technical bases, educational materials, and staffing. Lastly, it includes mechanisms for management and monitoring to ensure compliance with standards and effective oversight of the educational process.

The structure of SCES in Kazakhstan includes several broad parts:

1. Educational Standards:
   - These define the basic requirements for curricula, subjects, and teaching methods for primary, basic general, and secondary education. They also include requirements for educational programs for various professions and specialties, as well as the qualifications of educators.
2. State Educational Programs (SEP):
   - These programs are developed for each subject based on educational standards and include detailed requirements for educational content, teaching methods, and assessment of results.
3. State Curriculum (SC):
   - Establishes the structure of the educational process, the number of hours allocated for subjects, the sequence of classes, and other organizational aspects.
4. State Qualification Characteristics (SQC):
   - Define the requirements for the qualifications of graduates from educational

institutions, including the knowledge, skills, and abilities they should acquire.
5. Monitoring and Evaluation:
- SCES also includes mechanisms for monitoring and evaluating the quality of education, allowing for control and analysis of compliance with established standards.

The Ministry of Enlightenment of the Republic of Kazakhstan is responsible for the development, implementation, and updating of SCES. The Republican Center for Testing and other accredited organizations conduct monitoring and evaluation of educational quality. Educational Institutions (schools, vocational school) are required to comply with SCES in their activities and provide reports on meeting the standards' requirements.

Thus, SCES represents a comprehensive approach to standardizing and managing education in Kazakhstan, contributing to achieving high educational standards and preparing qualified specialists. The SCES includes the following necessary components to ensure comprehensive and quality education for students:

Subject-Based Content

At the heart of Kazakhstan's curriculum lies a carefully curated selection of subjects designed to provide students with a comprehensive education. These include core subjects such as Kazakh and Russian languages, mathematics, sciences, history, and literature. The content is tailored to each educational level, ensuring age-appropriate learning and progressive skill development.

Competency-Based Approach

Kazakhstan's modern curriculum emphasises a competency-based approach, focusing on developing practical skills alongside theoretical knowledge. This includes critical thinking, problem-solving, communication, and digital literacy. The aim is to prepare students for real-world challenges and the demands of a rapidly evolving global economy.

Cultural and Moral Education

An integral part of the curriculum is dedicated to fostering national identity, cultural awareness, and moral values. This includes lessons on Kazakh history, traditions, and ethics, as well as promoting understanding and respect for the country's diverse ethnic groups and cultures.

Extracurricular Activities

The curriculum extends beyond the classroom, incorporating a range of extracurricular activities. These include sports, arts, clubs, and community service projects, which aim to develop well-rounded individuals and promote holistic education.

STATE CURRICULUM
in Kazakhstan's Education

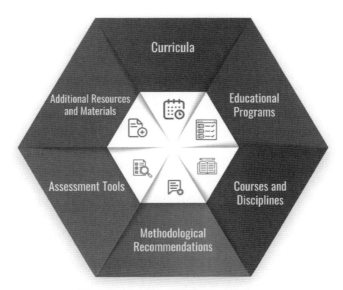

Figure 1: Structure of the Curriculum

STATE CURRICULUM (SC):

In its narrower meaning the notion "Curriculum" in Kazakhstan's Education means **a system of educational programs and plans** that defines the content and structure of the learning process at various educational levels.

These components are realized through the **structure of the curriculum which includes several key elements:**

1. Curricula:
Curricula define the number of hours allocated for each subject, the distribution of topics across semesters and years of study, and the sequence of teaching subjects.

2. Educational Programs:
Educational programs detail the content of each subject, including the topics to be covered, teaching methods, and forms of assessment. These programs are developed based on state educational standards and include specific learning objectives, skills, and knowledge that students are expected to acquire.

3. Courses and Disciplines:
The curriculum includes a list of compulsory and elective courses, disciplines, and modules that students must complete during their education. It may also include specialized subjects depending on the level of education and the field of study.

4. Assessment Tools:

Includes methods and instruments for assessing students' knowledge and skills. These may include tests, exams, projects, assignments, and other forms of assessment.

5. Methodological Recommendations:

These are recommendations for teachers on organizing the educational process, applying various teaching methods and technologies, and working with educational materials.

6. Additional Resources and Materials:

The curriculum may include recommendations on using textbooks, manuals, multimedia, and electronic resources to support teaching and learning.

Thus, the State Compulsory Educational Standard (SCES) in Kazakhstan represents the foundational system of standards that define general requirements and goals for education. It establishes the core framework for educational institutions across the country. Each year, the SCES is complemented by the Instructional-Methodological Letter (IML) from the National Academy of Education (NAE) of the Ministry of Enlightenment, which provides practical recommendations and methodological assistance to teachers and educational institutions on every aspect of the curriculum.

The Instructional-Methodological Letter and State Educational Compulsory Standards in Kazakhstan are important components of the education system that play different but interrelated roles. Instructional-Methodological Letter provides specific guidelines, recommendations, and methodological materials for implementing educational standards. Its purpose is to support and enhance the quality of the educational process through detailed instructions and methodological assistance. These letters include recommendations on teaching methods, new approaches and technologies, updates to educational programs, and practical advice for educators. They are designed to assist educational institutions in applying SCES in practice.

Lesson study approach is also reflected in the Instructional-Methodological Letter which each year provides practical recommendations and methodological assistance for using Lesson study in implementing these standards in the educational process.

This is the way the Instructional and Methodological Letter reflects Lesson Study as a guide for educational institutions and teachers:

✓ It gives description of the methodology of LS according to the accepted LS cycles (Pete Dudley, 2011):
  - Lesson Planning: Participating teachers collaboratively develop a lesson plan, defining goals, methods, and expected outcomes.
  - Conducting the Lesson: One of the teachers conducts the lesson in the presence of other group members.
  - Analysis and Discussion: After the lesson, an analysis is conducted, discussing the strengths and weaknesses of the lesson and proposing improvements.
✓ It specifies the role of School Administration in implementing LS:

- Support: The administration should support the implementation of the method, providing the necessary resources and conditions for its application.
- Evaluation and Control: The administration should be involved in evaluating the effectiveness of the method and monitoring its implementation process.

✓ It provides with recommendations for Evaluation and Monitoring:
- Evaluation Criteria: Criteria for assessing the success of the method are established, such as improvements in learning outcomes and teacher satisfaction.
- Monitoring: Recommendations for regular monitoring and adjustments to the process to achieve better results.

3. Which Components of the Kazakhstani Curriculum Can Be Influenced by Lesson Study?

The Lesson Study approach can influence several key aspects of the educational process in Kazakhstan, improving both teaching quality and overall education standards. However, the actual impact will depend on how this approach is implemented and adapted within the context of the Kazakhstani educational system.

1. Development of Educational Programs
- Enhancing Content: Lesson Study can help identify weaknesses and deficiencies in curricula and programs, leading to their update and improvement based on practical observations and data.
- Updating Materials: Educators can adapt teaching materials and programs to align with the real needs and interests of students, making them more relevant and effective.

2. Teaching Methods and Strategies
- Improving Methodologies: Discussion and analysis of lessons can contribute to the adoption of more effective teaching methods, improving interaction with students and the quality of material comprehension.
- Innovations in Teaching: Teachers can share successful methods and approaches, fostering the implementation of innovative educational practices.

3. Assessment and Monitoring
- Enhancing Assessment Tools: Lesson analysis can aid in developing more accurate and objective tools for assessing student performance and understanding.
- Reflection and Adjustment: Educators can better understand how their assessment methods impact the teaching process, helping to adjust approaches and improve results.

4. Preparation and Professional Development

- Skill Development: Lesson Study promotes teachers' professional growth through collaborative discussion and reflection, which can enhance their skills and competencies.
- Collaborative Learning: Teachers can work better as a team, share experiences, and find common solutions to problems, strengthening collective skills and knowledge.

5. Curriculum and Scheduling
- Optimizing Time: The method can help in more effective allocation of teaching time and resources, identifying aspects of the curriculum that require more attention.
- Balancing Workload: It can improve the balance of the academic workload, enhancing teaching quality and reducing student stress.

6. Integration of Subjects
- Interdisciplinary Approach: Lesson Study can promote a more integrated approach to teaching, helping to create coherent teaching blocks and projects that cover multiple subjects.

7. Adaptation to Changes
- Flexibility and Adaptability: The approach can enhance the flexibility of the education system in response to changes in the educational environment and student needs, allowing for rapid adaptation to new challenges and demands.

In 2024 the 17th annual international conference of the World Association of Lesson Studies was held in Astana, Kazakhstan. 398 abstracts were accepted to the conference from Kazakhstani educators. We analyzed them according to the aspects of the curriculum (shown above) they have connections with. We selected 220 abstracts connected in this or that way with curriculum implementation.

As the diagram below indicates, the equal part of the research deals with teaching methods and strategies (30%) and professional development (32.27%). A smaller proportion of research was done on assessment and monitoring (10%), integration of subjects (10%), and adaptation to changes (10%).

As for the last two aspects 'Development of educational programs and curriculum' and 'Scheduling' the teachers do not have a flexibility in making changes there, consequently they didn't do much research in these aspects as the number of hours of each subject, the distribution of topics, the sequence of teaching subjects, the content of each subject, and specific learning objectives are not subject to change.

When changes in education happen, teachers use Lesson study to research the challenges to search for solutions to their problems. The distribution above points to the adaptation of Kazakhstani educators to the introduction of the new updated curriculum in 2016 when teachers were exposed to the updated content of the educational programs, a new system of assessment—Criteria based assessment, innovative teaching methods, etc. As a preliminary step to the updated curriculum Kazakhstan launched in 2012 tiered professional development programs for teachers, marking a significant step

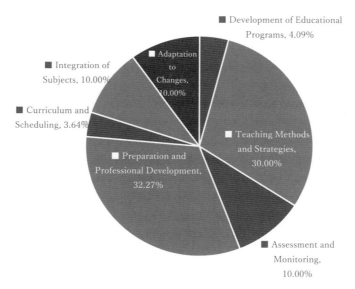

Diagram 1: Proportion of Lesson Study Research According to the Aspects of Influence

in the reform of its educational system. These programs were designed to enhance the professional skills of educators and align them with modern educational requirements. Teachers were introduced to seven modules, each covering various aspects of the educational process.

The first module focuses on New Approaches to Learning and Teaching, emphasizing dialogic teaching methods that encourage interactive communication in the classroom, and Learning How to Learn, which helps teachers and students develop metacognitive skills essential for effective learning. The second module, Assessment for Learning and of Learning, teaches educators how to implement assessment strategies that not only evaluate student performance but also support ongoing learning processes. The third module, Using ICT, explores the integration of information and communication technologies in the educational environment to enhance teaching and learning. Another important module is Teaching Critical Thinking, which aims to equip teachers with strategies to foster analytical and evaluative skills in students. The fifth module, Considering Age Characteristics, focuses on tailoring teaching methods to accommodate the developmental needs of students at different ages. The sixth module, Teaching Talented and Gifted Children, provides insights and strategies for effectively supporting high-achieving students. Finally, the module on Leadership and Management addresses the skills needed for effective educational leadership and school management. Together, these modules form a comprehensive framework for professional development, aimed at adopting and adapting the new curriculum, improving the overall quality of each lesson at each subject.

Out of all abstracts, admitted to the WALS conference 2024, the topics related to school subjects were selected. The diagram below represents the distribution of research done according to the subjects. The largest proportion of the topics are around language teaching (35.16%). It can be explained by the fact that Kazakhstan is a bilingual country,

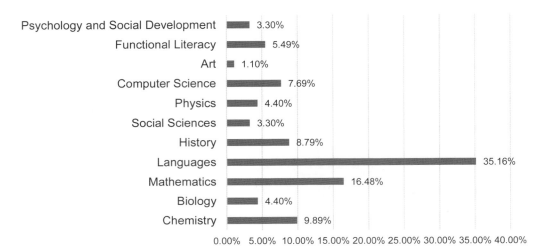

Diagram 2: Proportion of Lesson Study Research According to School Subjects

where Kazakh and Russian are both taught as the first language and the second one, depending on the language of instruction at a school. In addition, in 2019 the policy of trilingualism was announced in Kazakhstan. The English language has been taught as a foreign language for many years, but in 2019 the ideas of CLIL were introduced. This has led to the raise in the number of research done by the language teachers as well as subject teachers, who teach their subject in English.

The second place in the number of research conducted for the conference belongs to Math (16.48%) and then come sciences as Chemistry (9.89%), Computer Science (7.69%) and History (8.79%).

The implementation of Lesson Study and the curriculum development should be bilateral. First, it is essential to integrate Lesson Study with the broader context of the State Educational Standards (SCES). This integration should outline how Lesson Study aligns with specific standards or goals, such as enhancing teaching methods, improving curriculum delivery, or meeting educational benchmarks. At the same time lesson study should become an indicator that highlights shortcomings in all 7 aspects (see Figure 1).

Teachers need to ensure that the objectives of Lesson Study sessions directly reflect the goals of the curriculum. This alignment helps teachers focus on how their collaborative efforts can improve specific curricular outcomes. When planning lessons for Lesson Study, it is essential to integrate key content areas from the curriculum. This allows teachers to explore how different teaching strategies can enhance the understanding of curricular concepts.

Teachers should learn to utilize national curriculum standards as a framework for Lesson Study discussions. This ensures that the lessons being studied are relevant and address the required educational benchmarks.

Teachers should work together during Lesson Study to identify gaps in the curriculum or areas that need enhancement. Their collective insights can lead to the development of more effective and engaging curricular materials. After conducting a Lesson Study, feedback on the effectiveness of the lesson in relation to the curriculum should be collected to refine both the lesson plan and the curriculum content, creating a continuous improvement cycle.

Centering Lesson Study discussions around student learning outcomes as outlined in the curriculum will help teachers stay focused on the end goals and assess the effectiveness of their teaching strategies. Teachers should be encouraged to document their findings from each Lesson Study cycle, including how specific teaching practices impacted student learning related to the curriculum. Sharing these findings can foster a culture of continuous improvement and innovation in curriculum development.

And the last and probably most important step at this stage is to engage Stakeholders. It could be a good policy decision to involve curriculum developers and educational leaders in Lesson Study sessions. Their participation can help ensure that the insights gained from classroom practice are considered in future curriculum revisions as it is done in Japan.

4. Conclusion

In Kazakhstan, the wide application of Lesson Study approach has the potential to significantly improve education quality if implemented and adapted correctly. It can enhance teaching effectiveness, improve curricula and methods, and support teachers' professional development. It is important to consider the context and specific needs of the Kazakhstani educational system to fully leverage the benefits of this method.

The Lesson Study approach can help make the curriculum more dynamic and responsive to the real needs of students and teachers. It supports continuous improvement in the educational process, enhances the quality of teaching materials and methods, and fosters teachers' professional development.

References

Chichibu, T. (2013). Handbook for Teachers on Lesson Study, AEO 'Nazarbayev Intellectual Schools', Center of Excellence.

Dudley, P. (2011). Lesson Study: a handbook. https://lessonstudy.co.uk/lesson-study-a-handbook/

Fernandez, C., Yoshida, M. (2004). *Lesson Study: A Japanese Approach to Improving Mathematics Teaching and Learning*. Routledge.

Kuramoto, T. & Associate. (2014). *Lesson Study and Curriculum Management in Japan—Focusing on Action Research*. Fukuro Publishing.

Lewis, C., Takahashi, A. (2013). Facilitating curriculum reforms through lesson study. *International Journal for Lesson and Learning Studies.*

Lewis, C., Tsuchida, I. (1998). *A lesson is like a swiftly flowing river: Research lessons and the improvement of Japanese education*. American Educator.

Tanaka, K., Nishioka, K., Ishii, T. (2017). *Curriculum, Instruction and Assessment in Japan*. Routledge.

How does the Course of Study in Japan differ from other countries? Retrieved from: https://typeset.io/questions/how-does-the-course-of-study-in-japan-differ-from-other-1l65jkl29f

Introduction to the American Educational Curriculum. Retrieved from: https://medium.com/@ISSP_team/introduction-to-the-american-educational-curriculum-4ee9b1f62d4c

Об утверждении государственных общеобязательных стандартов образования всех уровней образования. Retrieved from: https://adilet.zan.kz/rus/docs/V1800017669

Образование в Казахстане. Retrieved from: https://www.gov.kz/article/128171?lang=ru

Overview. Retrieved from: https://www.mext.go.jp/en/policy/education/overview/index.htm

Basic Act on Education. Retrieved from: https://www.mext.go.jp/en/policy/education/lawandplan/title01/detail01/1373798.htm

Система образования Финляндии. Retrieved from: https://www.infofinland.fi/ru/education/the-finnish-education-system

Система общего образования Финляндии: современное состояние и перспективы. Retrieved from: https://kiro-karelia.ru/activity/journal/nomera/sistema-obshhego-obrazovaniya-finlyandii-sovremennoe-sosotoyanie-i-perspektivy

US Curriculum and Assessments. Retrieved from: https://www.nordangliaeducation.com/academic-excellence/curricula-guide/us-curriculum-and-assessments

Features of education in the UK. Retrieved from: https://www.unipage.net/en/education_system_uk

Teacher's Handbook. Third (Basic) Level (2012) AEO 'Nazarbayev Intellectual Schools', Center of Excellence.

Chapter 6

On-the-Job-Training (OJT) for Novice Teachers in Aichi Prefecture

Anthony RYAN, Nanzan University

1. Introduction

Across various Initial Teacher Education (ITE) programs offered by higher education institutions globally, the component known as "field experiences" or "teaching practicums" exhibits significant variability. It is generally accepted that participation in some form of field placement in schools is necessary before one can qualify or become licensed as a teacher. However, aspects such as the duration of these placements, the credits awarded to student-teachers, the structure of mentor-teacher arrangements, the involvement of university supervisors, and other program-specific elements differ not only between countries but also within different states, provinces, or educational jurisdictions within those countries. For instance, examining simply the duration of time spent in actual school settings—the teaching practicum period internationally shows a wide range of requirements. In the Asia-Pacific, where 4-year bachelor-degree ITE programs are standard, practicum durations include 12–20 weeks in Australia, 22 weeks in Cambodia, 10 weeks in Vietnam, 10–12 weeks in Hong Kong, and 10 weeks in Singapore. In contrast, Europe tends to favor post-graduate master's degree programs, where the length of teaching practicums also varies: the Netherlands sees trainee-teachers in schools for three days a week over a full academic year, the UK mandates a minimum of 24 weeks for those enrolled in the Post Graduate Certificate of Education (PGCE), France requires 18–24 weeks, and Finland, well-regarded for its education system, has training schools attached to its eight teacher training institutions where over a typical 5-year primary teacher program, student-teachers accumulate about 25 credit points for teaching practice, each point equivalent to 27 hours of study (Salovita, 2019), summing to roughly 20 weeks.

Two noteworthy exceptions in practicum length are Germany and Japan, which, at first glance, show parallels in their teacher training approaches. In Germany, depending on the state (Bundesland), the "University Phase" of the practicum can range from 4–6 weeks to an entire semester. During the "Referendariat Phase" of post-graduate training, trainee-teachers (referendare) engage in extensive fieldwork ranging from 18–24 weeks under mentorship at schools, participate in off-campus teacher-training seminars, and progressively assume more classroom responsibilities. This model closely mirrors the training structure in Japan, where during the university phase of 4 years, teacher trainees

93

typically undergo only 2 to 4 weeks of practicum. Most of their practical training is conducted post-graduation during a year-long induction program, where they work as probationary teachers in schools. This paper details the On-the-Job Training (OJT) system for novice teachers in a specific Japanese prefecture and discusses how this framework integrates into a lifelong professional development program for educators.

2. On-the-Job-Training (OJT) and Off-the-Job-Training (OffJT)

In Japan, during the late 1950s and early 1960s—a period marked by intense economic growth—Japanese businesses faced the challenge of keeping up with rapid technological advancements and aligning with global industry standards. They came to realize that a robust employee training system was needed: one that could accommodate staff from varied educational backgrounds, did not disrupt daily operations, and simultaneously provide the essential theoretical and practical skills required for employees' roles. This need led to the development of a dual-component training system for new employees (Koike, 1997) that remains prevalent across many Japanese industries today. This system includes "Off-the-Job Training" (OffJT) and "On-the-Job Training" (OJT). OffJT consists of structured programs conducted away from the workplace at locations like vocational schools or company-affiliated training centers, led by specialized instructors. OJT, derived from the apprenticeship tradition, takes place directly within the workplace, where trainees are guided by supervisors or experienced colleagues (Mitani, 1997). These components are designed to complement each other; for instance, a production trainee might learn machine operation through OJT and the underlying technology or machine mechanics through OffJT (Mitani, 1997). Thus, OffJT focuses on imparting theoretical knowledge and technical skills, while OJT emphasizes practical, job-specific skill development.

The education sector in Japan has adopted and adapted this bifurcated system, applying it to the ongoing professional development of teachers at all career stages. Legislative changes in the late 1980s significantly propelled this approach to the forefront of teacher training and development. Specifically, the "Law Concerning Organization and Management of Local Educational Administration" and the "Revision of the Special Law Concerning Public Education Personnel" in 1988, along with subsequent revisions in 2006 and 2007 to various education laws, transformed the landscape of teacher training and professional development in Japan. Initially, the "Law Concerning Organization and Management of Local Educational Administration" mandated that education boards implement a 1-year induction program for new teachers, aimed at equipping them with the practical and theoretical skills necessary to excel in teaching (Collinson & Ono, 1992). Additionally, the revisions to the "Special Law Concerning Public Education Personnel" asserted that teachers have both the right and the obligation to pursue ongoing professional development, leading the Ministry of Education, Culture, Sports, Science and Technology (MEXT) to encourage local education boards to develop systematic professional development programs beyond the induction year. The enactment of changes to the "Fundamental Law of Education" and the "School Education Law" in December 2006, and the "Education Personnel Certification Law" in 2007, introduced the "Teacher License Renewal" (TLR) system effective from April 2009, requiring teachers to periodically renew their licenses by undertaking advanced courses at universities with teacher-training programs.

While the MEXT's directives and these legislative changes have generally been effective, especially at the local level, the implementation has faced challenges. The programs require annual revisions due to various factors, including recent pandemic disruptions and the growing use of ICT in education. One significant challenge arose with the brief implementation and subsequent rescinding in April 2022 of the "Teacher License Renewal Law," which faced criticism for imposing excessive demands on teachers' time and finances, and for underestimating the specific needs of classroom teachers (Chapple, 2021).

The broad application of the OJT/OffJT system in Japan's education sector, as illustrated by detailed induction and professional development programs like those developed by the Aichi Prefectural Board of Education, underscores its adaptability and importance. Further details on these programs are provided in the subsequent sections, drawing from AI-assisted translations of guidelines and handbooks published by the Aichi Prefecture Board of Education and the Aichi Prefecture General Education Center.

1. 2023 To all New Teachers (「令和５年度 新しく先生となるみなさんへ」)
2. 2023 Guide for Novice Teacher Training (「初任者研修の手引き」)
3. 2023 Aichi Prefecture Teacher Training Plan (「令和５年度愛知県教員研修計画」)
4. 2023 Index of Aichi Prefecture Teacher Training Courses (「令和５年度愛知県教員研修計画一覧」)
5. 2023 'Carrying the Wind' To those Becoming Hub School Instructors (「令和５年度　風をはこぶ　拠点校指導教員となるみなさん」)

The description of the teacher-training system that follows is specific to compulsory education schools in Aichi Prefecture that are outside the training system for teachers in elementary and junior high schools, high schools, and special support schools of government-designated cities, as well as teachers in elementary and junior high schools of core cities. In Aichi prefecture, as of the time of writing, Nagoya is a government-designated city, while Toyota, Okazaki, Toyohashi, Ichinomiya and Kasugai are core cities. Teacher training in these cities, as well as that in other prefectures, is bespoke structured and implemented according to the training plans established by each city and each prefecture. For example, a novice-teacher in Kanagawa prefecture undergoes 210 hours of on-campus training and 18 off-campus sessions in his or her induction year, compared to those teachers in Aichi prefecture—excluding Nagoya and the core cities—who undergo 150 hours of on-campus training plus 17 days of off-campus sessions.

3. The Teacher Development System in Aichi Prefecture

The Aichi Prefecture "Teacher Development Index" (see Table 1 for Entry level and Stage 1 teachers) envisions that teachers will progress through a 3-stage developmental pathway over the course of their careers, progressing from (a) a Stage 1 early-career teacher working on building the foundations of his/her qualities and abilities as a teacher, to a (b) a Stage 2 mid-career teacher consolidating and developing the above qualities and abilities and taking on more leadership roles in the school, through to possibly becoming a (c) Stage 3 senior leader in a position of school management. For the teacher, the development index serves as a general guideline for developing, planning, and demonstrating specific capabilities pertaining to the stages of the teacher's career, the abilities that need to be demonstrated at each level, and what next-step the teacher should be aiming for next. The teacher training system of the Aichi Prefecture BOE does not make the hard-and-fast distinction between OJT and OffJT that industry does. All training is classified as OJT training and a distinction is then made between On-Campus OJT and Off-Campus OJT. This two-component system permeates the three development stages which are also referred to by the focus of the training sessions at each stage: "Skill-Up Training" at Stage 1, "Career-Up Training" at Stage 2, and "Leadership Training" at Stage 3. The goal is for teachers to work on continuously upgrading and upskilling through taking seminars at off-campus facilities and bringing what they have learnt into the classroom on-campus. According to the "2023 Aichi Prefecture Teacher Training Plan,"

"Teacher training can be broadly categorized into off-campus training and on-campus training. The integration of these two types of training allows for effective and efficient improvement in each teacher's qualities and capabilities. Initially, the content and tasks of on-campus training are organized based on the exercises and lectures scheduled for off-campus training. During off-campus training, teachers acquire new knowledge, learn practical methods, and find triggers for applying these methods. After returning to their schools, they apply what they've learned and further deepen their understanding through on-campus inquiry, leading to proactive and substantial training. Further enhancements are considered by bringing these experiences into subsequent off-campus training sessions, where deepened insights are discussed. This cyclical and organic linkage between on-campus and off-campus training enhances the overall effectiveness of the training" (Aichi Prefecture Teacher Training Plan, 2023, p.14).

This system is to serve as the core of a training system aimed at enhancing the qualities and abilities corresponding to each career stage, and includes mandatory training for newcomers, as stipulated by the "Special Measures Law for Education Personnel", and training for mid-career teachers aimed at improving their qualities, among others. In the "Skill-Up" Stage 1 this report in particular addresses, the documentation posits that "it's a comprehensive training designed to enhance the fundamental qualities and abilities needed by teachers at various career stages, whether due to their teaching experience or when they assume specific duties" (Aichi Prefecture Teacher Training Plan, 2023, p.13).

In 2023, the "Aichi Teacher Training Development Index" listed 255 seminars available to teachers across all 3 stages. While some are exclusively or mandatory for 1st,

2nd and 3rd year teachers (the latter two defined as "teachers with limited experience"), teachers with more than 3 years of experience can pick and choose seminars as they deem necessary for their personal professional development. Additionally, and as mentioned below, there are also mandatory seminars for those in mid-career stage 2 that are needed for leadership roles at schools. While the duration of time a teacher spends at each stage is not exactly clear in the documentation, prior to 2021, a Stage 1 teacher was someone with up to 5 years of experience, with a Stage 2 teacher classified as someone with 10 years or more experience. Extrapolating upon these figures, Stage 3 senior leaders would have required 20 or more years of experience (assuming a teacher had ambitions on such a role and had undertaken the required training courses) and enhanced training for these roles. Following recent revisions brought about by the recognition of the younger age profile of teachers and a shortage of middle leaders, necessitating training from an earlier stage to enhance the awareness and roles of middle leaders, Stage 2 teachers are now divided into "early-stage mid-career teachers" and "latter-stage mid-career teachers" with the teachers having 10 years of experience before entering the "early stage 2 mid-career" status.

"Starting in the 2021 fiscal year, the 5-year experience training for elementary, junior high, compulsory education schools, high schools, and special education schools has been abolished, and the 10-year experience training has been implemented as a mid-career teacher quality improvement training in an early and late-stage system. Both the early and late stages of mid-career teacher quality improvement training are legislated as statutory training" (Aichi Prefecture Teacher Training Plan, 2023, p.8).

A particular teacher's current stage largely depends upon the duration of time that has passed since beginning teaching and the number of required courses the teacher has undertaken, the school-based curriculum management roles undertaken to date (Kuramoto, 2024) and, presumably, the evaluations of the school's senior leaders and those at BOE-level familiar with the teacher. The detailed training records that are kept by both the teacher and Aichi Prefecture BOE are vital in regard (see Aichi Prefecture Teacher Training Plan, 2023, p.10 for a description) to the status of the teacher. Figure 1 shows the "Career Development Tree" (for want of a better English translation), as a diagrammatic representation of the development pathway of a teacher. It also shows some—not all—of the course training modules that teachers undertake at each stage of their career development.

In terms of the recruitment of Stage 1 teachers, Table 1, reproduced below in English, shows the "Entry Level" (i.e., what Aichi Prefecture is looking for upon entry to the profession) as well as the "Stage 1 Indicators" that teachers need to demonstrate across three key areas before progressing to Stage 2. The three key fields include "Fundamental Qualities", "Instructional Skills", and "Management Skills", each of which is further subdivided. "Fundamental Qualities", subdivided into four, includes demonstrating and developing (i) love of education, sense of mission and sense of responsibility (ii) logic, humanity and actions (iii) self-education and creative thinking, and (iv) communication ability. "Instructional Skills", also subdivided into four, includes (i) understanding of children (ii) instructional guidance (iii) student guidance, and (iv) understanding of

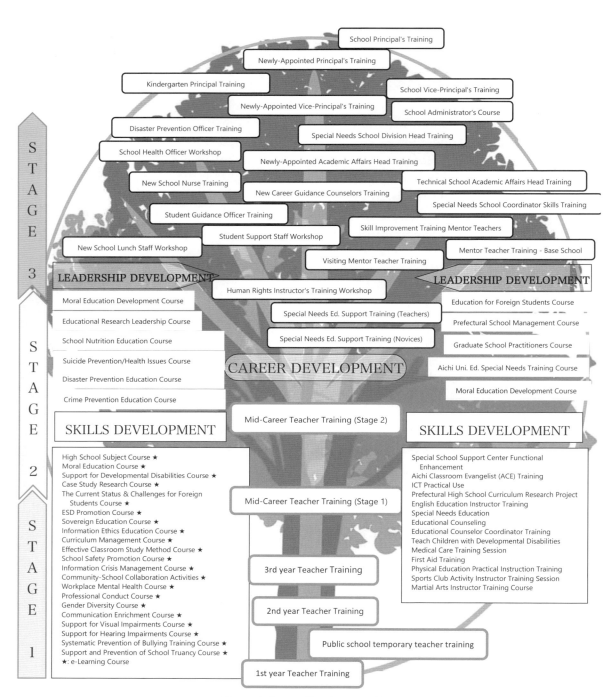

Figure 1: Career Development Tree

Table 1: Aichi Prefecture Teacher Development Indicators 2022– (Entry Stage and Stage 1)

Stage	Quality/Ability	Entry Stage — What Aichi Prefecture is looking for upon entry to the profession	Stage 1 — Solidify your foundations as a teacher
Fundamental Qualities	• Love of Education • Sense of mission • Sense of responsibility	In order to ensure the growth of students, the teacher continuously supports them with love, and feels joy in their growth.	
		While seriously thinking about the future of students, the teacher is aware of the sense of mission and responsibility that comes with taking on the development of students who will be responsible for the future.	
	• Logic • Humanity • Actions	The teacher strives to build trust with students by adhering to professional ethics, observing laws and regulations, and acting in a manner that serves as a role model for students.	
		The teacher strives to maintain an image that can become a goal and aspiration for students.	
		The teacher is proactive, persistent, and endeavors to fulfill the duties of a teacher.	
	• Self-Education Ability • Creative Thinking Ability	While possessing a wide range of knowledge and a high degree of expertise, the teacher engages in regular introspection and is motivated to continue self-learning and maintain strong motivation to improve.	
		Even when faced with unexpected problems, the teacher responds flexibly and always tries to approach such with creativity.	
	• Communication Ability	In addition to conveying one's own ideas, the teacher works collaboratively while taking into account the surrounding situation and the thoughts of the other person, while striving for common understanding.	
Instruction Skills	Understanding of Children	Acquire basic knowledge related to children's developmental stages and growth, recognize the significance and importance of understanding children, and strive to be proactive and involved with each person.	1. Treat each student with love and capture their feelings through your relations with the students. 2. Foster in students a sense of belonging to their class and grade. 3. Understand students based on their backgrounds such as their home environment. Aim to understand this and encourage growth tailored to each individual.
	Instructional Guidance	Based on the curriculum guidelines, the aim is to acquire fundamental teaching techniques such as questioning, black-board writing, and creating an engaging environment, as well as to follow the lesson plan and implement it in practice.	1. Develop fundamental teaching skills such as appropriate questioning, clear blackboard writing, effective use of ICT, and intentional classroom environment setup. Develop lessons that draw out students' autonomous learning and work on lesson improvement aimed at realizing personalized optimal learning and collaborative learning. 2. Understand the importance of lesson preparation—such as considering the students' actual conditions, clarifying the objectives of the lesson, and selecting teaching materials and aids—in order to facilitate an effective lesson. 3. Strive to improve one's teaching methods by learning from other teachers.

Instruction Skills	Student Guidance	Based on the importance of student guidance and career education, aim to understand and practice measures for teaching individuals and groups.	1. Respond to students with a perspective that aligns with "life skills education" and "career education," focusing on fostering individual growth, enhancing social competencies, and improving proactive behaviors. 2. Comprehend the issues of each and every student while understanding the concerns of their guardians. Collaborate with guardians and other educational staff to systematically and consistently support students.
	Understanding Diversity and Delivery of Educational Support	1. Possess a sense of human rights, recognizing the necessity to respect the individuality of children and students, and understanding the need for guidance and support tailored to each individual. 2. Make efforts to understand the diverse backgrounds of students who require special attention, such as those in special needs education and foreign students, while also acknowledging the importance of inclusive education.	1. Comprehend the individuals' actual situation appropriately while understanding individual characteristics and background. 2. Promote individualized instruction in a planned manner for students with special needs. 3. Through practice, deepen understanding of the diversity of students and provide guidance and support based on reasonable consideration.
Management Skills	Class management Grade management School management	1. Possess a vision of the ideal state for students and oneself, and strive to realize that vision in practice. 2. Actively try to obtain information related to education, such as the significance of school education and current issues related to education.	1. Understand school education goals, set policies for classroom management and subject management according to the actual situation of students, and provide uniform instruction. 2. Build good interpersonal relationships within the class group. 3. Participate in the management of the school year in cooperation with the school principal and other faculty members. 4. Be cognizant of your role within the school organization and carry out your duties in a systematic manner.
	School safety/ crisis management	Acquire basic knowledge about school safety and be able to detect dangers around students and try to avoid them or respond appropriately.	1. Put the safety and security of students first, foreseeing dangers and dealing appropriately with them. 2. Create an environment that takes safety and educational effectiveness into consideration, and ensure that "reporting, communication, and consultation" regarding issues is carried out.
	Coordination and collaboration with colleagues	As a member of society, act with common sense and try to build smooth interpersonal relationships.	1. As a member of a school, understand the role required of you and work collaboratively with your colleagues. 2. Proceed with self-improvement by actively engaging with other faculty members, discussing and sharing doubts and concerns.
	Collaboration and negotiation with local communities	1. Be aware of your role as an educational public servant and act with an awareness of your connections with society. 2. Understand the importance of collaboration with families, communities, and related organizations, and seek to be actively involved.	1. Build good relationships with families by making efforts to share information with them. 2. Respond appropriately by coordinating with the local community and related organizations as necessary and consider the advice of other faculty and staff.

diversity and educational support. The "Management Skills" include (i) class, grade and school management (ii) school safety and crisis management (iii) coordination and collaboration with colleagues, and (v) collaboration with the local community.

4. The Novice Teacher OJT system

A "novice teacher" in Stage 1, is defined as a beginning teacher in his or her first year of their teaching career who is subject to a one-year induction programme of initial training to be conducted while working in a school as a full-time teacher. In principle, 5 hours of the teacher's schedule per week are to be used as training periods during which the novice is under the guidance of mentor teachers. Some of the key features of the first-year induction programme, translated and summarized from the above sources, are outlined and commented upon below.

(a) Purpose
"As part of the ongoing professional development, a one-year training program is implemented for new teachers in order to cultivate the qualities and abilities necessary for teaching, such as personal development, leadership, and management skills, and to provide them with a broad range of knowledge. The training focuses on solidifying the fundamental skills of teaching as indicated in the first stage of the teacher development indicators" (2023 Aichi Prefecture Teacher Training Plan p.4).

(b) Types of training
(i) On-Campus Training
The current training plan calls for novices to undertake a total of 150 hours per year of on-campus training (i.e., at their workplace school) divided roughly into 5 hours per week over 30 weeks of the school year. In schools using the hub-school system, of the 5 hours, 2 hours are to be supervised at the instruction and direction of the home-school mentor teacher, with the remaining 3 hours allotted to supervision by the hub-school mentor teacher. In regard to the hours allotted to the hub-school mentor teacher, in principle the 3 hours are divided into 2 hours of lesson observations of the trainee's classes and 1 hour conducting post-lesson guidance sessions. Detailed records of their own visits to the school and the content of guidance sessions are to be kept by the hub-school mentor, both as records of the training sessions and as a record of the supervisor's working hours.

(ii) Off-Campus Training
Previous to the pandemic, the training plan called for 17 days of face-to-face sessions in off-campus training seminars for novice teachers in their first year, including sessions conducted during a 2-day *gasshuku* (training camp). However, with the restrictions on gatherings brought about by the pandemic, a more flexible and hybrid approach has been implemented recently with some of the 17 sessions being available asynchronously in

Table 2: Organization of Novice Teacher Training

On-Campus Training			Off-Campus Training	
System 1	System 2			
Home-School Mentor Teacher only	Home-School Mentor Teacher	Hub-School Mentor Teacher	Teacher-Lecturers (Each school/district has its own expert practitioners that are periodically seconded for lectures and practical workshops)	
5 hours per week x 30 weeks	2 hours per week x 30 weeks	3 hours per week x 30 weeks	face-to-face hybrid synchronous asynchronous school visitations	selected Wednesdays at Aichi Prefectural General Education Center, cooperating schools & facilities
150 hours	60 hours	90 hours		
Total = 150 hours			Total = 17 days	

e-learning sessions, online synchronous sessions, as well as face-to-face gatherings of the teachers at designated training facilities or visits to hub schools for lesson observations and training sessions. A recent ad hoc survey of 5 recent graduates of the author's seminar revealed an attendance rate range of 12 to 14 at face-to-face sessions on designated Wednesdays in their districts in 2023 with a further 3 available online asynchronously or synchronously. While attendance is mandatory in principle, the reality of the trainee's home school circumstances at particular times of the academic year often prevents full attendance at all 17 sessions in practice, so flexibility in incorporating asynchronous and hybrid modes into session delivery has become an essential and effective strategy in recent off-campus teacher training.

(c) Two Mentor Teacher Systems

There are two mentor teacher systems used for training novices in Aichi Prefecture. The "conventional method" (System 1), where one home-school mentor teacher guides the novice or novices in a single school, and the "hub school system" (System 2), where a mentor that uses a designated school as a base (i.e., hub) has been dispatched from that school to guide three to four new recruits from one or multiple schools. In System 1, a novice teacher is assigned a mentor from among their home school colleagues. The home-school mentor teacher is often the curriculum chief or deputy principal in elementary schools, while in junior high school where trainees are subject-specific teachers, the mentor is often the subject coordinator or a senior experienced teacher. In System 1, 4 hours are recommended to be set aside for direct training with the mentor per week, with the other hour to be spent on material development, lesson planning and self-study. In System 2, the training supervision is split between a home-school mentor (2 hours per week) and a hub-school mentor (3 hours per week). In regard to the allocation of training content in the System 2 programme for the novice (see "On-Campus Training Items" in Appendix A), either the home-school mentor can plan the entire 150 hours and apportion the topics for the 90 hours for the hub-school mentor to cover, or vice versa. Of the 3 hours per week assigned to the hub-school mentor in System 2, examples in the training guidelines reveal that it is recommended that 2 hours should be used on lesson observation and the other hour on guidance specific to the novice as well as lectures on topics from the 9 content domains for training (as above, Appendix A).

In terms of the selection of home-school mentors, hub-school mentors and off-campus instructors (see below), in general, the principal is responsible for all home-school mentors while the Aichi Prefecture BOE appoints hub-school mentors. The BOE has access to the up-to-date training records of all teachers in its jurisdiction which "enables the discovery of potential instructors" (2023 Aichi Prefecture Teacher Training Plan, p.12). Hub-school mentor teachers can also be selected from amongst experienced senior teachers in between transfers from schools who are sometimes attached to the Aichi Prefecture BOE for periods of one to two years to act as teacher-lecturers at training seminars and/or mentors for novice teachers. For example, a teacher that has served in a particular school for six years and who has been through a number of transfers and who may be due for or have requested another transfer, may be asked to serve as a mentor teacher for up to 3 or 4 novice teachers, rather than move to the new school. In recent times, however, due to a shortage of classroom teachers it is becoming increasingly difficult to release such experienced teachers from teaching duties in schools in order to act as mentor-teachers. Increasingly, the prefecture and municipalities are asking retired staff to take on roles as mentors. Ex-principals, vice-principals, senior leaders and subject teachers are being employed on casual employment contracts to act as mentor-teachers for the novice teachers (p.c. retired principal of elementary school). The mentors are assigned to a hub school to use as a 'base' and from there, they go out to visit the novices at their schools. Every Wednesday is a non-training day because the novices usually undertake off-campus training away from their schools, so the mentors work at their hub school for half the day on planning and record-keeping administration tasks. Depending upon how many hours the retiree wants to work per week, a hub-school mentor's workweek could be 2 and 1/2 or 4 and 1/2 days per week. While the system is noteworthy for its comprehensiveness and diligence, it is often the case that, even though most training time should be spent with the novice on 'subject instruction,' the major subject fields of the mentors are not the same as those of the novice teachers. The strain on human resources in recent times means that matching mentors and novices in this regard is not often possible, particularly when the mentor teacher is asked to take on more than one novice per year (p.c. retired principal of elementary school). It is usual for hub-school mentors to be training from 2 to 4 novices per year.

(d) Teacher's Manual

At the initial orientation sessions, the new teachers are given the "To all New Teachers" guidebook. Consisting of 4 sections, this 88-page handbook serves as a comprehensive instruction manual for the new teachers, dealing with everything from conducting morning class assembly meetings through to how to utilize various career support systems. Table 3 shows the table of contents of the "2023 To all New Teachers" handbook.

(e) Training Content

During their induction year, novice teachers in elementary schools receive On-Campus and Off-Campus guidance across 9 content domains. These are (1) Basic Knowledge

Table 3: Table of Contents of the "2023 To all New Teachers" Handbook

I Introduction	13 Guidance on problem behavior such as violent behavior	3 Cooperation with families
II Teacher's Mindset	14 What to do if an accident occurs	4 Life at home and in the community
III A Day in the Life of a Teacher	15 Health development	5 Class affairs
1 Start of the day	16 During recess times	6 Career education
2 Morning assembly	17 Make-up classes	7 In-service education
3 School education plan and instruction plan	18 School lunch guidance	8 School health
4 Lesson plan	19 Cleaning	9 School safety
5 Teacher's Remarks	20 Afternoon assembly	10 Guidance regarding food
6 Blackboard Writing & notebooks	21 How to spend time after school	11 Special needs education
7 How to ask questions	22 Club activities	12 Human rights education
8. The nature of evaluation	23 Various meetings	13 Manners as a member of society
9 Building trust - From a communication standpoint	24 Leaving work	14 Training and working conditions
10 Textbooks	IV What you need to know as a teacher	15 Educational administrative organization in Aichi Prefecture
11 How to prevent bullying	1 Classroom management	16 Status and duties of teachers
12 Guidance for truant children	2 Student guidance	17 Welfare system

(2) Classroom Management (3) Subject Instruction (4) Moral Education Instruction (5) Foreign Language Education (elementary school) (6) Integrated Studies Instruction (7) Special Activities (including extra-curricular activities) (8) Student Guidance (9) Career Guidance. Appendix A shows the specific topics within each domain. Junior High School novices do not receive training in #5, foreign language education.

Participation in and implementation of a "Research Lesson" (*kenkyu jugyo*) by the novice teacher falls into #1 basic knowledge and the research lesson is usually delivered at least once (Term 1in usually May or June) and sometimes once per other term (p.c. novice teacher) depending upon the individualized school-based training programme. In elementary schools, at least one of the research lessons is set aside for moral education. When conducting such lesson studies, the novice creates a teaching plan outline complete with plans for board writing and questioning strategies in consultation with their mentor. In creating the lesson plan, the teacher is expected to utilize his or her pre-study of the teaching materials, so as to implement a fulfilling lesson. The lesson plans also allow the mentor to focus their perspectives for class observations and apply these to the post-lesson guidance sessions. Prior to formal delivery of the lesson, a mock lesson may be staged with the mentor and supporting staff as advisers. If so, the plan is usually revised based on that advice. The lesson is then delivered and post-lesson discussions with the observers takes place. The goal is to improve practice and identify future research lesson focus possibilities. Such a process mirrors the "Lesson Study" procedures outlined elsewhere in this volume.

Aside from the formal "Research Lesson" period, over the course of the year, the novices are expected to be continuously creating and submitting lesson plans for all

Table 4: Training Content per Domain

Term	Term 1					Term 2				Term 3			Hours
Month	4	5	6	7	8	9	10	11	12	1	2	3	
① Basic Knowledge	2	2	3	2	2	1	1	1	1	2	2	1	20
② Classroom Management	2	1	2	1	0	2	1	2	1	1	1	1	15
③ Subject Guidance	4	7	8	4	2	7	7	8	5	8	8	2	70
④ Moral Education	1	1	2	1	0	2	2	1	1	1	1	0	13
⑤ Foreign Language Ed.	0	0	0	1	0	0	1	0	0	0	0	0	2
⑥ Integrated Studies	1	1	1	0	0	1	1	1	0	1	1	0	8
⑦ Special Activities	1	1	1	0	0	2	1	1	1	1	1	0	10
⑧ Student Guidance	1	1	1	1	1	0	1	1	0	1	1	1	10
⑨ Career Guidance	0	1	0	0	0	0	0	0	1	0	0	0	2
Total	12	15	18	10	5	15	15	15	10	15	15	5	150

subjects to mentors who can require as much detail in a lesson plan as he or she thinks the novice requires. Table 4 shows the recommended number of instruction hours set aside for each domain as well as a recommended plan for implementation per term.

As indicated above, Terms 1 and 2 are busiest for novices with 60 and 55 hours of training respectively, with the bulk of training hours (70) being for subject instruction.

In regard to Off-Campus guidance, the same domain fields are addressed in the Wednesday sessions that are led by expert "practitioners-lecturers", but as mentioned above, with a greater focus on imparting theory and knowledge to the novices, although some practical activities are also included at times.

(f) Forms of guidance

In terms of mentor forms of guidance with their novice/s, they include:

(i) Lecture: Mentors provide lectures to new recruits according to the training content.

(ii) Demonstration: Mentors guide new recruits by demonstrating best practices.

(iii) Observation: Mentors primarily guide through observing the lessons of the novice.

(iv) Collaboration: Mentors guide the novice through collaborative educational activities.

(v) Advice: Mentors give advice and guidance to the novice.

As noted above, out of the three hours of guidance per day by the hub-school mentor teacher, two hours are often spent observing lessons, making subject instruction the core of the guidance. That said, even though the guidelines also advise that it is desirable to cover all domains, it is acceptable to prioritize particular ones at particular junctures based upon the mentor's impressions of the hitherto novice's experiences and background.

5. Conclusion

There are few doubts that the OJT teacher training and professional development system that has been put in place for Stage 1 novice teachers (and also Stage 2 teachers, and Stage 3 leaders) is well-planned and is comprehensive in scope through what it addresses. Of course, the main question is whether or not the theory matches the practice. To what extent are the plans actually implemented? How successfully and effectively? Moreover, the very comprehensiveness of the system raises further questions for this ITE teacher-trainer.

The first questions are in regard to the role that universities play in Japan in ITE. What exactly is the role of the university in teacher-training in Japan? Why do trainees need to attend teacher-training institutions if the most relevant practical skills and theoretical knowledge are taught via the OJT/OffJT system during their first 3 years? If the university is necessary, what makes it so? Can the 'Entry-Level' stage be passed without attending a teacher-training institution? Is there anything the prefectures would like the universities to do more of?

A second set of questions is perhaps more important and pertain to the impact that OJT has on two major stakeholders in terms of delivering a quality education: namely, the children and their guardians. Does a child with a novice teacher as homeroom teacher (HRT) get as good an education as a child in the room next door with an experienced teacher? How do parents of a child with a novice teacher as a homeroom teacher feel about the fact that the person charged with educating their child has had perhaps only two weeks practical experience in schools prior to being tasked to teach, protect and counsel their child?

A final set of questions can be asked about the novices themselves. The author attended teacher's college in the 1980s in Australia when it was only possible to attain an initial 3-year diploma of teaching (Dip.T.) The bachelor degree in education, which required a further one year of study, could only be started after the teacher had had two years of experience in the classroom. In the Dip.T. programme there were 22 weeks of field and professional experience in schools during the 3 years. By graduation in 3rd year, we had *lost* more than one third of our entry cohort, most dropping out in 1st year when they quickly realized that teaching was not for them as a career. Others realized later that they and the profession were not suited. This begs the question for Japan teacher training. What happens to those novice teachers that do not *make it*, cannot cope with the pressure and workload, and find out in their first year of teaching that they were not meant to be teachers? What is the attrition rate for novice teachers? How effective is the OJT system with accommodating, assisting, and counseling struggling novice teacher? Would longer or more teaching practicums while a student in ITE programmes have better alerted the novice to their compatibility for the job, as well as the pressures it brings and the mental fortitude required, not to mention given them the chance to develop greater practical skills and required prior to starting their first year OJT induction programme.

Finally, there are a number of caveats about the text above. Due to space considerations, it is not possible to explain the system in greater depth than this broad outline of the main features of the novice teacher training system in Aichi Prefecture. In attempting to translate and summarize the meticulous detail of the published guidelines and handbooks, there was heavy reliance on as-not-yet-perfect AI translations of large sections of each, and so many details above must be considered as possibly inaccurate and misleading. Although the author consulted with three retired principals on some aspects of the text above, assumptions have been made and opinions expressed that might not be either accurate or deserved, and for this the author accepts total responsibility.

Handbooks & Guidelines

2023 To all New Teachers (「令和5年度 新しく先生となるみなさんへ」)

2023 Guide for Novice Teacher Training (「初任者研修の手引き」)

2023 Aichi Prefecture Teacher Training Plan (「令和5年度愛知県教員研修計画」)

2023 Index of Aichi Prefecture Teacher Training Courses (「令和5年度愛知県教員研修計画一覧」)

2023 'Carrying the Wind' To Those Becoming Hub School Instructors (「令和5年度 風をはこぶ　拠点校指導教員となるみなさん」)

References

Chapple, J. (2021). No need to renew: The end of Japan's teacher license renewal system and the future. *Asian Journal of Education and Training*, 9(2), 48–53. https://files.eric.ed.gov/fulltext/EJ1389493.pdf

Collinson, V., & Ono, Y. (2001). The professional development of teachers in the United States and Japan. *European Journal of Teacher Education*, 24(2), 223–248. DOI: 10.1080/02619760120095615

Koike, K. (1997). Human Resource Development. The Japan Institute of Labour, Tokyo.

Kuramoto, T. (2024). *School-Based Curriculum Management: Teacher Education and Lesson Study Perspective*. Okazaki, Japan: Fukuro Publishing.

Mitani, N. (1999). The Japanese employment system and youth labour market. Preparing youth for the 21st century: The transition from education to the labour market. (305–328). OECD.

Salovita, T. (2019). Outcomes of teacher education in Finland: Subject teachers compared with primary teachers. *Journal of Education for Teaching*, 45(3), 322–334. https://doi.org/10.1080/09589236.2019.1599504

Appendix A: Aichi Prefecture Yearly Training Plan for Novice Teachers

Domain	On-Campus Training Items	Off-Campus Training Items
	The role of public education 公教育の役割	
	◇ Related laws and realization of education goals ◇ Coordination and collaboration with social education and home education ◇ Development of educational measures and business	a ◆ Public education and mission b ☆ Current status of educational reform and school education
	Formulation, implementation, and evaluation of curriculum guidelines and curriculum 学習指導要領と教育課程の編成・実施ならびに評価	
	◇ Organization and implementation of curriculum guidelines and curriculum ◇ Participation in curriculum management according to the actual situation of our school	c ◆ Legal status and standards of the curriculum guidelines
	Efforts to realize school education goals 学校教育目標の具現化に向けた取組	
	◇ School education goals and student image ◇ School education goals and school management ◇ School education goals and instructional plans ◇ School education goals and educational activities ◇ School education goals and school evaluation	d ☆ School educational goals and educational activities
	The work of a teacher, how to be a civil servant, and how to live as a teacher 教員の勤務と公務員としての在り方・教員としての生き方在り方	
	◇ Our school's services and obligations (including prevention of scandals) ◇ Work and salary ◇ Personnel changes ◇ Attitude as a teacher at our school ◇ Participation in in-school training and research	e ◆ Service, duty f ◆ Attitude as a teacher g ◆ Views on the teaching profession h ◆ Training and personal growth s ◆ Workplace etiquette u ◆ Teachers' mental health and self-management
① Basic knowledge	School organization management 学校の組織運営	
	◇ Related laws and school organization ◇ Division of school duties and their functions ◇ Improving the educational environment ◇ Safety management and accident prevention at school ◇ Creating an open school ◇ PTA management	x ◆ Building relationships between schools, local communities, and parents
	Efforts to solve educational issues 教育課題の解決に向けた取組	
	◇ Human rights education at our school ◇ Environmental education (including ESD) ◇ Response to computerization, etc. in our school's education ◇ Development of information utilization skills (including programming education) ◇ Response to internationalization of education, etc. ◇ Response to education for returnees & foreign students ◇ How to proceed with school health, disaster prevention and safety education at our school ◇ How to proceed with food-related guidance (including school lunch guidance) ◇ Development and utilization of special needs education system ◇ Sovereignty education ◇ Consumer education	i ◆ Human rights education j ◆ Information moral education k ◆ Current status and challenges of foreign student education l ◆ How to proceed with school health guidance m ★ Special educational needs and instruction n ☆ Special support education system v ◆ How to proceed with safety guidance w ☆ Environmental education y ◆ SDGs
	Through experience at educational institutions, etc. 教育機関等における体験を通して	
		o ☆ Experiential training 体験的な研修
	Summary of training 研修の総括	
	◇ Summary of in-school training for new employees ◇ 校内初任者研修の総括	q ☆ Problem research r ◆ Summary of training for new employees

	Significance of classroom management 学級経営の意義	
	◇ Creating and utilizing class management plans	a ◆ Contents and roles of classroom management b ◆ Class management and grade management
	Practical management and ingenuity in classroom management 学級経営の実際と工夫	
	◇ Building class organization ◇ Creating a classroom environment ◇ Management of activities by students ◇ Interaction with students at our school ◇ Building a classroom community ◇ Daily guidance	c ★ Ways of interacting with students d ◆ Building a classroom community
② Classroom Management	Classroom management in collaboration with guardians 保護者と連携を図った学級経営	
	◇ Classroom visits and parent-teacher meetings ◇ Dissemination & collection of information to parents ◇ Advice to parents	e ◆ Building relationships between schools, communities, and parents
	Dealing with classroom administrative tasks 学級事務の処理	
	◇ Administrative tasks at the beginning of the school year and each term ◇ Classroom administrative tasks such as organizing official records ◇ Classroom administrative tasks including creating various ledgers related to grades, etc. ◇ Administrative tasks at the end of each term and the end of the school year ◇ Utilization of information processing in classroom administrative tasks ◇ Planning and streamlining of classroom administrative task processing	
	Techniques related to guidance and methods of conducting lessons 指導に関する技術・授業の進め方	
③ Subject instruction	◇ Basic techniques in subject instruction ◇ Techniques for practical teaching ◇ Creation of instructional plans ◇ Understanding students in the classroom ◇ Methods and realities of teaching material research ◇ Approaches to teaching material research ◇ Creation and evaluation of tests ◇ Utilization of ICT equipment in subject instruction ◇ Analysis and diagnosis of lessons ◇ Guidance on individualized learning and collaborative learning ◇ Learning evaluation for the integration of instruction and assessment ◇ Creation and utilization of teaching materials and educational tools ◇ Reflection and evaluation of lessons ◇ Creation of annual instruction plans ◇ Handling of the content of the course of study guidelines	a ◆ Intermediate techniques in subject instruction b ◆ Methods and realities of teaching material research c ★ Utilization of ICT equipment in subject instruction d ◆ Analysis and diagnosis of lessons e ◆ Approaches to individualized instruction (Elementary level) f ◆ Learning assessment for integrating instruction and evaluation (Intermediate level) g ◆ Creation of annual instructional plans
	Lesson observation and lesson study 授業参観・授業研究	
	◇ Perspectives on observing demonstration lessons 示範授業参観の視点 ◇ Lesson study 授業研究	h ☆ Perspectives on observing demonstration lessons 示範授業参観の視点 i ★ Lesson study 授業研究
	Basic understanding of moral education 道徳教育の基礎的理解	
④ Moral Education	◇ Basic policy for moral education in schools and communities ◇ Moral education in other subjects/areas, etc.	a ☆ Goals and significance of moral education b ☆ Aim of making morality a subject and how it should be evaluated
	Teaching time for "Special Subject: Morals" 「特別の教科 道徳」の時間の指導	
	◇ Theme concept & material research for ethics studies ◇ Creating a moral studies lesson plan ◇ How evaluation should be done in moral studies ◇ Perspectives on observing demonstration classes ◇ Moral Education lesson study 道徳科の授業研究	c ☆ Theme planning and document research that approaches "morality in thinking and discussion" d ☆ lesson study in Moral Education

Chapter 6
On-the-Job-Training (OJT) for Novice Teachers in Aichi Prefecture

⑤ Foreign language elementary school	◇ The significance and practice of FLA and foreign language classes (elementary) ◇ FLA and foreign language instruction (elementary school)	a ◇ The significance and practice of FLA and foreign language classes (elementary) b ◆ Key points of goals and content of FLA and foreign language classes (elementary) c ◆ Practical implementation of FLA and foreign language instruction (elementary school)
⑥ Integrated Study Period	Significance/Aim 意義・ねらい	
	◇ Aim of our school's integrated study time	a ☆ Significance of comprehensive study time b ☆ Aim of comprehensive study time
	How to create an overall plan and proceed with learning activities 全体計画の作成・学習活動の進め方	
	◇ Contents and handling of the overall plan ◇ Cross-sectional/integrative learning and exploratory learning ◇ Improving learning formats and teaching systems	c ☆ Need to create an overall plan d ☆ Development of learning activities e ☆ Cross-curricula/integrative learning and exploratory learning
	How to create an overall plan and proceed with learning activities 全体計画の作成・学習活動の進め方	
	◇ Characteristics of evaluation ◇ Evaluation methods and how to utilize them	f ◆ Relationship between evaluation methods and other learning and activities
⑦ Special Activities	Educational significance of special activities 特別活動の教育的意義	
	◇ Goals of our school's special activities ◇ Contents of our school's special activities ◇ Characteristics of special activities	a ◆ Special activity goals b ◆ Special activity details
	Improvements in special activity lesson planning, actual instruction, and evaluation of special activities 特別活動の指導計画と指導の実際・特別活動の評価の工夫改善	
	◇ Overall instruction plan and annual instruction plan ◇ Use of school library ◇ Children's association & student council activities ◇ Club activities ◇ School events ◇ School lunch guidance ◇ Cleaning instruction ◇ Improvements in committee guidance and evaluation ◇ Instruction and evaluation of staff activities ◇ Improving guidance & evaluation of meeting activities ◇ Use of Career Passport (Career Education Notes)	c ◆ Group Fieldtrip
⑧ Student Guidance	◇ Contents and methods for student understanding ◇ Human relations between teachers and students ◇ How to praise and scold children and students ◇ Enhancing guidance functions and educational consultation ◇ Efforts for the healthy development of children and students ◇ Student guidance system at school ◇ Collaboration with families, local communities, and related organizations ◇ Reflection and evaluation of student guidance ◇ How to prevent bullying and school refusal and how to provide guidance	a ◆ Significance of student guidance b ◆ Contents and methods for student understanding c ◆ Human relationships between teachers and students d ◆ How to praise and scold children (middle) e ☆ Case studies on problem behavior, etc. f ◆ How to provide guidance to students who are bullied or do not attend school
⑨ Career Education (Career guidance)	◇ Development of career education (career guidance) and case studies ◇ Actual guidance on enlightening experiential activities related to occupations and career paths ◇ Collection and utilization of career information ◇ Career education (career guidance) system at school ◇ Reflection and evaluation of career education (career guidance)	a ☆ Significance of career education (career guidance) b ☆ Enhancing guidance functions and educational consultation c ☆ Collaboration with families, communities, and related organizations

* Major items within the training area are listed based on the Ministry of Education, Culture, Sports, Science and Technology's training objectives and content examples for beginners (February 16, 2007).

* (Elementary) is only available for elementary schools and the first half of compulsory education schools, and (middle school) is only for junior high schools and the second half of compulsory education schools.

* ⑤ Elementary school foreign language includes foreign language activities and foreign language subjects (training related to foreign language subjects is not included in ③ subject guidance).

* Of the off-campus training items,

◆ is held at the General Education Center,

☆ is held at the education office/municipal board of education,

★ is implemented at both the General Education Center, the Education Office, and the Municipal Board of Education.

This research was also supported by:
「2024年度南山大学パッヘ研究奨励金Ⅰ－Ａ－２(Nanzan University Pache Research Subsidy I-A-2 for the 2024 academic year)」

Chapter 7

Empowering Learners: Cultivating Autonomy in Japanese University English Education

Jack RYAN, Shizuoka University of Art and Culture

Abstract

The concept of learner autonomy, defined as empowering learners to take control of their own learning, has long held significant attention in modern educational paradigms. This paper will explore the concept of learner autonomy and how educators can facilitate learning experiences that empower learners to become active participants in their foreign language education. Through a review of theoretical frameworks, an analysis of an action research project conducted at two universities in Japan, and a discussion of strategies to promote autonomy, this paper aims to both summarize and provide a deeper understanding of the principles and practices underpinning effective learner autonomy.

1. Introduction

This monograph reports on a small action research project into student opinions about autonomy undertaken in university English courses at two Japanese universities in the 2023 academic year. The paper will present a definition of learner autonomy and outline the theoretical framework of autonomy as well as the evolution of the concept of learner autonomy over the past half century or so. Then, the paper will discuss some of the cultural dimensions and considerations of autonomy as well as challenges, barriers and pedagogical practices that may limit the implementation or effectiveness of learner autonomy. Next, I will describe the action research project and discuss the results. After the discussion of the action research, the paper will outline some techniques for fostering learner autonomy. Finally, there will be a short conclusion reflecting on lessons learned and possible takeaways for educators.

2. Learner Autonomy

Learner Autonomy refers to the ability and willingness of learners to take control of their own learning processes. It involves learners actively participating in selecting their learning activities and monitoring and evaluating their progress. Learner autonomy is seen as beneficial insofar as it can empower individuals to set learning goals, select learning resources and reflect on their learning experiences. Holec (1981) is often credited with popularizing the concept of learner autonomy and defined it simply as "the ability to take charge of one's own learning."

Promoting learner autonomy in education can encourage students to become independent, self-directed learners who are capable of learning beyond the confines of traditional classroom settings. Learner autonomy can foster critical thinking skills and lifelong learning habits. Of course, formal classroom instruction plays only a small part, usually in the formative years, of the lifelong education of most people. As such, autonomy can enable learners to continue their education as they see fit after the leave formal education. In any case, teachers can play a supportive role in fostering autonomy by providing guidance, resources, and opportunities for reflection and self-assessment, as well as creating a supportive learning environment that encourages exploration and experimentation. Ultimately, however, autonomy is "the capacity to take control of one's learning" (Benson, 2011).

An important factor for many when considering how and to what extent to introduce learner autonomy, maybe even the raison d'être of learner autonomy, is whether it has any positive effect on student motivation. This is somewhat akin to the famous metaphorical proverb, "You can lead a horse to water, but you cannot make him drink." The point is that teachers can give learners autonomy but cannot force them to become motivated learners.

In any case, while there remains controversy about whether motivation is the result of autonomy or if it fosters autonomy (i.e., a chicken and egg problem; does the motivation come first or the autonomy come first?), the preponderance of research evidence across contexts suggests that motivation is enhanced when learners are given, or take, more control over their learning (Garcia, 1996). The research is not definitive on the question of whether motivation or autonomy comes first but it does suggest that autonomy and motivation are at least correlated if not causal. In any case, on a more basic, classroom-level, we teachers find it intuitive that when students know what is expected of them, and find the material enjoyable, they are more likely to respond in a positive manner to a lesson or course.

3. Theoretical Frameworks & Learner Autonomy

In this section, I will outline a few of the theoretical frameworks related to the concept of learner autonomy and how the concept of autonomy has developed over time.

3-1. Self-Determination Theory

Self-Determination Theory (SDT) is a psychological framework formulated by Deci and Ryan (1985) which asserts that individuals have a basic psychological need for autonomy, competence, and relatedness which serve as essential motivators for human behavior and well-being. SDT is relevant to learner autonomy in that it provides insights into the underlying motivational factors that drive autonomous learning behaviors. According to SDT theory, autonomy involves students having a sense of control and ownership over their learning activities, such as setting learning goals, selecting learning strategies, and evaluating their own progress. SDT suggests that, when learners feel empowered to make choices and decisions about their learning, they are more likely to engage in self-directed learning behaviors, take responsibility for their learning, and develop an intrinsic motivation towards learning.

'Competence' as an element of SDT emphasizes students seeing themselves as capable of mastering academic tasks, acquiring new knowledge and skills, and achieving success in their learning. When learners experience a sense of competence this can motivate them to seek out further opportunities for autonomous learning in a virtuous cycle.

'Relatedness' in terms of SDT refers to the need for social connection and support in fostering motivation and well-being. This involves students feeling connected to their peers, teachers, and learning community. When learners feel socially connected and supported, they are more likely to participate actively in the learning community. This sense of relatedness can enhance learners' motivation to engage autonomously in learning activities that contribute to their educational development.

Overall, Self-Determination Theory provides a theoretical framework for understanding the motivational dynamics underlying learner autonomy. An awareness of students' basic psychological needs for autonomy, competence, and relatedness can help inform educators as they work to create learning environments that promote autonomous learning behaviors and, ultimately, academic success.

3-2. Social Cognitive Theory

Social Cognitive Theory (SCT), as articulated by Bandura (1986), emphasizes the role of cognitive, behavioral, and environmental factors in human learning and behavior. SCT holds that individuals learn through observation, imitation, and modeling of others. SCT emphasizes individuals' beliefs in their ability to successfully perform tasks and achieve desired outcomes. Learners with high self-efficacy, or belief in themselves, are more likely to set challenging goals, persevere in the face of obstacles, and use effective learning strategies. These types of learners are motivated to take the initiative and exert control over their learning process, thereby demonstrating greater autonomy in their learning.

Social Cognitive Theory underscores the interplay between cognitive, behavioral, and social factors in fostering learner autonomy. By understanding this give-and-take, educators can create learning environments that empower learners to take greater ownership of their learning process and achieve academic success.

3-3. Other Perspectives

Constructivist perspectives of learning can offer valuable insights into autonomy in that learners are seen to actively construct their understanding of the world through their interactions and with each other and the environment. Constructivism emphasizes the importance of self-regulated learning, where learners take responsibility for setting goals, monitoring their progress, and evaluating their understanding. In this context, autonomy in learning involves the ability to regulate the learning process and make decisions about how, when, and what to learn based on one's interests, needs, and goals. While autonomy is emphasized, constructivism also recognizes that learners benefit from interactions with peers, teachers, and experts who provide scaffolding, support and feedback. Importantly, autonomy is not seen in isolation but rather as the ability to collaborate and engage in meaningful interactions with others to co-construct knowledge and understanding.

Socio-cultural perspectives highlight the influence of cultural norms, values, and practices on learning and development. In the socio-cultural paradigm, autonomy is viewed within the cultural context, where individuals' autonomy may be influenced by cultural expectations, societal norms, and community practices. Autonomy develops gradually as learners gain competence and confidence in their ability to contribute meaningfully to their communities. Learners navigate between individual autonomy and collective values, negotiating their autonomy within their socio-cultural context. This is relevant to the Japanese context in which the action research in this paper took place as we will see in the next section of this paper.

The concept of the Zone of Proximal Development (ZPD), proposed by Vygotsky (1978), suggests that learners develop autonomy by engaging in activities that are just beyond their current level of competence but achievable with 'scaffolding' and support. The ZPD is defined as the space between what a learner can do without assistance and what a learner can do with guidance or in collaboration with more capable peers. Autonomy is fostered through collaborative interactions with more knowledgeable others who provide the necessary support and guidance, or what is called 'scaffolding', to help learners stretch their abilities and achieve higher levels of autonomy. The ZPD and autonomy are linked through the idea of 'scaffolding,' which is central to Vygotsky's theory of cognitive development. While the ZPD initially involves external support, the ultimate goal is for learners to internalize the 'scaffolding' provided by others and develop the ability to regulate their own learning independently. This process fosters autonomy by gradually shifting the responsibility for learning from the teacher or more knowledgeable peer to the learner themselves. As the process evolves, the learner develops both more competence and more autonomy as their knowledge expands.

4. Challenges and Barriers to Learner Autonomy

It would probably be fair to say that as teachers, most of us would like our students to be autonomous, motivated and independent, and as learners, we would like to be the same. However, is this a culturally-specific idea held by a Western-educated and acculturated person like myself? Are there cultural dimensions to consider when attempting to implement learner autonomy in an East-Asian context like Japan with different educational and cultural norms? Further, are there pedagogical barriers or other challenges to be aware of that may limit the effectiveness of implementing autonomy? Finally, could there be institutional constraints that may hinder the effectiveness of learner autonomy? In this section, I will attempt to answer these questions.

Most students, in the course of their formal education, unconsciously balance their individual autonomy while conforming to their socio-cultural educational environment. When comparing cultural contexts of education, the concepts of individualism and collectivism can be relevant. To cite just one example, English as a Foreign Language (EFL) instructors in Japan face this cultural dichotomy. When teaching a foreign language, it is useful to consider the extent of cultural influences and preconceptions carried into the classroom by both educators and learners. At first glance, cultural norms in East Asian societies like Japan are generally more collectivist and, therefore, may not appear to foster individual autonomy (Hofstede, 1988). On the other hand, it is of course unwise to perpetuate cultural stereotypes by assuming that any culture is monolithic and inflexible. An example of this is cited in an article by Kubota (2002), commenting on a Japanese handbook for English teachers, "cultural dichotomies such as an emphasis on social hierarchy versus egalitarianism, collectivism versus individualism, and high context versus low context cultures are presented as differences between Japanese and Anglophone cultures and incorporated into communicative activities and assessment" (2001). Collectivism in particular can be seen as being in direct contrast to autonomy as a manifestation of individualism. In that respect, the English classroom in Japan could be viewed as a setting where cultural stereotypes are upheld and sustained rather than questioned or confronted (i.e. the foreign English teacher is outgoing and casual and their activities are fun while the Japanese teacher is more sober and their activities are more academic and focused on preparing for exams).

Similarly, Nozaki has noted that, traditionally, the Japanese view of a good student tended to value those who are "quiet, passive, and obedient youths who perform well on tests" (as cited in Hammond, 1993). The word 'passive' in the above quote could be read as almost an antonym for autonomous.

In fact, to this day, English language education in pre-tertiary Japanese schools predominantly adopts a teacher-centered approach. Commonly referred to as 'yakudoku,' or grammar translation, this entails teaching and learning English largely through translation of sentences. English classes taught via 'yakudoku' typically feature highly structured lessons, clear teacher and student roles, and Japanese as the primary language of instruction. A key point is that 'yakudoku' is very much a teacher-centered teaching method with limited opportunity for student autonomy. Therefore, it is probably safe to say (as my own anecdotal experiences suggest) that many Japanese university students may lack any experience in fostering autonomous learning in English classes.

However, when thinking about the Japanese context, it can be useful to refer to what Littlewood (1999) has coined 'reactive autonomy.' Reactive Autonomy can be described as the ability of learners to organize their resources autonomously in order to reach their goals even if they do not have complete control over their learning. This formulation of reactive autonomy could be seen as well-suited to the East Asian cultural context of Japan.

Differences in culture and teaching methods are of course factors in determining what is considered appropriate for learners in different context. However, these should not be seen as insurmountable impediments to the development of autonomy.

The years of formal classroom instruction play only a small part in the life and education of most people. As such, it follows that teachers should want students to develop skills such as autonomy that can be used outside of the controlled environment of the classroom context and without the overt support of a teacher. Therefore, teachers have a responsibility to encourage autonomy in students so that they can take some degree of control of their own learning after their formal education.

5. Action Research

In this section, I will describe an action research project undertaken from October 2023 to February 2024 at two Japanese universities. A total of 125 students in six courses participated in this research. The courses were of three types, four first-year English Communication classes, one English Composition course focused on essay writing and open to students of all grade levels and one English-medium global issues lecture course open to 2nd to 4th year students. The four English Communication courses can be further broken down into two courses consisting of students majoring in Intercultural Studies (a total of 28 students) and two English Communication courses consisted of students majoring in Engineering (19 students) and Information Systems (31 students). The English Composition course had 22 students and the global issues course had 25 students. The action research measures consisted of the following:

- submission of weekly written reflections after each class
- mid-course and post-course written online surveys administered using Google Forms
- post-course interviews with a select group of students

Weekly reflections and online surveys were submitted in a mix of English and Japanese. Japanese responses were translated by the author. Interviews were conducted in a mix of English and Japanese, depending on student preference. They were recorded, transcribed (and translated into English when necessary) by the author.

I will report on the results by going through the survey questions in order with a discussion of the responses broken down by course.

Question 1: Are you/Were you satisfied with the lesson pacing and activities? (Likert scale, 1-strongly disagree, 5-strongly agree)

This question was asked of students weekly on the course online lesson management system (known as 'Manaba') at the end of each lesson. The purpose of this question was two-fold:

118 | *Part 1.*
Illuminating International Research of Curriculum Study and Lesson Study for Teaching Training Development

- to give students an opportunity to contribute to their opinion of course content in terms of lesson activities and tasks on a weekly basis
- to allow students to place a numerical value at the end of the semester on their impression of the course methodology overall

It was hoped that this question would allow students to feel a certain level of ownership over the course contents while also encouraging the instructor to engage in self-reflection by giving them a chance to contemplate their teaching on a weekly basis.

The collated average responses to this question over the entire semester from each course respectively were as follows:

English Communication (4.9)
English Composition (4.4)
Global Issues (4.0)

Students in English Communication evinced a very high level of satisfaction with the pace and contents. Of the three courses, English Communication allowed for the most freedom in selecting and adapting course materials and activities based on student survey responses. English Composition (4.4) is focused on academic writing in which students write multiple essays over the semester. While the essay topics are adapted based on current events and student feedback, the lesson activities and tasks are harder to change on a dime. In the global issues course (4.0), students are assigned to read chapters from a book about current events each week and the lesson consists of a power point lecture about the contents of the book followed by pair work and discussion activities and a listening activity. The course is meant to simulate a lecture-style class at a university in North America. The global issues course moves at a fast pace with material that can be challenging for less proficient learners and with less scope to alter lesson activities based on student input. This could perhaps help explain why the responses were the lowest for the global issues course.

> Question 2: Is it appropriate for the teacher to choose the class materials each week (or for the entire semester) or should students be involved in choosing the course materials? (open-ended question written in both English and Japanese, asked two times, midway through the semester and at the end of the semester; also asked during post-course interview, students were free to answer in either English or Japanese, no preference was stated).

This question was the main focus of this action research project and responses (translated into English when applicable) from each type of course are discussed below.

English Communication
54% of respondents stated that they would prefer the instructor choose course materials. Responses included the following, "As long as the topics and activities are interesting the

teacher should choose. If the class is boring, I want to have more input." Another student wrote, "Good teachers sometimes let students participate in deciding what to study. I am grateful but the class is usually already interesting (because the teacher is good) so it is not so necessary. Bad teachers usually do not ask students their opinion or give them much freedom." This comment neatly describes a paradox about perhaps both good teaching and autonomy. A teacher likely to encourage autonomy may be considered a 'good' teacher because they are flexible and open to new ideas while a teacher unlikely to allow much autonomy may considered 'bad' or more inflexible and set in their ways.

During a post-course interview, one comment eloquently touched on the afore-mentioned connection between autonomy and motivation, "What students want to do should be reflected in class. Of course, sometimes we have to cover some material to prepare for our university entrance exams or for the teacher to fulfill their responsibility to teach us the required material. However, as much as possible, we should be allowed to follow our interests and if teachers allow this students will be more energetic and motivated in class." Also in the post-course interview, another student touched on the relationship between motivation and autonomy, albeit from a slightly different angle, "If what students want to do can be reflected in class I will respect and work hard for that teacher because they show that they care about and respect us." Another interviewed student suggested, "the teacher could give us a list of choices for course topics and activities and we could vote on those options. That would be a happy medium."

English Composition
74% of respondents stated they would prefer the teacher to choose course materials. This high number is striking as this was an open-ended question and leads one to wonder if it can be attributed to the cultural expectations of students in regard to teachers of more 'academic' courses in Japan. English Communication courses are often basic required courses and seen as less challenging and more 'fun' while a writing course may be seen as more serious and academic. A representative response was the following, "it is the teacher's responsibly. Students do not have enough knowledge and may choose something that is not appropriate for everyone." Another student wrote, "If we are allowed to choose topics and activities ourselves we will choose simple things like our favorite pop star instead of climate change and not challenge ourselves." These comments reflect the academic nature of this course and its focus on writing in contrast to an English Communication course which generally has more of a focus on speaking skills.

Global Issues
This is a challenging academic lecture-style elective course conducted in English with a considerable amount of homework. It tends to appeal to students with a high level of both English skills and motivation. Exactly 50% of respondents stated they would prefer the teacher to choose course materials. Perhaps understandably, one student wrote, "of course, when possible it is good to reflect student input and opinions in course materials but I don't see how that can be done in a course of this type. In a difficult academic course the teacher has to know how to best structure each lesson and the course overall.

We can't expect to have freedom when the teacher has to teach a certain amount of content." Another student with a practical perspective wrote, "We look at the course catalog and read the syllabus before choosing classes. The teacher is responsible for teaching the contents they put in the syllabus. Considering that, is it right for students to be involved in choosing course materials? It is a matter of quality control and the teacher should control the quality." These comments perhaps reflect a conventional view of the role of teacher and student, at least in Japan. However, a different opinion can be seen in the following comment, "I think it is very good to gather opinions of students but I think it's better if it's not completely student-centered."

In a post-course interview, one student acknowledged that in a demanding academic course the over-arching course material and topics should best be left to the teacher but suggested "classroom activities and tasks other than the main lecture could alternate week to week from teacher to student selected activities." Another interviewed student touched nicely on the idea of autonomy when commenting that, "it would be good to reflect student desires in class activities. This would show us that the teacher respects us and is willing to let us contribute to how the class is managed."

Notwithstanding the implications for teachers and their efforts to introduce autonomy in their classrooms, the scope and variety of responses demonstrate the value of soliciting student input, itself a type of autonomy, into courses. The exercise of soliciting student opinions in anonymous surveys can benefit teachers by encouraging reflection on their teaching while also promoting autonomy by demonstrating to students that their opinions matter to their teacher.

6. Strategies for Fostering Learner Autonomy

There are a number of intuitive, and some less intuitive ways teachers can promote autonomy among their students. A common-sense pedagogical approach is to cultivate a supportive learning environment in which students feel empowered to contribute. Providing students choice in selecting learning materials and activities and giving them a voice in course design can be an effective way of giving autonomy to students.

As seen in some of the survey question responses mentioned in the previous section, choice and flexibility can potentially be unsettling for both students and teachers. Even so, for students, opportunities to choose topics, materials, and activities can promote a sense of ownership and autonomy in the learning process. Incorporation of authentic materials like real-world texts and audio and video into the course can be especially motivating. For example, even though evidence suggests spending excessive time on social media may have negative mental health effects on students (Nazari et. al, 2023), creatively incorporating SNS into class, carefully and within reason, can make learning relevant to students and increase motivation. Peer collaboration and cooperative learning, group projects, and collaborative problem-solving tasks where students can support and learn from each other are also examples of how learning can be made more autonomous.

Metacognitive strategies such as persuading students to set realistic language learning goals and encouraging them to monitor their progress towards their goals are also powerful examples of autonomy. Examples include regular goal-setting sessions and periodic activities allowing students to reflect on their goals and reassess them as necessary based on their progress. Journals, learning portfolios, or reflective discussions with teacher guidance and feedback can give students more control over their learning. Teachers can also scaffold autonomy by gradually empowering students and fostering independence over time. Encouraging students to increase their learning capacity by developing learning strategies and making decisions about how to approach academic tasks can be a very effective way to engender greater autonomy.

Of course, as was discussed earlier, it is necessary to be culturally sensitive as well. It is important to be mindful of cultural factors that may influence students' attitudes toward autonomy and to adapt teaching strategies accordingly.

By providing a supportive and not overly-judgmental learning environment where students feel comfortable taking risks they are also likely to feel confident and comfortable exploring their autonomy.

7. Discussion

This paper has explored the concept of learner autonomy in university English courses at two Japanese universities through the lens of action research. A comprehensive examination of learner autonomy, its theoretical underpinnings, cultural dimensions, and challenges was offered. Learner autonomy was defined as the ability and willingness of learners to take control of their own learning processes and its potential benefits. The theoretical frameworks supporting the benefits of autonomy were investigated. Cultural considerations, societal norms and traditional teaching methodologies were revealed as things that could be potential challenges to autonomy. The concept of 'reactive autonomy' emerged as a possible avenue within challenging cultural contexts, emphasizing learners' ability to organize their resources autonomously despite external constraints.

The action research project provided insights into student preferences regarding autonomy in course materials selection. While a significant proportion of students expressed a preference for teacher-led material selection (as might be expected), there was also acknowledgment of the benefits of incorporating student input to varying degrees. This highlights the importance of finding a balance between teacher guidance and student autonomy, especially in demanding academic courses.

Strategies for fostering learner autonomy were discussed and emphasized the importance of creating a supportive learning environment, maintaining flexibility in learning activities, and incorporating metacognitive strategies to empower students in their learning journey. Culturally sensitive approaches were underscored as essential in navigating the complexities of autonomy within diverse educational settings.

Ultimately, this paper highlights the value of autonomy in education, not only for academic success but also for fostering critical thinking skills and lifelong learning habits. By embracing autonomy and adapting teaching practices to suit diverse cultural contexts, educators can empower students to take control of their learning and thrive both inside and, perhaps more importantly, outside the classroom, where they will spend most of their lives.

References

Bandura, A. (1986). *Social Foundations of Thought and Action: A Social Cognitive Theory*. Englewood Cliffs, N.J.: Prentice-Hall.

Benson, P. (2011). *Teaching and Researching Autonomy*. Harlow: Longman.

Ceylan, N. O. The Relationship between Learner Autonomy and Motivation. *TOJET: The Turkish Online Journal of Educational Technology*, October 2021.

Deci, E. L., & Ryan, R. M. (1985). *Intrinsic Motivation and Self-Determination in Human Behavior*. New York: Plenum.

Eliezer, J, & Marantika, R. Metacognitive Ability and Autonomous Learning Strategy in Improving Learning Outcomes. *Journal of Education and Learning*, 15(1), February 2021.

Gandhimathi, S. N. S. & Dr. Anitha Devi, V. Learner Autonomy and Motivation—A Literature Review. *Research on Humanities and Social Sciences*, 6(3), 2016.

Garcia, T., & Pintrich, P. The Effects of Autonomy on Motivation and Performance in the College Classroom. *Contemporary Educational Psychology*, 21(4), October 1996, 477–486.

Hammond, M. (2007). Culturally responsive teaching in the Japanese classroom: A Comparative Analysis of Cultural Teaching and Learning Styles in Japan and the United States. *Journal of the Faculty of Economics*, KGU, 17, 41–50.

Hofstede, G., & Bond, M. H. The Confucius connection: From Cultural Roots to Economic Growth. *Organizational Dynamics*, 16(4), Spring 1988, 5–21.

Holec, H. (1981). *Autonomy and Foreign Language Learning*. Oxford: Pergamon Press.

İçmez, S. (2007). Learner Autonomy: What we need to foster and how. *Çukurova Üniversitesi Eğitim Fakültesi Dergisi*, 3. Retrieved from: http://asoindex.com/journal-veiw?id=151

Jehanghir, M. Ishaq, K., & Ali Akbar, R. Effect of learners' autonomy on academic motivation and university students' grit. *Education and Information Technologies*, July 2023.

Kubota, R. (2002). *The Impact of Globalization on Language Teaching in Japan*. London: Routledge.

Littlewood W. (1999). Defining and Developing Autonomy in East Asian Contexts. *Applied Linguistics*, 20(1), 71–94.

Nazari, A., Hosseinnia, M, Torkian, S, & Garmaroudi, G. Social media and mental health in students: a cross-sectional study during the Covid-19 pandemic. *BMC Psychiatry*, 23, 2023.

Nishino, T., & Watanabe, M. (2008). Communication-oriented policies versus classroom realities in Japan. *TESOL Quarterly*, 42(1), 133–138. Retrieved from http://www.jstor.

org/stable/40264432.

Savage, T. (1999). *Teaching Self-control through Management and Discipline*. Boston: Allyn & Bacon.

Vygotsky, L. S. (1978). *Mind in Society: The Development of Higher Psychological Processes*. (Cole, M., John-Steiner, V., Scribner, S., & Souberman, E. Eds.) (Luria, A. R., Lopez-Morillas, M., & Cole, M. [with Wertsch, J. V.], Trans.) Cambridge, Mass.: Harvard University Press.

Wagner, A. (2013). Learner Autonomy In Japanese University English Classrooms. *Bulletin of Keiwa College*, 22.

Part 2.

Insights of Lesson Study in Teacher Education and Curriculum Development— Showcasing in the Context of Digital Transformation in Vietnam

Chapter 8

Exploring a Cost-Effective Online Teacher Training Model During the COVID-19 Pandemic: Insights from Vietnam

Thanh-Nga NGUYEN, Ho Chi Minh City University of Education, Vietnam
Hoai-Nam NGUYEN, Hanoi National University of Education, Vietnam
Thanh-Trung TA, Ho Chi Minh City University of Education, Vietnam
Viet-Hai PHUNG, The University of Da Nang - University of Science and Education, Vietnam
Thuy-Quynh LE-THI, Ho Chi Minh City University of Education, Vietnam

Abstract

As Vietnam continues to integrate internationally and update its educational curriculum, there is a developing interest in teachers' CPD (the continual professional development). This study seeks to investigate the influence of online professional development activities on the perceptions of Vietnamese educators during the COVID-19 pandemic. A structural equation model was used to identify the positive effects of training course factors on understanding and satisfaction, while reducing feelings of difficulty and increasing willingness to employ the new curriculum by analyzing data from 350 participating teachers. The findings indicate that the successful implementation of a professional development program can enhance teachers' comprehension, satisfaction, and willingness to innovate.

Keywords: *teachers' professional development, CPD model, online training, COVID-19 pandemic, structural equation modeling (SEM), PLS-SEM*

Paper type: Research Paper

1. Introduction

Continuous professional development (CPD) of teachers is a top priority (OECD, 1998; Shimahara, 1998) because teachers play a crucial role in ensuring the successful implementation of an educational program. Garet et al. (2001) cite training programs as an efficient method of professional development. In the context of international integration and the revision of the General Education Curriculum, continuing professional development (CPD) for instructors in Vietnam is of particular significance. Despite the fact

127

that training programs have had a positive effect on teachers' awareness, a number of obstacles exist, including excessive workload, financial issues, limited training opportunities, and fragmented training activities (Phan et al., 2020).

Currently, teacher training programs are administered in-person, online, or a combination of the two (Walsh et al., 2011). Learning management systems (LMS), social networking sites, and online seminars are available for online training (Lewis, 2020; Rensfeldt et al., 2018). As a result of the COVID-19 pandemic, online training has grown in popularity (Almutawa et al., 2021; Arnilla, 2021; Ng et al., 2021).

The new General Education Curriculum has been implemented since the 2020-2021 school year, with a shift from content-focused goals to developing learners' virtues and competencies. This has led to specific challenges and confusion among teachers. However, the Ministry of Education and Training (MOET) has issued guidelines for lesson preparation according to the new program (MOET, 2020) and has conducted several training courses for core and mass teachers within the framework of the ETEP program (MOET, 2019) for face-to-face learning under stable conditions during the COVID-19 pandemic.

Based on the needs of teachers and the context, researchers have conducted voluntary online training courses using low-cost training tools. This study aims to investigate the impact of online professional development activities on the perception of Vietnamese teachers in the context of COVID-19. The study found that training course factors positively affect understanding and satisfaction, reduce feelings of difficulty, and increase willingness to adopt the new curriculum. The results suggest that a well-implemented professional development program can improve teachers' understanding, satisfaction, and willingness to innovate (Pham et al., 2021; Wu et al., 2022).

2. Theoretical Framework

2-1. Online continuing professional development

Continuous Professional Development (CPD) refers to learning experiences and activities that are consciously planned for the benefit of individuals, groups, or schools, with the aim of improving the quality of education in classrooms (Day, 1999). CPD can be delivered through face-to-face sessions, online platforms, or a combination of both. Online CPD is a form of internet use that supports training, communication, and cooperation between learners and teachers when face-to-face meetings are not feasible (Binmohsen and Abrahams, 2020). Thanks to technological advancements, teachers have more options for participating in training courses that suit their professional development needs. Online platforms enable teachers to access and create digital resources, collaborate with colleagues, and support each other to build knowledge, without the geographic restrictions imposed by the pandemic (Gottlieb et al., 2020).

To ensure the effectiveness of online CPD for teachers, specific guidelines must be followed. According to Bayar (2014), effective teacher professional development should include elements such as needs-based appropriateness, active teacher participation in the design and planning of professional development activities, long-term engagement, and high-quality instructors. Teachers' needs are the most decisive factor in the effectiveness of the training course. Additionally, the training course should be tailored to the unique characteristics and levels of students in each school. Teachers must be involved in designing and planning professional development activities to avoid feeling disconnected from the course, and they need opportunities for active learning through practice. Finally, a team of high-quality instructors will inspire teachers to participate in the training, while low-quality instructors will reduce interest and affect their participation next time.

2-2. Online continuing professional development in Vietnam

Vietnam has implemented a new general education program starting from the 2020–2021 school year, which requires education administrators and teachers to be trained in order to overcome the challenges they face when implementing a new curriculum (Ekawati, 2017). To address this, the MOET has developed nine training modules for teachers, each aimed at a specific educational level (MOET, 2019). The modules provide guidance on various topics, such as teaching methods, IT applications, developing education plans, and evaluating students. The modules are digitized and hosted on the online LMS platform. The training is carried out in two stages, with the core group receiving a combination of online and face-to-face training, while the mass group receives mainly online training. Along with the implementation of the aforementioned training model, MOET has also issued guidelines to steer the program's implementation, with a special emphasis on cultivating high-quality development plans for teaching and education and enhancing students' abilities (MOET, 2020). Following MOET's schedule, teachers were scheduled to receive module 4 training on developing teaching and education plans from May to September 2021. However, due to the complicated COVID-19 situation, the Vietnamese government had to impose a lockdown to safeguard the health of the population, including teachers. As a result, face-to-face training had to be canceled, and many teachers encountered difficulties in devising innovative lesson plans while keeping up with their training activities amidst the pandemic. Therefore, the online teacher training format proved to be advantageous in this scenario.

The authors experienced lecturers from pedagogical universities, have developed an online training course to support Vietnamese teachers during the pandemic. The course simulates the ETEP program of MOET and focuses on four key elements for effective CPD. Unlike MOET's LMS, the authors use video conferencing via Zoom, which has grown massively during the pandemic (Bennett and Grant, 2020). Teachers actively participate in learning through practice and discussion with experts, and teaching assistants support the experts in training. The course features a team of expert lecturers who have experience in teacher training. The training course has a unique feature that sets it apart from others—it places great emphasis on the role of teaching assistants. These are teachers who have achieved good training results and possess the ability to share their expertise. During subsequent courses, they support the group of experts in training. This approach ensures that the experts focus on teaching theory while the teaching assistants guide the practical part. This stratification enables teachers to receive advice and answers from both experts and experienced teaching assistants. This multi-dimensional approach overcomes the limitations of the standard training model. The effectiveness of teaching assistants has been demonstrated in numerous studies worldwide, including during the pandemic (Mahmood, 2021). Moreover, teaching assistants are motivated to learn and develop their expertise over the long term when given the responsibility to share their knowledge with others.

2-3. CPD model evaluation

Assessing the effectiveness of training courses is crucial for identifying flaws and achieving a closer relationship between training and actual work. There are various evaluation means available, such as Kirkpatrick's model, CIPP model, Kaufman's 5-level model, and CIRO model, each with its merits and suitability for different fields (D. Kirkpatrick and Kirkpatrick, 2006). Among these, Kirkpatrick's four-level model is the most popular due to its simplicity, flexibility, and completion. Kaufman et al. (1996; 1994) proposed a five-level evaluation model that assesses impact for different subjects. This study focuses on analysing the effectiveness of teacher training using Kaufman's model, specifically the first three levels that evaluate factors affecting teachers' perceptions of training efficacy.

Input: Online resources

In the digital age, online resources have revolutionized the way we learn. Experts curate the online course content based on the teachers' learning activities during the course, such as sharing experiences, practicing lesson plans, and developing expertise. The quality of educational services is determined by several factors, but the human factor remains the most significant. It includes the experts and teaching assistants who are responsible for delivering the course. Learners evaluate them based on their knowledge, experience, and empathy toward different actions during the training process (Galanou and Priporas, 2009).

Process: Teachers' comments

Teachers who have completed the training are now able to comprehend the significance of new requirements for developing lesson plans, such as setting objectives, identifying students' learning products, and employing instructional strategies that promote capacity development (Bai et al., 2018). Nevertheless, some educators may experience negative emotions such as anxiety and feelings of incompetence when instituting new educational innovations (Thomson and Turner, 2019). This may involve transitioning to new guidelines for creating lesson plans that emphasize the development of students' virtues and skills (Pekrun, 2006).

Micro: Willingness

When a teacher lacks the motivation to embrace educational changes, it can lead to conflicts and hinder their progress. Although external factors such as school policies and requirements play a role in motivating teachers to adapt, internal factors such as understanding the significance of innovation should also drive positive change. This understanding can boost teachers' confidence, encouraging them to upgrade

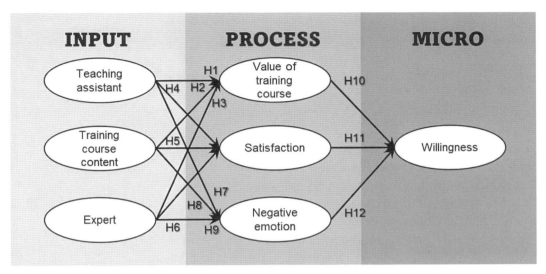

Figure 1: The Research Model

their skills and embrace new ideas (Botha and Rens, 2018). As a result, teachers will be more willing to utilize their newly acquired knowledge in practice, leading to increased confidence in their training content (Lessing and De Witt, 2007).

3. Aim and Research Questions

In accordance with MOET's ETEP program, Kennedy's CPD cascade model (Kennedy, 2014) has been adapted to create a voluntary and affordable online training program tailored to the Vietnamese context. This program was launched during the COVID-19 pandemic when in-person learning was not possible. The purpose of this study is to investigate how online professional development activities have affected the perception of Vietnamese teachers in regard to their training during the pandemic. The study aims to answer the following questions: RQ1. How can a low-cost teacher training model be designed to suit the context? RQ2. What is the impact of the training model on teachers' willingness to develop lesson plans that focus on virtue and competency development?

Methodology

This study surveyed 400 teachers across the country who were participating in an online training course. 350 questionnaires were collected and used for analysis, meeting the recommended minimum sample size as suggested by Hair et al. (2006). Of the respondents, 23.1% identified as male and 76.9% as female. The majority of teachers had more than five years of teaching experience (76%), while 24% had less. The largest group of teachers (40.9%) taught natural sciences. The questionnaire included questions about personal information as well as research concepts measured through statements using a 5-point Likert scale, with responses ranging from "Strongly disagree" to "Strongly agree."

Table 1: Scales of Research Concepts

Constructs	Items	Source
Training course content (CO)	(CO1) The course objectives are clearly written, have reasonable time, and are well organized.	(Galanou and Priporas, 2009)
	(CO2) The training course content is developed by the objectives and associated with the practice.	
	(CO3) Trainees are supported during the training process and evaluated on the course's final product.	
	(CO4) Positive energy and interaction in the learning process make learning easier.	
Expert (EX)	(EX1) Expert summarises during the session well.	(Kirkpatrick D. L. and Craig, 1970)
	(EX2) Expert keeps the session alive and exciting.	
	(EX3) Expert maintains a friendly and helpful manner.	
	(EX4) Expert provides suitable and helpful material.	
Teaching assistant (AS)	(AS1) Teaching assistants have a good understanding of the content to support teachers.	
	(AS2) Teaching assistants interpret, evaluate, and give suggestions that are easy to understand and close to the content of the lesson plan.	
	(AS3) Teaching assistants can point out the limitations and shortcomings and suggest solutions for trainees to overcome.	
	(AS4) Teaching assistants encourage teachers to share experiences to increase confidence.	
Value of training course (VA)	(VA1) The training course improves the capability of making lesson plans.	(Bai *et al.*, 2018)
	(VA2) The preparation of a good lesson plan will contribute to developing students' competency.	
Negative emotion (EM)	(EM1) Teachers find it difficult to determine the lesson's goal.	(Pekrun, 2006; Thomson and Turner, 2019)
	(EM2) Teachers find it difficult to prepare lesson plans.	
	(EM3) Teachers have negative emotions (boredom, frustration) when making the explicit content of lesson plans.	
Satisfaction (SA)	(SA1) The training content meets the expectations of individual teachers.	(Dorner and Karpati, 2010)
	(SA2) Teachers are satisfied with the quality of the training course.	
	(SA3) Teachers want to introduce the training course to their colleagues.	
	(SA4) Teachers will participate in the next training courses organised.	
Willingness (WI)	(WI1) Teachers are confident in developing ideas for lesson plans.	(Lessing and De Witt, 2007)
	(WI2) Teachers are confident in making lesson plans.	
	(WI3) Teachers are ready to implement lesson plans into practice.	
	(WI4) Teachers are willing to use lesson plans as illustrations in professional activities.	

The research followed a two-phase process, namely qualitative and quantitative research. To begin with, the theory and related works were analyzed to extract a preliminary set of scales. Next, a group discussion technique was employed, involving three experts who were highly experienced lecturers in the university of pedagogy, and a group of 20 teachers who participated in the first training course.

After the preliminary research, a quantitative evaluation was carried out to assess the reliability and scale value of the research concepts. The initial research findings were obtained through questionnaires that were used for official research purposes.

Table 2: Process of Evaluation

Step	Criteria
Evaluate the internal consistency reliability	• Cronbach's Alpha: CRA > 0.7: acceptable
	• Composite reliability is obtained from the difference in the outer loading coefficient between observed variables. CR ≥ 0.7: good (Nunnally and Bernstein, 1994) 0.6 < CR < 0.7: acceptable (Hair *et al.*, 2014)
Evaluate the convergent validity	• The outer loading of observed variables must be greater than 0.708.
	• Convergent validity is used to evaluate the stability of the scale. AVE > 0.5 (Fornell and Larcker, 1981)
Evaluate the discriminant validity	• Fornell-Larcker (1981): $\sqrt{AVE}$ > inter-construct correlations. • Heterotrait–monotrait ratio: HTMT < 0.85 (Henseler *et al.*, 2015).
Evaluate the nomological validity	• Evaluating the nomological validity scale tests the validity of the meaningful relationship between concepts in the measurement theory, which is performed based on testing the relationship between concepts in the structural model (Gerbing and Anderson, 1988).
Test the model fit	• RMSEA (root mean square error approximation): RMSEA < 0.08: suitable; RMSEA < 0.03: very suitable. • Standardised root means square residual (SRMR) index of the difference between the actual data and the predicted model: SRMR < 0.08: suitable (Hu and Bentler, 1998). • NFI (normed fit index) of the normally distributed difference of χ^2 between the independent and multi-factor models: NFI > 0.9: suitable. • Some other indicators need to be met, such as d_{ULS} < 95%; d_G < 95%.

The official study took place between June and September 2021, and data was collected through online platforms, including interviews with teachers who participated in the training course, using a questionnaire.

The collected data will be further evaluated through analysis of the measurement and structural models, which will help to obtain a comprehensive understanding of the research outcomes.

In this study, a statistical analysis program called partial least squares is utilized to estimate the linear structural model (SEM) by employing standard indices that are not reliant on the assumption of normal distribution. Furthermore, these indices are flexible enough to be adapted to small sample sizes.

4. Results and Discussion

The measurement model has been evaluated for reliability and convergence value. This is achieved through the use of outer loading, CRA, CR, and AVE. Table 3 indicates that all outer loading coefficients surpass the recommended value of 0.6, thereby demonstrating the reliability of the observed variables. The results of the CRA coefficient of the factors have values from 0.861 to 0.949, and the CR coefficients with values from 0.915 to 0.963 are all greater than 0.7, showing that internal consistency reliability is ensured. The AVE coefficient has a value from 0.783 to 0.928 greater than 0.5, thus indicating sufficient convergence among the scales.

Table 4 shows that all HTMT indexes are below 0.85, which again proves the

Table 3: Measurement Model Results

Constructs	Items	Outer loading (min - max)	CA	CR	AVE
Training course content (CO)	CO1-2-3-4	0.904 - 0.943	0.943	0.959	0.853
Expert (EX)	EX1-2-3-4	0.902 - 0.953	0.949	0.963	0.868
Teaching assistant (AS)	AS1-2-3-4	0.906 - 0.945	0.941	0.957	0.849
Satisfaction (SA)	SA1-2-3-4	0.877 - 0.921	0.918	0.942	0.803
Value (VA)	VA1-2	0.963 - 0.964	0.922	0.963	0.928
Negative emotion (EM)	EM1-2-3	0.849 - 0.913	0.861	0.915	0.783
Willingness (WI)	WI1-2-3-4	0.897 - 0.920	0.927	0.948	0.820

Table 4: HTMT Validity Results

Constructs	EX	EM	SA	AS	CO	VA	WI
Expert (EX)							
Negative emotion (EM)	0.321						
Satisfaction (SA)	0.669	0.426					
Teaching assistant (AS)	0.748	0.349	0.638				
Training course content (CO)	0.302	0.322	0.323	0.273			
Value (VA)	0.218	0.214	0.258	0.160	0.718		
Willingness (WI)	0.428	0.575	0.654	0.483	0.299	0.233	

discriminant value of the scale in this study.

To evaluate the strength of the structural model in PLS-SEM analysis, researchers often use the structural path and R^2 of the dependent variable. To ensure accuracy, a non-parametric analysis using bootstrapping techniques was repeated 5000 times on a sample size of 350 observations. R^2, which ranges from 0 to 1, indicates the predictive ability of the structural model. Establishing an acceptable R^2 value is difficult since it depends on the research context and model complexity. A value around 0.75 is considered substantial, while 0.50 is average and 0.25 or lower is weak (Hair et al., 2011; Henseler et al., 2009). Findings show that the expert, teaching assistant, and training course content concepts explained 45.2% of satisfaction variation, 45.2% of value perception variation, and 14.9% of negative emotions variation among online course teachers. Satisfaction, value perception, and emotion concepts also explained 46.3% of the willingness of teachers to apply trained skills into practice. However, the remaining 54.7% was not explained due to the exclusion of other factors in the model (Table 5).

The Q^2 predictive significance is a supplementary evaluation of model fitting (Geisser, 1974; Stone, 1974). PLS utilizes the Blindfolding method to measure Q^2. Our study results indicate that Q^2 has predictive relevance greater than zero for all constructs (Chin, 2009), suggesting that all dependent variables in the model can be predicted.

Figure 2 presents the results of the path weighting in the linear structural model of SEM. The model has a statistical value of $\chi^2 = 1043.052$ with a p-value of 0.000, which is less than 0.005. According to Hu and Bentler (1998), a model coincides with the actual data if the SRMR value is less than 0.08. In this case, the research model is suitable for the

Table 5: R², Q² Results

Constructs	R²	Remark	Q²	Overall Predictive
Value (VA)	0.452	Average	0.407	Yes
Satisfaction (SA)	0.452	Average	0.352	Yes
Negative emotion (EM)	0.149	Weak	0.111	Yes
Willingness (WI)	0.463	Average	0.371	Yes

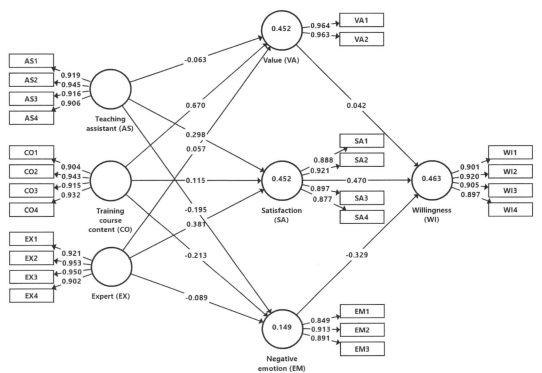

Figure 2: Items Loading, Path Coefficient, and R²

study area in Vietnam, with an SRMR of 0.040, which is less than 0.08. Additionally, the results indicate that the collinearity between predictive research variables is not a problem in the structural model, as the variance inflation factor (VIF) of both endogenous and exogenous variables is less than three (with the highest being 2.064).

PLS investigates data that is believed to be non-normally distributed. Therefore, the parametric significance test for coefficients like path coefficients cannot be used in regression analysis. Instead, PLS employs a non-parametric bootstrapping analysis to determine coefficient importance and calculate t-values to check if the path coefficient is significantly different from zero. In this study, a non-parametric bootstrapping technique was evaluated using 350 observations and 5000 repeats to confirm the condition for evaluating the linear structural model. The reliable estimates in the model are supported by the significant original weights with mean weights of bootstrapping, all within the 95% confidence interval, as shown in Table 6. The results of the structural model support hypotheses H2, H4, H5, H6, H7, H8, H11, and H12, while rejecting H1, H3, H9, and

Table 6: Summary Results of Path Coefficient and Hypothesis Testing

Path Coefficient	Original Sample	t-value	p-value	Results
Direct effect				
H1: Teaching assistant → Value	- 0.063	0.941	0.347	Not Supported
H2: Training course content → Value	0.670	8.373	0.000	Supported
H3: Expert → Value	0.057	0.806	0.420	Not Supported
H4: Teaching assistant → Satisfaction	0.298	4.812	0.000	Supported
H5: Training course content → Satisfaction	0.115	2.143	0.032	Supported
H6: Expert → Satisfaction	0.381	4.049	0.000	Supported
H7: Teaching assistant → Negative emotion	- 0.195	2.592	0.010	Supported
H8: Training course content → Negative emotion	- 0.213	3.250	0.001	Supported
H9: Expert → Negative emotion	- 0.089	1.122	0.262	Not Supported
H10: Value → Willingness	0.042	0.875	0.382	Not Supported
H11: Satisfaction → Willingness	0.470	8.207	0.000	Supported
H12: Negative emotion → Willingness	- 0.329	6.538	0.000	Supported
Indirect effect				
Teaching assistant → Willingness	0.202	4.309	0.000	Supported
Expert → Willingness	0.211	3.630	0.000	Supported
Training course content → Willingness	0.152	3.435	0.001	Supported

H10. The linear structural model estimation shows that hypotheses H2, H4, H5, H6, and H11 have positive regression weights, and hypotheses H7, H8, and H12 have negative regression weights.

Table 6 indicates that the training course resources (including teaching assistants, experts, and training course content) had a significant impact on teachers' willingness, despite varying indirect effects. The study found that online learning curriculum only affects teachers' awareness of students' quality and competence when designing lesson plans. However, teachers respond positively when presented with well-designed and thoroughly researched courses that align with the training content. Berlach (2011) proposed that program reform often creates a gap between relevant factors, leaving teachers uncertain about the reform's intentions. Additionally, the Concerns-Based Adoption Model (CBAM) suggests that teachers' perceptions and behaviors undergo six stages. Therefore, it is crucial to provide adequate time and frequent measures to bring about noticeable changes in teachers' perceptions.

When teachers learn new skills, they tend to connect with reality on a cognitive level. As a result, they require a process to modify their skills and gradually adapt to these changes (Yazdi et al., 2017). Participating in online program activities has been found to positively impact teachers' perceptions. Compared to traditional courses, human factors have a lesser impact on online courses due to reduced interaction between learners and instructors. This has a negligible effect, as the path coefficients of these factors are of little statistical significance. The study also found a weak connection between teachers' positive perceptions of creating virtue and competency-based lesson plans and their willingness to put them into practice. Factors influencing their eagerness include objective ones such as pandemics, the manager's direction, and debates in the teacher community, as well as subjective ones like self-doubt, lack of flexibility, and work pressure.

One psychological barrier that affects teachers is negative emotions, such as worry, difficulty, and lack of confidence when facing new teaching requirements (Pekrun, 2006; Thomson and Turner, 2019). This study focuses on teachers' uncertainty about implementing a new requirement and how it can be addressed. Research has shown that providing teaching assistant resources and training courses can alleviate negative feelings and boost confidence (Yazdi et al., 2017). The proposed training program includes engaging activities to enhance the practical experience and flexible application of professional activities through an online platform. In addition, supporting activities and suggestions on practical products foster a sense of cooperation and sharing between teachers. This creates a community of teachers with a common goal of learning, practicing new things, and solving educational problems, aligning with the research's intention to improve the teacher training process.

The satisfaction of participants in the training model is influenced by all available resources. The study shows that both the human resources and the training programs have successfully met the expectations of teachers who enrolled in the courses. To enhance teacher satisfaction, synchronous solutions are necessary. These solutions will improve the quality of the team of experts and teaching assistants and adjust the training program according to the teachers' needs. In terms of satisfaction-related paths, experts have the most significant impact while training content has the least significance. This reflects that teachers usually have high expectations of experts, possibly due to a long process of traditional teaching and training. The satisfaction of teachers has a decisive impact on their willingness to apply the innovations they have learned in practice (Dorner and Karpati, 2010). When their expectations are met, they are more willing to employ the teaching skills they have acquired.

The resources of the low-cost online training model have generally positive indirect effects on teachers' willingness to implement innovative teaching practices. Although experts are the most important factor, their influence is not substantially greater than other factors. This finding emphasizes the necessity of including additional resources, such as teaching assistants and training content, to enhance the quality of teacher training.

5. Conclusion and Practical Implications

Vietnam's education system is undergoing a significant reform, and to support this, the implementation of CPD models to assist teachers is being extensively adopted throughout the country. A recent study suggests that one should contemplate a cost-effective model for online teacher training. The study also found that a number of factors, with varying degrees of influence, motivate teachers to implement innovations. It is essential to address these issues and provide the necessary resources to help teachers be ready for change. The involvement of a team of experts is crucial since Vietnamese teachers are not used to self-improvement and require support. However, the experts' role should be limited to designing training processes, assessing quality, and advising on wicked problems, with teaching assistants providing support for self-study and self-improvement. Educational managers should focus on training teaching assistants, creating a network of practice communities, and empowering them to promote dynamism. Policymakers must recognize the positive effects of CPD programs in increasing awareness, satisfaction, and willingness to innovate. Based on feedback, the next phase involves building a community of creative teachers with specialized training courses corresponding to different subjects and grades, forming strong connections between teachers, education experts, and management agencies.

Limitations

The study's limitation is its inability to incorporate objective factors, such as teachers' lesson design skills' evaluation results, into the SEM model. The evaluation scale for this factor has only been legally applied and lacks empirical data-based standardization, making its inclusion in the model's reliability uncertain. The next step is to re-evaluate the model's scale, assessing teacher training form effectiveness with standardized factors added to the current scale. The training model is still in the early stages of testing with a limited scale, requiring in-depth studies to assess its effectiveness when widely replicated. Additionally, the study can re-test the effectiveness evaluation model scale of a low-cost online teacher training course with prerequisites and current scale results added or expand the test for higher-rated factors per Kaufman's theory.

Co-Author Contribution

The authors affirmed that there is no conflict of interest in this article. All the authors took part in carrying out the field work, preparing the literature review, writing the research methodology, doing the data collection and analyses, interpreting the results, and reviewing the writeup of the whole article. All authors commented on the manuscript at all stages. All authors read and approved the final manuscript.

Statements and Declarations

We confirm that this work is original and has not been published elsewhere, nor is it currently under consideration for publication elsewhere.

Ethics Approval Statement

All subjects participated voluntarily. The participants provided their written informed consent to participate in this study. The Declaration of Helsinki was adequately addressed, and Ho Chi Minh City University of Education, Vietnam, approved the study.

Acknowledgments

Thanh-Trung Ta was funded by the Master, Ph.D. Scholarship Programme of Vingroup Innovation Foundation (VINIF). Hoai-Nam Nguyen thanks to the support of the

Mekong-Lancang Project.

References

Almutawa, N. A. M., Mahmoud, M. H., Rao, C., and Main, M. (2021). Continuing Professional Development: Provision and Adaptation of Clinical Education within the Primary Health Care Setting in Qatar during the COVID-19 Pandemic. *Principles and Practice of Clinical Research*, 7(1), 40–45. https://doi.org/10.21801/ppcrj.2021.71.6

Arnilla, A. K. (2021). Coaching Teachers Remotely during COVID-19 Pandemic: Perspectives and Experiences from a Developing Country. *AUBH E-Learning Conference 2021: Innovative Learning & Teaching—Lessons from COVID-19*. https://doi.org/10.2139/ssrn.3873980

Bai, Y., Li, J., Bai, Y., Ma, W., Yang, X., and Ma, F. (2018). Development and validation of a questionnaire to evaluate the factors influencing training transfer among nursing professionals. *BMC Health Services Research*, 18(1), 1–9. https://doi.org/10.1186/s12913-018-2910-7

Bayar, A. (2014). The Components of Effective Professional Development Activities in Terms of Teachers' Perspective. *International Online Journal of Educational Sciences*, 6(2), 319–327. https://doi.org/10.15345/iojes.2014.02.006

Bennett, D. and Grant, N. (2020). Zoom Goes From Conferencing App to the Pandemic's Social Network, available at: https://www.bloomberg.com/news/features/2020-04-09/zoom-goes-from-conferencing-app-to-the-pandemic-s-social-network (accessed 20 July 2022)

Berlach, R. G. (2011). The Cyclical Integration Model as a Way of Managing Major Educational Change. *Education Research International*, 2011, 963237. https://doi.org/10.1155/2011/963237

Binmohsen, S. A. and Abrahams, I. (2020). Science teachers' continuing professional development: online vs face-to-face. *Research in Science and Technological Education*, 40(3), 1–29. https://doi.org/10.1080/02635143.2020.1785857

Botha, C. S. and Rens, J. (2018). Are they really 'ready, willing and able'? Exploring reality shock in beginner teachers in South Africa. *South African Journal of Education*, 38(3), 1546. https://doi.org/10.15700/saje.v38n3a1546

Chin, W. W. (2009). How to write up and report PLS analyses. In *Handbook of partial least squares: Concepts, methods, and applications* (pp.655–690). Berlin, Heidelberg: Springer Berlin Heidelberg. https://doi.org/10.1007/978-3-540-32827-8_29

Day, C. (1999). *Developing teachers: The challenges of lifelong learning.* London, UK: Routledge Press. https://doi.org/10.4324/9780203021316

Dorner, H. and Karpati, A. (2010). Mentoring for innovation: key factors affecting participant satisfaction in the process of collaborative knowledge construction in teacher training. *Journal of Asynchronous Learning Networks*, 14(4), 63–77.

Ekawati, Y. N. (2017). English teachers' problems in applying the 2013 curriculum. *Journal of English Education*, 6(1), 41–48. https://doi.org/10.25134/erjee.v6i1.769

Fornell, C. and Larcker, D. F. (1981). Evaluating structural equation models with unobservable variables and measurement error. *Journal of Marketing Research*, 18(1), 39–50. https://doi.org/10.1177/002224378101800104

Galanou, E. and Priporas, C. V. (2009). A model for evaluating the effectiveness of middle managers' training courses: evidence from a major banking organization in Greece. *International Journal of Training and Development*, 13(4), 221–246. https://doi.org/10.1111/j.1468-2419.2009.00329.x

Garet, M. S., Porter, A. C., Desimone, L., Birman, B. F., and Yoon, K. S. (2001). What makes professional development effective? Results from a national sample of teachers. *American Educational Research Journal*, 38(4), 915–945. https://doi.org/10.3102/00028312038004915

Geisser, S. (1974). A predictive approach to the random effect model. *Biometrika*, 61(1), 101–107. https://doi.org/10.1093/biomet/61.1.101

Gerbing, D. W. and Anderson, J. C. (1988). An Updated Paradigm for Scale Development Incorporating Unidimensionality and Its Assessment. *Journal of Marketing Research*, 25(2), 186–192. https://doi.org/10.1177/002224378802500207

Gottlieb, M., Egan, D. J., Krzyzaniak, S. M., Wagner, J., Weizberg, M., and Chan, T. (2020). Rethinking the Approach to Continuing Professional Development Conferences in the Era of COVID-19. *The Journal of Continuing Education in the Health Professions*, 40(3), 187–191. https://doi.org/10.1097/CEH.0000000000000310

Hair, J. F., Anderson, R. E., Tatham, R. L., and Black, W. C. (2006). *Multivariate data analysis*, New Jersey, USA: Prentice Hall.

Hair, J. F., Hult, G. T. M., Ringle, C. M., and Sarstedt, M. (2014). *A primer on partial least squares structural equation modeling (PLS-SEM)*. Thousand Oaks, CA, US: SAGE Publishers.

Hair, J. F., Ringle, C. M., and Sarstedt, M. (2011). PLS-SEM: Indeed a silver bullet. *Journal of Marketing Theory and Practice*, 19(2), 139–152. https://doi.org/10.2753/MTP1069-6679190202

Henseler, J., Ringle, C. M., and Sarstedt, M. (2015). A new criterion for assessing discriminant validity in variance-based structural equation modeling. *Journal of the Academy of Marketing Science*, 43(1), 115–135. https://doi.org/10.1007/s11747-014-0403-8

Henseler, J., Ringle, C. M., and Sinkovics, R. R. (2009). The use of partial least squares path modeling in international marketing. *New Challenges to International Marketing (Advances in International Marketing)*, 20, 227–319. https://doi.org/10.1108/S1474-7979(2009)0000020014

Hu, L. T. and Bentler, P. M. (1998). Fit indices in covariance structure modeling: Sensitivity to under-parameterized model misspecification. *Psychological Methods*, 3(4), 424–453. https://doi.org/10.1037/1082-989X.3.4.424

Kaufman, R. and Keller, J. M. (1994), Levels of evaluation: Beyond Kirkpatrick. *Human Resource Development Quarterly*, 5(4), 371–380.

Kaufman, R., Keller, J., and Watkins, R. (1996). What works and what doesn't: Evaluation beyond Kirkpatrick. *Nonprofit Management Leadership*, 35, 8–12, https://doi.org/10.1002/pfi.4170350204

Kennedy, A. (2014). Models of Continuing Professional Development: a framework for analysis. *Professional Development in Education*, 40(3), 336–351, https://doi.org/10.1 080/19415257.2014.929293

Kirkpatrick, D. and Kirkpatrick, J. (2006). *Evaluating training programs: The four levels*. San Francisco, CA, US: Berrett-Koehler Publishers.

Kirkpatrick, D. L. and Craig, R. L. (1970). *Evaluation of training. Training and Development Handbook*, Oregon, CA, US: University of Oregon.

Lessing, A. and De Witt, M. (2007). The value of continuous professional development: Teachers' perceptions. *South African Journal of Education*, 27(1), 53–67.

Lewis, S. (2020). Providing a platform for 'what works': Platform-based governance and the reshaping of teacher learning through the OECD's PISA4U. *Comparative Education*, 56(4), 484–502. https://doi.org/10.1080/03050068.2020.1769926

Mahmood, S. (2021). Instructional strategies for online teaching in COVID-19 pandemic. *Human Behaviour and Emerging Technologies*, 3(1), 199–203. https://doi.org/10.1002/hbe2.218

MOET. (2019). Decision 4660/QD-BGDDT, dated December 4, 2019, on promulgating the list of training modules for core teachers and administrators of general education institutions to carry out the regular training for teachers, administrators of general education institutions.

MOET. (2020). Official dispatch 5512/BGDĐT-GDTrH, dated December 18, 2020, guiding the formulation and implementation of educational plans for junior high schools, high schools and high schools with multiple levels of education.

Ng, V., Gupta, A., and Erlich, D. (2021). Brought about by necessity: how the pandemic accelerated a transformation of continuing professional development. *Education for Primary Care*, 33(1), 2–5. https://doi.org/10.1080/14739879.2021.1920474

Nunnally, J. C. and Bernstein, I. H. (1994). The Assessment of Reliability. *Psychometric Theory*, 226, McGraw-Hill, New York.

OECD. (1998). *Staying ahead: in-service training and teacher professional development*. Paris, France: Centre for Educational Research and Innovation, available at: http://hdl.voced.edu.au/10707/36767

Pekrun, R. (2006). The control-value theory of achievement emotions: Assumptions, corollaries, and implications for educational research and practice". *Educational Psychology Review*, 18(4), 315–341. https://doi.org/10.1007/s10648-006-9029-9

Pham, P. T., Thi Phan, T. T., Nguyen, Y. C., & Hoang, A. D. (2021). Factor associated with teacher satisfaction and online teaching effectiveness under adversity situations: a case of Vietnamese teachers during COVID-19. *Journal of Education*, 00220574211039483. https://doi.org/10.1177/00220574211039483

Phan, T. T. T., Ta, N. T., Duong, V. A. P., and Hoang, A. D. (2020). Dataset of Vietnamese teachers' habits and motivation behind continuous professional development programs participation. *Data in Brief*, 33. https://doi.org/10.1016/j.dib.2020.106525

Rensfeldt, A. B., Hillman, T., and Selwyn, N. (2018). Teachers 'liking' their work? Exploring the realities of teacher Facebook groups. *British Educational Research Journal*, 44(2), 230–250. https://doi.org/10.1002/berj.3325

Shallcross, T., O'Loan, K., and Hui, D. (2000). Developing a School Focused Approach to Continuing Professional Development in Sustainability Education. *Environmental Education Research*, 6(4), 363–382. https://doi.org/10.1080/713664694

Shimahara, N. K. (1998). The Japanese model of professional development: teaching as craft. *Teaching and Teacher Education*, 14(5), 451–462. https://doi.org/10.1016/S0742-051X(97)00055-3

Stone, M. (1974). Cross-Validatory Choice and Assessment of Statistical Predictions. *Journal of the Royal Statistical Society*, 36(2), 111–133. https://doi.org/doi:10.1111/j.2517-6161.1974.tb00994.x

Thomson, M. M. and Turner, J. E. (2019). The role of emotions in teachers' professional development: Attending a research experience for teachers (RET) program. *Education Research International*, 2019(9), 1–12.

Walsh, C. S., Bradshaw, P., and Twining, P. (2011). E-Learning through collaborative teacher professional development in primary and secondary schools in England, In *IADIS International Conference E-Learning 2011*.

Wu, W., Hu, R., Tan, R., & Liu, H. (2022). Exploring Factors of Middle School Teachers' Satisfaction with Online Training for Sustainable Professional Development under the Impact of COVID-19. *Sustainability*, 14(20), 13244. https://doi.org/10.3390/su142013244

Yazdi, M. T., Motallebzadeh, K., Ashraf, H., and Baghaei, P. (2017). A latent variable analysis of continuing professional development constructs using PLS-SEM modeling. *Cogent Education*, 4(1), 1355610. https://doi.org/10.1080/2331186X.2017.1355610

Authors

Thanh-Nga Nguyen[1], Hoai-Nam Nguyen[2*], Thanh-Trung Ta[1], Viet-Hai Phung[3], Thuy-Quynh Le-Thi[1]

1 Faculty of Physics, Ho Chi Minh City University of Education
2 Faculty of Technology Education, Hanoi National University of Education
   namnh@hnue.edu.vn, orcid: 0000-0003-1064-7468
3 Department of Physics, The University of Da Nang - University of Science and Education

*Corresponding Author

Chapter 9

Curriculum Management in Teacher Education: Visualized in Vietnam with Lens of Digital Transformation

Nam-Phuong NGUYEN, Hanoi National University of Education, Vietnam
Van-Tu NGUYEN, Northeast Normal University, China
Quoc-Khanh MAI, Hanoi National University of Education, Vietnam
Trung-Kien PHAN, Hanoi Metropolitan University, Vietnam

Abstract

This chapter delves into the intricacies of curriculum management within teacher education in Vietnam, particularly through the lens of digital transformation. As the educational landscape evolves, driven by rapid technological advancements, there is an increasing need to reexamine and reform the existing frameworks of teacher education to align with contemporary demands. This chapter conducts a thorough literature review, tracing the historical and educational milestones that have shaped Vietnam's approach to teacher training curricula. The qualitative research methodology employed focuses on analyzing the processes, requirements, and transformations that are essential for curriculum management in the digital era. The chapter is structured around three pivotal research questions: (1) What are the perspectives on digital transformation and its impact on the curriculum in Vietnamese universities, specifically within universities of education? (2) How have teaching competencies been defined and adapted in the context of curriculum management under the influence of digital transformation? (3) In what ways should the teacher education training process be adapted to meet the critical demands of the digital era? Through these inquiries, the chapter reveals significant insights into the contextual factors that affect curriculum management in teacher education. It highlights the shift from traditional content-based approaches to competency-based approaches, which are increasingly being adopted globally to ensure sustainable educational outcomes, reduce resource strain, and alleviate pressures on both educators and learners. The study emphasizes the need for a holistic transformation in educational philosophy, goals, and methods, underscoring the centrality of the learner in this new paradigm. The analysis extends to the specific competencies required of teachers in the digital age, drawing from both domestic and international perspectives. The chapter discusses the four core teaching competencies—lesson design, teaching organization, assessment, and teaching management—that are necessary for effective curriculum delivery in universities of education. These competencies are further broken down into sub-competencies, reflecting the nuanced demands of modern education. In addition to addressing the competencies, the chapter explores the broader implications of digital transformation on educational practices. It argues that the integration of digital literacy into teacher education is not merely an option but a necessity in preparing future educators for the challenges of the 21st century. The study proposes a structured approach to developing these digital competencies, emphasizing the importance of ongoing evaluation, flexible training programs, and robust support systems to facilitate continuous professional development. Moreover, the chapter outlines the challenges and opportunities presented by the digital transformation of education, including the need for adequate infrastructure, the development of digital literacy among both educators and students, and the alignment of educational practices with global standards. The recommendations provided aim to guide policy makers, educators, and institutions in effectively navigating the complexities of digital transformation in teacher education. In conclusion, this chapter offers a comprehensive overview of the current state of curriculum management in teacher education in Vietnam, highlighting the critical role of digital transformation in shaping the future of educational practices. The findings underscore the importance of adopting a forward-looking approach that integrates digital competencies into the core of teacher education, ensuring that educators are well-equipped to meet the demands of a rapidly changing educational landscape.

Keywords: *teacher education, teaching competence, digital transformation, curriculum development, curriculum management*

1. Context of Teacher Education in Vietnam Amidst Digital Transformation

As society evolves and changes, education has undergone significant improvements. During the Feudal era, education was distinctly class-based, with access to education being a privilege reserved for the ruling class, and the content of instruction was largely dependent on the knowledge and experience of the teacher. As the Feudal system declined, education began to transition towards becoming a universal right, no longer an exclusive privilege of the ruling class. However, in the early capitalist period, contemporary ideologies were disseminated through educational activities, where education served as a tool of the capitalist regime. It was not until the remnants of the Feudal system were entirely eradicated that mass education models found the space to develop, gradually extending education to all members of society.

Today, education has become an essential activity, continuously adjusting to establish suitable learning pathways and laying the foundation for the concept of lifelong learning.

Countries worldwide have been transitioning from content-based educational programs to competency-based approaches. This shift aims not only to ensure sustainable educational outcomes but also to save time and resources in training, while simultaneously reducing the pressures of teaching and learning for both educators and students. The transformation of education is closely linked to the industrial revolutions, and it can be summarized as follows[1]:

Characteristics of Industrial Revolutions	Industrial Revolution1.0: Mechanization with machines powered by hydraulics and steam engines	Industrial Revolution 2.0: The advent of electric engines and assembly lines, leading to mass production	Industrial Revolution 3.0: The era of computers and automation	Industrial Revolution 4.0: Integration of systems that connect the real and virtual worlds
Characteristics of the Education System	Before 1980s Education 1.0	1980s Education 2.0	1990s Education 3.0	2000s Education 4.0
Focus	Knowledge transmission	Teaching for employability	Knowledge creation	Innovation and value creation
Educational Management	Top-down	Top-down with feedback	Top-down and horizontal	Tilted, horizontal, and bottom-up
Curriculum	Single-discipline	Interdisciplinary	Multidisciplinary	Transdisciplinary
Technology	Paper and pen	PCs & Laptops	Internet and mobile devices	Internet off Everything (IoE)
Teaching and Learning	One-way	Two-way	Multi-directional	Personalized
Outcomes	Skilled labor	Knowledgeable workers	Co-creators of knowledge	Innovators and lifelong learners

In Vietnam, the Party and the State consistently affirm that education and training are of paramount importance as national policies; investment in education is an investment in development, and education must be prioritized, leading other sectors. Under the influence of the Fourth Industrial Revolution, specialized knowledge becomes outdated rapidly, while new knowledge and scientific information are generated exponentially and can be stored compactly through digitalization. In this digitized environment, education will undergo significant transformations—from its philosophy and objectives to the role of educators, from teaching methods to the "central" position of learners. Consequently, educational reform in general, and higher education reform in particular, is a global trend that Vietnam cannot ignore. To meet the urgent demands of reality, the Central Committee of the Communist Party of Vietnam adopted Resolution No. 29-NQ/TW on November 4, 2013, on "Fundamental and Comprehensive Renovation of Education and Training, meeting the requirements of industrialization and modernization within the context of a socialist-oriented market economy and international integration." Since then, the process of higher education reform in Vietnam has been underway, aiming to achieve a fundamental and significant transformation in the quality and effectiveness of education. The first task in this reform process is the establishment of a suitable educational philosophy. This shift involves moving from an education system primarily focused on imparting knowledge to one that emphasizes teaching skills, self-directed learning, and critical thinking. Following Resolution No. 29-NQ/TW, the Ministry of Education and Training officially announced in 2018 a comprehensive program that includes 27 subject curricula and educational activities under the new general education curriculum.

The 2018 general education curriculum reflects the goals of general education, stipulates the required competencies and qualities students should achieve, outlines the educational content, teaching methods, and assessment procedures, and serves as a basis for managing the quality of general education. Additionally, it represents the State's commitment to ensuring the quality of the entire general education system and each educational institution. This necessitates innovations in teacher training as well. To achieve this, universities, especially those specializing in teacher education, must enhance the quality of teacher training—future teachers should take on an active role, while lecturers serve as guides, directing students on how to acquire knowledge and providing support when necessary. This innovation entails a series of fundamental changes, from the framework program to the curriculum and teaching methods. To ensure this, it is essential to innovate the approach to the components of the teaching process:

- **Teaching objectives**: Shift from primarily imparting knowledge to developing learners' qualities and competencies.
- **Teaching curriculum**: Transition from centralized control to decentralization, with frameworks set by the Ministry, local programs, and school-based curricula.
- **Teaching content**: Move from academic content to streamlined, selective, and integrated material that meets the requirements for practical application and international integration.
- **Teaching methods**: Shift from predominantly one-way transmission where students passively receive information (teacher-centered) to organizing learning activities where students are active and self-directed (student-centered, with teachers as supporters and guides).
- **Teaching formats**: Transition from traditional classroom-based instruction to a diversified approach that combines in-class and out-of-class learning, including heritage education, instruction linked to production and business, increased social activities, enhanced use of information technology, scientific research, and creative experiential activities. This also involves a shift from whole-class instruction to a combination of small group, individual, and whole-class learning.
- **Assessment and evaluation**: Shift from primarily testing knowledge retention to evaluating competencies; from focusing solely on academic results to combining academic performance with the assessment of learning processes and student progress.
- **Learning conditions**: Move from relying solely on in-school educational resources to creating conditions that allow students to learn from diverse and rich societal resources, particularly through the Internet. This aims to develop students' self-study and research abilities and prepare them for lifelong learning.

Part 2.
Insights of Lesson Study in Teacher Education and Curriculum Development
—Showcasing in the Context of Digital Transformation in Vietnam

In the era of digital education, the competencies that need to be developed must be grounded in the context of the digital society. By analyzing teaching competencies and their specific manifestations in combination with the social context, it is possible to establish criteria and indicators that have not yet been clearly defined in current teacher competency and outcome standards. Ultimately, this will lead to the development of implementation processes and solutions to overcome challenges in the current Vietnamese educational context, providing a scientific basis for other countries to reform their educational and training programs.

2. Teaching Competency and Its Development in Teacher Education in Vietnam within the Context of Digital Transformation

2-1. Teaching competency and its development in teacher education

According to the provisions of the General Education Program issued under Circular 32/2018/TT-BGDDT, the concept of competency as defined in the 2018 General Education Program is as follows: *Competency* is an individual's attribute that is formed and developed through innate qualities and the process of learning and practice. It enables individuals to effectively mobilize and integrate knowledge, skills, and other personal attributes such as interests, beliefs, willpower, etc., to successfully perform a specific activity and achieve desired outcomes under certain conditions.

Thus, teaching competency is a type of competency that is formed and developed through learning and practice, allowing individuals to mobilize and integrate knowledge, skills, and personal attributes such as interests, beliefs, and willpower to successfully conduct the teaching process. The concept of teaching competency has been discussed by numerous scholars both domestically and internationally, including P. N. Gonobolin (1979), Denyse Tremblay (1999), Bernd Meier (2020), Nguyen Ngoc Bich (1998), Pham Minh Hac, Le Duc Phuc (2004), Le Van Hong et al. (2001), among others. While there are varying perspectives, teaching competency can generally be characterized by the following features:

i. Teaching competency is a crucial component of pedagogical competency.
ii. Teaching competency pertains to the effectiveness of the teaching activity.
   A competent teacher is one who can effectively address the following questions:
   - Does the teacher have a strong command of the subject matter they teach?
   - Is the teacher capable of adapting and modifying instructional materials?
   - Does the teacher accurately apply appropriate teaching methods?
   - Does the teacher interact effectively with their students?
   - Can the teacher anticipate and manage teaching scenarios?

According to Circular 20/2018/TT-BGDDT, the professional standards for teachers in general education institutions include five key standards: Teacher Ethics; Professional Development; Creating a Positive Educational Environment; Developing Relationships

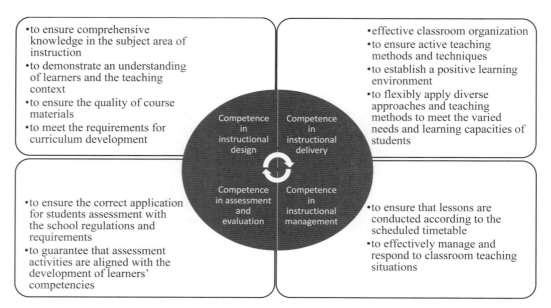

Diagram 1: Components of teaching competences mentioned in training curriculum in universities of education

between Schools, Families, and Society; and the Use of Foreign Languages or Ethnic Languages, Information Technology Application, and the Use of Technological Devices in Teaching and Education. However, when examining the elements specific to teaching competency, it can be broken down into four main components: Teaching Design Competency, Teaching Organization Competency, Assessment Competency, and Teaching Management Competency. These four competencies encompass various sub-competencies.

In accordance with the regulations from the Ministry of Education and Training, Vietnam National University (2023) has also proposed a framework for evaluating teaching competencies based on three components, which notably do not include Teaching Management Competency.

In summary, teaching competency can be conceptualized as comprising four specific competencies: Teaching Design Competency, Teaching Organization Competency, Assessment Competency, and Teaching Management Competency. Each of these competencies contains specific criteria, which are illustrated in Digram 1.

The competency in instructional design is demonstrated through the process by which teachers prepare for a successful lesson, encompassing several criteria: ensuring a solid knowledge base in the subject area; understanding the learners and the teaching context; ensuring the quality of instructional materials; and meeting the requirements for constructing and designing teaching activities. According to the current output standards assessments of teacher training institutions in Vietnam, instructional design competency is materialized through several component competencies.

First, the competency in lesson preparation includes understanding the learners, researching educational programs (from the national to the school level), compiling teaching materials, and conducting relevant research. Second, the competency in lesson design involves translating pedagogical theories and principles into specific lesson plans and teaching activities, effectively utilizing and leveraging teaching materials and tools, and accurately aligning objectives with the curriculum and the competency development goals of the students.

The competency in instructional delivery refers to the ability to actualize the instructional design plan by organizing and managing learners' activities to help them acquire knowledge, skills, and professional attitudes. To meet the criteria for instructional delivery, such as effective classroom management, applying active teaching methods and techniques, creating a positive learning environment, and flexibly adopting various teaching approaches to meet the diverse learning needs and abilities of students, the teacher must possess several fundamental competencies. These include the ability to apply both traditional and modern teaching methods, utilize instructional materials and equipment, organize learning activities, and communicate effectively.

The competency in assessment and evaluation requires teachers to ensure the objectivity, fairness, and accuracy of the evaluation process, thereby accurately assessing students' abilities and development. To meet these requirements, teachers must possess several component competencies, such as the ability to develop assessment tools, use these tools effectively, and analyze and compare results, ensuring that the assessment process is aligned with competency-based approaches, the learning objectives, and the requirements of the educational program.

Finally, **the competency in instructional management** ensures that the teaching process aligns with the instructional goals. This competency not only involves ensuring that classroom activities proceed smoothly but also that the instructional plan is implemented according to the intended objectives. It requires teachers to have the competency to handle pedagogical situations and resolve any issues that arise during the preparation, organization, and assessment phases of the teaching process.

The development of teaching competencies is a process that enables students to form and enhance these specific competencies through educational activities both within and beyond the school setting.

2-2. Structure of teaching competence in teacher education in Vietnam

Currently, Hanoi National University of Education outlines specific graduate outcomes for its students, which encompass 6 qualities, 6 general competencies, 5 pedagogical competencies, and 6 specialized competencies.

The **six qualities** include: Love for nature, homeland, and country; Affection for students and belief in their potential; Passion for and pride in the teaching profession; Honesty and trustworthiness; Responsibility and dedication; A commitment to lifelong learning and self-research.

The **six general competencies** are: Self-management and adaptability to change; Communication and collaboration; Leadership; Problem-solving and creativity; Cultural and social awareness; Critical thinking.

The **five pedagogical competencies** include: Teaching competence; Educational competence; Competence in guiding student development; Social activity competence; Professional development competence.

The six specialized competencies are: Specialized competence in a specific field; The ability to apply general educational knowledge and specialized knowledge to thoroughly explain specific teaching content in the General Education Program; The ability to apply general educational knowledge and specialized knowledge in practice; Research competence in specialized fields and educational sciences; The ability to use foreign languages in professional activities; The ability to utilize information and communication technology in professional activities.

(*Source*: Teacher Education Program Graduate Standards,
Hanoi National University of Education, 2023)

It is evident that the current graduate standards at Hanoi National University of Education are still constructed based on *three core elements*: knowledge, skills, and attitudes. These can be summarized as follows:

For the development of teaching competence in teacher education, the graduate outcomes concerning *knowledge* should ensure: (i) knowledge of natural sciences, society, and history to support professional development and personal improvement; (ii) Theoretical and practical knowledge in the specialized field aimed at solving professional problems; (iii) In-depth, detailed professional knowledge.

The graduate outcomes concerning *skills* should ensure: (i) Cognitive skills, professional practical skills such as problem communication and problem-solving skills; (ii) Necessary communication and interpersonal skills in the field to perform professional duties corresponding to the career position; (iii) The ability to work independently and in teams.

The graduate outcomes concerning *attitudes* should ensure a sense of responsibility towards oneself, the community, and the country, as well as professional ethics.

These contents can be summarized in Diagram 2.

However, with the advancement of technology, the organization of teaching activities has diversified into various forms, most notably including traditional face-to-face teaching, online teaching, and blended learning. Consequently, the demands on teaching competencies are inevitably influenced, particularly by the need for students to acquire digital competencies. Killen (2018) argued that every job position will be "digitized", and the ability to use technology will become a fundamental requirement across all professions. In this context, both educators and students must leverage the benefits of technology while supporting the community and fostering innovation and creativity in future generations.

The work "Framework of Student Digital Competence"[2] identifies seven pillars of digital competence for students, including: Operating devices and software; Information and data literacy; Communication and collaboration in digital environments; Digital safety and well-being; Digital content creation; Learning and developing digital skills; and Using digital competence for professional purposes.

(*Source*: Framework of Student Digital Competence,
Vietnam National University, 2023)

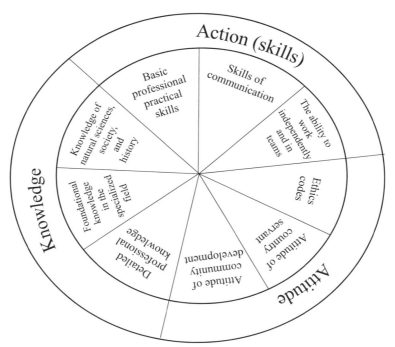

Diagram 2: Components of Teaching Competences in Teacher Training Curriculum of Universities of Education

In conjunction with teaching competencies, the digital competencies of education students must be cultivated and meet specific criteria.

In the context of digital transformation, teacher training must go beyond merely developing teaching competencies; it must also ensure the development of digital competencies among students. The four essential teaching competencies should intersect and integrate with the seven pillars of digital competencies. Through this integration, a competency framework for teaching in the digital context can be constructed, which will then serve as the foundation for developing digital competencies, applying them in the teaching process, and enhancing teaching competencies within the digital transformation context.

2-3. The process of developing teaching competencies in teacher education within the context of digital transformation

A student is an individual enrolled in an undergraduate program at a higher education institution, having completed their general education. When considering the development of teaching competencies, it is essential to recognize that these students have already been exposed to an educational environment, meaning that starting their teaching competency development from scratch would be inefficient. Thus, the process of cultivating and advancing teaching skills in teacher training can be divided into three stages.

Stage 1 (Pre-pedagogical stage): During their general education, students begin to

Table 1: Students' Digital Competence (Vietnam National University, 2023)

Digital competence	Criteria
1. Operating equipment and software for teaching	• Operating digital devices in teaching • Utilizing software and digital services in teaching
2. Utilizing information and data for teaching	• Identifying information needs for teaching • Searching for information for teaching • Evaluating information relevant to teaching activities • Managing and storing information for teaching • Using and distributing information for teaching
3. Communication and collaboration in digital environments for teaching	• Communicating, recognizing behavioral norms, and understanding the audience (empathy) for teaching • Effectively participating in online communities/groups/forums for teaching • Practicing rights and public services through digital platforms for teaching • Conducting oneself on the internet in accordance with ethical standards and legal regulations for teaching • Collaborating in work through digital technology for teaching
4. Digital safety and well-being for teaching	• Protecting digital identity and privacy for teaching • Safeguarding the environment during the use of digital devices and services for teaching
5. Creating digital content for teaching	• Practicing innovative thinking in the creation of digital content for teaching • Creating digital content (tools and methods) for teaching • Applying legal frameworks in the development and use of digital content for teaching • Participating in the development of applications on digital platforms for teaching
6. Learning and developing digital skills for teaching	• Recognizing trends and opportunities in online education for teaching • Digital learning (tools and methods) for teaching • Open access to learning resources for teaching
7. Applying digital competencies in professional teaching practices	• Utilizing specialized digital technology for teaching • Recognizing and evaluating specific content and data for teaching • Applying technology in entrepreneurial ventures for teaching

develop essential skills as they absorb knowledge. This competency formation occurs regardless of the educational reforms in place or whether students are actively planning or passively acquiring these skills. For example, when a teacher calls on a student to answer a question, the student practices presentation skills such as articulating ideas and problem-solving. Similarly, when a student solves a problem on the board, they passively develop skills in board writing and presentation. Through observation, students also gain insights into the procedural structure of a lesson.

Stage 2 (Learning at teacher training institutions): In this phase, students undergo structured and well-planned training designed to instill essential pedagogical competencies. This includes specialized courses and foundational subjects such as psychology, education, theory, and instructional methodologies, all of which contribute to a well-rounded competency development.

Stage 3 (Teaching practice in general education schools): At this stage, students directly engage in designing and implementing educational activities in schools through practicum and internships. This critical phase allows them to apply and refine the competencies acquired during their training, providing practical experience that enhances their teaching capabilities until they achieve proficiency.

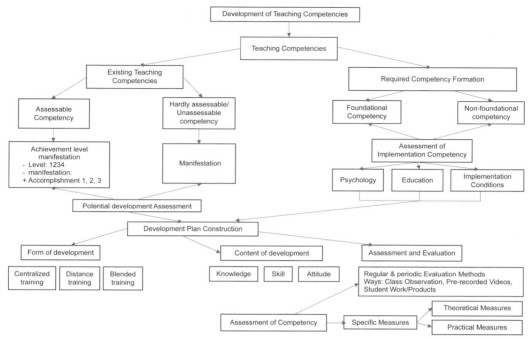

Diagram 3: Developing the Teaching Competencies for Teacher Education in Digital Transformation

To foster teaching competencies in teacher education within the context of digital transformation, several factors must be ensured: First, establish a knowledge foundation and identify factors influencing the development of teaching competencies among students. Second, focus on teaching and enhancing both existing and emerging competencies in students. Third, maintain regular competency assessments (theoretical and practical). These elements are illustrated in Diagram 3.

Firstly, it is essential to identify the teaching competencies of learners in relation to their specific fields of study. These competencies include both general and specialized skills, with general competencies such as board writing and presentation skills, and specialized competencies such as defining objectives and designing instructional plans for the specific subject area. It should be noted that some competencies may not be directly assessable. These competencies need to be evaluated using a scoring rubric to determine which criteria of the profession have been met.

After assessing the existing competencies, it becomes clear which competencies have been achieved and can be further developed, and which competencies have not yet been attained, thereby requiring formation. From these competencies in need of development, the ability to execute tasks should be evaluated based on three key criteria.

Once the evaluation is complete, the planning process begins. The first step involves selecting an appropriate mode of delivery (online, offline, hybrid, modular, credit-based, course-based, etc.) to design the content, ensuring that it covers the three essential components: knowledge, skills, and attitudes. This step also includes developing an evaluation plan and assessment methods.

Identifying limitations and influencing factors is crucial for conducting a backward evaluation and finalizing the plan. The constraints of traditional teaching contexts have gradually been mitigated as education adapts to the changes brought by digital transformation. However, digital transformation also presents significant challenges to the development of teaching competencies in teacher education.

- **Requirement of definition**: More diverse, secure, and selective methods are needed, with a higher comfort level for participants to provide feedback.
- **Considerations**: Multiple evaluation methods should be considered, along with a comprehensive understanding of institutional needs and conditions (as schools have digitized, and information regarding faculty, facilities, and practical connections has been digitalized).
- **Training delivery**: Can be conducted online, offline, or in a hybrid format (including practical exams and electronic lesson plans).
- **Extended training duration**: Increased training time is necessary due to disparities in pre-service training; some participants may be familiar with digital tools while others are not, leading to the need for additional instruction based on varying starting points.
- **Conference delivery (online, offline, hybrid)**: Facilitates openness and easier access to a broader range of experts.

This process ensures that teachers not only possess a strong foundation in technology but are also capable of effectively integrating it into their teaching practices, thereby supporting the holistic development of teacher student.

2-4. Recommendations for ensuring the implementation of the teaching competency development process in teacher training within the context of digital transformation

To overcome these challenges, teacher training programs must provide technical support, abundant resources, and continuous learning opportunities to help teachers develop and update their skills.

In the context of digital transformation, teacher training for the development of teaching competencies requires the following conditions:

i.   **Technical infrastructure**: Provide adequate and modern information technology infrastructure to enable teachers to access and utilize digital tools and resources in the teaching and learning process.

ii. **Supporting resources**: Ensure the availability of comprehensive supporting resources, such as instructional materials, guides, educational videos, and software, to facilitate effective training activities and competency enhancement.

iii. **Flexible training programs**: Design flexible training programs that can be adjusted to reflect new trends, emerging technologies, and learner needs.

iv. **Modern teaching methods**: Ensure that teachers are trained in modern teaching methods that align with the digitalized environment, such as flipped classrooms, video-based instruction, and gamified learning.

v. **Continuous feedback and evaluation**: Establish mechanisms for regular feedback and evaluation from learners and administrators to improve the quality and effectiveness of the training process.

vi. **Technical support**: Ensure that sufficient technical support is available to help teachers address technology-related issues during the teaching process.

vii. **Supportive and encouraging environment**: Create conditions where teachers feel encouraged and supported in experimenting with and applying new technologies in their work.

viii. **Knowledge sharing and collaboration**: Provide opportunities for teachers to connect, share experiences, and learn from each other through forums, research groups, or online communities.

ix. **Time and space for learning**: Facilitate conditions where teachers have the time and space to engage in training activities without disrupting their daily teaching responsibilities.

x. **Leadership commitment**: Educational organization leaders must demonstrate strong commitment and support for the development of teaching competencies in the context of digital transformation, from providing resources to fostering an environment conducive to change and growth.

3. Conclusion

In conclusion, this chapter has explored the critical role of digital transformation in shaping curriculum management within teacher education in Vietnam. As the educational landscape rapidly evolves due to technological advancements, it becomes increasingly imperative to reconfigure teacher training programs to meet contemporary demands. The analysis reveals that a shift from traditional content-based approaches to competency-based models is essential to ensure sustainable educational outcomes and to alleviate the pressures on both educators and learners. The chapter highlights the necessity of integrating digital competencies into teacher education as a core component of curriculum management. This integration is not merely an option but a fundamental requirement to prepare future educators for the challenges of the 21st century. By emphasizing the development of teaching competencies, such as lesson design, teaching organization, assessment, and teaching management, within the context of digital literacy, the study proposes a comprehensive approach to enhance the effectiveness of teacher education in Vietnam. Furthermore, the recommendations provided address the infrastructural, pedagogical, and administrative adjustments needed to support the successful implementation of digital competencies in teacher training. These include the provision of modern technological infrastructure, flexible and up-to-date training programs, continuous feedback mechanisms, and strong leadership commitment. By adopting these strategies, educational institutions can better equip teachers to navigate the complexities of digital transformation, ultimately contributing to the broader goal of educational reform in Vietnam. The findings underscore the importance of a forward-looking approach that not only responds to current educational needs but also anticipates future challenges. This chapter serves as a call to action for policymakers, educators, and institutions to embrace digital transformation as a driving force for innovation and excellence in teacher education.

This chapter utilizes the results of the project "Developing Blended Teaching Competence for Students in Universities of Education"
(Code B2024-SPH-05, project leader: Dr. Nam-Phuong Nguyen).

Notes
1) Nguyen Thi Tuyet Hanh (2017). [Vietnamese: *Phát triển năng lực thích ứng cho đội ngũ giáo viên đáp ứng yêu cầu thực hiện nhiệm vụ giáo dục trong bối cảnh mới*. Development of adaptability for the teacher staff meeting the requirement of educational tasks in the new context]. Dong Thap University. *Journal of Science*. No 29 (13–18).
2) https://daotao.sis.vnu.edu.vn/bo-sach-ve-nang-luc-so-va-khung-nang-luc-so-danh-cho-sinh-vien/772/

Reference
Bui, M. H. (ed.) (2016). *History of international education* [Vietnamese: *Lịch sử giáo dục thế giới*]. University of Education Publishing House.

Gonobolin, P. N. (1979). *Teachers' psychological qualities*. Hanoi, Vietnam: Publishing House of Education.

Hanoi National University of Education (2021). Outcomes of the teacher training curriculum http://daotao.hnue.edu.vn/forum/newscontent.aspx?id=1492&pg=0 Retrieved on February 16, 2024.

Killen, C. (2018). Collaboration and Coaching: Powerful Strategies for Developing Digital Capabilities. In Digital Literacy Unpacked (29–44). Facet.

Le, V. H., Le, N. L., & Nguyen, V. T. (2001). *Developmental psychology and Educational psychology*. Hanoi National University of Publishing House.

Meier, B., & Nguyen, V. C. (2020). *Modern teaching methodology*. University of Education Publishing House.

Nguyen, N. B. (1998). *Psychology of Personality* (252–257). Hanoi, Vietnam: Publishing House of Education.

Nguyen, T. T. H. (2017). Development of adaptability for the teacher staff meeting the requirement of educational tasks in the new context [Vietnamese: *Phát triển năng lực thích ứng cho đội ngũ giáo viên đáp ứng yêu cầu thực hiện nhiệm vụ giáo dục trong bối cảnh mới*]. *Dong Thap University Journal of Science*, 29, 21–24.

Pham, M. H., & Le, D. P. (2004). *A number of issues in research of personality*. Hanoi, Vietnam: Publishing House of National Politics.

Tremblay, D. (1999). Aborder l'enseignement et l'apprentissage par le biais des compétences: les effets dans la pratique des enseignants et des enseignantes. *Pédagogie collégiale*, 13(2), 24–30.

Vietnam National University (2022). Framework of digital literacy. https://daotao. sis.vnu.edu.vn/bo-sach-ve-nang-luc-so-va-khung-nang-luc-so-danh-cho-sinh-vien/772/ Retrieved on February 15, 2024.

Authors

Nam-Phuong Nguyen[1]*, Van-Tu Nguyen[2], Quoc-Khanh Mai[1], Trung-Kien Phan[3]

1   Hanoi National University of Education, Vietnam
2   Northeast Normal University, China
3   Hanoi Metropolitan University, Vietnam
*Corresponding author: ORCID 0000-0001-7344-1470
*Corresponding email: phuongnn@hnue.edu.vn

Chapter 10

Practice of 'Lesson Study' in Japan and Vietnam within the Contemporary Era

Dinh Chien TRAN, Hung Vuong University, Vietnam
Nam-Phuong NGUYEN, Hanoi National University of Education, Vietnam

Abstract

This chapter provides a comprehensive analysis of the concept of "Lesson study", a professional development practice that originated in Japan and has been recently introduced in Vietnam. Utilizing a methodology centered on literature review and comparative analysis, this chapter reveals significant academic and practical findings. Despite cultural and human commonalities between Japan and Vietnam, the implementation of "Lesson study" in Vietnam exhibits a more limited and narrowly focused approach compared to its widespread application in Japan. As the foundational chapter in this section, it delineates three critical research dimensions within the context of cross-cultural studies: (i) The aspects of the contemporary era as educational contextually in Vietnam in which have set the requirements for the move of teachers' professional development, (ii) Analysis of "Lesson study" drawn through the practice in Japan, and (iii) How "Lesson study" helps Vietnamese school teachers in their professional development as contemporary educators. By concentrating on in-service teacher education, this chapter offers both academic and practical frameworks for research in teacher education, addressing the diverse and evolving needs of contemporary education. It provides insights into "Lesson study" as a tool for continuous professional development among school teachers in Vietnam, while also considering its broader implications for school curriculum development and management, as extensively practiced in Japan.

Keywords: *Lesson study, perspectives, Japan, Vietnam, comparisons*

1. Introduction

Japan and Vietnam, two nations with rich cultural heritages, share notable similarities in educational values, particularly in the structure and objectives of teacher training and student-centered pedagogies (Saito, 2015; Sato, 2011; Kuramoto et al., 2020, Nguyen et al., 2021a). Both countries place a significant emphasis on education as a critical pillar for societal development, underpinned by Confucian principles that prioritize collective well-being, respect for authority, and continuous self-improvement. These shared values foster an environment where teaching is not just a profession but a lifelong commitment to personal and societal betterment, creating a robust foundation for cross-cultural educational initiatives like Lesson Study.

Lesson study is the issue that has lately appeared in Vietnam (Ha, 2018; Le, 2014; Nguyen, 2018; Pham et al., 2018; Vu & Nguyen, 2010), while there has been a long-term research period till now in Japan devoted to this issue. The practice of Lesson Study—collaborative teaching improvement and reflective teaching practices—originated in Japan and has become a cornerstone of in-service teacher education globally. In Japan, Lesson Study is implemented through a cyclical process of planning, teaching, observing, and reflecting, allowing teachers to enhance their skills through practical classroom experiences (Sato, 1996; Takano, 1988; Kuga, 2007; Fernandez & Yoshida, 2004; Kuramoto et al., 2009, 2014).

Since 2018, Vietnam has embraced educational innovation with the implementation of the General Education Curriculum (GEC), which seeks to modernize the educational system and shift from content-based to competency-based learning (Nguyen et al., 2021b; Nguyen, 2020; Vu, 2020). Vietnam's educational reforms have increasingly focused on integrating collaborative learning and professional development methods like Lesson Study, inspired by Japanese models, to address the evolving demands of contemporary education. In today's globalized and rapidly advancing world, Vietnam faces new challenges and opportunities in education. Technological advancements, changing societal expectations, and a growing emphasis on critical thinking and problem-solving skills require innovative approaches to teaching and professional development. In this context, Lesson Study emerges as a vital mechanism for Vietnam's in-service teacher education. Rooted in real-world classroom practice, Lesson Study enables teachers to engage in a structured yet flexible process that emphasizes continuous improvement, reflection, and collaboration.

Given the considerably similar cultural educational background, the scholars in Japan and Vietnam still have had a number of different points including the issue of "Lesson study" to some extent. Within this chapter, focusing on in-service teacher education theoretically and practically, the three research questions should be answered are:

(1) What are the aspects of the contemporary era as educational contextually in Vietnam in which have set the requirements for the move of teachers' professional development?
(2) What is the analysis of "Lesson study" drawn through the practice in Japan as the way of teacher education?
(3) How does "Lesson study" help Vietnamese school teachers in their professional development as contemporary educators?

The focus is on how Lesson Study serves as a critical pathway for in-service teacher development, examining both its potential and challenges in the context of Vietnam's educational landscape. By drawing on Japan's extensive experience with Lesson Study, this chapter provides valuable insights into adapting this model for Vietnam's unique cultural and educational environment, paving the way for more effective, context-specific teacher development practices that can elevate the quality of education across the country.

2. Research Results

2-1. Aspects of the educational context contemporarily in Vietnam and the requirements for the move of teachers' professional development

In contemporary Vietnamese education, the digital transformation is a significant factor in reshaping vocational and higher education. Decision 2222/QD-TTg targets expanding digital integration in vocational education by 2025 and aims for full digital adaptation by 2030 (MOET, 2021). This strategy focuses on creating a digital ecosystem to facilitate online learning, data-driven educational practices, and digital literacy among educators and administrators. By 2025, the program anticipates that 50% of educational institutions will operate on digital platforms, with the goal of achieving complete digitization across all vocational training institutions by 2030. This transformation aligns with national ambitions to raise productivity and improve workforce competitiveness in the context of international economic integration.

Teacher autonomy and school autonomy are also evolving in response to national reforms in higher education. The 2018 amendment to the Higher Education Law enhanced autonomy for universities, specifically by empowering academic institutions to manage their finances, curricula, and human resources independently. Consequently, over 97% of public universities have established autonomous governing councils, which are instrumental in implementing self-directed policies that align educational objectives with market demands (Le & Tran, 2023). School autonomy has thus facilitated more adaptable and responsive educational models, supporting continuous quality improvements and aligning Vietnamese higher education institutions with global standards.

Career development for educators, especially regarding vocational and higher education standards, has received attention through policy reforms that define career advancement pathways. Decision 2003/QD-BGDDT, for example, outlines structured career development programs for secondary school teachers, emphasizing skills in digital pedagogy, student support, and adapting to changes in educational practices (MOET, 2023). These programs align with the national goal of fostering a skilled, adaptable teaching workforce. Furthermore, the Circular 05/2024/TT-BGDDT has clarified promotion criteria for university lecturers, stipulating requirements such as quality performance ratings and advanced qualifications (MOET, 2024). This structure supports career mobility within education while addressing the need for expertise in digital and modern teaching methodologies, thus contributing to improved educational standards.

The requirements for teachers' professional development in contemporary Vietnam emphasize digital competency, collaborative learning, and adaptation to global educational standards. Vietnam's 2021 digital transformation strategy sets ambitious goals for integrating technology across educational institutions, which necessitates teachers' proficiency in digital tools and platforms to enhance their teaching effectiveness. This digital shift complements the introduction of innovative practices, such as "Lesson Study," a collaborative and reflective approach to teaching rooted in Japanese educational reforms. This approach, increasingly practiced in Vietnam, encourages teachers to engage in structured lesson planning, observation, and feedback cycles, fostering a collaborative learning environment. Professional development programs, such as the competency-based guidelines established in 2023, also highlight the need for teachers to master skills in adaptive pedagogy and student-centered teaching. These programs not only focus on enhancing instructional skills but also promote the development of a reflective teaching practice aligned with the country's shift towards competency-based education.

In summary, Vietnam's contemporary educational reforms, marked by digital transformation, increased school autonomy, and robust teacher career development norms, underscore a commitment to adapting its education system to modern demands. These initiatives collectively contribute to a more dynamic, competitive educational landscape poised to meet future workforce needs in Vietnam's rapidly evolving economy.

2-2. Lesson study in Japan: Lens and the practice

Conversely, researching "Japanese Lesson study" is internationally becoming an important issue in the fields of teacher education, curriculum and instructional design, school management, and in other fields. Lesson study has its origins in Japan (Fernandez & Yoshida, 2004; Akita & Lewis, 2008; Lewis et al., 2011), which is a direct translation of the Japanese *Jugyo-Kenkyu* (translated as 'lesson adapted till it is perfect' in English).

Lesson study is one of the most remarkable achievements to come out of Japanese educational culture.

Firstly, in the very first time of research on Lesson study, as the original meaning of the Japanese word, *Jugyo-Kenkyu*, it has the main point in teacher education. This time, the goal of Lesson study is to effectively improve the *quality of teaching*, such as by demonstrating *teachers' model techniques* for other teachers. Working in groups, teachers collaborate with one another by, meeting to discuss learning goals, planning actual classroom lessons, observing how lessons work in practice, and then revising and reporting on the results so that other teachers can learn something new through their practical research. Since Lesson study means a Japanese style of researching curriculum and instruction, or in-service teacher training in the school, the concept will contribute to supporting school improvement (Lewis & Tsuchida, 1998; Stigler & Hiebert, 1997,1999; Akita & Lewis, 2008; Le, 2014).

Identified by NASEM (National Association for the Study of Educational Methods), Lesson study is the science of educational method "clarifies the aim, content, and method and tries to contribute to teaching practice" (Sato, 1996, p.270). Teachers who practice teaching make Lesson study for the purpose of *promoting professional vocation of teacher*

162 | *Part 2.*
Insights of Lesson Study in Teacher Education and Curriculum Development
—Showcasing in the Context of Digital Transformation in Vietnam

and *developing practical ability of teaching*, and make teaching practice an object of Lesson study to do so and develop professional ability through its study (Inagaki & Sato, 1996).

Since the 1960's the term "Lesson study" has characterized one of its figures: reflecting results of science to educational content as accurately as possible and to fundamentally recompose educational content with non-government educational research movement as the center of its movement of Lesson study (Sato, 1996)

An important issue of Lesson study in Japan is how it combines what is called today teacher education connected with teacher education and in-service teacher training (Sugiyama, 1969, p.112), including of "analysis of teaching-learning", "instruction" and "learning" (NASEM, 2011).

In the second aspect, regarding a literature review initially, the historical definition of Lesson study and the school's common educational goals and content, should be established by managing the school's organization performance. Also, the quality of Lesson study must be developed to create strategic teaching and curriculum (Plan), to implement the curriculum and the actual teaching of lessons (Do), and to evaluate teaching effectiveness (Check). Finally, improving the quality of curriculum design and teaching strategies (Act) should be completed for students and teachers within a school year. This typical PDCA paradigm is called "curriculum management with Lesson study" (Takano,1988; Nakatome, 2001, 2005; Kuramoto, 2018). Significant steps have been made since the introduction of Lesson study to the international teaching community through the establishment of the World Association of Lesson Studies (WALS) in 2008.

Since the international recognition of WALS as a profound teaching methodology was first established, educators meet every year at an annual conference in various worldwide locations to discuss research and to further develop pedagogical methods. Therefore, Lesson study is a necessary component of the concept of curriculum management. Based on the principles of the new "course of study" from 2020, the official school curriculum guideline, the following approaches are recommended to ensure that school management understands "curriculum management with Lesson study" (MEXT, 2016). It is classified with further explanation:

- The standard educational content for students must be approached from each subject's interrelation, and an integrated curriculum must be systematically developed based on school goals.
- A Plan-do-check-act (PDCA) cycle with a planned series of steps: Plan (formulate curriculum), Do (practice), Check and Act (evaluate and improve), that must be established to develop teaching skills based on examinations concerning the conditions of the entire school, and various data for improving the quality of school education (This means that Lesson study is a critical strategy).
- The standard educational content, teachers and students, and material must be effectively managed as internal resources in schools, and external resources in the community must be utilized.

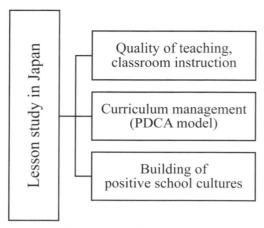

Diagram 1: Aspects of "Lesson study" in Japan through the Literature Review

Furthermore, *thirdly*, the concepts of Lesson study and curriculum management indicate the building of positive school cultures (O' Neill & Kinston,1996; Steven, 1998), and lastly, being accountable for the communities (Kratzer & Teplin, 2007; Kuga, 2007; Kuramoto & Tsuyuguchi, 2009). A number of books written by Japanese scholars on Lesson study that was translated into Vietnamese mostly have focused on its practice in learning community, in holistic schooling innovation (Saito et al., 2015; Sato & Sato, 2011).

In general, Lesson study refers to the ability of developing the curriculum management through a holistic approach, rather than individual teachers making improvements independently. Japanese Association for the Study of Educational Administration (JASEA) says school curriculum management leads to improved teachers' quality and fulfillment of educational guidance in their teaching (NASEM, 2011; JASEA, 2008). In other words, a key element of curriculum management is Lesson study to facilitate teacher training and improvements in teaching quality in schools.

2-3. Lesson study in Vietnam: Insights and the practice

Recently Vietnam education has engaged in educational innovation according to the implementation of the 2018 General Education Curriculum in this country. Though being newly revealed, a number of academic works has given some aspects to identify "Lesson study" critically as below.

Firstly, Lesson Study is defined in terms of its terminology and roles within teacher education in Vietnam. "*Nghiên cứu bài học*" (Lesson Study/Lesson Research) refers to the process of researching and improving teaching activities through specific lessons, themes, subjects, and classes conducted by a group of teachers within a school. This approach is designed to optimize the quality of learning for each student. During Lesson Study, teachers form small groups, collaboratively select a lesson for research from the curriculum, jointly develop a comprehensive and detailed lesson plan, observe one of the group members teaching the lesson, and then engage in discussion and analysis of the lesson, sharing results and applying the findings to practical teaching. The primary focus of Lesson Study is on researching and analyzing student learning through specific lessons, themes, subjects, and classes. Teachers in the subject-based group participate in organizing the lesson's teaching process, reflecting, sharing insights, and deriving methods for the most effective organization of teaching activities.

The characteristics of Lesson Study involve teachers organizing the teaching of individual lessons or themes within the curriculum, with prior preparation, collaboration, and cooperation throughout the entire Lesson Study process. This process is systematic and continuously improves and evolves. Lesson Study serves a dual purpose: it aims to enhance both teaching and educational practices, while simultaneously developing the professional competencies of teachers.

Secondly, the objectives of Lesson Study have been predominantly considered within the scope of in-service teacher education. According to global research, the three fundamental philosophies of Lesson Study are: (1) Ensuring learning opportunities for all students; (2) Ensuring professional development opportunities for all teachers; and (3) Building a learning community to innovate school culture. The World Association of Lesson Studies (WALS) highlights several benefits of Lesson Study: (1) It brings teachers, who often work in isolation, back to collaborative work; (2) It serves as the foundation for building collegiality, developing subject-based groups, and transforming the school into a "learning community," an "organization that learns"; (3) It prompts teachers to reconsider and improve their practices rather than assuming that their current methods are optimal; and (4) While teachers cannot change others or the past, they can change themselves and their future vision through Lesson Study (Ministry of Education and Training, 2014).

Thus, Lesson Study fundamentally differs from traditional teacher training methods. It is not about producing perfect lesson plans, nor is it a solitary activity conducted by individual teachers. Lesson Study is not a one-time process; it involves continuous improvement and development throughout each teacher's teaching and educational practice.

Lesson Study is a collaborative activity where teachers learn from the real-world learning experiences of students. In this process, teachers jointly design lesson plans, observe, reflect, and share their observations (primarily focusing on student learning). They also provide feedback on how the teaching strategies employed (e.g., lectures, questions, learning tasks assigned by the teacher) impact student learning. Based on these observations, teachers share their experiences, learn from one another, and make adjustments to lesson content and teaching methods for more effective daily instruction.

Lesson Study, according to this practice, is not intended for evaluating or ranking teaching sessions. Instead, teachers are encouraged to learn from each other, collaboratively identify why students are or are not learning, and propose measures to ensure that all students genuinely engage in learning. Through this process, teachers develop the ability to adapt lesson content and teaching methods flexibly, tailored to the specific needs of their students.

Thirdly, in the context of ongoing professional development for Vietnamese school teachers, Lesson Study is widely implemented with a structured and systematic process,

Chapter 10
Practice of 'Lesson Study' in Japan and Vietnam within the Contemporary Era

particularly within the framework of professional teacher meetings.

2-4. Designing demonstration lessons

- Demonstration lessons are either voluntarily registered by teachers or selected through discussion and consensus within the subject-based group, based on the specific objectives of the professional development session. The selection process ensures that all teachers within the group participate in turn.
- The teacher responsible for the demonstration lesson studies the subject curriculum, teaching plans, textbooks, and related teaching materials, collaborating with other teachers in the group to co-develop a detailed lesson plan. The design of the demonstration lesson plan, aimed at developing students' qualities and competencies, follows specific steps.

+ *Identifying learning objectives*: To define learning objectives that align with the required outcomes of the curriculum and serve as the foundation for constructing content and learning activities suitable for the current level of students, it is necessary to assess their existing knowledge, skills, and experiences. The objectives should be articulated using action verbs so that when these actions are performed, students exhibit specific behaviors that can be observed and measured. The learning objectives are evaluated across four levels: *1) Recognition: Recalling and repeating according to a model; 2) Comprehension: Presenting and explaining according to personal understanding, following instructions; 3) Application: Solving familiar problems or similar situations in learning and life; 4) Higher Application: Solving new problems or providing reasonable feedback in learning and life in a flexible manner.*

+ *Analyzing lesson content*: This step involves analyzing the content units specified in the curriculum and the lesson corresponding to the required outcomes expressed through action verbs. The analysis must clarify the content and logic of the content within the students' learning activities. The results of the analysis guide the selection and implementation of teaching methods, assessment of learning outcomes, selection of teaching materials, and design of the learning environment.

+ *Designing learning activities*: The design of learning activities must align with the objectives, required competencies, and learning qualities of the students, as well as the structure of the lesson content and the characteristics of the students. Learning activities should be designed with an approach that fosters and develops student competencies, organizing learning through a sequence of active, independent, and creative learning activities with appropriate organization, guidance, and support from the teacher. The sequence of learning activities includes: *1) Initiation activities, 2) Exploration, connection, and reflection activities, 3) Practice and drill activities, 4) Application, extension, and enhancement activities.*

+ *Assessing school infrastructure and teaching resources*: An assessment of the available school infrastructure, teaching equipment, and resources, such as classroom layout, student desks, teacher desks, blackboards, projection equipment, the condition of libraries, laboratories, subject-specific classrooms, and existing teaching tools, will help teachers develop plans to effectively utilize these resources and select appropriate teaching methods.

Based on the unified lesson plan design steps within the subject group, the demonstration teacher may proactively and flexibly adjust content, duration, teaching aids, methods, and teaching techniques, as well as the assessment of student learning processes, to suit the student population and teaching conditions, aligning with the development of student competencies and qualities. The demonstration teacher may exchange ideas and lesson content with colleagues within the subject group to improve the quality of the demonstration lesson. The discussion typically focuses on:

- *What type of lesson is this? (Is it for the introduction of new knowledge, review, practice, or hands-on activities?);*
- *How should this lesson be introduced? (Directly or indirectly? What is the most natural way to begin the lesson?);*
- *Is there a problem-based scenario used to introduce this lesson? (What kind of scenario? What are the anticipated solutions?);*
- *How is the lesson content divided into knowledge units? What corresponding teaching activities are planned? How will the teacher use questions to stimulate students' creative thinking?;*
- *What classroom organization is appropriate? How can teaching methods and teaching tools be used most effectively? What teaching techniques need to be employed? What are the specific words, actions, and gestures of the teacher? What content will be presented on the board?;*
- *What related educational content is appropriate to integrate? How does this impact student learning? How do students learn? What thoughts, words, actions, and behaviors are expected from students during the lesson? What are the anticipated products of student learning in this lesson? What are the expected challenges students might face in these learning activities? What are the anticipated situations, and how should they be handled? How should the lesson conclude? How will student learning outcomes be assessed during the lesson? What evidence will be used to evaluate student learning outcomes?*

After this discussion, the demonstration teacher will further develop the lesson plan, independently deciding on the lesson objectives, content, teaching tools, structure, and process, while analyzing and incorporating feedback as needed. Other members are responsible for detailed planning for observation and discussion during the lesson study.

Demonstration teaching: Based on the developed lesson plan, the demonstration teacher represents the group in conducting the lesson for the subject group to observe and analyze. During the lesson, if student learning situations arise that deviate from the planned design, the demonstration teacher may flexibly adjust the content, format, and teaching methods to align with student learning needs, ensuring that the lesson objectives are met.

- The demonstration teacher should closely observe student learning, paying attention to students who struggle with the material to provide timely guidance and optimal support for all students' learning.
- The demonstration teacher should avoid pre-teaching or rehearsing the content of the demonstration lesson to maintain student engagement and allow observers to analyze authentic learning situations during the lesson. Pre-teaching is discouraged as the primary goal of Lesson Study is for collaborative learning and experience-based understanding.

+ *Lesson observation*:

- Observers should sit in positions that allow easy observation, note-taking, filming, and diagramming of student seating arrangements (from either side, front, or back of the classroom).
- During observation, the focus should be on observing student learning activities combined with observing the organization and guidance of the teacher, based on the following criteria:
- Transferring learning tasks: Learning tasks should be clear and appropriate to the students' abilities, reflected in the expected product students must complete during the task; the method of task delivery should be lively and engaging, stimulating students' cognitive interest, and ensuring all students receive and are ready to perform the task.
- Executing learning tasks: Encourage students to cooperate and assist each other during the task, promptly identify any difficulties students face, and provide timely, appropriate, and effective support; ensure no student is «left behind».
- Presenting results and discussion: The format for presenting task results should align with the learning content and active teaching techniques employed, encouraging students to discuss the learning content with one another; any pedagogical situations that arise should be handled appropriately.
- Feedback and evaluation of task performance: Provide feedback on the process of task completion, analyze and evaluate the task performance and discussion contributions of students, aiming to build students' interest and confidence in learning, and improve learning outcomes; clarify the knowledge students have gained through the activity.

During observation, teachers are encouraged to take notes and record student learning activities to use during lesson analysis, without disrupting the teaching and learning process. Utilize techniques such as listening, observing, thinking, note-taking, filming, and photographing to collect data for analysis to answer questions like: *How do students learn? What difficulties do students encounter? Why? What changes are necessary to improve student learning outcomes?* Understanding how students learn is often challenging for observers, and the ability to sensitively observe student learning develops only after multiple observations within a Lesson Study context. Teachers can create seating charts to facilitate observation, combining overall classroom atmosphere observations with focused attention on selected student groups. Observing student behavior, facial expressions, gestures, and speech is crucial for understanding the relationship between student learning and the impact of teaching methods and content.

+ Discussion and analysis of the demonstration lesson

- The demonstration teacher shares the lesson objectives, new ideas, content changes, adjustments in teaching methods, and reflections on the lesson, including both satisfying and unsatisfying aspects of the demonstration.
- The subject group discusses and analyzes the demonstration lesson, focusing on:
Student learning activities: Students' readiness to complete learning tasks, their active, independent, creative, and cooperative engagement in the learning tasks, their active participation in presenting, discussing, and reflecting on their learning outcomes, and the accuracy and relevance of their learning products, as well as their attitudes and emotions during each activity.
Organizing learning activities: Methods of transferring learning tasks, observation, monitoring and identifying students' difficulties, strategies to support and encourage self-learning and cooperation among students, and analysis and feedback on student learning processes.
Factors influencing student learning activities: Lesson plan design (required outcomes, teaching aids, learning activities, etc.), interactions between students, student-teacher interactions, students' psychological and physiological conditions, classroom atmosphere, etc.

The criteria for analyzing the demonstration lesson include evaluating the effectiveness of student learning activities, assessing the organization and guidance provided by the teacher, and analyzing the outcomes. When analyzing classroom activities, the «Regulation 5555» (MOET, 2014) serves as a key reference tool in contemporary Vietnamese education.

Lesson study, within the way of professional teacher meetings (PTMs) considered as the critical dimension for in-service teacher education in Vietnam, would be successfully implemented with these working conditions.

In terms of **awareness, proficiency, and competence of management personnel**: In the context of reforming Lesson Study to meet the requirements of the 2018 General Education Curriculum, local education administrators and school management personnel need to shift their awareness, attitudes, and behaviors. They must take a proactive role in fostering confidence among teachers regarding the positive changes brought about by the new approach to Lesson Study, particularly in their relationships with colleagues and educators. Management personnel must accurately understand the significance and objectives of Lesson Study under the new requirements, master the new Lesson Study model, and possess the competence to manage, organize, and direct Lesson Study. They should also have the ability to persuade, support, and facilitate teachers' participation in Lesson Study, while flexibly addressing any challenges that arise during the process.

Secondly, **responsibilities of principals and vice principals** includes:

- Directing the development and approval of the professional activities plans within the subject groups; participating in, supporting, monitoring, and evaluating the effectiveness of these activities within their institutions.
- Organizing the implementation of professional activities according to regulations, with a sense of responsibility, self-awareness, and proactiveness in proposing content and methods to enhance the quality of these activities, ensuring the effective implementation of the General Education Curriculum.
- Timely identifying challenges and taking appropriate measures to address issues in professional activities within the subject groups; consolidating feedback from these groups and reporting to the Department of Education and Training during the implementation of professional activities at the school.

Thirdly, **responsibilities of subject group leaders** are:

- Proactively developing plans to innovate Lesson study according to the requirements of the 2018 General Education Curriculum.
- Encouraging teachers to register for specialized topics and demonstration lessons, ensuring that all teachers participate in Lesson study, attend classes, engage in discussions, and apply the lessons learned into practice.
- Organizing teachers to participate in the design and discussion of lesson plans, conducting demonstration lessons, attending classes, reflecting, and analyzing lessons based on student activities, and organizing meetings to draw lessons from these activities to improve teaching methods, assessment practices, and build a repository of practical experiences for daily application.

Then, fourthly, **awareness, proficiency, and competence of teachers**. Teachers are the "central figures" in the implementation of Lesson Study, both in specialized topics and lesson research. Teachers must shift their awareness, attitudes, and behaviors, taking an active role in participating in and implementing the Lesson Study process according to the new approach. They need to fully understand the significance and objectives of Lesson Study under the new requirements, master the new Lesson Study model, and possess the competence to execute the steps in the Lesson Study process.

In terms of the teachers, their **specific responsibilities** are:

- Understanding the content and methods of implementing professional activities according to the new requirements (specialized topics, Lesson Study).
- Registering to participate in groups that design specialized topics and demonstration lessons, actively thinking and creatively constructing new ideas/content and methods for lesson design.
- Learning to observe students, take notes, listen, share opinions, build collegial

relationships that are friendly, cooperative, and constructive, and drawing personal lessons from these activities.

Awareness, proficiency, and competence of students. Students should change their understanding of the purpose and significance of learning, developing the right motivations, interests, and drive for their studies. Active and proactive learning and collaboration among students will create favorable conditions for teachers during demonstration lessons.

Last but not least, **School Conditions** which conditions include the availability of materials, timetables, educational tools, and equipment. Additionally, the support and agreement obtained from students' families are also considered crucial components of the conditions necessary for the effective implementation of Lesson Study among Vietnamese school teachers.

3. Reflection

We find it quite familiar in researches of Lesson study in Japan and Vietnam that they mention, in a certain extent, the perspective of teacher education, specifically in-service teacher education. Works in both countries (contemporarily in Vietnam and the previous Japan) have focused on critically classroom observation. That's why, up to now, once Lesson study regarded, we mostly think of crucial classroom activities observed, analysed and the syllabus revised and adapted. Both countries consider Lesson study as the very good way to foster human resource in education, mainly focused on in-service teachers, their practice in classroom and improving their performance in career of teaching, thanks to PTMs and the regular deep discussions on teacher performance in physical classroom. Either understood in Vietnam or Japan, Lesson study is for the purpose of promoting professional career of educators and developing practical ability of teaching. It includes of analysing teaching and learning, instruction and learning. Those works mentioned above have showed that Lesson study is the science of educational method «clarifies the aim, content and method and tries to contribute to teaching practice» (Sato, 1996, p.270). Lesson study might probably be considered the connection between teacher education and in-service teacher training.

In terms of *scope in educational development*, in Vietnam, Lesson study has mainly been concerning a critical subject, engaged with a real classroom and crucial incidents happened in there. It might be supposed that works of Lesson study in Vietnam have mainly focused on *micro-term educational process* as how to zoom students' responses in classroom, what are the best standing points in classroom for the most effective observation, how the teachers response to students' unexpected behaviors. That explains the reason why Lesson study regarded in Vietnamese papers mentions a lot of teaching techniques including teaching methods, classroom observation as well as classroom behavioral management. Meanwhile, Lesson study in works of Japanese cultural background has mentioned a larger perspective, not only within a classroom, it spreads its scope to holistic school improvement, curriculum management, as well as contribution of learning community. To some extent, Lesson study refers other factors impacting education and schooling such as families, parents' involvement with their children and the teachers' activities. It means that the scope of Lesson study includes *in-class* and *off-class* dimensions, in *macro term* of education.

In terms of *vision in educational development*, Lesson study in Vietnam plays an important role in in-service teacher education. The literature review above mentions these works with teacher students (in-service teacher education), novice teachers as well as professional development for school teachers (namely in-service teacher education). Whereas, works in Japan have regarded Lesson study as an essential component in curriculum management and through a holistic approach of learning community, rather than individually and independently teachers' improvements.

4. Recommendations to Lesson Study Delivery in Vietnam as Continuing Professional Development for In-Service Teachers

Focusing on in-service teacher education, this book chapter gives a number of recommendations for terminology development of "Lesson study" in Vietnam as continuing professional development for K12 teachers.

Enhancement of school leadership and management capacity

It is essential to conduct training workshops aimed at enhancing the awareness and competencies of school managers regarding Lesson Study. This training should emphasize the importance of Lesson Study in fostering a culture of continuous professional development and school improvement. School leaders, including principals and vice principals, should be equipped to support and encourage Lesson Study initiatives, promoting teacher autonomy and leadership within a collaborative, bottom-up management model.

Comprehensive teacher training programs

Implement extensive training programs for teachers that focus on both the theoretical understanding and practical application of Lesson Study. These programs should aim to deepen teachers' comprehension of the methodology, its scope, and its relevance to classroom practices, particularly in alignment with Vietnam's 2018 General Education Curriculum (GEC). Teachers should be encouraged to participate actively in Lesson Study groups, fostering a collaborative learning environment that supports their professional growth.

Integration of lesson study in pre-service teacher education

Incorporate Lesson Study into the curriculum of pre-service teacher education programs. This integration would provide teacher students with hands-on experience in Lesson Study, preparing them for their future roles as educators. By engaging in Lesson Study during their training, pre-service teachers can develop critical reflective practices and collaborative skills that are essential for their professional development

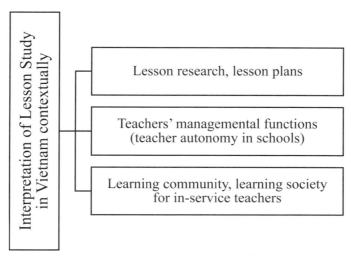

Diagram 2: Interpretation of Lesson Study in Vietnam Contextually for Teachers' Professional Development

and effective classroom management.

Improvement of school infrastructure and resource allocation

To facilitate the effective implementation of Lesson Study, it is crucial to ensure that schools are adequately equipped with the necessary infrastructure and resources. This includes optimizing classroom conditions, reducing student-teacher ratios, and enhancing the availability of teaching materials and technology. Additionally, fostering greater engagement from students' families and the wider community can provide valuable support for the Lesson Study process, contributing to a more holistic approach to educational development.

5. Conclusion

In conclusion, this paper has provided a critical examination of the cross-cultural perspectives on Lesson Study, specifically comparing its implementation and impact in Japan and Vietnam. The analysis highlights the significant differences in how Lesson Study has been adapted and integrated into the educational systems of both countries, despite their cultural and educational similarities. In Japan, Lesson Study has evolved into a comprehensive tool for professional development, curriculum management, and school improvement, whereas in Vietnam, its adoption remains more limited, focusing primarily on in-service teacher education within a narrower scope. The recommendations proposed in this paper emphasize the need for a broader and more strategic approach to Lesson Study in Vietnam. This includes enhancing the competencies of school leaders, providing extensive training for teachers, integrating Lesson Study into pre-service education, and improving school infrastructure to support this initiative effectively. By adopting these measures, Vietnam can leverage the full potential of Lesson Study as a means of continuous professional development for teachers, ultimately contributing to the advancement of its educational system. The findings and recommendations of this study underscore the importance of cross-cultural research in understanding and optimizing educational practices. Future research should continue to explore the contextual factors that influence the effectiveness of Lesson Study and other educational innovations, providing further insights that can inform policy and practice in diverse educational settings.

References

Akita, K., & Lewis, C. (2008). *Jyugyo no Kenkyu, Kyosi no Gakusyu* (Learn from Lessons, Teacher Inquiry and Lesson Study). Tokyo: Akasisyoten.

Fernandez, C., & Yoshida, M. (2004). *Lesson Study: A Japanese Approach to Improving Mathematics Teaching Learning.* NJ: Lawrence Erlbaum Associate.

Ha, V. T. (2018). Applying micro-teaching and jugyou kenkyuu (Lesson study) enhance students' teaching skills through the module of Geography teaching methodology at high schools. *Ho Chi Minh City University of Education, Journal of Science (Education Science)*, 15(5b), 105–116.

Huynh, T. T. D., & Thathong, K. (2017). Applying Lesson study among high school Biology teachers in Vietnam. *International Journal of Educational Science and Research*, 7(4), August 2017, 7–18.

Kratzer, C. C. & Teplin, A. S. (2007). From Lesson study to lesson link: Classroom-based professional development. 2007 Annual meeting of the American Educational Research Association (Chicago, IL, April 9–13).

Kuga, N. (2007). A study about the "model of reflective practitioner" in the specialty of the teacher: Based on the suggestion from the knowledge study of the teacher. *Bulletin of Center for Collaboration in Community*, Naruto University of Education 22.

Kuramoto, T. (2007). *The course of study and textbook, The Encyclopedia of Education Administration*, Japanese Association for the Study of the Education Administration, [JASEA], Thomson Learning Publisher.

Kuramoto, T., et al. (2014). *Lesson study and Curriculum Management in Japan.* Japan: Fukuro Publishing.

Kuramoto, T. (2018). *Amerikaniokeru karikyuramu manajimennto no kennkuyuu* (Curriculum Management in the USA; From the Perspective of Service-Learning). Japan: Fukuro Publishing.

Kuramoto, T., Ryan, A., Nguyen, N. P., & Takahashi, M. (2020). Initial Cross-Cultural research: Lesson study for Pre & In-service teacher education, presented in the symposium of the 2020 online international conference of WALS (World Association of Lesson study).

Le, T. M. H., & Tran, D. M. (2023). Innovation in Vietnam higher education in approaching to education for sustainable development. Intensive documents of Central Propaganda and Education Commission.

Le, T. T. H. (2014). Sinh hoat chuyen mon dua tren nghien cuu bai hoc – cong cu doi moi nha truong. *Vietnam Journal of Education*, 332(2), April 2014, 26–28.

Lewis, C. C., Perry, R. R., & Friedkin, S. (2011). Using Japanese Curriculum Materials to Support Lesson study Outside Japan: toward Coherent Curriculum. *Educational Studies in Japan International Yearbook*, 6, Japanese Educational Research Association.

Ministry of Education, Culture, Sports, Science and Technology in Japan (MEXT) (2016). *Syougakko to tyuugakkou tono rennkeinituiteno jittai tyousa* (The survey for integration between elementary schools and junior high schools).

Ministry of Education and Training of Vietnam (2014). Dispatch No. 5555/BGD-DT-GDTrH (signed October 18, 2014)—*huong dan sinh hoat to chuyen mon va doi moi kiem tra danh gia va phuong phap day hoc* (Guidelines of activities in subject-based teacher groups and innovation in assessment and teaching methods).

Ministry of Education and Training in Vietnam (2021). Decision 2222-QD-TTg in launching the program of digital transformation in vocational education up to the year of 2025 with the orientation of 2030.

Ministry of Education and Training in Vietnam (2024). Documents of intensive training "Development of education meeting the requirements of high quality labor resources"

Nakatome, T. (2001). *Sougouteki na gakusyuu nojikann, karikyruamu manajimennto no souzou* (Integrated Curriculum: How to create Curriculum Management). Tokyo: Nihonn kyouiku sougou kennkyuusyo.

Nakatome, T. (2005). *Karikyuramu manejimennto no teityaku katei* (The process of implementation for Curriculum Management). Tokyo: Kyouiku kaihatu kennkyuusyo.

National Association for the Study of Educational Methods (2011). *Lesson study in Japan*. Keisuisha, Hiroshima University, Japan.

Nguyen, T. D., & Nguyen, P. N. (2021). Social resources mobilization for general education development: A case study for secondary schools in Ho Chi Minh City, Vietnam. *Vietnam Journal of Education*, 5(2), 21–28. https://doi.org/10.52296/vje.2021.34

Nguyen, N. P., Ngo, V. T. H., & Nguyen, H. A. (2021a). *Huong dan to chuc sinh hoat chuyen mon thuc hien chuong trinh giao duc pho thong 2018—cap Tieu hoc* (Guidelines to process professional development for primary school teachers meeting the requirements of the 2018 GEC). Hanoi: University of Education Publisher.

Nguyen, N-P., Nguyen, D-T., & Kuramoto, T. (2021a). Reviews of 'Lesson study' reflected from works in Japan and Vietnam. Proceedings of Innovation in Learning Instruction in Teacher Education (ILITE). Hanoi National University of Education, 11th & 12th December 2021. ISBN 978-604-54-8739-6, 287–296.

Nguyen, T. K. (2018). Van dung nghien cuu bai hoc de phat trien nang luc thiet ke giao an day hoc mon Toan cho sinh vien chuyen nganh Giao duc tieu hoc o Dai hoc Dong Thap (Applying Lesson study for developing the competence of syllabus designing for undergraduates majored in Primary Education in Dong Thap University). *Vietnam Journal of Education*, 2, 61–65.

Nguyen, T. K. D. (2020). Phat trien nang luc giang day cua giao vien moi vao nghe thong qua hoat dong chuyen mon dua tren "nghien cuu bai hoc" (Contributing to the novice teachers' competences of teaching through lesson-study-based professional development). *Hanoi National University of Education, Journal of Science—Educational Sciences*, 65(4C), 49–56.

Pham, T. T. H., et al. (2018). Van dung nghien cuu bai hoc de phat trien cong dong hoc tap, nghien cuu truong hop tai truong trung hoc co so Nguyen Truc, Ha Noi. *Vietnam Journal of Education*, 430, 42–46.

Sato, M. (1996). *Kyouikuhouhougaku* (Educational Methodologies). Tokyo: Iwanamisyotenn.

Saito, E., Murase, M., Tsukui, A., & Yeo, J. (2015). *Nghien cuu bai hoc vi cong dong hoc tap—Lesson study for Learning community: A guide to sustainable school reform.* Translated by Khong Thi Diem Hang. Hanoi: University of Education Publisher.

Sato, M., & Sato, M. (2011). *Cong dong hoc tap: Mo hinh doi moi toan dien nha truong* (Learning community: The model for holistic school innovation). Translated by Khong Thi Diem Hang. Hanoi: University of Education Publisher.

Khong, T. D. H. (2021). Teacher Learning Through Dialogue: The Cases of Vietnamese Teachers. In D. Bao & T. Pham (Eds.), *Transforming Pedagogies Through Engagement with Learners, Teachers and Communities* (169–188). Springer Singapore. https://doi.org/10.1007/978-981-16-0057-9_11

Saito, E. (2021). The evolution of joint teacher observations and reflections as sites of heteroglossia and heteroopia: an actor–network theoretical discussion. *Reflective Practice*, 1–15. https://doi.org/10.1080/14623943.2021.1964946

Saito, E., Atencio, M., Khong, T. D. H., Takasawa, N., Murase, M., Tsukui, A., & Sato, M. (2018). The teacher as a 'colony': a case study of agentive responses to 'colonising' education policy in Vietnam. *Cambridge Journal of Education*, 48(1), 65–86. https://doi.org/10.1080/0305764x.2016.1240151

Saito, E., & Khong, T. D. H. (2017). Not just for special occasions: supporting the professional learning of teachers through critical reflection with audio-visual information. *Reflective Practice*, 18(6), 837–851. https://doi.org/10.1080/14623943.2017.1361921

Saito, E., Khong, T. D. H., & Tsukui, A. (2012). Why is school reform sustained even after a project? A case study of Bac Giang Province, Vietnam. *Journal of Educational Change*, 13(2), 259–287. https://doi.org/10.1007/s10833-011-9173-y

Saito, E., & Tsukui, A. (2008). Challenging common sense: Cases of school reform for learning community under an international cooperation project in Bac Giang Province, Vietnam. *International Journal of Educational Development*, 28(5), 571–584. https://doi.org/10.1016/j.ijedudev.2007.12.006

Saito, E., Tsukui, A., & Tanaka, Y. (2008). Problems on primary school-based in-service training in Vietnam: A case study of Bac Giang province. *International Journal of Educational Development*, 28(1), 89–103. https://doi.org/10.1016/j.ijedudev.2007.08.001

Takano, K. (1988). *Kyouiku katei keiei no rironn to jissai* (The theory and practice of Curriculum Management) Tokyo: Kyouiku kaihatu kennkyuusyo.

Tsukui, A. (2019). What makes a teacher 'act'. In M. Murase & A. Tsukui (Eds.), *Lesson study and Schools as Learning Communities: Asian School Reform in Theory and Practice* (90–109). Routledge. https://doi.org/10.4324/9781315690322

Tsukui, A., & Saito, E. (2018). Stroll into students' learning: Acts to unload teachers' values through the practices of Lesson study for learning community in Vietnam. *Improving Schools*, 21(2), 173–186. https://doi.org/10.1177/1365480217717530

Tsukui, A., Saito, E., Sato, M., Michiyama, M., & Murase, M. (2017). The classroom observations of Vietnamese teachers: mediating underlying values to understand student learning. *Teachers and Teaching*, 23(6), 689–703. https://doi.org/10.1080/13 540602.2017.1284055

Vu, T. T. H. (2020). Tang cuong sinh hoat chuyen mon theo nghien cuu bai hoc de phat trien nang luc day hoc doc hieu van ban thong tin cho giao vien Ngu van trung hoc (Developing high school teachers' competences of Comprehensive Reading by enhancing professional development through Lesson study). *Vietnam Journal of Education*, 472, 18–20.

Vu, T. S., & Nguyen, D. (2010). Nghien cuu bai hoc—mot cach tiep can phat trien nang luc nghe nghiep cua giao vien (Lesson study—a perspective of professional development for teachers). *Journal Science of Education*, 52, 45–48.

Yamasaki, H. (2016). Teachers and teacher education in Japan. *Graduate school education, Hiroshima University*, part III, 65, 19–28.

Authors

Dinh Chien TRAN[1], Nam-Phuong NGUYEN[2]*
1 Hung Vuong University, Vietnam
2 Hanoi National University of Education, Vietnam
*Corresponding author: ORCID 0000-0001-7344-1470
*Corresponding email: phuongnn@hnue.edu.vn

Chapter 11

Classroom Management: A Dimension of Lesson Study Encountered in Vietnam

Duc Giang NGUYEN, Hanoi National University of Education, Vietnam
Thi Phuong NGUYEN, Vietnam National University, Vietnam
Van Hai TA, National Academy of Educational Management, Vietnam
Minh-Yen NGUYEN, Scholar Vietnam Education System, Vietnam

Abstract

This chapter explores another facet of lesson study, namely classroom management, within the context of high school education in Vietnam. Classroom management encompasses a teacher's actions to organize students, space, time, and resources to enhance student learning in the classroom. The chapter delves into key aspects of classroom moderation, classroom behavioral management, and positive discipline in high school settings in Vietnam. It also emphasizes the importance of incorporating lesson study techniques and principles into classroom management. The chapter addresses three research questions: (i) Defining classroom management in the context of lesson study; (ii) Describing the dimensions for classifying classroom management in Vietnamese schools; and (iii) Illustrating insights into classroom management as a dimension of lesson study through practical examples from Vietnam. In consideration of the Japanese origins of the terminology associated with lesson study, this chapter explores its application within the Vietnamese school culture, offering recommendations and guidance of classroom management for in-service teachers currently working in schools.

Keywords: *Classroom management, classroom moderation, student behavioral management, positive discipline, high school student, Vietnam*

1. Introduction

Teacher education and classroom management are inextricably intertwined elements within the realm of education. Classroom management, the art of creating a conducive learning environment, and teacher education, the process of preparing educators, share a symbiotic relationship that profoundly impacts student learning outcomes.

In-service teacher education and continuing professional development (CPD) serve as vital avenues for enhancing educators' skills in classroom management. These programs provide opportunities for teachers to refine their strategies, update their knowledge base, and engage with contemporary pedagogical theories. Effective classroom management techniques not only foster an environment conducive to learning but also minimize disruptions, allowing teachers to focus on delivering quality instruction.

Moreover, teacher education programs increasingly integrate coursework and practicum experiences focused explicitly on classroom management strategies. By equipping educators with a repertoire of effective management techniques, these programs empower teachers to create inclusive, engaging, and structured learning environments.

Ultimately, the correlation between teacher education and classroom management underscores the significance of ongoing professional development in ensuring educators possess the requisite skills and knowledge to effectively manage diverse classroom settings, thereby optimizing student learning experiences.

This chapter would like to give the answers to three research questions including:

1. What should be the dimensions to describe the classification of classroom management?
2. What are the manifestations of classroom management in schools in Vietnam, and some techniques would be shown in terms of teachers' roles in their occupation?
3. How to illustrate the insights of classroom management as a dimension of Lesson Study with the examples provided in practice of Vietnam?

In this diagram:

- "Classroom Management" is depicted as a fragmental competence belonging to systematically the teaching competence (Freeman et al., 2014).
- "Lesson Study" is another standalone concept, representing the collaborative professional development approach where teachers work together to plan, observe, and refine lessons. Lesson study can enhance long-term learning in classroom teaching by analyzing teaching methods and focusing on individual learning outcomes (Tall, 2007).
- Classroom Management influences Lesson Study: Effective classroom management creates an environment conducive to collaborative activities like lesson study. When teachers can effectively manage their classrooms, they have more time and mental space to engage in professional development activities like lesson study (Freeman et al., 2014; Tall, 2007).
- Lesson Study influences Classroom Management: Through lesson study, teachers can discover and implement new classroom management techniques. They can observe how different management strategies affect student behavior and learning outcomes, leading to improvements in their classroom management skills (Freeman et al., 2014; Tall, 2007).

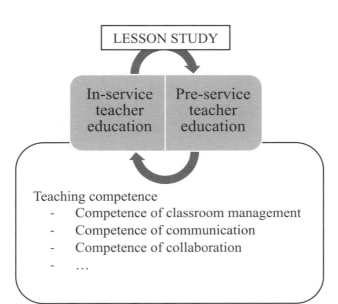

Diagram 1: The Correlation between Lesson Study and Classroom Management—Namely as One Component of In-Service Teacher Competence

This diagram illustrates the dynamic relationship between classroom management and lesson study, emphasizing how they support and enhance each other in the context of teacher professional development and instructional practice.

2. Overview of Classroom Management

2-1. What is classroom management?

Classroom management encompasses all the actions undertaken by a teacher to arrange students, space, time, and resources in a way that facilitates student learning. According to Brophy and Evertson (1976), classroom management skills hold paramount significance in determining teaching success, as evidenced by various teacher effectiveness surveys, whether assessed through student learning outcomes or evaluations. Hence, these skills are fundamental and indispensable. A teacher lacking proficiency in classroom management skills is likely to encounter limitations in achieving productive outcomes (Brophy & Evertson, 1976). Classroom management proficiency entails actions directed towards two primary objectives:

1. To encourage student participation and collaboration across all classroom activities.
2. To establish an environment conducive to effective learning.

An effectively managed classroom features a set of procedures and routines that structure the learning environment (Simonsense et al., 2008). These procedures and

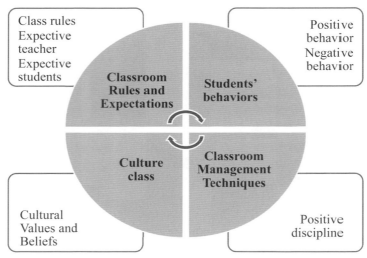

Diagram 2: Components of Classroom Management

routines streamline the myriad activities occurring in the classroom, promoting smooth functionality and minimizing stress. These activities encompass reading, note-taking, group work, class discussions, interactive games, and content creation. An adept teacher ensures active involvement and cooperation from each student in these activities and beyond.

2-2. Structure of classroom management

The structure of classroom management refers to the organization and strategies that teachers use to create a positive and effective learning environment for students (Freeman et al., 2014). Effective management is essential for maintaining order, fostering student engagement, and promoting a conducive atmosphere for learning.

Classroom rules and expectations

Establish clear and concise classroom rules and expectations. Make sure they are communicating to students at the beginning of the school year or term.

Discuss the reasons behind these rules and the importance of adhering to them.

Behavioral expectations

Clearly define behavioral expectations for students. Let them know what behaviors are acceptable and what consequences may follow if they violate the rules.

Be consistent in applying consequences and rewards.

Positive behavior in students is characterized by actions, attitudes, and conduct that contribute to a productive, respectful, and conducive learning environment. It reflects not only academic success but also personal and social growth. Here are some examples of positive student behavior: Active Engagement; Responsibility; Effective Communication; Cooperation; Problem-Solving; Empathy; Help-Seeking Behavior; Conflict Resolution; Goal Setting; Self-Motivation; Resilience; Positive Attitude; Appreciation for

Diversity; Time Management; Courtesy; Honesty and Integrity; Accountability; Active Listening.

Negative behavior in students refers to actions, attitudes, or conduct that disrupt the learning environment, hinder academic progress, or exhibit disrespect and disregard for rules and expectations. Understanding and addressing negative behaviors is important for maintaining a conducive and safe educational setting. Here are some examples of negative student behavior: Disruptive Behavior; Lack of Respect; Insubordination; Bullying; Cheating and Plagiarism; Tardiness and Absenteeism; Disengagement; Destructive Behavior; Disrespecting Personal Boundaries; Irresponsibility; Fighting; Habitual Lying; Disrespect for School Property.

Classroom Management Techniques

Positive discipline is an approach to child or student behavior management that focuses on teaching appropriate behaviors and promoting a positive and respectful learning or family environment. It aims to foster self-discipline, responsibility, and social skills in children or students, rather than relying on punitive measures. Here are some key principles and strategies of positive discipline:

Clear Expectations: Set clear and age-appropriate expectations for behavior. Make sure children or students understand what is expected of them.

Effective Communication: Encourage open and respectful communication between adults and children or students. Listen actively and provide opportunities for them to express their thoughts and feelings.

Teaching and Modeling: Teach appropriate behaviors and values through modeling. Demonstrate the behaviors you want to see in children or students.

Logical Consequences: Instead of punishment, apply logical consequences that are related to the misbehavior. For example, if a child refuses to clean up their toys, they may temporarily lose access to those toys.

Problem-Solving: Involve children or students in problem-solving when conflicts or misbehavior occur. Encourage them to brainstorm solutions and make choices.

Consistency: Be consistent in applying rules and consequences. Children or students need to know that rules are consistently enforced.

Encouragement and Positive Reinforcement: Acknowledge and praise positive behaviors and efforts. Positive reinforcement can be more effective than punishment in encouraging desirable behavior.

Time-In vs. Time-Out: Instead of using time-outs as a form of punishment, consider using "time-ins" where you spend time with the child or student to discuss their behavior and feelings.

Empathy: Show empathy and understanding towards children or students. Recognize and validate their emotions, even when correcting behavior.

Natural Consequences: Allow children or students to experience natural consequences when appropriate. For example, if a student doesn't complete their homework, they may receive a lower grade.

Choices and Autonomy: Offer choices within limits. This helps children or students feel a sense of autonomy and control over their decisions.

Family or Classroom Meetings: Hold regular family or classroom meetings to discuss rules, expectations, and address concerns collectively. Encourage everyone's input.

Learning Moments: View misbehavior as an opportunity for learning and growth. Discuss what went wrong and how to make better choices next time.

Parent/Teacher-Child/Student Relationship: Build strong, trusting relationships with children or students. A positive relationship can enhance the effectiveness of positive discipline.

Self-Reflection: Adults should also engage in self-reflection to evaluate their own reactions and behaviors. Model self-awareness and the ability to admit mistakes.

Positive discipline aims to create a nurturing and respectful environment where children or students develop a sense of responsibility for their actions and learn to make positive choices. It focuses on long-term behavioral and character development rather than short-term compliance through punishment.

Culture class

Cultural values in a classroom context refer to the beliefs, customs, and norms that shape the behavior, interactions, and expectations of students and educators within a particular cultural or educational setting. These values play a significant role in shaping the classroom culture and influencing how teaching and learning occur. Here are some ways cultural values can manifest in the classroom: Respect for Diversity; Inclusivity; Cultural Sensitivity; Language and Communication; Teaching Styles; Hierarchy and Authority; Parental Involvement; Conflict Resolution; Dress Code; Cultural Celebrations.

It's essential for educators to be culturally responsive and adaptable in their teaching to create an inclusive and respectful classroom environment that values and respects the cultural diversity of their students. Acknowledging and understanding these cultural values can enhance the teaching and learning experience for all students.

In recent years, there are many behavioral issues of Vietnamese students that need attention, in which the issue of school bullying is one of the most alarming and needs attention.

Research results at Hanoi high schools show the phenomenon of actively committing violence against friends and being subjected to violence have become quite common in high schools with more than 50% of students. Reported having experienced violence in at least one form and more than 33% of students reported having experienced direct peer violence (hitting each other, threatening) or indirectly through social networks. Students tend to abuse social networks related to violence online is more common, which includes both proactive violence against friends as well as being subjected to peer violence (threats, threats), through social networks. Bullying friends takes the form of both physical and mental violence, in both direct and indirect forms indirectly through social networks can have negative consequences and impacts on learning, physical health and mental health, affecting the psychology and development of students (Duong, 2017).

Picture of classroom management in Vietnam—visualization in Lesson Study of junior high schools
Reality in Vietnam: challenges in classroom management
Illustration for student activities in high schools

(Source: Vinschool Education System, Hanoi City, Vietnam)

A study on 1,040 middle and high school students in Hanoi and City. Ho Chi Minh City in 2019 showed that 75.7% of students participated in traditional bullying and 32.5% of students participated in online bullying to varying degrees, from 1 to 2 times during the school year. to everyday, with different roles as perpetrator, victim or both.

A study conducted in 2019 on 482 students at 4 middle schools showed that these students all experienced at least 1 incident of school bullying in the previous three months up to the time of the study. In that case, many students choose to respond with negative thoughts, negative emotions and negative actions. This affects the mental health, learning and life of students, even they become the perpetrators of violence to others (Nguyen, 2020).

Statistical data at the Conference to evaluate the prevention and control of school violence held in 2022 (data compiled from reports of 49/63 provinces and cities) show that, in 5 years (from the school year) 2017–2018 to the 2021–2022 school year), the total number of school violence cases occurring is 2,624 cases, with 7,209 subjects involved. In particular, the school years 2017–2018 and 2018–2019 had the highest number of school violence cases and tended to decrease in both the number of cases and the number of participants. The school year 2021–2022 has a total of 386 cases/1,161 related subjects, the number of students at risk of being involved in school violence is 935 students.

Although reported data shows that school violence in Vietnam in recent years has gradually been limited, experts believe that the current situation of school violence is complex. Many incidents involve a large number of participants, using dangerous weapons, leading to serious consequences. Many school violence cases are committed by female students. Many incidents were videotaped and distributed on social networking platforms or shared on associations and groups. The forms of school violence are also becoming more and more diverse (slandering each other online, using, grouping treatment, dividing into associations, groups right in a collective, ...).

Facing that situation, education experts made recommendations to schools to strengthen the work of building school culture; seriously implement cultural behavior in schools. Educating students on ethics, lifestyle and life skills so as not to be affected by school violence in particular and social evils. Schools also need to strengthen the relationship between families and schools in student education management; regularly two-way communication between the school and family about the school's activities, learning and training situation, abnormal signs to coordinate in implementing measures to educate students on ethics and behavior born.

Classroom management techniques
Classroom moderation that includes class rule setting, seating assignments, and building positive classroom climate.

Meanwhile the ***behavioral management techniques*** is about maintaining and reinforcing appropriate student behaviors, while limiting and stamping out inappropriate student behaviors. Corresponding to these two tasks are the component skills: Attention, guidance and encouragement skills; Active ignorance and navigation skills; Silence discipline skills; The skill of determining logical consequences.

Practical guidance on building classroom management strategies: A showcase of a multiple-level school in Hanoi, Vietnam
It is divided into five levels: preschool, primary school, secondary school, high school, and higher education. Formal education consists of twelve years of basic education. Basic education consists of five years of primary education, four years of secondary education, and three years of high school education. The majority of basic education students are enrolled on a daily basis. The main goals are general knowledge improvement, human resources training and talent development.

A private school in Hanoi can be considered a prime example of building a positive discipline model and effort in committing to a learning environment where exemplary behavior is a top priority.

Students at this school are educated to become individuals with good character; to live with ideals and responsibilities; to have a developing mindset, ready to face and overcome life's challenges; to possess the ability to handle issues related to social interaction based on moral standards, social rules, and legal regulations; thereby becoming useful citizens contributing to the common development of the community and society. To achieve this educational goal, five core values are set for students to guide the entire curriculum, training methods, and the school's involvement with students, including discipline education. These values are: Inquisitiveness, Proactiveness, Integrity, Creativity, and Respect.

The highest value that positive discipline brings to the school is to make the school and teachers proud of their students, and each student is proud of their school. To achieve this, it is necessary to create a friendly and harmonious environment where students are always enthusiastic and make an effort to present their best selves, both in and outside the classroom. In addition, the school also encourages, praises, and rewards good behavior. With this direction, the school has built a behavior management model and student discipline guidance, encouraging students to cultivate self-discipline and express core values, emphasizing integrity and respect through a system of conduct points. The school aims to promote a collaborative approach in managing students with inappropriate behavior, helping teachers and staff support students positively, while providing information to students about the form and level of punishment when they engage in inappropriate behavior that needs correction.

The objectives of the conduct point management model
This behavior management model aims to achieve three objectives:

- Cultivate a positive behavioral culture by guiding and supporting students to meet high standards in all aspects of school life.
- Help students develop a sense of right and wrong, which serves as a foundation for building and nurturing relationships, as well as awareness of the rights, emotions, and physical and mental health of everyone around them.
- Enable students to self-regulate their behavior and practice responsibility for the consequences of their actions.

The principle of encouragement and praise
At this school, any behavioral regulations emphasize a positive approach such as encouragement and praise, rather than criticism and punishment. Teachers, support staff, and advisors provide constructive advice to students as part of focusing on positive approaches to maintain and improve students' behavior and life skills. It cannot be denied that praising students to build a positive learning environment, and praise extends to the support process, stimulating students to reflect and draw lessons for

themselves. There, teachers and staff can praise and adjust students' conduct points if they show improved actions beyond expectations and a change in their conduct, which can serve as an example for other students. Teachers and staff can praise students in various ways, for example:

- Provide positive feedbacks or encouraging smiles;
- Write positive comments on students' assignments;
- Acknowledge positive actions in group activities, events, and locations outside the classroom;
- Give positive feedback to parents about students through verbal and written communication;
- Increase student responsibilities;
- Display meaningful and eye-catching examples of students' good work;
- Share the tasks that students have excelled in with the whole class;
- Display students' official awards, honors, and certificates.

Delivery of the student behavior management system using conduct points

- Students who adhere to the School Rules will earn 100 conduct points in one month;
- Students who violate the School Rules will be subject to appropriate disciplinary actions, including the deduction of conduct points;
- The deduction of conduct points for students will be updated in the School's Education Management software and carried out by any teacher or staff member involved in the student behavior education process;
- The semester's conduct point is the average conduct point for the months in that semester.

If students wish to improve their conduct points, they can participate in the school's projects, community projects, or individual projects proposed by students themselves that bring value to the community. These projects will be assessed by the homeroom teacher and approved by the School Principal. Depending on the project's results, role, and level of contribution, the School Principal will decide the reward points for students. Students who show significant improvement may be upgraded by a maximum of one behavior grade or evaluation result for that semester.

Please note that projects can be carried out within the school or in the community, but they are not academic projects, as the goal is to cultivate moral awareness in students.

Projects that students have undertaken or participated in to contribute value to the community, with the aim of improving behavior include activities such as raising awareness among adolescent students aged 10 to 15 in the Hai Ba Trung District about the dangers and consequences of electronic cigarettes. Community fundraising projects involving handmade scented candles were conducted, with all funds raised being donated by the student group to a volunteer fund that supports underprivileged ethnic minority children in attending school.

Guidance on how to support and stimulate students to reflect and learn from their actions for themselves

The ultimate purpose of disciplinary education is not punishment but to provide support and stimulate students to reflect and learn from their actions. This practice empowers students, helping them learn from their mistakes, understand the impact of their behavior, and ultimately, develop themselves. It enables students to take ownership of their actions, learn from errors, grasp the consequences of their behavior, and, in turn, helps them grow personally. It teaches them how to make better decisions and problem-solve effectively. There are many benefits to supporting and stimulating students to reflect and learn from their actions, such as:

- Building relationships;
- Helping everyone feel respected;
- Providing opportunities for fair exchange and decision-making;
- Involving students, teachers, and parents in problem-solving;
- Encouraging everyone to take responsibility for their behavior.

One common mistake made by many teachers in various schools is not dedicating enough time and necessary patience when dealing with inappropriate student behavior. It is easy to react with anger and immediately apply punishment, bypassing the step of providing support and stimulating students to reflect. Asking the right, appropriate questions plays a pivotal role in helping students feel heard, express themselves, have the opportunity to reflect, adjust their behavior, and rectify their mistakes.

Conclusion

In conclusion, the symbiotic relationship between teacher classroom management and lesson study unveils a profound synergy essential for fostering effective teaching practices and student learning outcomes. Classroom management serves as the bedrock upon which the edifice of lesson study stands, providing the structure, discipline, and conducive environment necessary for meaningful educational experiences. Conversely, lesson study, with its collaborative, reflective, and iterative approach to instructional design, fortifies classroom management by empowering teachers with pedagogical insights, strategies, and a deep understanding of student needs.

Through meticulous planning, observation, and reflection inherent in lesson study, teachers refine their classroom management techniques, identifying areas for improvement and implementing evidence-based interventions tailored to individual and collective student dynamics. Moreover, lesson study cultivates a culture of continuous improvement and professional growth among educators, enriching their repertoire of classroom management strategies with innovative approaches rooted in research and best practices. Ultimately, the integration of teacher classroom management and lesson study engenders a dynamic ecosystem where effective discipline, student engagement, and academic achievement flourish. By embracing this holistic approach, educators cultivate vibrant learning communities where every student thrives, underscoring the transformative power of synergy between pedagogy and practice.

References

Brophy, J. E., & Evertson, C. M. (1976). *Learning from Teaching: A Developmental Perspective*. Allyn and Bacon. https://books.google.com.vn/books?id=pGQkAQAAMAAJ

Conroy, M. A., Sutherland, K. S., Snyder, A., Al-Hendawi, M., & Vo, A. (2009). Creating a positive classroom atmosphere: Teachers' use of effective praise and feedback. *Beyond Behavior*, 18(2), 18–26.

Duong, H. T. T. (2017). School violence in high school students: research results and recommendations [Vietnamese: Hành vi bạo lực ở học sinh trung học phổ thông: Kết quả nghiên cứu và đề xuất giải pháp]. *Journal of Educational Sciences*, 136, 93–97.

Freeman, J., Simonsen, B., Briere, D., & Macsuga-Gage, A. (2014). Pre-Service Teacher Training in Classroom Management. *Teacher Education and Special Education*, 37, 106–120. https://doi.org/10.1177/0888406413507002.

Gulbrandson, K. (2012). *Three Ways to Foster a Positive Classroom Climate*. https://www.cfchildren.org/blog/2012/08/key-factors-in-creating-a-positive-classroom-climate/

Ministry of Education and Training (2020). *Promulgate regulations for junior high schools, high schools and multiple-level high schools*. Hanoi, Vietnam. Retrieved from https://vanban.chinhphu.vn/default.aspx?pageid=27160&docid=201098

Nguyen, H. T. M. (2020). Manifestations of negative responses of students who are victims of school bullying in junior high schools in Hanoi City [Vietnamese: Một số biểu hiện ứng phó tiêu cực của học sinh bị bạo lực học đường tại các trường trung học cơ sở ở thành phố Hà Nội]. *Vietnam Journal of Education*, 491, 22–27.

Simonsen, B., Fairbanks, S., Briesch, A., Myers, D., & Sugai, G. (2008). Evidence-based Practices in Classroom Management: Considerations for Research to Practice. *Education and Treatment of Children*, 31, 351–380. https://doi.org/10.1353/ETC.0.0007.

Tall, D. (2007). Setting lesson study within a long-term framework of learning. https://doi.org/10.1142/9789812835420_0003.

Authors

Duc Giang NGUYEN[1]*, Thi Phuong NGUYEN[2], Van Hai TA[3], Minh-Yen NGUYEN[4]

1   Hanoi National University of Education, Vietnam

2   Vietnam National University, Vietnam

3   National Academy of Educational Management, Vietnam

4   Scholar Vietnam Education System, Vietnam

*Corresponding author: ORCID 0000-0002-4616-5199

*Corresponding email: giangnd@hnue.edu.vn

Part 3.

School-Based Curriculum Management
from the Perspective of Lesson Study and
Teacher Education in Japan

Chapter 12

Creating Learning Communities for Home Economics Teachers and Knowledge Management: Under the Times of Rapid Change and Unpredictable Society

Kaoru HORIUCHI, Yokohama National University
Sachiko NAKANISHI, Yokohama National University

Abstract

The Society 5.0 era is ongoing, and people's work and lifestyles must change dramatically. Amid such rapid societal changes, improving teachers' abilities has been emphasized as a response to school education. It is proposed that students realize optimal individualized and collaborative learning. Along with teachers promoting ICT-based instruction, in-service teacher education has also permeated for introduced online implementation.

In such a social situation, we researched home economics teachers' knowledge creation mechanisms to utilize each teacher's "knowledge" and help them grow as teachers. We analyze actual voluntary training sessions to determine the kind of place needed for new "knowledge" through collaborative thinking and dialogue with others and for home economics teachers' growth.

We analyzed case examples to explain how a place where the "knowledge" inherent in each teacher is created into new "knowledge" and where the learning of home economics teachers leads to their growth should be.

1. The Social Background and the Improvement Trends of Teachers' Qualifications

The ongoing Society 5.0 era is a technological revolution and a societal transformation expected to change people's work and lifestyles dramatically. These technological innovations and social transformations are about economic development and solving pressing social issues such as aging societies and declining populations.

The Sustainable Development Goals, adopted at the UN Summit in September 2015, are not just goals to be achieved by 2030 but a global mission to solve social issues such as poverty, conflict, climate change, and infectious diseases. Central ministries, agencies, local governments, universities, corporations, NPOs, and NGOs are crucial in this endeavor.

Amid such rapid societal changes, improving teachers' abilities has been emphasized as a response to school education. The final report of the Central Council for Education (CCE) presented the importance and necessity of the "establishment of an image of teachers who continue to learn" in the "Policy for the Comprehensive Improvement of Teachers' Quality and Ability throughout their Teaching Careers" published in August 2012 (Ministry of Education, Culture, Sports, and Technology: MEXT 2012).

Another critical report on teachers' abilities and career development from the CCE was presented in December 2015 (MEXT, 2015). As it was only written in Japanese, the translated title in English was "Improvement of the Qualified Competencies of Teachers for Future School Education: Toward the Establishment of a Teacher Training Community where teachers learn and enhance each other."

The critical report on teachers' abilities and career development from the CCE in December 2015 highlighted the urgent need for systemic reform to support teachers who continue to learn. The report suggested collaboration and cooperation among education boards and universities, promoting the enhancement of in-school training and supporting voluntary training at educational centers.

The recent CCE report published in January 2021 was "Toward the Construction of 'Contemporary Japanese-Style School Education (Reiwa no Nihon-gata gakkou kyouiku): Realization of Optimal Individualized and Collaborative Learning that draws out the Potential of All Children." The role of schools has been reaffirmed during the COVID-19 pandemic and the rapid changes in society. Great attention has been paid to distance and online education to guarantee learning, and ICT is essential as a fundamental tool to support school education. Therefore, along with the acceleration of the Global and Innovation Gateway for All (GIGA), the report calls for measures to improve the ICT-based instructional skills of in-service teachers and training programs at the national and local levels and promote collaboration with universities in training programs for education boards and other organizations. Practical methods, such as ICT equipment and online implementation, are needed (MEXT, 2021).

Furthermore, the teacher license renewal system, in effect since 2009, requires these licenses to be renewed every ten years, however, the system dissolved in July 2022. Subsequently, the system's future direction was set so that teachers could learn to optimize individual and collaborative learning on their initiative (MEXT, 2022).

In this context, the expansion of online training, training methods that use the Internet and independently select learning content—is recommended. A system that teachers can access and learn in their free time has been promoted.

2. Initiative-Taking Training Opportunities to Support "Teachers Who Continue to Learn"

In the future, teachers with autonomous learning attitudes must provide proper learning in response to changing societies and environments. Especially for public school teachers, each municipality has set up teacher development indicators for the qualities and abilities teachers should get, and based on the system, teacher training programs have been implemented for new and other career-oriented teachers.

Based on this reform trend, Kitada (2017) examined the conditions necessary to guarantee teachers' learning as professionals using three questions: "Why do they learn?", "What do they learn?" and "Where do they learn?" She said, "To guarantee learning as a profession, teachers must train themselves based on the public mission of the teaching profession as professionals." She also noted that "promoting the construction of standards and reforming schools into places where professionals can learn will be important issues," Further, she emphasized that "this is an urgent task that cannot be postponed."

While teacher development is accelerating, Geshi (2013) highlighted that passive training will not lead to developing an attitude of "continuing to learn." He argued that teachers' voluntary training should be allowed so that the system can produce "teachers who continue to learn."

Sato (2015), in a survey of what was most effective in improving classroom practice, found that "the most effective innovative teaching was reflection on one's classroom practice, followed by case studies of classes taught by colleagues in the same subject or the same grade. The next most effective method was in-school classroom training. The second most effective approach was training by the municipal board of education or union. Furthermore, he has said that "teachers do not learn and mature alone" and the importance of "the school becoming a community of professional learning" (ibid., 119).

However, Imazu (2012) highlighted that learning motivation occurs "only when each teacher is intrinsically motivated to learn despite challenges at the school site" and stated that there should be flexibility in preparing the learning opportunities that should be provided and how. Teachers must take part in training with the will to learn independently to develop their abilities. They need a place to learn together to pursue their educational issues.

3. Current Situation and Issues Surrounding Home Economics Teachers

Home economics education in Japan is included in the curriculum as a required subject for boys and girls from the fifth grade of elementary school through high school. The subject has changed in response to the social movement toward a gender-equal society. In addition to knowledge and skills related to food, clothing, and housing, economics education has become a problem-solving study that addresses various issues necessary for living and decision-making, including lifestyle design, consumer economics, sustainable lifestyles, infant development, the welfare of older people, and family relationships. Due to the variety and specificity of the content, teachers must devise daily teaching materials and refine their lessons.

According to an earlier study, teachers are extremely busy with daily preparations for practical training and work, and there is no teacher in the school with whom they can consult about their subject matter (Horiuchi, 1999). The national trend in teacher allocation is that one full-time teacher is always present in areas with the most significant schools. However, in areas with many small schools, teachers in charge of non-licensed subjects and part-time teachers are employed (Uesato et al., 1999). Gathering the latest information on teaching topics such as welfare and the environment, which change over time, is challenging (Ogura et al., 2009).

Bias in expertise and busyness have also been highlighted (Takagi, 2013). There is insufficient support for non-licensed teachers, such as training to improve teaching skills, and limitations in improving teaching skills caused by this situation (Hikage et al., 2019).

Horiuchi (2008) focused on male home economics teachers, who are a minority among home economics teachers; she pointed out that for them to enhance their competence as "home economics teachers," there is a need for a network and exchange among teachers who can study and learn from each other. Such a network allows collaborative learning among teachers that transcends gender. Horiuchi (2018) surveyed university teachers in charge of home economics education at teacher-training universities and faculty nationwide about the actual state of teacher training and support.

The results showed three main problems: (1) lack of time to research teaching materials owing to busy schoolwork, (2) lack of opportunities for class support and information exchange, and (3) lack of knowledge. This suggests that teachers, including part-time teachers who do not have training opportunities, should be encouraged to undertake new tasks in areas where they are weak or strong.

Support is needed to provide a place for various home economics teachers, including part-time teachers with no training opportunities, teachers with weak or strong areas, and veterans who seek new knowledge. Such training opportunities will become cooperative places where every teacher can connect across schools and share wisdom and information gained from their experiences.

4. Knowledge Creation Mechanism of Home Economics Teachers

Each home economics teacher has a different expertise and skill. In addition, through practical and experiential lessons, students expanded their learning perspectives from home to the community and society. Students also consider their own lives through home economics lessons. Home economics is not limited to knowledge and skills but asks students questions with more than one correct answer, leading to decision-making with value.

Through these practical experiences, we have accumulated much "knowledge." However, the amount of this "knowledge" remains closed in teachers' minds. Teachers do not update their knowledge. They struggle to learn and exchange knowledge gained through their careers and expertise. Their knowledge is not fully used to build competence.

One reason may be that teachers do not recognize that knowledge should be shared with other teachers and, therefore, do not express it or that some knowledge may be

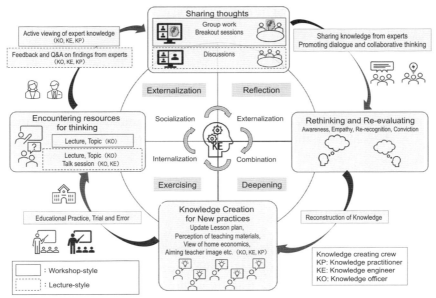

Figure 1: Knowledge Management Model for Home Economics Teachers

challenging to convey. Although there is a will to share, there are few opportunities. As home economics is a subject that deals with life itself and has multiple correct answers, simply repeating practices based on each home economics teacher's limited "knowledge" is insufficient to conduct proper classes. Therefore, home economics teachers must continue to develop their knowledge. We need an unprecedented place and mechanism to use each teacher's "knowledge" and help them grow as teachers.

In an earlier study in business administration that focused on knowledge, especially tacit knowledge, Nonaka and Takeuchi (1996) theorized that "knowledge creation management" is essential to create organizational knowledge for innovation in business management and disseminate it to the world. Consequently, knowledge has become a global movement. They divided human knowledge into two categories: explicit knowledge, expressed in formal and systematic language, and tacit knowledge, which is personal and rooted in each person's experience.

They also considered the interaction between formal and tacit knowledge, individual and organizational, as "organizational knowledge creation," explaining that it involves experience, trial and error, thinking, and learning from others to generate ideas. They proposed the "SECI model" as a knowledge transformation process.

The "knowledge management" proposed by Nonaka and Takeuchi (1996) does not confine the <knowledge> inherent in everyone, but rather, through the interaction of tacit and formal knowledge, individuals and organizations, it is utilized by learning together among home economics teachers, shared and refined in "a place of learning through horizontal relationships = home economics teacher community," and individually acquired as new.

This leads to getting new knowledge, developing the ability to continue thinking and questioning, and supporting their practice to realize their personal growth. We propose a variant of the SECI model shown in Figure 1, devised in response to the community of home economics teachers.[1]

We analyze actual voluntary training sessions to figure out the kind of place needed for new "knowledge" through collaborative thinking and dialogue with others and for home economics teachers' growth. Next, case examples are introduced to explain how a place where the "knowledge" inherent in each teacher is created into new "knowledge" through collaborative thinking and dialogue with others and where the learning of home economics teachers leads to their growth should be.

5. Case Study: How Teachers Improve Their Competence with Knowledge Management Systems

In this case study, the author organized a voluntary training program. This workshop is held once a month for home economics teachers from elementary to high school, those involved in home economics teacher training at universities, and those connected with the author.[2] The third workshop in September 2023 was held online. The workshop consisted of selecting Internet content that could be used as home economics teaching materials, introducing them to the participants, and having them discuss and report in groups on how they could use the content in their classes. The participants were also asked to discuss and report back to each other on how these contents could be used in their classes. The seven participants in this session did not include the organizers.

After the breakout session, the entire group shared their opinions. In response to the post-training survey, all participants showed satisfaction with the training session's content and the tips for their classes and teaching materials.

The workshop theme, which was held five months later, was a report by a teacher who had used the Internet content and ICT methods introduced in an earlier workshop. Ten middle and high school home economics teachers took part in the workshop. Because of the online nature of the event, the participants living in various locations, from the Tohoku region to the Tokai region of Japan, took part. They were teachers working in schools in distant cities where they would not usually see each other. Many teachers were acquainted with the author through previous public workshops or were university graduates, but many did not know each other. Even so, they could exchange ideas on topics familiar to them as home economics teachers. This feature of ease of participation can only be achieved online.

The workshop content was a report by a high school teacher who taught based on the information she had gained from taking part in the third workshop. The content included a video recipe created by students who learned about snacks for toddlers and an initiative in which students posted reports on the cloud using Google Classroom and reviewed them with others. Participants listened to the reports, compared them to the situation in their schools, and considered how they would conduct their classes.

After the reports, the presenters and knowledge engineers held a short talk session to answer participants' frequent questions and deepen the content of the practices. In the breakout sessions, they exchanged opinions based on practice reports and shared their views.

In the post-workshop survey, all the participants showed that they could incorporate the content of the day's workshops into their classes. One participant said, "It was very informative to talk with teachers from other prefectures. I want to incorporate videos into my classes next school year." Some participants commented that they were inspired by the presenter's practices and gained insights and learning from the exchange of ideas in the breakout sessions, such as "talking with teachers from other school types and schools with different student achievement levels was an opportunity to gain many insights."

6. Conclusion

The state of education is being questioned in the backdrop of rapidly changing and uncertain social conditions and remarkable advances in science and technology, including AI. Teachers are expected to continue to learn and improve their abilities as mediators to respond to the new era and provide education that leads to children's futures. Home Economics teachers are no exception. They need to understand the ever-changing lives of their students and empower them to shape their futures as independent consumers.

With only one home economics teacher assigned to each school, there are few public opportunities for teachers to reflect on their teaching and gain insights for improvement. Therefore, there is an urgent need to set up a place where aspiring teachers can gather on their initiative and take part in informal training sessions that are planned and organized as informal training sessions.

We conducted a training session incorporating online and face-to-face opportunities for home economics teachers to gather and examine the insights and learning gained by the teachers who participated. The results showed that teachers reflected on their practices and obtained hints about future lessons by listening to and exchanging opinions about others' lessons.

Dialogues about teaching among teachers from different schools in the same position are critical. However, teachers need to have knowledge engineers who can interpret practices, understand values, and find issues in their development. The modified SECI model proved to be an effective model for training home economics teachers. In the future, we would like to examine teachers' learning opportunities, what they gained from the program, and how they tried and were able to connect it to their future as teachers.

Notes
1) Sachiko Nakanishi's dissertation thesis authorized the Knowledge management model for home economics teachers.
2) This work was supported by JSPS KAKENHI (grant number 22K02110).

References

Geshi, A. (2013). "Manabi tsuzukeru kyoshi-zo" genjitsu ka no tameni: shogai gakushu shakai to riron jissen mondai (「学び続ける教師像」現実化のために――生涯学習社会と理論・実践問題). *Journal of the Society for Educational Research of Nihon University*, 48, 56–60.

Hikage, Y., Aoki, K., Shimura, Y. (2019). Findings from a Survey About Training for Unlicensed Home Economics Teachers in Junior High School (中学校の家庭分野を担当する免許外教員に対する研修の実態). *Journal of Association of Home Economics Education*, 62(3), 170–180.

Horiuchi, K. (1999). The Actual Situations and Teachers' Consciousness on Home Economics Education in Junior High Schools in Kanagawa Prefecture (神奈川県における中学校家庭科教育の実態と教員の意識). *Journal of the Center for Educational Research and Practices, Faculty of Education and Human Sciences, Yokohama National University*, 15, 63–77.

Horiuchi, K. (2008). Career Development of a Male Home Economics Teacher: Beyond the Token of Gender-Equalized Society (男性家庭科教員のキャリア形成――男女共同参画の象徴を超えて). *Japanese Journal of International Society for Gender Studies*, 6, 25–41.

Horiuchi, K. (2018). The Present Situation and Challenges in Home Economics Training and Teacher Support: A Survey of Teachers in Charge of Home Economics Education at Teacher Training Colleges (家庭科関連研修と教員支援にみる現状と課題――教員養成系大学家庭科教育担当教員への調査から). *Journal of Education Design, Graduate School of Education, Yokohama National University*, 9, 187–193.

Imazu, K. (2012). *Kyoshi ga sodatsu joken* (教師が育つ条件). 41. Tokyo: Iwanami Shoten, Publishers.

Kitada, K. (2017). Senmon shoku toshite no kyoshi no manabi (専門職としての教師の学び). The Association of Teacher Education ed., *Handbook on teacher education*, Tokyo: Gakubunsya, 262–265.

Ministry of Education, Culture, Sports, Science and Technology (MEXT) (2012). Kyoshoku seikatsu no zentai wo tsujita kyoin no shishitsu-noryoku no sogoteki na kojo hosaku ni tsuite (教職生活の全体を通じた教員の資質能力の総合的な向上方策について（答申）). https://www.mext.go.jp/component/b_menu/shingi/toushin/__icsFiles/afieldfile/2012/08/30/1325094_1.pdf (2024.3.22)

Ministry of Education, Culture, Sports, Science and Technology (MEXT) (2015). Korekara no gakko-kyoiku wo ninau kyoin no shishitsu-noryoku no kojo ni tsuite—: Manabi-ai, takame-au kyoin ikusei komyunitei no kochiku ni mukete (これからの学校教育を担う教員の資質能力の向上について〜学び合い，高め合う教員育成コミュニティの構築に向けて〜（答申）). https://www.mext.go.jp/component/b_menu/shingi/toushin/__icsFiles/afieldfile/2016/01/13/1365896_01.pdf (2024.3.31)

Ministry of Education, Culture, Sports, Science and Technology (MEXT) (2021). "Reiwa no Nihon-gata gakko-kyoiku" no kochiku wo mezashite: subete no kodomotachi no kanosei wo hikidasu, kobetsu-saiteki na manabi to kyodo-teki na manabi no jitsugen (「令和の日本型学校教育」の構築を目指して〜全ての子供たちの可能性を引き

出す，個別最適な学びと，協働的な学びの実現～（答申）). https://www.mext.go.jp/content/20210126-mxt_syoto02-000012321_2-4.pdf (2024.3.22)

Ministry of Education, Culture, Sports, Science and Technology (MEXT) (2022). Kyoin menkyo koshin sei no hatten-teki kaisho to "Arata na kyosi no manabi no Sugata" (教員免許更新制の発展的解消と「新たな教師の学びの姿」). https://www.mext.go.jp/a_menu/14167461.htm (2024.3.22)

Nonaka, I. and Takeuchi, H. (1995=1996). The Knowledge-Creating Company. Umemoto, K. (trans) *Chishiki sozo kigyo* (知識創造企業), Tokyo: Toyo Keizai Inc.

Ogura, I., Miyazaki, Y., Ohmoto, K., Omote, M., Kishimoto, Y., Nagaishi, K. Yoshii, M. (2009). Home Economics Education Teacher's Recognition of Home Economics and the Problems of the Scene of Home Economics Education (家庭科教員の家政学認識と教育現場の課題). *Kasei-gaku Genron Kenkyu*, 43, 30–38.

Sato, M. (2015). *Senmon ka toshite no kyoshi wo sodateru: The Grand Design of the Teacher Education Innovation* (専門家としての教師を育てる). Tokyo: Iwanami Shoten, Publishers, 117–119.

Takagi, N. (2013) Theme 4: Chugakko kateika kyoin jittai chosa/chukan hokoku (中学校家庭科教員実態調査・中間報告). *Journal of Association of Home Economics Education*, 56(3), 161–165.

Uesato, K., Konno, C., Watahiki, T., Kojima, K., Horiuchi, K., Tsuruta, A., Takagi, N., Hukutome, M. The Situations and the issues of the Home Economics Education in the Junior High School in 12 Prefectures in Japan (1): Home Economics Teacher's Actual situations （12の都道府県調査からみる中学校家庭科教育の実施状況（1）——家庭科教員の実態). *Journal of Association of Home Economics Education*, 42(2), 17–22.

Chapter 13

Strategizing and Developing Lesson Study through Systems Thinking Using the Curriculum Management Model

Tomoko TAMURA, Osaka Kyoiku University

Abstract

This chapter introduces the Curriculum Management Model (CM-Model), a theoretical framework developed by the author representing the overall structure of School-Based Curriculum Management (SBCM). We demonstrate how the CM-Model is a foundational structure for implementing Lesson Studies (LS) in high schools unfamiliar with this approach. Through a detailed case study, we showcase the successful adoption of LS to enhance both classroom and school environments. Furthermore, we explore the synergistic relationship between SBCM and LS, underscoring their mutual reinforcement in educational settings.

1. A Theoretical Model for School-Based Curriculum Management

1-1. Examination of the preceding models

School-Based Curriculum Management (SBCM) is defined as "a strategic and problem-solving organizational activity in which curriculum development and practice are systematically dynamic through a management cycle with evaluation at its core, while each school develops and utilizes various conditions and resources inside and outside the school to realize its educational goals" (Tamura, 2018). This complex activity involves numerous intertwined elements, hindering its understanding, and has led practitioners and researchers to repeatedly state, "I do not understand SBCM," or ask, "What is SBCM after all?" Therefore, we set the construction of an apparent structural model depicting the overall structure of SBCM as our research topic. We set up a hypothetical model based on previous studies and models and verified the relationships among the elements through a quantitative survey. Furthermore, we conducted case studies to interpret practices using the model and developmental studies to support the practitioners (Tamura, 2004; Tamura, 2005; Tamura, 2011).

We encountered diverse perspectives while exploring existing theoretical curriculum development and management models globally. Abiko (1983) highlighted the interplay between the educational goals, the teaching and learning process, and the curriculum and management processes, emphasizing the primacy of academic goals. However, this model lacked clarity regarding the processes' inner workings and effective management of resources and conditions. In contrast, Takano (1989) introduced a model focusing on the curriculum content within a Plan-Do-See (PDS) cycle and its relation to school management conditions, particularly emphasizing lesson management. Takano's model, however, depicted a linear, time-bound process without explicitly addressing educational goals. Nakadome (2002) expanded this model by integrating educational goals, outcomes, cultural factors, and the school's external environment into curriculum management, proposing a more strategic approach involving evaluation, relevance, and collaboration.

1-2. Embracing systems thinking in School-Based Curriculum Management

School-Based Curriculum Management (SBCM) originates from foundational philosophies and theories and transcends mere practice. A deeper understanding and application of these underlying principles enables adapting and creating methods tailored to diverse educational settings. Systems thinking is central to SBCM, providing a framework for viewing curriculum management not in isolation but as an integral component of the broader educational ecosystem.

Takano's efforts to imbue curriculum management with a scientific basis led to the advocacy for systemic thinking. He conceptualized curriculum management as a sub-system within the overarching school management system, further distinguishing lesson management as a sub-subsystem within this framework (Takano, 1989). Similarly, Nakadome characterized schools as open systems that dynamically interact with their environments to transform inputs into educational outcomes, emphasizing the system's adaptive nature (Nakadome, 1991).

"A system is an interconnected set of elements coherently organized in a way that achieves something" (Meadows, 2008, p.11). This definition shows that a system consists of the "purpose," "elements," and "connections between elements." In Meadows' view, the order of importance is the purpose, connection, and elements. Systems thinking offers invaluable insights into the complexities and diversities of educational practices and aids in comprehending the purposes behind these practices, the characteristics of their constituent elements, and how these elements interact and influence each other to achieve educational objectives. Within the SBCM framework, this systemic perspective highlights the interconnectedness of curriculum, teaching methodologies, organizational support, leadership, and community involvement, all aligned toward fulfilling the school's educational goals.

1-3. Elements and interconnections within the School-Based Curriculum Management

Drawing on preceding discussions, this section outlines the architecture of the Curriculum Management Model (CM-Model). In this model, illustrated in Figure 1, the upper segment ([1] to [5]) delineates direct educational undertakings, whereas the lower

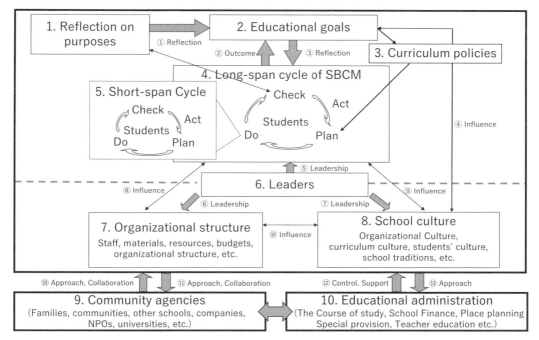

Figure 1: Curriculum Management Model (Tamura, 2005, 2011, etc., revised)

segment ([6] to [10]) encapsulates management endeavors that shape these educational activities. This dual structure underscores the intrinsic link between educational and management processes, a hallmark of the SBCM approach.

[1. Reflection on Purpose and Reality]
Central to SBCM is the goal of fostering educational growth in students. In accordance with the Fundamental Law of Education, other laws, and the Courses of Study, Japanese schools tailor their curricula to reflect with their unique mission and the nuanced characteristics of their local community and student body. This alignment is referred to as [1. Reflections on Purpose and Reality] involves critically evaluating the school's objectives against social realities, encouraging a reassessment of the philosophies and principles of school administration and staff (VanMannen, 1977).

[2. Embodiment and Realization of Educational Goals]
Following the reflective process, each school articulates and disseminates its educational objectives, grounded in the reflection above. English (1980) cautioned against conflating goals, such as student learning, with the means to achieve them, such as teacher support, and advocated for specific goal articulation. Therefore, the [2. Embodiment and realization of School Educational Goals] are placed at the top of the model, whereas the curriculum management cycle is opposed as a means to realizing these goals.

[3. Curriculum Policy]
The [3. Curriculum Policy] is positioned between [2. Realization of Educational Goals]

and [4. Long Span Cycle of SBCM]. This policy highlights and defines the curriculum's characteristics, serving as the core of the school's strategic management. It guides the allocation of resources, conceptualizes organizational structure, and fosters external relations.

[4. Long Span Cycle of SBCM]

The curriculum management cycle, a crucial component of SBCM, is a process categorized into long and short spans—the [4. Long Span Cycle of SBCM] operates on an annual basis. The CM-Model is unique as it places an assessment at the top of its cycle and expresses its linkage with the educational goals reflected in the curriculum. In contrast, achieving academic goals is the outcome of the curriculum.

In recent years, the PDCA cycle (P=Plan et al.) has been introduced and is taking root in the Japanese educational administration and school settings. However, numerous concerns and criticisms regarding the application of PDCA originate from factory production to education (Yui, 2012). For example, "reflection" is more appropriate for educational evaluation than "check" to determine if progress is being made as planned. The reason why "Act" is depicted in a subtle position outside the cycle is that the process does not necessarily proceed linearly from "Check (evaluation)" to "Act (improvement)." Instead, it is closer to the actual situation and more efficient if evaluation and improvement or improvement and planning are carried out in an integrated manner.

[5. Short Span Cycle of SBCM]

The annual curriculum cycle includes short-term management cycles for units and lessons at the individual unit, lesson, and lesson studies levels. This approach allows for the integration of contemporary methodologies such as the Anticipate-Act-Reflection (AAR) cycle proposed by the OECD or the Observe-Orient-Decide-Act (OODA) loop developed by military strategist John Boyd, enabling more detailed and nuanced management strategies.

[6. Leaders]

SBCM's primary driving force is leadership, and the model advocates for a distributed leadership model. Leaders, including the principal, vice principal, curriculum coordinator, and year-head teacher, are the linchpins of the curriculum management process, emphasizing the leader's pivotal role within the model.

[7. Organizational Structure]

The [7. Organizational Structure] encompasses formal management resources such as personnel, materials, finances, structural organization, time, and information. The magnitude and management of these resources critically influence educational activities delineated in the upper part of the model.

[8. School Culture]

In the CM-Model, school culture is formed by the organizational culture of teachers and staff, student culture, and school culture, which links teacher and student culture (Kudomi, 1996; Nakadome & Tamura, 2004; Tamura, 2009). Organizational culture is differentiated into curriculum culture (shared views of children and teaching) and organizational culture in a narrow sense (organizational characteristics such as collegiality and collaboration) (Nakadome & Tamura, 2004). Furthermore, the influence of individual values, which considerably affect the organization but have not yet reached organizational culture, is also considered. This [8. School Culture] is influenced by and reflects the school's educational objectives and achievements. Factors from community agencies, such as the school district's local characteristics, also influence school culture.

[9. Community Agencies]
Focusing on elements outside school [9. Community Agencies] has increased in importance with the 2017 revised course of study based on the philosophy of "curriculum open to society." This includes daily communication with parents and community members to understand their needs, their participation in school evaluation and management, and the school's accountability. Curriculum implementation can increase social capital between schools and communities. It is hoped that a mutually beneficial partnership will be established between the two.

[10. Educational Administration]
This element refers to the Ministry of Education, Culture, Sports, Science and Technology, prefectural boards of education (MEXT), and municipal boards of education. The curriculum standards set by the national and local governments, as well as prior guidance and reporting confirmation of curricula, regulate the educational practices of schools. In addition, the discretion of school principals regarding budgets and personnel matters is also recognized to some degree, although it is relatively limited in Japan compared with some other countries. SBCM materializes when curriculum standards are generalized and flexible and the autonomy and independence of schools are guaranteed (Nakadome, 2005). Hence, expanding school discretion is a prerequisite for SBCM. Educational administration provides various forms of "⑫ control and support," such as providing human and material resources, training, and school visits by supervisors. The schools "⑬ approach the educational administration to get support."

2. A Case Study of a High School—The Strategic Implementation Process of Lesson Studies using the CM-Model

In this section, we examine the case of X High School, which successfully implemented LS. We analyze the actual situation and develop strategies by applying the CM-Model. This section clarifies the effectiveness of the integration between CM and LS by describing and analyzing the school improvement process at X High School.

X High School is a state school in a mountainous region that offers regular and specialized courses. It is a small Japanese high school with approximately 300 students, 25 full-time teachers, and 25 part-time teachers, and it has faced its share of challenges.

Several years ago, the school encountered numerous issues related to student guidance. In response, grade-level teaching teams collaborated closely to support students, which has since improved student behavior. Nevertheless, the perceptions of the school among local community members remained unfavorable. Many students from local junior high schools chose to attend high schools in other areas. Consequently, many who enrolled at X High School were reluctant to attend classes and exhibited lower academic achievements. The number of applicants for admission fell short of the available slots. X High School continued to be under capacity, and the Board of Education considered consolidating the school.

2-1. Initiating reform at X High School: Principal Y's strategic approaches and communication challenges

In this subsection, we delve into the initial six months of reform efforts at X High School, spearheaded by Principal Y, whom the Board of Education appointed to lead the school. Upon his arrival, Principal Y embarked on a comprehensive reform, beginning with evaluating the school's dynamics and assessing the students as quiet, patient, and without the energy to run out of the classroom even if they didn't understand the lessons. The faculty, while knowledgeable in their respective subjects, struggled to engage students, leading to a growing concern about how to support underachieving learners. Principal Y deduced that the faculty had not fully grasped the unique educational needs of the school's students.

To address these challenges, Principal Y introduced two key strategies. The first was to begin mutual observation of lessons. He encouraged all teachers to observe their colleagues' classes and provide feedback through comment cards. However, almost all teachers at X High School had no experience in LS and were reluctant to participate in mutual observation. Despite some initial resistance, Principal Y's persuasive efforts led to some engagement in this program. From April to September, ten teachers opened their classrooms for 304 hours. However, there were only 78 observers, and most open classes were held without observers.

The second strategy focused on functionalizing the school's evaluation process. Principal Y set a goal to achieve 70% progress in identifying issues and 30% in developing solutions by the end of the school year. To realize this, he formed a "vision committee" of eight teachers relatively receptive to enhancing the school's evaluation.

Furthermore, X High School also had problems communicating with its teachers and staff. With four staff rooms designated for different grade levels and general use, the main staff room remained underutilized. This physical division reflected a broader issue of siloed communication, where grade-level teams were highly focused on student guidance but found engaging with colleagues from other grades challenging. This sometimes resulted in a confrontational atmosphere, hindering cross-grade collaboration.

2-2. Analysis of the actual situation using the CM-Model

At the request of the Board of Education, we engaged in a three-year consultancy with

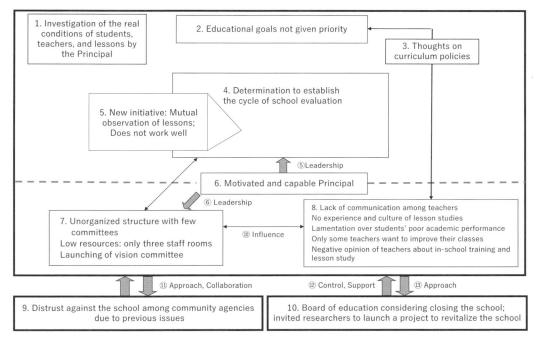

Figure 2: Analysis by the CM-Model of the first conditions of X high school

X High School. We visited the school board members approximately once a month (10 times), interviewed administrators and teachers, and facilitated discussions on improvement strategies. In addition, we oversaw the planning and execution of in-school training programs, offering guidance and consultation throughout. With permission, all discussions, interviews, and training activities were recorded and transcribed for comprehensive analysis.

Our initial step involved gathering insights from Principal Y, the school's administration, and other stakeholders. We employed the CM-Model as a framework for our analysis (refer to Figure 2).

[1. Reflection on Purpose and Reality], [2. Embodiment and Realization of Educational Goals], and [3. Curriculum Policy]
Like most schools in Japan, X High School had educational goals, but most teachers were unaware of them. Therefore, even in the classroom, there was no awareness of the "qualities and abilities we wanted to cultivate in these students. Based on this reality, Principal Y established a "Vision Committee" to "reflect on purpose and reality," "set educational goals," and formulate "curriculum policy."

[4. Long Span Cycle of SBCM] and [5. Short Span Cycle of SBCM]
At X High School, traditional lecture-style teaching was prevalent, although some teachers ventured into active learning approaches. In addition, the school lacked a structured mechanism for evaluating and improving individual lessons and the broader curriculum. As a result, the quality of instruction depended mainly on each teacher's skills. In

contrast, the cohesive cycle of curriculum management in both the long and short span remained unestablished.

[6. Leaders]

Principal Y provided robust and top-down leadership. The curriculum coordinator and the principal also provided leadership and established a "vision committee."

[7. Organizational Structure] and [8. School Culture]

The existence of multiple staff offices (organizational structure) seemed to hinder communication among faculty members and inhibit a collaborative organizational culture. A "vision committee" was newly established; however, some of its members were concerned about the opinions of other faculty members. There was a limited division of school duties, and no one was in charge of in-school training. One of the teachers at the time said this might have reflected the lack of school culture for organizing training, however the training content was left decided. In addition, there was a feeling that the voices of a few teachers and staff members who strongly condemned the low academic performance of students cast a shadow over the school's collective morale.

[9. Community Agencies]

X High School strived to become a school trusted by the local community and realize integrated junior and senior high school education in cooperation with neighboring junior high schools. However, as mentioned above, the school struggled to reestablish trust within the local community.

[10. Educational Administration]

The school board identified X High School as a potential candidate for consolidation but decided to allow the school to renew their program before taking any definitive action. To assist in this endeavor, the board enlisted the help of several university researchers, including the authors, to guide the school through its reform process.

3. Second Half of the First Year of Reform—External Support Focusing on In-School Training

In the first year, we conducted six in-school training sessions (as described below) after repeated discussions with the administration and a review of teacher responses and training outcomes. All training sessions were workshop-style in-school training (hereafter referred to as "WS"), in which small groups of teachers discussed issues using sticky notes and worksheets. The small groups were intentionally formed to mix members from different departments and grade levels to promote the exchange of opinions across subjects, departments, and grade levels. In addition, the sticky note method was used to allow everyone to express their opinions. In this way, we aimed to revitalize communication among teachers, which had tended to stagnate (approach to [8. Organizational

Culture]).

The first WS was held at the school. Under the theme "Learning from each other's lessons," each teacher wrote on sticky notes what they did in their lessons, and then the group organized them using the KJ method. The keywords that emerged from the WS were "love," "care," "hands-on," "eliciting children's voices," and "encouraging and building confidence." In most sticky notes, descriptions of the teaching methods were general. Based on the questionnaire results and discussions with administrators, most teachers evaluated their participation positively. However, they generally did not feel that they had a positive response. It is assumed that the workshop's design was inappropriate for teachers with no experience in systematic training and research on teaching methods and were suddenly asked to share their wisdom and experience.

Before the second WS, Principal Y sent middle-level teachers to an elementary school and a university in other prefectures. Although inspection tours and debriefing sessions had been held in the past, they tended to end up as mere reports. Therefore, we confirmed that the purpose of the debriefing session was to "learn from the advanced practices of other schools and think about concrete measures that can be applied to the practices of our schools." Participants listened to the reports while adding sticky notes onto items they could (or would like to) implement in their schools. Then, they narrowed down the items to be implemented and classified them into different time and organizational levels. The whole group then reviewed the results of the discussion. Not only were the discussions on this day more active than in the previous sessions, but a consensus was reached on future actions.

In the third WS, in response to the principal's proposal at the steering committee meeting (what should be done during the current school year), we discussed how to make the school unique and work on its profile. In this process, the school's organization, such as the division of tasks, was reviewed, and the workshop-style in-school training was recognized as one of the school's decision-making tools.

During the fourth meeting, the challenges previously identified in the workshops and the principal's strategic vision were categorized under different elements of the CM-Model. These elements included [2] Clarifying the school's educational goals, particularly the desired characteristics and skills of graduates; [4] Developing a curriculum designed to develop students' diverse skills and abilities; and [4] Examining and refining the school's internal meeting structures, committees, and approaches to time management. Each educator identified the issue to which they could contribute most, formed specialized groups, and began discussions to operationalize the identified challenges. The principal then identified the department responsible for leading each initiative and formally delegated tasks to the groups.

The series of strategic meetings continued with the fifth meeting in December, which was dedicated to an in-depth examination of student-centered concerns and a deliberate articulation of the skills to be nurtured in students. This session was structured around two critical dimensions: ([1. Reflections on Objectives and Actual Conditions] and [2. Educational Goals of the School])

At the sixth meeting in March, an innovative approach was adopted to increase transparency and community engagement: classrooms were opened to the public. This initiative marked the first opportunity to conduct research dialogues through workshops centered on these open classroom experiences. The deliberations that took place during this meeting were organized around two integral components of the CM-Model: [4] Curriculum Implementation and Evaluation, which emphasizes the implementation and evaluation of the curriculum in fostering a conducive learning environment, and [7] Organizational Structure, with a specific focus on Lesson Study, which aims to refine the institutional framework and processes to support effective pedagogy and professional development.

The workshops were consistently organized around the central theme of promoting student growth. Various initiatives' content focus and prioritization were deliberated and established during these sessions. This process demonstrated to faculty the effectiveness of workshops in minimizing the time investment required to launch new projects. Notably, these deliberations had already led to tangible improvements by the second year, fostering an inclusive environment where all participants, including the more reticent junior faculty members who had previously abstained from meeting discussions, felt empowered to voice their perspectives. When eight faculty members were interviewed about the WS, they highly evaluated "the fact that it is a training program in which they are proactive rather than passive participants" and "the fact that they can listen to the opinions of other faculty." In addition, the results of the questionnaires administered after each workshop indicated that many of them provided positive evaluations of the workshops (e.g., enjoyable, practical, and educational).

Reflecting on the first year's efforts and emerging outcomes, the curriculum coordinator articulated successes and challenges. Analysis revealed the following insights into the accomplishments achieved:

1. A dynamic of casual and substantive discussion emerged, fostering an environment conducive to open dialogue and collaborative problem-solving.
2. Strategies were developed for Wednesday after-school time, considerably reducing the frequency of non-essential meetings.
3. The introduction of open lessons has begun to improve the quality of teaching.
4. A dedicated in-school training department was established, marking a crucial step toward continuous professional development.
5. The frequency of daily "conversation" has increased, improving the school's operational communication.

The challenges to be addressed are as follows:

1. Discussions on how to improve teaching were sometimes found to lack depth and practical content.
2. Attendance at workshops (WS) showed room for improvement, suggesting improving engagement and participation strategies.

4. Second Year of Reform—Emphasizing the Role of Middle Leaders

While the external support mechanisms introduced in the first year were successful overall, they also met some resistance from a subset of teachers. Feedback from post-training questionnaires indicated that between 10 and 20 percent of teachers evaluated the training sessions negatively. This dissatisfaction was not limited to verbal or written feedback; a slight but notable group of teachers chose to take annual leave on the days designated for training, thereby physically absenting themselves from the reform processes.

Therefore, from the second year on, a coordinator for in-school training (a young teacher, Z) was appointed. The coordinator was responsible for planning and implementing the WS and school evaluation, whereas the authors provided logistical support (changes in [6], [7], [9]).

Coordinator Z proposed a strategy to align annual planning with school evaluation. He asked each department for an annual plan that included the year's improvement initiatives. These plans were compiled into a list and shared at a staff meeting, clarifying initiatives for each department and grade level and identifying opportunities for collaboration. The principal used this list to set the school's reform agenda for the year, linking School-Based Curriculum Management (SBCM) with school assessment to focus on systematic improvement, particularly in areas [4] and [7].

This effort demonstrated how principal leadership and teacher input could operate together. Under the leadership of coordinator Z, top-down and bottom-up efforts were combined to drive school improvement, leading to the improvement of [6].

The second year of the workshop focused on improving instruction to enhance individual teachers' teaching skills and have each teacher teach according to a plan. Therefore, the first step was to establish goals that would serve as standards for instructional improvement because neither the teachers nor the students were aware of the school's educational goals. Although they had been established at X High School, we clarified the skills teachers wanted to develop in students. Because the teachers' wishes had already been discussed at the 5th WS in the first year, in the second year, we conducted a questionnaire survey asking students what they wanted to be taught and what they wanted to be able to do by the time they graduated. A questionnaire was also sent to the parents of incoming students, asking them what they wanted their children to learn in the next three years. The student survey results, and the teachers' wishes identified in the first year were organized in the WS and summarized in 21 goals. Beginning in the second semester, the 21 goals were posted in every classroom and hallway. The following was posted on the school's website: "Classes at X High School are conducted with an awareness of the 21 Goals for Teachers and Students." In addition, as part of the lesson evaluation linked to the school evaluation, a questionnaire on the level of achievement of the "21 Goals" for students was planned to be conducted in March and July, whereas a management cycle was planned to reflect on this year's efforts and link them to improvements for the next school year. In this way, a system was established for school personnel to be aware of their educational goals.

During the current academic year, X High School has created syllabuses for its curriculum. However, the school faced a considerable challenge: the lack of a defined annual curriculum for each subject and initiatives that leveraged such a curriculum. To remedy this, a targeted approach was adopted. For each subject, specific, most relevant goals to that subject were selected from the established "21 goals." These selected goals were the basis for developing a comprehensive annual instructional plan for each subject. These carefully crafted plans were presented to the faculty to foster collective improvement. To ensure that the plans were shared and accessible for ongoing reference, they were uploaded to the school's server. This gave faculty members the flexibility to view and review the plans as needed, fostering an environment of continuous learning and adaptation. This process culminated in the creation of a structured curriculum organization policy. It addressed both the specific teaching policy for each subject and the overarching annual School-Based Curriculum Management (SBCM) plan, thereby enhancing the educational strategy with a focus on enriching areas [3] and [4].

Following unveiling the annual lesson plans based on the "21 Goals," X High School began the practical phase in which teachers began implementing the lessons derived from these plans. Three lessons were openly demonstrated throughout the year in June, October, and January, covering nine subjects annually. These sessions were open to the school's faculty and outside educators, fostering an environment of collaborative learning and sharing insights. Following these open classes, workshop-style research conferences were organized to deepen the pedagogical approaches presented. To ensure broad reach and facilitate asynchronous learning, all open classes were recorded from multiple angles within the classroom. These recordings and the corresponding lesson plans were made available to all faculty members via the school's server, allowing them to engage with the material at their convenience.

The workshops were structured to maximize engagement and learning outcomes through a series of interactive and reflective activities:

1. An initial briefing by coordinator Z.
2. Teachers' note-taking of their observations and thoughts using sticky notes.
3. Small group discussions to compile and organize these notes on a worksheet.
4. Sharing discussion highlights with all participants.
5. A closing discussion includes trainers' insights and participants' feedback.
6. Time for personal reflection on the day's learning and how to apply it.

Recognizing that many teachers were new to Lesson Studies, the focus was on identifying and discussing positive aspects and actionable insights rather than on criticism. Teachers from affiliated junior high schools were also invited to participate to enrich the discussions with different perspectives. In addition, comprehensive training schedules were distributed well in advance to create a conducive learning environment and ensure that participants were well-prepared and could manage their time effectively. Sessions were held strictly on schedule to minimize any sense of time pressure. Refreshments such as tea and cakes were provided to create a welcoming atmosphere. The results of these discussions were promptly documented and distributed as same-day feedback, ensuring that the insights gained were actionable and readily available to all participants.

In conjunction with these initiatives, the school engaged in biannual evaluation cycles designed to foster continuous improvement and reform. Substantial organizational and programmatic changes were implemented during the school year to improve educational outcomes. These included reorganizing departments, using achievement and general knowledge assessments to identify areas for instructional improvement, and opening the school festival to the community to improve its communication with X School.

In addition, the school implemented various programs to meet the diverse needs of the students and the community. Initiatives such as cross-curricular learning opportunities for students concerned about their academic abilities, after school study sessions, and an emphasis on career education from the first grade onward were launched. Internship programs were introduced for second-grade students. The school festival was opened to the local community to promote inclusion and involvement, and volunteer activities, including community clean-ups, were organized. Efforts were also made to promote literacy, such as providing reading tutorials and updating the mobile phone website with new book introductions.

However, despite these multifaceted efforts, the results of the 21 Goals questionnaire did not show statistically significant changes before and after implementing these instructional improvement strategies within the second year. Nevertheless, a notable change in student attitudes was observed. Students demonstrated an increased awareness of their aspirations to improve their skills in alignment with the 21 Goals. This newfound clarity enabled them to articulate their developmental efforts and goals more concretely during job interviews and other evaluative scenarios. They learned to provide detailed explanations of their goals and the steps taken to achieve them based on the framework provided by the 21 Goals.

5. Evolution of Faculty Perspectives

In the first year of the reform, the author heard the comment, "Our students are not capable," made by a teacher at X High School several times. Furthermore, during one group interview, the author witnessed teachers nodding in agreement when a veteran teacher said, "High school is not compulsory education, so students who want to learn can do so on their own. I was allowed to participate in the workshop group, and I wrote on sticky notes and put them on the model papers, for example, to bring actual objects to class and to have students conduct research. However, before I knew it, they were rejected (removed from the model papers). "Although some teachers desired to improve their classes, the negative comments often drowned their voices. However, in the second year of the WS (class study), one teacher exclaimed, "Because it is our school, we must study classes. " In contrast, another teacher regularly underlined, "We are class professionals," and held voluntary training sessions. Throughout the reform process, the discourse and atmosphere of the group of teachers changed (transformation of [8]). Figure 3 visually summarizes these reformative steps, organized according to the CM-Model.

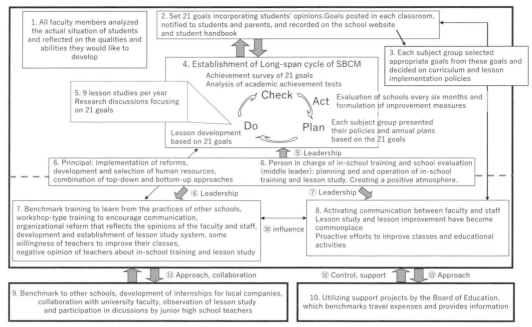

Figure 3: Organization of School Reforms at X High School

In the third year, Principal Y was transferred to another school, but Teacher Z continued to provide leadership as a middle teacher. He continued to improve in-school training, lesson research, and school evaluations. As a result, the student satisfaction survey results for the lessons improved and exceeded 80%. The "amplified stress in silence" commonly observed in the past among teachers was reduced. In the fifth year of the reform, the school faced challenges, including the departure of teachers present since the beginning of the reform and a stagnation in professional development initiatives. However, despite these hurdles, the school successfully navigated these difficult times. It emerged as a beacon of progress, gaining recognition from other high schools in the prefecture for its exceptional in-house training programs. In addition, the school stood out for its innovative approaches to teaching, particularly in developing classes for students with lower academic achievement up to junior high school, enabling them to re-engage in learning effectively.

6. Implications from the Case Study

Integrating Lesson Study (LS) into educational settings unfamiliar with its practices poses critical challenges. Key barriers include teachers' and staff's psychological reluctance to expose their teaching methods to the scrutiny of administrators and peers, the substantial amount of time required for lesson planning, the logistical and time demands of arranging peer observations, and the lack of dedicated leadership to organize and oversee the LS process. These barriers can considerably impede the successful implementation of LS.

In addition, even when conditions are conducive to opening and observing classrooms to the public, it is critical to define the perspectives and goals that guide instructional design and identify focal points for discussion during observations. These elements are essential to facilitate productive and meaningful dialogues about teaching practices.

Despite these hurdles, Principal Y's vigorous advocacy led to the reluctant agreement of teachers and staff to open their classrooms for public observation. However, this initiative initially attracted few visitors, making the effort less impactful than anticipated. This experience underscores the need for strategic planning, clear communication, and persistent leadership to effectively implement LS, along with measures to ensure that the process is as inclusive and beneficial as possible.

Prior to the full implementation of the LS program, a preparatory phase was critical. This phase included workshops that brought together all teachers and staff to reflect on the current state of student learning, the competencies and qualities to be fostered throughout the school's curriculum, and the specific skills to be developed in each subject area. These discussions also addressed necessary reforms to the school's organizational structure. Barriers were addressed on an individual basis through iterative dialogues. In particular, integrating student feedback into the development of general competencies alongside subject-specific knowledge and skills considerably improved both the LS and classroom teaching. This series of workshops (WS) gradually improved communication among teachers and staff and created an environment where discussions about students and teaching practices became a natural part of everyday conversations.

By shifting leadership roles from the principal to middle-level leaders and involving coordinator Z in planning, conducting, and evaluating LS, X High School achieved self-directed LS without outside assistance. The coordinator, who played a central role, not only facilitated the immediate management cycles of LS but also engaged in the annual cycles of school evaluation. This dual engagement allowed for the seamless integration of short-term actions with long-term strategic planning.

The collective impact of several critical elements-principal leadership, articulation, and shared understanding of educational goals informed by direct student voices and the actual classroom environment, workshops designed to foster teacher communication, bottom-up reform of the school system, and the distribution of leadership to middle-level teachers-synergized to advance school-based curriculum management (SBCM) using LS as a core tactic at X High School. These components worked harmoniously and contributed substantially to successfully integrating SBCM and LS as strategic approaches within the institution.

7. Integrating LS and SBCM

The Curriculum Management model (CM-Model) plays a vital role in the successful implementation of Lesson Study (LS) and the revitalization of School-Based Curriculum Management (SBCM). To facilitate this, worksheets based on the CM-Model were developed and used in teacher training sessions organized by the National Institute for School Teachers and Staff Development (NITS) during national training periods and in teacher training centers in various municipalities. A comprehensive survey of training participants confirmed the usefulness of the CM-Model in providing a comprehensive overview of school practices. This method allows for structural analysis, emphasizes the Plan-Do-Check-Act (PDCA) cycle, and helps identify strengths and areas for improvement in current practices while also outlining future challenges and action strategies (Tamura & Homma, 2014). In addition, this approach has been recognized for its effectiveness in promoting a synergistic blend of LS and SBCM, thereby enhancing the overall educational framework.

References

Abiko, T. (1983). "Management of Curriculum" in *Curriculum Encyclopedia: General Edition* (教育課程事典　総論編). supervised by Morihiko Okatsu. Tokyo: Shogaku-kan, 368–398.

English, F.W. (1980). *Improving Curriculum Management in the Schools*. Council for Basic Education.

Kudomi, Y. (1996). "The Structure and Characteristics of School Culture" in *School Culture as a Magnetic Field* (講座学校6──学校文化という磁場). Eds. by Horio, T., & Kudomi, Y. Tokyo: Kashiwa Shobo, 7–41.

Kuramoto, T. (2024). *School-Based Curriculum Management—Teacher Education and Lesson Study Perspective*. Fukuro Publishing, 1–233.

Meadows, D. H. (2008). *Thinking in Systems: A Primer*. Ed. by Diana Wright. White River Junction, VT: Chelsea Green Publishing Co.

Nakadome, T. (1991). *Strategies for School Improvement for School Leaders: Shifting Perspectives Toward New Educational Curriculum Management* (スクールリーダーのための学校改善ストラテジー──新教育課程経営に向けての発想の転換).　Tokyo: Toyokan Publishing Co.

Nakadome, T. (2002). *Comprehensive Learning Connecting Schools and Communities—Strategies of Curriculum Managemen*t (学校と地域とを結ぶ総合的な学習──カリキュラムマネジメントのストラテジー).　Tokyo: Institute for Educational Development.

Nakadome, T. (2005). *The Process of Establishing Curriculum Management* (カリキュラムマネジメントの定着過程). Tokyo: Institute for Educational Development.

Nakadome, T., & Tamura, T. (2004). *Curriculum Management Changes Schools* (カリキュラムマネジメントが学校を変える). Tokyo: Gakujutsu Publishing.

Takano, K. (1989). *Theory and Practice of Educational Curriculum Management* (教育課程経営の理論と実際). Tokyo: Institute for Educational Development.

Tamura, T. (2005). Model Development of Curriculum Management. *Journal of the Japan Association for Educational Media Study*, 29 (Supplement), 137–140.

Tamura, T. (2011). *Practice of Curriculum Management* (実践・カリキュラムマネジメント). Tokyo: Gyosei.

Tamura, T. (2018). "Progress and Future Challenges in Curriculum Management Research" in *Trends in Educational Management Research* (カリキュラム・マネジメント研究の進展と今後の課題). Ed. by the Japanese Association for the Study of Educational Administration. Tokyo: Gakubunsha, 24–35.

Tamura, T. (2022). *Theory and Practice of Curriculum Management* (カリキュラム・マネジメントの理論と実践). Tokyo: Japan Standards.

Tamura, T., & Homma, M. (2014). Development and Evaluation of Analytical Methods for the Practice of Curriculum Management. *Curriculum Research* (カリキュラム研究), 23, 43–55.

Yui, H. (2012). "PDCA Cycle": It's Spread and Catachreses without Consideration of Its True Meanings, Making Reference to University Evaluation, *The Journal of Business Studies Ryukoku University* (龍谷大学経営学論集), Vol. 52, No. 2/3, 37–54.

VanManen, M. (1977). Linking Ways of Knowing with Ways of Being Practical. *Curriculum Inquiry*, Vol. 6, No. 3, 205–228.

Chapter 14

Analysis of the School Improvement Process within the Framework of Curriculum Management

Toshiya CHICHIBU, National Institute for Educational Policy Research

Abstract

Previous studies on Curriculum Management include those that discuss how to establish conditions for school management in studies of curriculum development, those that focus on curriculum development in studies of school management such as school improvement and school-based management, and those that integrate them into Curriculum Management. This paper contrasts the unique perspectives of Tetsuo Kuramoto and Tomoko Tamura, both of whom consider curriculum development and school management. Their work emphasizes the totality of school management while focusing on curriculum development.

1. Introduction

This paper discusses the school improvement process based on the theme of Curriculum Management. It aims to achieve a situation in which both school improvement and curriculum development are achieved.

Kuramoto (2008) found that some studies that aim at curriculum development discuss the conditions for school management (Wilws & Bondi, 2011; Wraga, 1996; Martinello & Cook, 2000) and that some studies that discuss school management, such as school improvement and school-based management (Aikin, 1942; Sayles, 1964; Kurt, 1951; Lipitt et al., 1958; Skilbeck, 1984), and Curriculum Management theory (English, 2000; Hinojosa, 2001), which integrates the two studies (Wilws & Bondi, 2011; Wraga, 1996; Martinello & Cook, 2000). 2000; Hinojosa, 2001; Henderson, 2000).

The American Curriculum Management theory, as analyzed by Kuramoto, aligns with the findings of previous studies in Japan. This alignment, as demonstrated by Tamura's citations of Tadahiko Abiko, Toji Tanaka, Keiichi Takano, Takeaki Nakadome, and Shigeru Amagasa, underscores the global relevance of the research presented in this paper.

Kuramoto (2014) describes Curriculum Management as a threefold circle structure, a key concept in this paper. This structure consists of a primary circle for curriculum development and direct educational matters, a secondary circle for indirect instructional

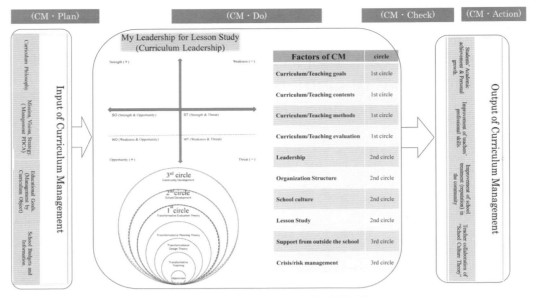

Figure 1: Curriculum Management Model by Kuramoto

factors, and a tertiary circle for external factors that influence schools. Understanding this structure is crucial for comprehending the Curriculum Management framework and its application to the school improvement process.

Kuramoto (2024) shows his idea of curriculum management in Figure 1.

Tamura (2022) shows the structure of various factors related to curriculum management extracted by Kuramoto, as shown in the figure. Like Kuramoto's theory, she identifies schools' internal and external structures; the overall related structure is similar.

Kuramoto and Tamura's diagrams are different, but their elements of curriculum management are very similar.

Using the Curriculum Management framework by Kuramoto and Tamura, this paper analyzes the trajectory of school improvement in a case study school. It examines how the school improvement process can be explained from a Curriculum Management perspective and strategies to further school improvement from a Curriculum Management perspective.

Tamura	Kuramoto
Setting education goals	1st circle: teaching goals, teaching contents, teaching methods
Management cycle of curriculum	
Structure of organization	2nd circle: leadership, organization structure, school culture, lesson study
School culture	
School leaders	
Community agencies	3rd circle: support from the outside of school, risk management
Administration	

Figure 2: Curriculum Management Model by Tamura

2. School Improvement at T Junior High School

T Junior High School is a school that underwent a significant transformation from the 2015 school year when Principal F was in office to the 2021 school year. T Junior High School was in rough shape in the 2015 school year when Principal F moved in, and teacher W, who had been in the school the year before Principal F was assigned to the school, reported that "many teachers were on sick leave or retired," she said. Around 2017, teacher W said, "The number of students who were out of the classrooms decreased a lot," and in the staff room, "thick, high mental barrier between teachers which initially existed disappeared at that time."

The most important key to this school's improvement was the leadership of Principal F. He focused on keeping in mind that anyone can do it. His first efforts were to greet the campaign in the morning when students came to school and to deal with the students who were out of the classrooms. He called on students outside their classrooms and asked them to paint the shoe boxes. He asked only those who said, "I will help you." Some students did not want to help, saying, "Why should I do that?" He tried to co-operate with students gradually. Eventually, one teacher started to help the principal, who was coaching the tennis team, work with students outside the classroom to clean the gutters of the tennis court. Through such efforts, the number of students who did not enter the classrooms decreased dramatically, and the school became calmer.

In 2016, the school received a grant for Universal Design Education from the city administration. Principal F focused on improving the classroom environment, remembering that everyone can do it again as in the previous year. As with the previous year, he asked all teachers to be involved, but some teachers still needed to comply. Even though he instructed the teachers to remove all the postings around the blackboard on the advice of a universal design specialist, many teachers still need to do so. After several warnings, they still did not remove them, so the principal and vice principal finally went to remove them. Although the method was top-down, the teachers felt the school was calming down.

In 2017, T Junior High School received the city's grant for ICT education. Teachers' reactions differed by subject area. Social studies, science, and English teachers were initially favored, while mathematics teachers were hesitant. There was strong opposition from Japanese language teachers. This is because reading and writing are the main content of the Japanese language, and they do not think ICT is useful for Japanese language lessons. There were many positive opinions about introducing ICT, so we became a pilot school.

In the use of ICT, "we focused on methods that anyone can use and had teachers work on a method of taking pictures of students' notes and projecting them on a projector." The use of ICT in the classroom "made the students look up and listen" and "changed the teachers who had been opposed to the use of ICT" (Principal F).

The ICT education has stimulated communication among the staff. Teachers would ask each other, "How did you use that?" Principal F said, "Until my third year as principal, I think there was a feeling that the teachers were forced to do things by the administration. In the third year of the ICT initiative, we began to see teachers opposed to the idea of change.

Starting in 2019, T Junior High School worked on sharing educational goals. The school that teacher W visited in 2018 was impressed by the school's efforts to share educational goals. When teacher W reported to Principal F about the school, Principal F immediately began to think about working on sharing educational goals.

T Junior High School worked with teachers to create an image of the students they aimed for in the 2019 school year. As a result, they came up with "8 student images" (self-determination, coordination, imagination, thinking, foresight, judgment, action, and social contribution).

In 2020, they narrowed down the skills to be nurtured in each grade level to three of the eight student images and engaged in integrated learning. Because the classroom teachers lead integrated learning, there was a possibility that different teachers would take different approaches. Therefore, it was decided that the curriculum for integrated learning would be developed collaboratively at each grade level. At that time, the teachers knew the three abilities to be developed. However, while the subject lessons would follow the textbooks only, the teachers decided to make the lessons in the integrated studies at least aware of the children's three abilities.

Each grade level narrowed down the three abilities to be nurtured in integrated learning this school year. Teacher W's narrative above focuses not on the integrated learning lesson itself but on transforming the consciousness of the group of teachers. Teacher W's respect for each teacher's agency may have deepened the group's trust and commitment to shared educational goals. The school culture during this period was as follows.

Teachers who had previously been reluctant to participate in in-school training began to say, "I thought it was good because the training gave me confirmation that I wanted to do these things and that I was happy to be doing these things."

In October 2021, T Junior High School opened lessons to the public. Teaching materials were presented to attract students' interest. The way the teaching materials were created differed from subject to subject, showing traces of each teacher's unique considerations.

The teaching plan for the open lesson was discussed during the summer vacation. First, each teacher who would give an open lesson prepared a lesson recipe ("I took about 20 minutes to prepare it," he said, "so I did not make them take that much time"), and then "each subject area would get together and present what kind of lesson they were going to give, and then the teachers who would provide the open lessons would look at what they had prepared and discuss what they thought. After that, "each subject gathered to present what kind of lesson they would give, and then we discussed what they thought of the open lesson by having them look at what the teacher was offering.

Teacher Y, appointed in the 2020 school year, said that compared to his previous school, T Junior High School's in-school training system "provided more opportunities to get together in each subject area. When asked if he did not feel burdened by this system, he replied, "It is not so much a burden, but I have my problems, and I get to hear from my seniors about various classes, ideas like this, and practical examples of how they did what I did, so I appreciate that. I am very grateful for that.

The above transformation of T Junior High School can be interpreted within the framework of Curriculum Management as follows.

(1) Principal's leadership

The most crucial factor in this case is Principal F. At first, Principal F went alone to the students who did not enter the classrooms. The principal's leadership was also the main factor in this case. The principal's decision to get an ICT education grant for the 2017 school year was also his initiative, despite the opposition of some staff members.

Principal F's school reforms were initially top-down. However, as the school settled down and communication among the staff became more active, he shifted to respecting the staff's initiative. What was initially top-down leadership has morphed into servant leadership. This transformation of the principal can be interpreted as a response to the transformation of the school's organizational culture, which will be discussed below.

Many previous studies have noted the relationship between principal leadership and organizational culture. This case shows that the school's commitment to Curriculum Management is linked to transforming the principal's leadership.

(2) Teacher W's middle leadership

The middle leadership demonstrated by teacher W, in this case, is also significant: Teacher W had been assigned to T Junior High School one year earlier than Principal F but was a new hire. Principal F appointed the young teacher as a lead teacher in 2017, her fourth year of employment. At first, the teacher acted mainly under the principal's direction but gradually began to take a proactive leadership role; the frequency of in-school training at T Junior High School is eight times a year, which is a lot compared to the city's average of about three times yearly. When teacher Y was asked about this by teacher W, he replied, "Isn't that because of your personality?

(3) Organizational Culture

The school culture at T Junior High School was transformed under the leadership of Principal F and Teacher W. At the beginning of the reform, the school culture was "poor relationships among staff members, and there were thick and high walls." In 2017, when teacher W became the lead teacher and was designated an ICT pilot school, information was exchanged in the staff room on how to use ICT; it was around this time that teacher W said, "The high, thick walls of the staff room that I felt when I first arrived were gone."

(4) Sharing of educational goals

The organizational culture of T Junior High School was gradually transformed under the leadership of Principal F. The subsequent phase of shared educational goals brought together not only the organizational culture but also the consciousness of teachers. In 2020, the first year in which efforts were made to share educational objectives, the school focused on three of the eight student images to be nurtured at each grade level and engaged in integrated learning. The following year, they narrowed down the skills to be cultivated throughout the school. While respecting the independence of the grade groups, Principal F gradually brought the staff's awareness together.

(5) Improvement of teaching methods

The initial focus at T Junior High School was on student guidance. First, students who did not enter the classroom were calmed down, and then the classroom environment was improved from the perspective of universal design. Once the students had settled in, the next step was to improve the teaching methods, which included using ICT to increase students' interest in learning. At the stage of working on shared educational goals, the school engaged in integrated learning, during which grade-level groups reviewed instructional plans. The gradual evolution from student guidance to improving teaching methods has interacted with the transformation of the organizational culture. Principal F worked to improve teaching methods while monitoring the transformation of the organizational culture.

(6) PDCA of curriculum

Although T Junior High School worked on improving teaching methods with an awareness of the ability to nurture, the efforts were limited to integrated learning, and no unique curricula were developed for other subjects. The trend of curriculum development for integrated studies is expected to spread to different subjects, and a cross-curricular curriculum will be developed. However, T Junior High School has yet to reach this point.

(7) Support from the Board of Education and local community

The city's grant was the catalyst for the transformation of T Junior High School, and the city's board of education supports the school by dispatching lecturers to frequent in-school training sessions. Although the support of the Board of Education in this case exists, it is difficult to say that it has had a particularly significant impact on the transformation of T Junior High School since the Board of Education works with all schools in the city similarly. Principal F kept his position for nine years. This is a very long tenure, as a principal's term of office is usually three to four years. This could be interpreted as the school board's high regard for Principal F's leadership, but it could also be because the local community wanted him to continue.

3. Dynamic Process of Curriculum Management

It is difficult to say that T Junior High School's improvement processes are more than the result of management or improved teaching methods. In the context of everything being interrelated, it is appropriate to interpret this case as a school where school improvement through Curriculum Management was established.

In T Junior High School, the leadership of Principal F and Teacher W changed organizational culture and shared educational goals were decisive factors. These influences have improved teaching methods. It is also possible to consider that further school improvement at the middle school is expected.

The school improvement process at T Junior High School is characterized by the transformation of Principal F's leadership and school improvement strategies. As the organizational culture changed, Principal F's leadership was initially top-down but gradually became servant-like. The school's efforts were initially focused on student guidance, followed by using ICT and other lesson technology, and then the clarification of the image of the students to be nurtured. This points out the challenge of discussing leadership theory, student guidance theory, and pedagogy separately. It indicates that they are transformative in their interactions and that school improvement must be dynamic.

4. Direction of Training from a Curriculum Management Perspective

The above discussion raises a new perspective on the nature of in-service training for school improvement. It shows the limitation of providing training at educational centers or in-school training programs in a reductive manner, such as subject pedagogy, methodology of lesson study, and understanding of students. The school situation constantly changes dynamically, and strategies must be considered according to the problem at any given time. Training aimed at acquiring such a way of thinking will be required.

Kuramoto and Tamura require participants in training courses at education centers or school-based training to analyze the school situation according to the model diagram shown in Figures 1 and 2. Their training does not provide knowledge but aims to acquire a way of thinking to understand the total school situation according to the framework of curriculum management.

Managers and teachers' thinking toward school improvement will be to dynamically analyze the school curriculum management situation and formulate strategies whose effectiveness is transformative in interaction with the problem. In this context, developing strategies and deepening the thinking of the organization's members should be necessary.

References

Aikin, W. N. (1942). *The Story of Eight-Year Study*. New York: Hasper & Brothers.

Kuramoto, T. (2008). *A study of curriculum management in the USA: From the service-learning perspective* (アメリカにおけるカリキュラムマネジメントの研究——Service-Learningの視点から). Japan: Fukuro Publishing.

Kuramoto, T. (2014). *Lesson Study and Curriculum Management in Japan*. Fukuro Publishing.

Kuramoto, T. (2024). *School-Based Curriculum Management*. Fukuro Publishing.

Kurt, L. (1951). *Field theory in social science*. New York: Harper.

Lipitt, R., Watson, J., & Westley, B. (1958). *Dynamics of planned change*. New York: Harcourt, and Brace.

Martinello, M. L., & Cook, G. E. (2000). *Interdisciplinary Inquiry in Teaching and Learning*. Merrill Prentice-Hall.

Tamura, T. (2022). *The Theory and Practice of Curriculum Management* (カリキュラムマネジメントの理論と実践). Nihon-Hyojun.

Wiles, J., & Bondi, J. (2011). *Curriculum Development: A Guide to Practice*. Columbus: A Bell & Howell Company.

Wraga, W. G. (1996). "A Century of Interdisciplinary Curriculum in American Schools," in Hlebowitsch, P. S., & Wrage, G. W. (eds.), 1996, *Annual Review of Research for School Leaders*, National Association of Secondary School Principals.

Chapter 15

A Study on the Future of Lesson Study in Japan— An Individual Lesson Plan Using "Zaseki-hyo"

Kiyotaka SAKAI, University of Teacher Education Fukuoka

Abstract

This chapter attempts to examine the development of the qualities and abilities required of teachers in Japan in the future through a Lesson Study using seating charts. Specifically, in the Lesson Study using the seating chart conducted at the school where the author was enrolled, we could catch glimpses of the collaboration of a group of teachers, a shift in the teachers' philosophy of teaching based on "understanding students" and their attempt to think through students learning while overcoming their different views of education and teaching.

1. Introduction

In Japan, where generational changes in school settings have been accelerating in recent years due to the mass retirement of veteran teachers and the mass hiring of young teachers (in their 20s and early 30s), there has been active debate over "improving teacher quality" and "developing and upgrading the expertise of the teaching profession."[1] In "Creating Compulsory Education for a New Era" (MEXT 2005), which can be said to be the genesis of this debate, MEXT said that "it is no exaggeration to say that the success or failure of education (reform) depends on teachers" and emphasizes the issue of "it is essential to train and secure high-quality teachers who are widely respected and trusted by society." It also points out three "conditions for excellent teachers": "strong passion for the teaching profession" "solid competence as an education specialist" and "comprehensive human skills."[2] This point is becoming even more critical in school education, which is rapidly becoming more diverse and complex after the COVID pandemic.

According to TAILS (2018), an international OECD survey focusing on the learning environment of schools and the working environment of teachers, Japan, compared to other participating countries, has a good number of teachers (= mentors) who guide schools and teachers (= mentees) who receive support, so to say, informal professional development is possible This human resource situation is a result of the fact that Japanese schools have a large number of teachers (Mentors). This human resource situation is supported by the practice of in-school training and Lesson Study in Japanese schools.[3]

229

However, it will be challenging to continue to develop systematic professional development as in the past under the current situation where large numbers of young people continue to be hired along with the retirement of large numbers of veteran teachers. The question is how to improve the quality of young teachers' professional development and abilities. In other words, Japan is undergoing a significant change in how in-school training sessions and the development of teacher qualifications and skills are conducted in various types of schools.

Lesson Study is an activity that involves constant efforts to improve the quality and competence of teachers as professionals in educational practice, and its character is one of obligation, rights, and autonomy. Therefore, it is significant to explore the future of Lesson Study that promotes the growth of teachers as "Action Researchers"[7] "who are important role models for students" and "teachers who continue to learn."[8]

2. Achievements and challenges of Lesson Study in Japan

In Japan and abroad, Lesson Study is recognized as a model for training preservice teachers and an effective method for developing teachers' competence and classroom improvement. In particular, the significance of Lesson Study in Japan lies in the fact that it is not forced upon teachers but self-evident to them. For this reason, the Japanese Lesson Study system is said to function as a culturally embedded practice for teachers' collaborative professional development.[9]

As a general lesson study model in Japan, "research classes" and "lesson study sessions" are often conducted as a set. The former refers to classes that offer suggestions for solving school and student problems. The latter is to deepen the "research class" contents through discussions based on the participants' interests. In Lesson Study, for example, the content of discussions ranges from the creation of teaching materials, questions, and instructions in class, specific involvement of students, the content of writing on the board, and understanding of student's level of comprehension. By accumulating such Lesson Study, Japanese teachers have improved their practical competence centering on teaching techniques while receiving advice and appropriate suggestions from experienced teachers.[10] [11]

However, it has been pointed out that these "research classes" have become a mere formality and routine, as they are often open to the public as classes that lack proposals or in which the teachers themselves have little awareness of the issues involved. It is also pointed out that the essence of the class is not sufficiently discussed in the lesson study sessions, with observers criticizing the class based on their own experiences and making comments based on their impressions and emotions rather than the facts of the class[12]. Many other comments touch on superficial rhetoric and trivial details of the classes.

In light of the challenges of the Lesson Study described above, in recent years, there has been a shift from the teacher-centered Lesson Study to the "workshop" type Lesson Study in which all members participate. In a workshop-type Lesson Study, after a self-review by the teacher, small group discussions are held based on the pillars of the debate, and the results are presented. Shared.[13] Therefore, the "workshop" method of Lesson Study is not about the quality of the teacher's teaching techniques but about the discovery of students' unique ways of thinking, future development of learning, transformation of the teacher's awareness, and new insights of the observers that are the subject of discussion. As Jeanne Wolf and Kiyomi Akita have stated, "Although the class is the window for inquiry, it does not end with that particular class; rather, a lesson study is a place where discussions can be held, and questions can be asked about the curriculum, teaching materials, and long-term transformation of children and teachers."[14] it is essential that lesson study is not limited to improving individual teachers' teaching skills but is also intended to improve teachers' collaboration and school organization.

On the flip side, the class has the characteristics of "one-occurrence," "unrepeatable," "complex," and "contextuality,"[15] and in light of these characteristics, it is necessary to enhance not only the universal rational approach but also the individual situational approach. In the current revision of the Courses of Study, a shift in the view of goals = qualitative abilities, a shift in the view of evaluation = assessment for learning[16] and formative assessment[17], a shift in learning methods = self-regulated learning[18] and the use of ICT, and a shift in learning content = cross-curricular learning content are presented, which is the most significant tonal shift in the revision to date. This is the most significant change in tone among the previous revisions of the Courses of Study. In light of the revised Courses of Study and global educational trends, we have shifted from "teaching" to "learning," from "What and how did we teach?" to "What and how did they learn?". This means shifting the subject of lesson study from teachers to students.[19]

Therefore, these days, when "individualized optimal learning" and "collaborative learning" are required, it is necessary to update "Lesson Study" to focus on "students" once again.

3. Lesson Study using a Seating Chart

3-1. What is a seating chart?

Generally, in Japanese school classrooms, the seats where students sit are fixed. Therefore, a "chart" shows which students sit in which seat. The chart is called a "seating chart." In Japan, Lesson Study utilizing this "seating chart" has been widely conducted, especially by a private educational research group, "Syakaika no Syoshi wo Thuranuku Kai (The Society for the Preservation of Social Studies' Initial Aspirations)."[20] During these studies, various arrangements have been made to the seating chart, such as writing the student's abilities, interests, characteristics, points to be noted, relationships with others, and wishes for the student along the temporal and spatial axes.

The aim of the Lesson Study using the seating chart is twofold. The first is to provide concrete clues for guiding students' learning. The second is to show the possibilities for students' learning when developing classes. In other words, the seating chart is not only a tool to show the actual condition of the students but also a tool to show the strategy for developing a class that makes the most of each student's individuality. Therefore, the seating chart has the function of dynamically grasping the transformation of the students along the development of their learning.

There is also a method of utilizing the seating chart as "lesson plan" for Lesson Study, which suggests a new style of Lesson Study in the future.

3-2. Today's significance of lesson study using a seating charts

In the 2000s, the Japanese Lesson Study emphasized "how teachers teach," "research on teaching materials," and "class development based on lesson plans" rather than "how to understand individual students" amid the domestic trend to guarantee "solid academic ability." Therefore, the seating chart no longer shows the viewpoint of making the most of each student or their unique thinking situation but mainly indicates the student's level of understanding of the content and the actual state of learning. Under such circumstances, teachers began to use the seating chart to evaluate students' knowledge of the content rather than dynamically utilize it in class development.

However, in the context of recent global trends, such as the Key Competencies outlined in the OECD's Education 2023 and the 21st-century skills of the ATC21s, the seating chart, which contributes to the promotion of individual and collaborative learning in class development, is being reevaluated as a component of Lesson Study that places students at the core.

Undeniably, the seating chart has been trivialized to assess students' understanding of their learning status by the cynical view of the comprehension-centered class, which has led to "evaluation for evaluation's sake" and "evaluation fatigue." However, a careful examination of the essence of the evaluation cannot deny that it includes viewpoints that are indispensable for understanding and evaluation. Simply put, the significance of seating charts today is to "capture students' thinking and apply it to class development." There is no doubt that the seating chart has significant value both as a function for activating class development and as a function for evaluating learning. This is because it aims to overcome teacher-centered learning development and contributes to class activation and student understanding through students' experiences, thoughts, perspectives, conflicts, and gaps in perception. In addition, recent school education is undergoing various changes, such as a shift from "lesson plan" that prioritizes teaching materials to "learning design" based on students' learning trends, from "educational evaluation" that focuses on achievement to "learning assessment" that focuses on the learning process, and from teachers' "teaching methods" to students' "learning methods"[21].

Using the seating chart could be an opportunity for applying this shift in school education.

3-3. How to conduct a lesson study session using a seating chart

However, even if a seating chart is used in a class, lesson study sessions are not very sensible based on the traditional teacher's teaching method. Therefore, it is necessary for both the teacher and the observers to participate in the lesson study sessions using the seating chart with a Student-First mindset. In this sense, the lesson study sessions method should be shifted to conference type[22] instead of the conventional meeting type.

The term "conference" here is similar to the "care conference" that takes place in the field of medical care and nursing care. A "care conference" is a meeting of doctors, nurses, caregivers, and other administrative positions at medical and nursing care facilities to develop a plan to provide better treatment and care for patients in hospitals and nursing care facilities. In light of this, "care conference" in Lesson Study is an opportunity for both the teacher and the observer to develop strategies to promote understanding of the students and to utilize the learning potential of the students in the classroom.

3-4. Types of seating charts and points to consider in their preparation

This section presents a model of a seating chart that the author has practiced.

Type A: Blank seating chart.
Figure 1 shows the Type A seating chart model. Only the student's name is written in the Type A seating chart, and the space below the name is left blank. By leaving the space blank, the observer can observe the students without preconceptions. It also makes it easier to keep a record (i.e., more accessible to write down who said what) and allows the observer to trace the students they are interested in.

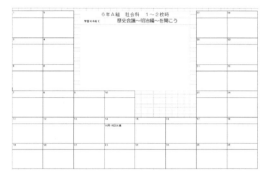

Figure 1: Type A Seating Chart Model

In Lesson Study, each observer can interpret the students' learning that the observer has locked on to, which can lead to discoveries through sharing.

Type B: Extracted student-written seating chart.
Figure 2 shows a Type B seating chart. The Type B seating chart selects two or three students ("Extracted students") before the class. On the seating chart, the teacher writes the student's pre-study information, current study status, particulars, and the teacher's wishes for the student.

Figure 2: Type B Seating Chart Model

The observer observes the interaction with other students, mainly the extracted students, and records what they notice. In this way, while taking into account the students' prior information, the change of the students during the class, the deviation from the previous lesson plan, the development of learning, and comments that may serve as an opportunity to develop the class can be written down and used in the conference after the class. Posting the extracted students will make it easier to grasp the teacher's intention and lead to understanding the extracted students.

Figure 3: Type C Seating Chart Model

Type C: All-student write-in seating chart.
The seating chart in Figure 3 should contain various information for all students. Of course, it also provides a holistic view of the students and a preview of the teacher's intentions.

Creating this seating chart is a significant burden for the classroom teacher. However, this seating chart is extremely important in keeping track of the learning status and various interactions of all students in the class.

*   *

As shown in Figure 4, a seating chart can be created using the Microsoft Excel spreadsheet software, and by adding sheets to the chart, it is possible to grasp the development of each student in the context of the class. By adding sheets in this way, it is also possible to learn the dynamic nature of the student-student and student-teacher

Figure 4: Excel Sheet

learning relationships in the development of the unit. In addition, using such a series of sheets is a practical strategy for understanding students' ways of seeing and thinking for an hour and throughout the unit. This leads to understanding the transformation of students' ways of seeing and thinking and the knowledge of the student's way of learning.

Type D: Student-created seating chart.
Types A–C are all seating charts prepared by the teacher. The C-type seating chart, in particular, requires much work, as the teacher must write down the student's thoughts and opinions by themselves. However, the recent conversion to GIGA schools has allowed students to use computers in all Japanese schools. Therefore, the photo proposes a D-type seating chart filled in by each student using a Google Spreadsheet on the cloud. The teacher prepares a spreadsheet frame with students' names. Then, each student can access the spreadsheet and enter their thoughts and opinions in the frame with their name. They can always access and input their thoughts and opinions while studying, during breaks, or even from home, and they can also make corrections.

Photos: Type D Seating Chart

The seating chart written by the students is printed and distributed in class. With this D-type seating chart, the teacher can concentrate on developing a lesson plan based on the completed seating chart since the students fill it in.

3-5. Extracted students and seating chart

In the seating chart, extracted students may be selected by the class and observers as "students of concern."

In particular, the B-type posts the extracted students on the seating chart and observes and examines the class development centering on the extracted students. As Tanoue (2004) indicates, extracted students have three functions: i) an evaluative function to grasp students' learning based on their specific individual goals, ii) a supportive function to enable specific instruction based on students' stumbling blocks and potential for growth up to the previous period, iii) and a verification axis focusing on extracted students' words and actions[23]. Thus, setting the extracted students as the target of the class is like shining a light on them. It is impossible to watch all students equally in class. Therefore, by shining light on a few students, it is possible to grasp the relationship with the students in the surrounding area. Instead, starting from that student, it will be possible to grasp the relationship with the material, to others, and to the responses to the teacher's questions based on the specificity of that student.

3-6. Seating chart and lesson plan

In Japan, there exists a formal "Lesson Plan = study guide" consisting of a student's view (actual condition of students), a view of teaching materials (value and essence of teaching materials), a view of teaching (specific teaching methods), goals of the unit, a lesson plan, and a time development plan. Many variations of this type of lesson plan have been developed in Japan. Training in preparing such lesson plans is part of the curriculum for pre-teacher training programs and is undoubtedly a part of the qualities and abilities required of a teacher. However, as discussed in 3-4, there are some cases in which the preparation of lesson plans has become a formality or the preparation of lesson plans has become an objective. Sometimes, the vital task of creating lessons is neglected by spending too much time on lesson plans. In addition, when a group of teachers works together to create a lesson plan, the knowledge and experience of veteran teachers are given priority, and the intentions, ideas, and other ideas of younger teachers are sometimes excluded. On the other hand, in terms of the lesson plans' contents, the student viewpoints describe prevalent student situations, and the teaching material viewpoints are sometimes taken directly from the textbook.

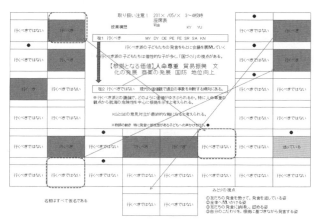

Figure 5: Seating Chart-type Lesson Plan

Therefore, to solve this problem, we would like to propose a "Seating Chart-type Lesson Plan" that uses the "Zentai no Keshiki = overall scheme" (Ueda, 1977)[24] as an aid. Figure 5 shows a model of a seating chart-type lesson plan. The C-type seating chart clearly states the issues of contention in the class (differences or conflicts of opinions and ideas) and the students' ideas to be utilized during this time. The most significant feature of this type of seating chart-type lesson plan is that it is created with the idea of using the students, especially in the development of the class (unit), rather than just understanding the content of the current class. The teacher tries to anticipate as much as possible when and how the students will react and where their interactions with others will occur. Of course, depending on the development of the class, it may not be possible to follow this lesson plan. However, it is effective in dynamically capturing the fundamental transformation of the students on the spot and in writing the trajectory of modifications during the development of the class.

In turn, such a seating chart-type lesson plan is effective for participating in teachers in encouraging a shift from teacher teaching to student learning.

4. Practice and Consideration

In this chapter, the author reports on the case study of in-school Lesson Study using the seating chart described so far at a school where the author works (hereafter referred to as "our school").[25]

4-1. Student understanding and student learning

"Learning" in our school is an activity that transforms one's behavior and abilities to a higher level. In other words, shifting from a passive to an active learning attitude is essential for developing higher-order qualities and skills. This transformation will lead students to have dreams and hopes for the future and continue learning throughout their lives. To achieve this, it is crucial to make students aware of their current strengths and weaknesses through cooperative and active learning that emphasizes diverse interactions with others and aims for self-realization while envisioning new possibilities for themselves.

At the core of the educational practice is an understanding of the student. This "understanding of students" is the cornerstone of academic training and is the teacher's work to create interactive intellectual and physical transformation of the students while having educational intentions. Therefore, the educational practice needs to be mindful of the student's intellectual curiosity, awareness of the gap with the outside world, and involvement with others rather than putting them into a teacher's "frame," even if intentionally.

4-2. Involvement, connection, and linkage

In recent years, Japan has been amid significant trends such as a declining birth rate, an aging population, advanced information technology, and declining local communities. In education, there is concern about the lack of normative awareness among students and the weakening of human relationships, as it has been pointed out that relationships at home and in the community are declining. In light of this current situation, the Courses of Study emphasize the importance of fostering the skills necessary for independent and self-reliant participation in society as a community member. In addition, each individual is expected to create new values as a bearer of a sustainable society. Therefore, our school will implement educational practices that aim to foster the acquisition of essential knowledge and skills through the three cyclical elements of "involvement, connection, and linkage" shown in the diagram on the right, as well as the ability to think, judge, and express to find and solve problems by utilizing these skills.

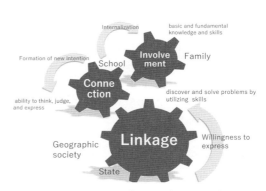

Figure 6: Involvement, Connection, and Linkage

To realize this kind of education, it is necessary to provide guidance and support according to the individuality and needs of each student and to develop educational activities that allow students to feel a sense of existence and the joy of self-realization through independent learning, referred to as "Manabiai = learning together."

In light of the above, a qualitative shift is required to transition from research on teachers' "teaching methods" to research on "understanding students."

4-3. Lesson study system

Our school has a buddy system, where lesson study is conducted mainly in grade divisions. In the grade divisions, veteran teachers and young teachers form buddy pairs. They aim to build a relationship to mutually enhance each other's skills by sharing ideas for classes and discussing daily classroom management and work-related problems.

Because our school is private, we need help participating in training programs sponsored by local government education centers or boards of education. Our school cannot "outsource" training to enhance practical skills, so we must train young teachers. Therefore, our school adopts "On the Job Training" (hereinafter referred to as OJT) for in-school training, which is widely used in many companies as a method of human resource development through daily duties. By implementing OJT at our school, we have tried to create a foundation for teacher development that looks five to ten years into the future. Specific OJT includes, for example, instruction on how to conduct classes, classroom management, preparation of materials for school events and other proposals, personal instruction by the administration and other staff members on school service days, and consultation on work-related matters.

4-4. Teachers as reflective practitioners

The school has two groups of teachers: veteran teachers and younger teachers, and their interaction could be a driving force for improving the school's educational capacity and the quality of its teachers.

Therefore, we devised a model in which the four elements of "expertise," "practical leadership," "collegiality," and "reflective practitioner" are circulated,

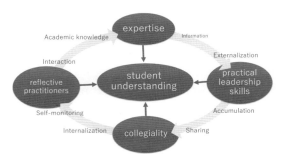

Figure 7: Teachers as Reflective Practitioners

as shown in the figure on the right. First, the "expertise" of individual teachers is accumulated as they demonstrate their "practical leadership skills." Next, individual practical skills are shared through "collegiality." Then, they monitor their educational practices and internalize them as "reflective practitioners." Finally, they improve their "expertise" while acquiring further academic knowledge (or PCK).

At the core of this process is "student understanding." "Currently," "ambition," "communication skills," and "practical ability" are being severely questioned concerning the inner nature of teachers' practical competence. Therefore, the characteristics of the "qualities and abilities" required of teachers necessitate that they are "reflective practitioners." A good teacher updates their framework of perception and experience of a problem and then attempts to solve it. By accumulating such practical knowledge, they enhance their professional knowledge and techniques. Teachers' expertise and practical knowledge result from collaborative practice mediated by dialogue, in addition to = reflection on the problem.

Therefore, from the perspective of fostering "reflective practitioners," our lesson study will not be limited to general and universal discussions of class creation but will aim at a style of teacher learning in which practical knowledge is discovered, shared, and accumulated while confronting various class situations.

4-5. Raising teachers' awareness for understanding students

As we have mentioned, lesson study, in general, has pursued improving teaching methods. However, the recent drastic tonal shift in the view of academic achievement from measurable knowledge and skills, thinking, judgment, and expression to qualities and abilities inevitably calls for a change in teachers' mindset in-class research.

What kind of lesson study is needed to promote a change in teachers' awareness? Lesson study aims at improving classes. The substance of this "improvement" is the pursuit of its effect on the students. Therefore, it is natural for teachers to enhance the quality of their teaching techniques. However, focusing on how students learn, which changes moment by moment, will change teachers' awareness.

Therefore, our lesson study discusses "how the students' learning was" about the classes. We believe this kind of "organizational awareness" by a group of teachers visualizes student learning and leads to a better understanding of students throughout the school. Furthermore, based on the results and reflections of the open classes, we can improve the quality of instruction by improving the courses according to the actual conditions of the students.

4-6. Use of seating chart for student understanding

Our school will utilize seating charts in research classes (as well as in daily courses). This records the students' behavior up to the previous period, their actual conditions, readiness, and the teacher's wishes. It can be used as a document for reflection after the class or for the class workshop by writing down the changes of the students in the class, discrepancies from the teacher's plan in advance, and comments that might be the occasion for the development of the class. In addition, it has a dynamic function that allows the user to freely write down the students' movements during the lesson (especially the discrepancies from the teacher's expectations and the discovery of the growth potential).

4-7. Study of the transformation of teachers' awareness

In this section, we examine data from a questionnaire survey (semi-structured questionnaire method) for teachers on class research and data from the recording of statements in lesson study from the two perspectives of i) efforts in lesson study and ii) self-growth.

For ethical reasons, the alphabetical names of the teachers are pseudonyms.

2011 Regarding i)

"I would like to see more class research that focuses on 'how to teach'" (K)

"I am not sure if this will lead to the improvement of young teachers' teaching skills" (H)

"I want to know how to conduct basic classes" (Y)

"I want to know how to conduct a basic class" (S)

"I want to observe many teachers' classes" (A)

"I want to know what to say to students that I should pay special attention to in their interactions with each other" (H)

The responses are more skeptical than negative about efforts to conduct student-centered lesson studies. Related to ii) above, since many of the teachers are young, emphasis should be placed on basic class creation and improving teaching techniques. Only 30% of the respondents commented on "student learning" in class research. On the other hand, there were some comments that students' growth was realized, although only slightly, which gives us hope for the following year.

Regarding ii)

"I could talk about lesson planning in daily conversations with the younger teachers" (K)

"I learned a lot from working with veteran teachers on lesson planning, especially how to pay attention to students who have difficulty learning" (S)

"We were able to learn basic teaching techniques during the afterschool hours" (A) and "I appreciated the many times we had to participate in the mock classes" (K).

Many teachers feel that there is an organic relationship between veteran teachers and younger teachers. The buddy method of training has produced some positive results. In addition, the fact that the school is newly established, with only four out of six grades, and that there is more space in the school's operation itself has contributed to the relaxed after-school training.

2012: Regarding i),

"The number of open classes increased due to the increase in the number of staff, and I was able to observe many classes" (K)

"It was perfect that the range of subjects in the classes was wider than last year" (N)

"The way the interactive board was presented was helpful" (K)

"The teachers' awareness of the issues in the academic activities class was excellent" (T)

"I can write the students' movements in class on the seating chart, which makes it easier to speak up at the workshop" (H)

"I do not know how to use the seating chart" (N)

"I want to know how to write the seating chart before class" (K)

Rather than "student learning," many comments touched on the novelty of classroom materials, questioning the ingenuity of presenting materials on interactive boards, and teachers' teaching methods, indicating continued interest in teachers' teaching techniques. There was a slight increase in comments regarding their use (there were no comments regarding seating charts in 2011). This suggests that teachers have begun to take an interest in creating classes that make the most of "students" due to the seating chart creation. On the other hand, comments regarding "teacher questioning," "writing on the board," and "using the interactive board" still accounted for 80% of the comments in the lesson study sessions, suggesting that teachers' awareness of "understanding students" has not changed.

Regarding ii)

"How they could not see the students" (K)

"I aimed at developing a class concept with an awareness of the connections between students" (A)

"I can always talk about classes with teachers in the same grade" (S)

"The points raised at the lesson study were not only about teaching methods, but also about students whom I could not see myself, so my view of students expanded" (H)

"More training outside the school" (Y)

"It is important to have opportunities to observe classes at other schools" (N).

Young teachers who had not previously been in charge of their classes are now aware of the importance of observing students daily and applying this knowledge to the development of their classes. In addition, the young teachers feel a sense of fulfillment as they engage in research classes with flexible ideas that only young teachers can develop. On the other hand, many requested training opportunities outside of school. This suggests that they feel that school-centered teacher education has reached an impasse.

2013 Regarding i)

"When I made a study question about XX particulars, his comments became very active" (S)

"I was able to use the predictions of students' relationships with each other on the seating chart in class" (T)

"A naughty student began to speak up to support his friends, and his attitude toward life became more relaxed" (L)

"I would have watched closer to XX" (M)

"XX's special interest was utilized in the class" (Y).

Compared to 2012, the number of teachers discussing class creation and development while naming specific students in surveys and class workshops has increased. In particular, by naming selected students in advance on the seating chart, observers can trace them and deepen their understanding even if they are not the students in charge. It can be seen that many of the observers in the lesson study sessions are tracing the students' learning spontaneously or consciously.

Regarding ii)

"I was able to observe classes in all grades and observe the developmental stages and growth of students in detail" (N)

"I would like to bring up grades and further improve students" (K)

"The advice from XX was beneficial. I was able to use it to improve my classes" (O)

"The young teacher's ideas revitalized my class" (Y)

"I was able to develop a class that made use of the students' ideas by learning how to use the interactive board" (F)

"It is important to raise the level of question research and interpretation of teaching materials as well as the use of ICT equipment" (Y).

In 2013, with all six grades in place, 23 lesson study sessions were held. It is evident that young teachers are gradually gaining confidence in their class development after having their classes observed many times and by observing other teachers' classes. Both young and experienced teachers are aware of their growth through the many class study sessions. On the other hand, veteran teachers pointed out the importance of educational technology, which has been highly valued in the past, and there is still a strong tendency toward a rational-technical approach to teaching.

2014 Regarding i)

"I was able to anticipate specific lesson developments by adding arrows and marks to the seating chart to anticipate student interactions" (K)

"I can see the changes in student awareness by attaching the seating chart from the previous period" (S)

"The ingenious seating chart allows me to understand the intentions of the teacher" (L)

"I can clearly understand the intention of the teacher through the ingenious seating chart" (F)

In 2014, an evolutionary seating chart was created that showed the relationships among extracted students and the particulars of extracted students. In addition, an instructional seating chart was also developed, which included a diagrammatic seating chart with arrows, lines, and indicators. Comments regarding the diversity of students' thinking and the potential for developing students' thinking have increased in surveys and class workshops. In addition, many teachers have gained insight into the differences between students' expected and actual movements, which has led to further understanding of students. Although there are still some comments on teachers' questions, instructions, and writing on the board in the survey, there are indications that teachers' understanding of the school's student-understanding-centered lesson study is becoming more widespread.

Regarding ii)

"The students were more than happy to have so many teachers observe their classes" (S)

"I realized the importance of basing development on the student's awareness of problems while experimenting with various learning methods" (O)

"I was inspired by the efforts of the young teachers" (T)

"I have to change my view of teaching" (N).

In 2014, more young teachers voluntarily opened their classes to the public and conducted challenging classes. For example, courses in which students are moderators and ICT is utilized indicate that the teachers are growing while learning new teaching methods. In lesson study, role models of teachers who continue to learn are represented, such as a teacher who showed the difference between a preliminary lesson plan and the actual lesson development and analyzed the difference, a young teacher who opened up the entire unit to the public, and a teacher who developed experiential learning with a guest teacher. On the other hand, among the veteran teachers, some teachers were inspired by the challenging practices of younger teachers and promoted a shift in their views of teaching and education, suggesting that the informal, buddy-style training was also practical.

4-8. Summary

The first is a shift in the teacher's view of teaching based on "student understanding." Over the past five years, through trial and error, we have been shifting from a teacher-driven view of teaching. This shift in their view of teaching has contributed to their daily improvement. This results from our search for and realization of classes where students can live and breathe.

Looking again at our school's approach to teaching, we see that it is not a planned and scheduled approach to learning that aims for the acquisition and mastery of objective knowledge and skills as given, but one that encourages interactive and collaborative learning that creates a world of meaning for each student. This, of course, does not mean that the systematic view of learning is easily eliminated. Instead, while including the value of the teacher's image as a "technically proficient" teacher, it promotes a mutually complementary relationship with the empiricist view of learning that our school emphasizes, making it "the two wheels of learning," so to speak.

The second point is about the possibility of teacher education in the future. As the feedback from teachers who have participated in our in-school research indicates, the collective consciousness of the teaching staff regarding "student learning" and "student understanding" is transforming. This implies the growth of teachers as well as that of students. In other words, we can say that teachers are finding the possibility of personal development as "reflective practitioners" by not only understanding their students but also relativizing them by examining them from the viewpoint of class creation.

In addition, through OJT, a sense of collaboration among young and veteran teachers was fostered regarding the management of lesson study, and an atmosphere was created in which they could talk about classes daily, including their daily interactions. In other words, it can be said that OJT has been able to make an organization in which daily small-group gatherings enrich the content related to student understanding. For the younger teachers, learning from other teachers in their daily teaching activities was a way to improve their teaching skills and acquire a wide range of practical skills. On the other hand, it is thought that it gave the veteran teachers an opportunity to look back at their practice objectively, using the younger teachers as a mirror and encouraging them to improve their teaching.

5. Conclusion

It has long been said that we live in an unpredictable and uncertain society. The global spread of the novel coronavirus (pandemic) is a symbolic event of this. In the future, we must respond flexibly to the unknown while demonstrating the knowledge and skills we have acquired. In other words, those who have acquired such abilities will be the future leaders of society. It is well-known that knowledge memorized is not the same as knowledge that can be used in society. To solve the problems, we must customize and update our knowledge (information) and try it out in various situations. We must collaborate with others with different lifestyles, religions, cultures, and customs. This paper proposes using a seating chart to overcome the problems of conventional lesson study in Japan and to explore classes that develop the qualities and abilities required in the future and students' individuality. This lesson study using a seating chart is familiar and is a practice that has been handed down from generation to generation in various parts of Japan. However, by reconsidering the present-day meaning of this type of lesson study, we hope that it will provide an opportunity to create classes that make the most of students' individuality in various educational settings in the future.

Teachers are required to make split-second decisions in the development of their classes. In this context, Pedagogical Content Knowledge-based methods are necessary. The teacher faces students who move in complex and diverse ways and make decisions moment by moment concerning the learning content. This is the "Pedagogical Tact" that they have to keep wielding. In light of this embodied and tacit knowledge of teaching methods, capturing students' thoughts and ideas is the essence of class development. Therefore, the seating chart is a tool to visualize students' thoughts, ideas, and preoccupations.

The seating chart shows the students' condition and captures their views and ideas. It opens the way for their learning and draws out the students' learning. Lesson study using a seating chart is efficient, and it is necessary to show the accumulated results to avoid fixation and superficiality of the practice (= packaged practice).

Packaged classes do not produce creative classes but rather stagnate the practical competence of teachers. In the future, teachers and students will be required to have a flexible and variable mindset and to "cultivate an awareness/agency"[27] to change as a subject that contributes to our future society.

References

1) Central Council for Education. (2015). Improving the Qualified Competencies of Teachers for Future School Education—Toward building a community of teacher development in which we learn from and enhance each other—. p.3. https://www.mext.go.jp/component/b_menu/shingi/toushin/__icsFiles/afieldfile/2016/01/13/1365896_01.pdf

2) Central Council for Education. (2005). Creating Compulsory Education for a New Era, Chapter 2: Establishing Unwavering Trust in Teachers: Improving Teacher Quality. https://www.mext.go.jp/b_menu/shingi/chukyo/chukyo0/toushin/attach/1347059.htm

3) National Institute for Educational Policy Research (ed.). *International Comparison of Teacher Environments: Report of the OECD International Teachers' Teaching Environment Survey (TALIS) 2018 [Volume 2]—Teachers and Principals as Professionals.* Akashi Shoten.

4) Partial Amendment Act to the Law on Special Provisions for Education Public Officers promulgated in November 2016 (to be enforced in April 2017). https://www.mext.go.jp/b_menu/hakusho/nc/mext_00051.html

5) Central Council for Education. (2015). The School as a Team and Future Improvement Strategies. https://www.mext.go.jp/b_menu/shingi/chukyo/chukyo0/toushin/__icsFiles/afieldfile/2016/02/05/1365657_00.pdf

6) Central Council for Education. (2022). Measures for the comprehensive improvement of teachers' quality abilities throughout their teaching life. https://www.mext.

go.jp/b_menu/shingi/chukyo/chukyo3/079/sonota/1412985_00004.htm

7) Central Council for Education. (2012). Measures for the Comprehensive Improvement of Teachers' Qualification and Competence throughout their Teaching Life. https://www.mext.go.jp/component/b_menu/shingi/toushin/__icsFiles/afieldfile/2012/ 08/30/1325094_1.pdf

8) Yokomizo, S. (2000). *Action Research for Japanese Language Teachers*. Bonjinsha.

9) Kawano, M. (2020). The Cultural system and Society for Lesson Study Implementation: What is Lesson Study? *Joetsu University of Education Research Bulletin*, 40(1), 45–55.

10) Nakatome, T. (2002). In-school training. In Abiko, T et al. (eds.), *Encyclopedia of Modern School Education 2*, Gyosei, 71.

11) Kiyomi, A., & Manabu, S. (2006). *An Introduction to Teaching in the New Era*. Yuhikaku Alma.

12) Sakai, K. (2013). Consideration of In-school Lesson Study in Elementary Schools: Through Case Studies of Public A Elementary School and Private S Elementary School. *Kyushu Educational Management Society Research Bulletin Kyushu Educational Management Society*, 19.

13) Graduate School of Education and Developmental Sciences, Nagoya University. (2004). Educational Practice Problem Support Project: Methods and Procedures of Participatory Class Study Workshop as Collaborative Problem Solving. https://ocw. nagoya-u.jp/files/44/edu_method13-14ref_a. pdf

14) Akita, K., & Lewis, K. (eds.). (2007). *Lesson Study: An Introduction to Teachers' Lesson Study*. Akashi Shoten, 29.

15) Konishi, M. (2022). *Kangenroku*. ERP Corporation, 14.

16) MEXT. (2017). General Courses of Study for Elementary Schools.

17) OECD Center for Educational Research and Innovation (ed.). (2008). *Formative Assessment and Academic Achievement*. Akashi Shobou.

18) Ito, T. (2018). *The formation process of self-regulated learning: the role of learning strategies and motivation*. Kitaoji Shobo.

19) Sato, M. (2015). *Nurturing Teachers as Experts: Grand Design for Teacher Education Reform*. Iwanami Shoten.

20) Kosakai, A., & Ohtsubo, H. [Syakaika no Shoshi wo Tsuranuku Kai (eds.)]. (1991). *(Series 2) Seating Chart Lesson Plans in Vitality: Practice in Ando Elementary School*. Reimei Shobo.

21) Ishii, T. (2015). *What is the academic ability and learning required now—the light and shadow of competency-based curriculum*. Nippon Keidanren booklet.

22) Tsukano, H. (2013). A Study on Class Conferences in Teacher Training: An Elementary School Social Studies Class for Trainee Teachers. *Research Bulletin of the Center for Educational Practice, Faculty of Education, Iwate University*, 12, 171–183.

23) Tanoue, S. (2004). A Study on Case Studies in Teacher Education: Focusing on the Functions of Extracted Students (18 Teacher Education A). *JSAE Research and Presentation Handbook*, 63, 194–195.

Tanoue, S. (2009). A Basic Study on Extracted Students in Lesson Study: Focusing on

Comparison with Target Students. *Graduate School of Education Research Bulletin*, 11, 111–123, Graduate School of Human Environment Studies Kyushu University, Department of Education, Graduate School of Human Environment Studies, Kyushu University.

24) Ueda, K., Ando Elementary School. (1977). *Every Child Should Live: From Medical Records and Seating Charts to 'ZENTAI NO KESHIKI'*. Meiji Books.
Ueda describes a dynamic view of the unit as a "whole picture" of the learning unit that shows the students' ideas and problems, the teacher's wishes, and the learning content in a structured and elastic manner.

25) Sakai, K. (2020). An Attempt of In-school Research with 'Student Understanding' at the Core. *Annual Report of the Graduate School of Teaching Practice, University of Teacher Education Fukuoka*, 10, 267–274.

26) Schön, D. A., translated by Sato, M. (2001). *Expert Wisdom: Reflective Practitioners Think While Acting*. Yumiru Publishing Co.

27) OECD. (2019). Future of Education and Skills 2030 project. https://www.oecd.org/education/2030project/teachingandlearning/learning/learningcompass- 2030/OECD_Learning_Compass_2030_ concept_note.pdf

Chapter 16

Student Attitude Shifts within the International Baccalaureate Curriculum: Insights from Student Narratives

Yuya AKATSUKA, Sagami Women's University

Abstract

This study provides a perspective on the transition of Japanese students from the traditional Japanese National Curriculum Guidelines (JNCG) to the International Baccalaureate (IB) curriculum. Focusing on three Japanese students in grades 5 and 7 at an IB school in Jakarta, the research highlights their adaptation to the IB's student-centered, active learning environment. Significant shifts were noted in their attitudes towards freedom in learning, active participation, fostering a caring mindset, and independent learning. The study underscores the importance of constructivist principles in promoting a caring and engaging educational environment, emphasizing their value in shaping students' attitudes and learning experiences.

Keywords: *attitude change, constructivism, positivism, International Baccalaureate curriculum, Japanese national curriculum*

1. Backgrounds

Due to the rising need to foster student competencies, the Japanese national curriculum was revised and implemented in AY 2020 for elementary schools and AY 2021 for junior high schools. The revised curriculum referenced the OECD's Definition and Selection of Competencies (DeSeCo) project's theoretical and conceptual foundations of competencies (Mizuhara, 2017). The Japanese Curriculum Planning Special Committee 2015 described the revised Japanese National Curriculum Guidelines (JNCG) as representing an unprecedented and significant change since 1958, when the guidelines were first released in Japan. Consequently, the revised JNCG requires schoolteachers to shift toward fostering students' autonomy through methodologies centered on dialogue and deeper learning.

At the first meeting of the Japan Special Committee on Curriculum Planning on

January 29, 2015, the International Baccalaureate (IB) curriculum was mentioned as a potential reference, which could influence the revision of JNCG. Sieve (2018) noted that the IB curriculum is recognized for its emphasis on students' competencies through dialogue and deeper learning.

Traditionally, IB programmes primarily targeted students who move internationally due to their parents' jobs (Hill, 2010). In recent years, IB programmes have been widely open to students who wish to enroll (Lowe, 1999). However, even today, international students remain the primary attendees at some IB schools. These students have experienced a transition from national curriculum-based programmes to the IB curriculum. Davidson (1998) clarifies that students from some cultural backgrounds may experience difficulties with lessons driven by active inquiry, especially in fostering critical thinking. This observation leads to the hypothesis that Japanese students who move internationally may also face specific challenges as they adjust to the IB curriculum. These potential challenges, including adapting to a more student-centered learning environment, underscore the need for further research in this area, and this chapter aims to clarify the shift in Japanese student attitudes when transitioning to the IB curriculum.

2. Learning Transition from Positivism to IB Constructivism

The IB curriculum fosters student competencies, especially in improving critical and creative thinking; the curriculum is designed based on the constructivism principles developed by theorists such as J. Piaget and L. Vygotsky (International Baccalaureate Organization, 2015). To realize these principles, the IB adopts four teaching approaches: 'deeper learning,' 'inquiry-based learning,' 'project-based learning,' and 'problem-based learning' (Sieve, 2018). These approaches shape the question-driven lessons, advocating for a student-centered and active learning environment. This framework views students as active learners who collaborate with peers, engage in dialogue, and learn through exploration and inquiry. Within the IB curriculum, teachers facilitate learning, encouraging student-led exploration and dialogue.

In Japanese schools, however, the practice of constructivism-based pedagogy remain limited[1]. Kubota (2003) employs the concept of "positivism" as the antithesis of constructivism, while Tada (2017) utilises the notion of "essentialism". According to Tada (2017), essentialism places a strong emphasis on the acquisition of universal knowledge, whereas constructivism is characterised by a learner-centred, dialogue-driven approach. Tsuneyoshi (2009) introduces the concept of "subject-based learning", in which the role of the teacher is to provide direct instruction through whole-class teaching, offering explanations and presenting the correct answers. These concepts—positivism, essentialism, and subject-based learning—have been invoked to describe approaches that stand in opposition to constructivism. All three highlight a focus on knowledge acquisition through teacher-led instruction, which had traditionally been the predominant educational model in most Japanese schools.

In other words, capturing the attitude shift from traditional JNCG to IB curriculum

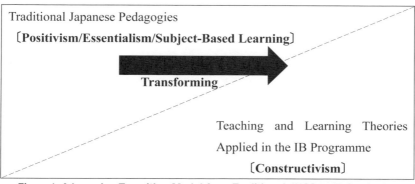
Figure1: A Learning Transition Model from Traditional JNCG to IB Curriculum

can be described as a transition from positivism to constructivism (see Figure 1). This transition is significant as it represents a shift from a traditional, teacher-centered approach to a more student-centered, active learning environment. This transition is significant as it represents a shift from a traditional, teacher-centered approach to a more student-centered, active learning environment. Previous research on learning experiences within the IB curriculum, such as that conducted by Wilkinson and Hayden (2010), discussed how students' attitudes change in the Diploma Programme. In addition, Shibuya (2018) analyzed how culturally diverse children are embraced and what practices are implemented concerning cultural diversity. However, these research did not delve into perspectives such as how attitudes towards learning have occurred regarding learning style transition.

The significance of capturing attitude changes in this research lies in the understanding that the act of thinking is fundamentally comprised of skills and attitudes (Perkins, 1992). Kusumi (2011) asserts that thinking comprises both non-cognitive elements (attitudes) and cognitive elements (skills and knowledge). He discusses the structure in which cognitive elements are founded upon non-cognitive elements. That is, with the development of appropriate attitudes, skills will be effectively acquired. Therefore, cultivating attitudes is paramount, and this study contends that capturing attitude shifts holds significant value.

3. Methods

3-1. Participants

The study examines three native Japanese-speaking students currently enrolled in grades 5 and 7 at an IB School in Jakarta, Indonesia (see Table 1). These students have transitioned from the JNCG to the IB curriculum due to their parents' work-related relocation. The decision to enroll in the IB school was made by the parents rather than the students. All three participants primarily speak Japanese at home, while their school utilizes English as the medium of instruction and communication. All other instruction is provided in English except for second-language classes in Bahasa Indonesia. Before their exposure to the IB curriculum, they had engaged with the JNCG for over three years.

3-2. Methods

The semi-structured interviews were conducted in February 2024 by the researcher and were audio-recorded to ensure accuracy and thoroughness. Each session lasted approximately 15 minutes. Informed consent was obtained from the students and their parents before the interviews, granting permission to use the audio recordings and any data from the sessions. It is noted that Student A and Student B had previously attended a government school in Japan operating under Article 1[2]. In contrast, Student C was educated at the Japanese School in Malaysia. Despite the geographical differences, the curriculum at the Japanese School in Malaysia adhered to the standards of the JNCG.

Table 1: Each Student Backgrounds

	Student A	Student B	Student C
Years of Experience in JNCG	6.5 years	4.5 years	3 years
Years of Experience in IB	0.5 years	0.5 years	2.5 years
Grade	Grade 7 (MYP 2)	Grade 5 (PYP 5)	Grade 5 (PYP 5)
Gender	M	M	F
English Proficiency Level	Beginner	Beginner	Intermediate

3-3. Results and findings

3-3-1. Embracing freedom in learning

One aspect of the IB curriculum is its focus on cultivating an open-minded learner profile (International Baccalaureate Organization, 2015). Student C noted, "Schools here are very free-spirited. I was used to listening to the teacher and engaging with the lessons as the norm (at Japanese school), so when I came to this school, I was surprised." Similarly, student A remarked on the distinct learning environments, "Everything is decided by rules (at Japanese school). (But in this school), it has an open vibe, which is very open and free." Student B compared the emphasis on exams in Japanese schools to the approach at their IB school, "In Japan, classes are often focused on preparing for exams, but here, without tests, it feels like we have the freedom to learn in a more open-ended way." Additionally, student B recognized a more lenient attitude towards mistakes, "It is more relaxed, like as long as you know this, you are good, which feels kinder." They also noted a different reaction to errors in the classroom, "There was a feeling of dread if you make a mistake in a Japanese school, like 'Oh no,' but here, it is more like, 'Oops, haha.'"

However, three students also noted that classroom management by the IB subject teachers are somewhat lenient compared to their previous schools. They mentioned that IB teachers should place greater emphasis on creating a classroom environment where all students can study their subjects in a calm and focused atmosphere.

These student reflections underscore the emphasis on freedom, openness, and a more relaxed approach to learning and handling mistakes within the IB curriculum. Although the IB documents do not explicitly state the importance of fostering a sense of freedom or a safe environment for making mistakes, the students' narratives indicate that the IB curriculum facilitates a learning environment suffused with freedom, and they have shifted their attitudes towards learning to embrace freedom of thinking.

3-3-2. Transitioning to active learning

In the IB programmes, students actively engage in group work and problem-solving activities, a method explained by Sieve (2018). Student C shares her experience with this model, "We will share our opinions, consolidate them, and then present them to the teacher." Student C further details that this approach extends to tackling global issues: "To improve the Earth, what should we do? In that context, we are divided into groups, and my group is working on reducing the number of people without food, focusing on Zero Hunger. We do much research, which can be quite bothersome."

Student A reflects on the initial challenge of this active learning environment, "At the beginning, it felt overwhelming. There was so much to think about, and the idea of presentations was just too bothersome." However, student A also shares an adaptation and skill development, "But now, I have gotten used to it. What once seemed like a huge task, just doing the research, now seems no big deal. The reason? I have gotten better at using the internet. It used to be hard to think of what keywords to search for, but now, they just come to me instantly."

This narrative illustrates a shift from passive to active learning. Despite initially perceiving group work and research as bothersome, students eventually find value in these activities, developing inquiry skills and gaining confidence in navigating complex tasks.

3-3-3. Fostering a culture of caring

The 10 IB learner profiles are at the core of the IB curriculum. "Caring" stands out as a pivotal trait, reflecting Peterson's (1972) assertion that being humane is at the heart of the IB's philosophy.

Student C finds the manifestation of this caring ethos in her school environment, "Everyone is so kind and incredibly friendly. Today, a friend with a leg injury sat in this chair. Everyone helped them out, expressed concern, pushed their chair, and even lent a hand when climbing stairs. I think there is much kindness around here." This anecdote highlights the school's commitment to embodying the "caring" learner profile in practical, everyday school actions.

Similarly, student B contrasts their experiences with social interactions in Japan to those at their current school, "Everyone is friendly here. Interactions were minimal in my previous school, and people often say hello, but in the current school when you meet someone, it is common to ask their name and chat casually."

These reflections from students B and C underscore the impact of the IB curriculum's emphasis on caring and fostering a school culture where kindness, friendliness, and supportive interactions are in daily school life.

3-3-4. Empowering independent learning

The IB curriculum emphasizes independent research in all subject areas (International

Baccalaureate Organization, 2015). Student A describes the process: "In the IB programmes, you must research independently, making compiling and organizing information challenging. You set a goal to create something and plan towards achieving it. You plan and eventually complete the project." This method encourages students to take initiative and set and pursue their own goals. "Design classes are about actual designing, from planning to creation," explains student A, illustrating the hands-on, project-based nature of the curriculum.

Student B emphasizes the practical application of knowledge in design classes, "It is different from (Japanese) art (lesson); you create things using study. For instance, figuring out how to make something like a propeller flies higher." This approach requires students to apply cross-disciplinary knowledge, such as mathematics, to solve real-world problems.

Furthermore, student A reflects on the pedagogical approach within the IB programmes, "The teaching method here encourages active participation rather than the teacher just leading the class one-sidedly; it is like the students and the teacher together create the class." This collaborative environment contrasts with the experience as quieter and more teacher-led. "Here, in a good way, it is lively. Right now, we are studying Medieval Europe, and we come up with our questions about their country's history and answer them ourselves,"

The emphasis on student-led inquiry enables a deeper connection with the material, as students are not only recipients of knowledge but also active participants in its discovery. "It is not so difficult to come up with questions because I have a lot to know," mentions student A, indicating his natural curiosity. However, he also acknowledges a potential drawback: "In Japanese schools, we are taught various things directly, so knowledge automatically comes to you without thinking deeply. Here, though, you need to research by yourself, which leads to a sense of achievement and makes the knowledge stick. However, things you do not manage to research yourself might not be learned."

This narrative indicates the IB curriculum's commitment to fostering independent thinkers who take ownership of their learning. It also suggests balancing self-directed study with guidance to ensure a comprehensive understanding of the subject matter.

4. Conclusion

The study reveals that students transitioning to the IB curriculum primarily notice differences in freedom, a more caring mindset, active learning participation, and encouragement of thoughtful engagement in their learning. The findings suggest that a constructivist curriculum is crucial for creating an environment that fosters a sense of care and safety, allowing students to deepen their learning experience. Additionally, the results indicate that while students struggle with question-driven lessons, they gradually become accustomed to and shift their attitudes to this new learning style.

The results also suggest that in the constructivism approach, while students appreciate the freedom of learning, they also desire a balance between effective classroom management and the enjoyment of learning. Furthermore, the findings indicate that adequate student support will be essential for the transition to inquiry-based learning, particularly in fostering self-directed learning; otherwise, challenges may arise.

However, this research is subject to limitations, including personality and family life background differences and small samples, which means the results should be viewed as suggestions rather than definitive conclusions. For future research, increasing the number of student participants and considering their personality is recommended, as this could significantly impact their engagement with and adaptation to the IB curriculum.

References

Davidson, B. (1998). Comments on Dwight Atkinson's 'A critical approach to critical thinking in TESOL': A Case for Critical Thinking in the English Language Classroom. *TESOL Quarterly*, 32(1), 119–123.

Hill, I. (2010). *The International Baccalaureate: Pioneering in Education*. A John Catt Publication.

International Baccalaureate Organization. (2015). Approaches to learning. Retrieved from https://ibpublishing.ibo.org/dpatln/apps/dpatl/guide.html?doc=d_0_dpatl_gui_1502_1_j&part=2&chapter=2

Iraha, T. (2021). A study into the history of the Ryukyus Junior High School: A shift in pedagogical models one time vol.1. *Bulletin of Teacher Center of University of Ryukyus*, 3, 117–128.

Kubota, K. (2003). New educational practices based on constructivism. *Computer and Education*, 15, 12–18.

Kusumi, T. (2011). Hihan teki shiko towa- Shimin literacy to generick skill no kakutoku [What is critical thinking: Acquisition of civic literacy and generic skills]. In Kusumi, T., Koyasu, M., & Michita, Y. (Eds.), *Hihan teki shiko wo hagukumu—gakushiryoku to shakaijin kiso ryoku no kiso keisei* [Fostering critical thinking: Forming the foundations of academic and professional skills] (140–148). Yuhikaku.

Lowe, J. (1999). International Examinations, National Systems, and the Global Market. *Compare*, 29(3), 317–330.

Mizuhara, K. (2017). *Kyoiku katei seisaku no genriteki kadai: Competency to 2017 gakushu shido yoryo katitei* [Fundamental problems of curriculum policy: Competencies and courses of study revision in 2017]. Journal of Educational Research, 84(4), 421–433.

Perkins, D. N. (1992). *Smart school: From training memories to educating minds*. New York: Free Press.

Peterson, A. (1972). *International Baccalaureate*. London: George G. Harrap & Co. Ltd.

Shibuya, M. (2018). Bunkatekini tayona kodomo kara kokusaitekina shiyawo motsu ningen e: Kokusai baccalaureate ni okeru bunkateki tayosei [From Culturally Diverse Children to Individuals with a Global Perspective: Cultural Diversity in the International Baccalaureate]. *The Journal of Child Study*, 24, 43–60.

Sieve, C, M. (2018). Teachers' experiences in using constructivist pedagogies in the International Baccalaureate Diploma Programme [Doctoral dissertation, College of

Professional Studies Northeastern University]. Northeastern University Repository. https://repository.library.northeastern.edu/files/neu:m044c765r/fulltext.pdf?fb-clid=IwAR3InWueFRvInGVaGV-FpgRsTzjHAK2NP5Hg-ySX5Wfn2eAS_Cri8eQa-dzg

Tada, T. (2017). *Global jidai no taiwagata jugyo no kenkyu- jissen no tameno 12 no yoken* [Research on dialogue-based lessons in the global era: 12 requirements for practice]. Toshindo.

Vygotsky, L. S. (1978). *Mind in society: The development of higher psychological processes.* Cambridge, MA: Harvard University Press.

Wilkinson, V., & Hayden, M. (2010). The International Baccalaureate Diploma and student attitudes: An exploratory study. *Journal of Research in International Education, 9*(1), 85–96.

Note

1) For instance, a practical example can be found at the University of the Ryukyus Affiliated Elementary and Junior High Schools (Iraha, 2021)

2) Article 1 School: In Article 1 of the Japanese School Law, the definition of a school is provided. These schools must adhere to the national curriculum. In contrast, most international schools are not covered by Article 1 and do not follow the Japanese national curriculum.

Chapter 17

Transformation of Student Consciousness through Service-Learning Focused on Hip Hop

Takeshi BABA, Baiko Gakuin University

Abstract

This study examines the consciousness transformation students bring through Service-Learning focused on Hip Hop. Service-Learning (SL) is an experiential educational approach that involves applying students' knowledge to community activities tailored to local needs, reflecting on activities through deliberate structured reflection, and expanding learning through reflection. A characteristic of SL is prioritizing consideration for students' interests. Thus, the author focuses on "Hip Hop," which has explosively spread among young people in Japan. Since Hip Hop is popular among Japanese youth, it can be a factor in appealing to the "interests" of students. Considering these backgrounds, the author has developed and engaged in SL practices with the theme "social contribution through Hip Hop." Then, the author examines the consciousness transformation brought by students through SL focused on Hip Hop, which was targeted to appeal to students' interests.

1. Introduction

The first introduction of Service-Learning (hereafter SL) in Japanese higher education was undertaken by International Christian University, and the year of its introduction in 1999 coincided with the period when the University Council (1998) outlined a policy emphasizing the utilization of practical education in university education through the establishment of courses incorporating experiences outside the classroom. During this period, when this policy was articulated, Japanese higher education was transitioning from quantitative expansion to ensuring quality, and there was a shift from teaching-centric approaches by educators towards student-centric learning (Central Council for Education, 2005, 2008, 2012; Science Council of Japan, 2010). Adding this backdrop, the "Center of Community" (COC) project was initiated in 2013 to strengthen collaboration between universities and local communities and evolve into the "Center of Community +" (COC+) project (Ministry of Education, 2013, 2016), thereby community-engaged learning including SL was promoted in Japanese higher education to date.

SL is an experiential educational approach that involves applying students' knowledge to community activities tailored to local needs, reflecting on activities through deliberate, structured reflection, and expanding learning through reflection (Kuramoto, 2008; Baba, 2022). A characteristic of SL is "prioritizing consideration for students' interests" (Kuramoto, 2008, p. 227). Thus, the author focuses on "Hip Hop," which has explosively spread among young people in Japan. While Hip Hop is often perceived as a genre of music or a form of dance, it is a "culture" consisting of four elements: rap, DJing, breakdancing, and graffiti (murals). Since these four elements are popular among Japanese youth, they can be a factor in appealing to the "interests" of students. Indeed, in the birthplace of Hip Hop in the United States, Hip Hop Based Education, a teaching method incorporating elements of Hip Hop into course content, has begun to spread (Hill, 2009). Considering these backgrounds, the author has developed and engaged in SL practices with the theme "social contribution through Hip Hop." While previous studies have demonstrated that SL yields learning outcomes such as enhancing students' self-understanding, improving self-efficacy, and transforming perspectives on social issues (Eyler & Giles, 1999), the learning outcomes resulting from the incorporation of Hip Hop remain unknown. Therefore, this study aims to examine the consciousness transformation brought by students through SL focused on Hip Hop, which was targeted to appeal to students' interests.

2. What is Hip Hop?

2-1. The background of Hip Hop's emergence and the essence of Hip Hop

Jeff Chang's "Can't Stop Won't Stop: A History of the Hip-Hop Generation" (2007) stands out as a seminal work summarizing the development of Hip Hop from its early stages to around 2000. Therefore, the discussion on the background of birth of Hip Hop primarily relies on information from this work.

In the early 1950s, urban development began in New York City laid the groundwork for the emergence of Hip Hop. This urban development aimed to create a circular network connecting Manhattan with the suburbs, transforming Manhattan into a center of wealth. As part of this effort, construction began on the Cross Bronx Expressway, a highway extending from the South Bronx to Manhattan. In this urban development scheme, clearing impoverished areas (ghettos) in Manhattan was essential to transforming it into a center of wealth. Officials involved in urban development abused their rights, displacing lower-class racial minorities such as African Americans and Puerto Ricans from Manhattan to the booming public housing areas in East Brooklyn and the South Bronx. Consequently, the urban development in New York during the 1950s and 60s led to the exodus of middle-class white residents to suburban white residential areas. At the same time, the poor (primarily racial minorities) moved into public housing. As a result, public housing in the South Bronx, where people experiencing poverty resided, gradually deteriorated.

By the 1970s, New York City faced a financial crisis, with job losses in manufacturing industries in the South Bronx reaching as high as 600,000, leading to the disappearance of 40% of the industrial sector. In such circumstances, public housing became rife with corruption, with unscrupulous landlords resorting to arson to collect insurance money. These landlords neglected heating and water supply to apartments, defaulted on property taxes owed to the city, and eventually set fire to vacant apartments. Consequently, between 1973 and 1977, 30,000 cases of arson in the South Bronx were plunging the area into severe decay during the 1970s.

In the severely deteriorated South Bronx, numerous gangs emerged, effectively dominating the area. Between 1968 and 1973, when gangs ruled supreme, gang wars were rampant. However, the situation gradually improved due to the activities of Africa Bambaataa, a charismatic leader who became the youthful leader of the formidable gang Black Spades. Bambaataa embarked on activities to stop violence by rallying many young people and appealing to cease hostilities. Bambaataa then established the organization known as the "Zulu Nation," where anti-violence and cessation of hostilities became the core activities. Members from various gangs, including Black Spades, joined the Zulu Nation, primarily composed of rappers, DJs, breakdancers, and graffiti writers. These individuals eventually became the core of what would be known as the "four elements of Hip Hop."

Thus, with the activities of the Zulu Nation, rap, DJing, breakdancing, and graffiti were encapsulated under the framework of "Hip Hop" leading up to the present day. Consequently, the essence of Hip Hop has been significantly influenced by the ideals of the Zulu Nation. The organization's motto was "Peace, Love, Unity, and Having Fun." Similarly, KRS-One (2009), a rapper who has walked through the dawn of Hip Hop alongside Bambaataa, states that "Peace, Love, Unity, and Having Fun" are the principles of Hip Hop from its early stages. Despite the presence of aggressive lyrics in rap and the glorification of delinquent culture in gangster rap, Hip Hop's core values include peace and love, positioned diametrically opposite to violence.

2-2. The spread of Hip Hop in Japan

The influx of Hip Hop into Japan dates back to the 1980s. During this era, Yoyogi Park in Tokyo became a gathering place for street musicians and young people performing music, with dancers engaging in breakdancing among them. Various artists practicing Hip Hop elements began to mix with these dancers, recognizing this small group as the first generation of Japanese Hip Hop (Condry, 2009).

Today, nearly 40 years since the first generation, freestyle rap battles have gained popularity in terms of rap, and rap battle TV shows have begun to be broadcast. The existence of TV programs as terrestrial broadcasts can be seen as an indicator of the high demand in the Japanese rap market. Additionally, with the proliferation of Internet television, the number of rap TV programs in Japan has increased across multiple media platforms, and rap-based TV commercials have become more common.

Regarding breakdances, the population of street dance enthusiasts, including breakdancing, has reached as high as 6 million (Street Dance Association, 2021). Furthermore, due to the revision of the curriculum guidelines in 2008, dance became a mandatory subject in physical education in junior high schools. In the revised guidelines, dance is composed of "creative dance," "folk dance," and "modern rhythmic dance," with "modern rhythmic dance" described explicitly as "dancing to modern rhythmic songs such as rock and Hip Hop" (Ministry of Education, 2008). In other words, exposure to Hip Hop is standardized within the educational curriculum.

As for graffiti, due to its high affinity with comics (manga), it has developed through the medium of manga. Manga focusing on graffiti, such as "Tokyo Graffiti" (Inoue, 2017), "Shounen in the Hood" (SITE, 2020), and "Illbros" (TABOO1, 2019), have been published, with authors like SITE and TABOO1 being graffiti writers themselves. Furthermore, unlike in the United States, the birthplace of Hip Hop, no manga focused solely on graffiti, making it a unique development in Japan, known for its manga culture.

In summary, over approximately 40 years, Hip Hop has steadily permeated Japan, becoming as ingrained in the daily lives of young people as baseball and soccer from the West have been in Japanese society.

3. Hip Hop Based Education

3-1. What is Hip Hop Based Education?

Hip Hop Based Education (HHBE) is an instructional method used in formal and informal educational activities, incorporating elements of Hip Hop while teaching subject matter (Hill, 2009). Instructional methods using Hip Hop elements may also be called Hip Hop Pedagogy (O'Connor, 2016) or Hip Hop Education (Emdin & Adjapong, 2018). However, since these names may lead to misconceptions about "teaching Hip Hop elements," this work adopts the name coined by Hill (2009), emphasizing "based on Hip Hop."

HHBE began to spread in the United States, and numerous practical examples have been reported (Morrell & Duncan-Andrade, 2002; Hill, 2009; Emdin, 2013; Love, 2015). For example, the case of Emdin's (2013) high school science class is widely known. This practice aims to increase interest and motivation in science by using rap among high school students who lack interest or enthusiasm. Students in this class write rap lyrics using scientific terms and compete with each other. The key to this practice is that in creating lyrics using scientific terms, students must research the meanings of those terms and understand them thoroughly. Without a solid understanding of the meanings of the terms, students cannot deepen the relationships between terms or the lyrics' coherence (narrative structure). Therefore, students study scientific terms to complete the lyrics, enhancing their motivation to learn science.

3-2. Theoretical background of Hip Hop Based Education

The theoretical background of HHBE is rooted in Culturally Relevant Education (CRE). CRE is an educational theory designed to address the needs of students from diverse cultural backgrounds, including race, ethnicity, and language. The origins of this theory can be traced back to the 1960s, as summarized by Kodama (2018). In American elementary and secondary education during the 1960s, issues arose concerning the academic achievement gap between minority students, particularly those from impoverished families such as Black and Hispanic minorities, and their White counterparts. To address these disparities, compensatory education programs were initiated. By the late 1960s, compensatory education had evolved into multicultural education, focusing not only on theoretical and methodological aspects but also on the role of teachers as advocates for multicultural education. Since then, there has been a growing disparity between the demographic makeup of teachers—predominantly White, female, and from middle-class backgrounds—and the increasing diversity of students in American schools, a trend that has continued since the 1990s. Most aspiring teachers lack significant experience interacting with culturally diverse groups during their upbringing, schooling, or prior experiences, and they often receive inadequate guidance on how to interact with children from different cultural backgrounds during their teacher education programs. As a result, newly appointed teachers face challenges adapting to schools with diverse student populations, including students of color. Against this backdrop, attention has increasingly turned to Culturally Relevant Education.

While this educational theory has been referred to by various names such as Culturally Appropriate (Au & Jordan, 1981), Culturally Congruent (Mohatt & Erickson, 1981), Culturally Responsive (Cazden & Leggett, 1981), and Culturally Relevant Pedagogy (Ladson-Billings, 1995), it has become commonly known as Culturally Relevant Education (Dover, 2013; Aronson & Laughter, 2016). Among these theories, Ladson-Billings' (1995, 2009) Culturally Relevant Pedagogy (Teaching) is particularly influential. Culturally Relevant Pedagogy is "pedagogy that empowers students intellectually, socially, emotionally, and politically by using cultural references to impart knowledge, skills, and attitudes" (Ladson-Billings, 2009, p.20). As mentioned earlier, since Hip Hop originated from cultures such as African American and Hispanic American, there is a risk of misinterpretation that HHBE is intended only for "African American and Hispanic American" students. However, Hip Hop has adapted to multiple cultures and has been localized to fit regional contexts, making HHBE adaptable regardless of race or ethnicity (Love, 2015). In other words, given that Hip Hop has become entrenched as youth culture in Japan, incorporating Hip Hop into education can be highly effective as a "culturally relevant material" for Japanese students.

4. Practice

The practice targeted in this study was conducted as part of the fourth-year seminar course at Baiko Gakuin University, where the author is affiliated, located in Shimonoseki City, Yamaguchi Prefecture, Japan. This seminar focused on "social contribution through Hip Hop," aiming to resolve marine litter issues and enhance tourism appeal in Yamaguchi Prefecture by promoting "ethical tourism." Ethical tourism is "travel that considers people, the environment, and the destination/region for the sake of sustainable society and future" (Kinki Nippon Tourist, 2022). The background to the focus

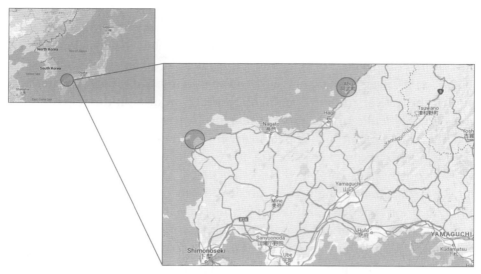
Figure 1: Tsunoshima (left) and Abu-cho (right)

on ethical tourism stems from the fact that Yamaguchi Prefecture faces two significant challenges: the "marine litter issue" and the "tourism issue."

Yamaguchi Prefecture, located on the Sea of Japan side, is affected by the Tsushima Current flowing between Japan and Korea. Due to this current, not only domestic waste from Japan but also waste from China and Korea drifts ashore in Yamaguchi Prefecture. The amount of waste washed ashore in Yamaguchi Prefecture is considered the highest in Japan. According to the results of the 2019 marine litter survey, Shimonoseki, ranking first among the ten monitoring survey locations nationwide, had 21,648 liters of washed-up garbage, significantly exceeding the 5,334 liters in Hakodate (Hokkaido), which ranked second (Ministry of the Environment, 2021). As for the "tourism issue," Yamaguchi Prefecture faces challenges such as stagnation in inbound tourism growth and inadequate dissemination of the charms of Yamaguchi Prefecture to other prefectures. Regarding the number of tourists from other prefectures, there is a difference of about one million people compared to Hiroshima Prefecture, also in the same region. Yamaguchi Prefecture ranks 39th in the ranking of prefectures people want to visit (DIAMOND online, 2021).

Against this backdrop, the seminar selected Tsunoshima and Abu-cho (Figure 1), facing the Sea of Japan, as activity sites. The 21 seminar participants were divided into Tsunoshima and Abu-cho teams, engaging in coastal cleanup while experiencing local tourist resources. Based on the experiences in both areas, a "Yamaguchi Prefecture PR rap video" was created, and crowdfunding campaigns were conducted to attract tourism and address marine litter issues by utilizing the PR video. In this seminar, partners from both areas, NPO Cobalt Blue Shimonoseki Life Saving Club (hereinafter referred to as Cobalt Blue) for Tsunoshima and ABU Camp Field for Abu-cho, formed a team, offering return gifts aimed at promoting tourism to Tsunoshima and Abu-cho. Ten percent of the support funds were allocated to reducing marine litter.

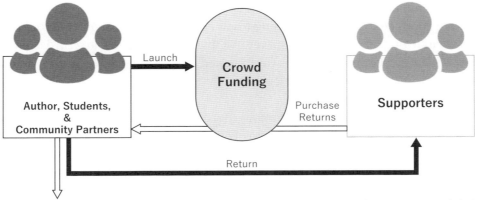

Ten percent of the support funds will be allocated to support reducing marine debris.

Figure 2: Composition of Crowdfunding

Additionally, both the Tsunoshima team and the Abu-cho team are divided into subgroups within the team (divided by the type of activity), consisting of three subgroups (a total of six subgroups for both teams combined): the "Rap Creation Team" for creating the Yamaguchi Prefecture PR rap, the "Video Creation Team" for producing the Yamaguchi Prefecture PR rap video, and the "Promotion Team" for promoting crowdfunding.

5. Analysis

5-1. Data collection

As for the analysis targets, six of the 21 seminar participants were selected. As mentioned, these six individuals served as leaders for each activity type subgroup (six subgroups). The reason for targeting these six individuals is twofold: firstly, as leaders, they have overseen the activities of each subgroup, making their transformation in attitude towards this practical activity more noticeable compared to other members, and secondly, it was believed that diverse opinions could be gathered based on the activities of each subgroup. Furthermore, these six individuals were divided evenly between those exposed to Hip Hop daily and those without, allowing for a balanced representation. Considering these points, it was deemed appropriate to select these six individuals.

The distinction between those who had been exposed to Hip Hop in their daily lives and those who had not was made because, among the 21 participants, some regularly engaged with one or more of the four elements of Hip Hop and had a pre-existing interest in Hip Hop, as well as those who had not engaged with any of the four elements and chose the seminar either out of interest in social contribution or simply because they found it intriguing. Therefore, in this study, in addition to verifying the transformation of students' consciousness, the differences in the transformation between the "Hip Hop group" and the "Non-Hip Hop group" will also be examined. Subsequently, "Hip Hop group" will refer to those exposed to Hip Hop daily, while "Non-Hip Hop group" will refer to those who have not.

Data collection involved conducting interviews with these participants. The interviews were conducted individually using a semi-structured interview method with an interview guide prepared before the survey. All interview content was recorded using an IC recorder, and verbatim transcripts were created.

5-2. Analysis method

SCAT (Steps for Coding and Theorization), devised by Otani (2007, 2011, 2019), was adopted as a qualitative method. SCAT involves coding transcribed audio data through four steps to extract conceptual structures, generate storylines, and attempt theoretical descriptions by fragmenting the storyline. It is worth noting, as stated by Otani (2011), that the term "theory" here refers to "what can be said from this data" rather than universal or generally applicable principles.

SCAT is effective for analyzing relatively small-scale qualitative data, and its process leaves explicit traces, compelling the analyst to confirm the validity of the analysis. It delves into the context of the "manifest" data groups and systematically describes them as the context of the "latent" data groups in the storyline, which is excellent for theorization. Therefore, this method was adopted. SCAT involves four basic coding steps: (1) listing noteworthy phrases in the data, (2) listing phrases outside the data to paraphrase those in step (1), (3) entering concepts to explain step (2), and (4) entering emerging themes or conceptual structures from steps (1) to (3). This study followed this procedure for the coding process (Figure 3). Furthermore, as Otani (2019) states, the purpose of analysis using SCAT is strictly to obtain theory, and the storyline is an intermediate product. When conducting theoretical descriptions, it is suggested to "write theory using the words contained in the storyline." Therefore, both the storyline and theoretical descriptions would overlap. Hence, due to space constraints, only the theoretical descriptions are provided in this paper's "4. Analysis Results" section. It is important to note that all these analysis processes were conducted in Japanese, and the theoretical descriptions were translated into English for this paper.

5-3. Ethical considerations

The interviewees targeted in this study were verbally informed about the interview recording and the intention to utilize the data for academic presentations, journal publications, etc. They sought their consent (the consent process was recorded on tape). Furthermore, the names of the interviewees have been anonymized to ensure confidentiality.

5-4. Analysis results

Table 1 presents the theoretical descriptions obtained from the analysis results for both the Hip Hop and Non-Hip Hop groups. The numbers [1] to [4] listed in the table's left column correspond to the interview questions outlined below.

<Questions for Interview>

[1] How did the impression of "social contribution" change when "Hip Hop elements" were added? (How did it affect the motivation to take the course?)

No.	Speaker	Text	<1>Noteworthy words or phrases from the text	<2>Paraphrases of <1>	<3>Concepts from the text that account for <2>	<4>Themes, constructs in considerations of context	<5>Questions & tasks
1	Author	山口県の海洋ゴミ問題や観光魅力度問題に対する興味関心度合は、4年ゼミ開始前と比較し、どのように変化したか？また、その変化にヒップホップ（ゼミのテーマ「ヒップホップを通した社会貢献」）が影響していると思うか？	・興味関心度合 ・開始前と比較 ・変化 ・ヒップホップ ・影響	・ゼミ活動前後での興味関心の変化 ・ヒップホップによる影響	・興味関心の変化 ・ヒップホップによる要因	・興味関心の変化要因	
2	Student 1	興味関心度合いは凄く上がったと思います。門司に住んでいるのでちっちゃい頃から角島とか行くこともちょこちょこあって、でまあ山口県も隣の県なんで下関とかだけでも来ることはあったんですけど、やっぱりこのゼミに参加して初めて、ゼミとあと先生の授業ですけど、この海洋ごみ問題とか観光魅力度問題っていうのが、山口県内で結構おっきい問題になっているっていうのは初めて知ったと思います。だから、ゼミを通してその解決策を探すっていうことで、自分の中でこうしたらいいんじゃないかとか、そういったアイディアを考えたりはしたので、やっぱりそういうところに関する興味関心度合いは大きく変化したと思います。	・山口県内で結構おっきい問題になっているっていうのは初めて知った ・興味関心度合いは大きく変化	・問題に対する知識の少なさ ・問題に対する興味関心の高さ ・興味関心の変化	・地域問題に対する見識不足 ・地域問題に対する興味関心度合いの低さ ・興味関心度合の変化要因	・地域問題に対する興味関心度合の低さ故の問題に対する見識不足 ・興味関心の変化要因	
3	Author	ヒップホップのどういう側面が影響していると思いますか？	・ヒップホップ ・側面 ・影響	・ヒップホップの影響力	・ヒップホップによる影響要因	・ヒップホップによる影響要因	
4	Student 1	ヒップホップの、それそこそこないだいだパワーポイントを作ってて、先生のパワーポイントにもあったんですけど、四つの、あのDJとかのほうじゃなくて、四つの要素ってあるじゃないですか。楽しむのかとか、っていうのが自分の中では結構大きい側面だったなぁって思って、やっぱ海洋ごみ問題とか観光魅力度の問題っていうのが、普通に取り扱ったら多分シリアスな内容になりがちだと思うんですけど、やっぱりヒップホップの要素を取り入れることで、例えばこうゼミの中でラップの動画とか作ったり、みんながこう動画だけじゃなくてラップの歌詞とか考えてるのを見ると、みんななんか楽しみながらやれてたなーって思って、だからやれなかったら、単に、じゃあこの問題を解決するにはどうしたらいいだろうみたいな考えて、もうめっちゃ真剣に考えて終わりみたいな感じになりそうだなーと思ったんですけど、そういうヒップホップの楽しむ要素っていうのがあったので、そこが凄いゼミ全体の活動に、その側面が結構貢献したんじゃないかなって思います。	・四つの要素 ・楽しむのかとか、っていうのが自分の中では結構大きい側面 ・普通に取り扱ったら多分シリアスな内容 ・みんなんか楽しみながらやれてた ・もうめっちゃ真剣に考えて終わりみたいな感じ ・ヒップホップの楽しむ要素	・Peace, love, unity, having fun ・ヒップホップの本質 ・シリアスな内容 ・真面目な内容 ・楽しい	・ヒップホップの本質 ・地域の「問題」というシリアスな内容 ・楽しい	・「楽しむ」というヒップホップの本質 ・地域問題というシリアスさ	

· (Omitted due to space constraints)

No.	Speaker	Text	<1>Noteworthy words or phrases from the text	<2>Paraphrases of <1>	<3>Concepts from the text that account for <2>	<4>Themes, constructs in considerations of context	<5>Questions & tasks
10	Student 3	ヒップホップとゴミ問題は、ここの繋がりっていうのがまずいじゃないですか、そもそも。そういうところで、こういうちょっと、ほぼ対義語みたいな二つが合わさったところがやっぱ惹かれたところかなぁと思います。	・ヒップホップとゴミ問題は、ここの繋がりっていうのがまずいない ・ほぼ対義語みたいな二つが合わさった ・惹かれたところ	・二つの事象の関連性のなさ ・対極 ・魅力	・関連性のない対極性 ・対極性が生み出す魅力	・関連のない対極性が生み出す魅力	

Story-Line	授業開始前には、地域問題に対する興味関心度合の低さ故の問題に対する見識不足が顕著であるが、興味関心の変化要因としてヒップホップが機能する。地域問題というシリアスさ故に、地域問題解決への取組に高いハードルを感じていたが、ヒップホップを通すことにより身近な問題へと変化した。その変化には、「楽しむ」というヒップホップの本質や、ヒップホップと地域問題解決という関連のない対極性が生み出す魅力という部分が、ヒップホップによる影響要因として関与している。
Theory	・授業開始前には、地域問題に対する興味関心度合の低さ故の問題に対する見識不足が顕著であり、地域問題というシリアスさが地域問題解決への取組に対する高いハードルとなるが、ヒップホップを通すことで地域問題が身近な問題へと変化し、ヒップホップが興味関心の変化要因として機能する。 ・地域問題が身近な問題へと変化する過程において、「楽しむ」というヒップホップの本質や、ヒップホップと地域問題解決という関連のない対極性が生み出す魅力が、ヒップホップによる影響要因となる。

Figure 3: Example of SCAT Analysis

[2] How did the motivation to engage in the initiative change as a result of addressing local issues under the theme of "social contribution through Hip Hop" rather than just "beach cleaning" or "tourism promotion"?

[3] How did the level of interest and concern regarding the marine litter issue and tourism attractiveness issues in Yamaguchi Prefecture change compared to before the start of the course? Also, do you think Hip Hop influenced this change?

[4] How did your motivation towards the course change after taking classes that incorporated Hip Hop elements?

Table 1: Theoretical Descriptions Obtained from the Analysis Results

Q	Hip Hop Group	Non-Hip Hop group
[1]	• Hip Hop serves as an appealing element to the "desire for enjoyment" and becomes a determinant factor in the decision-making process regarding course enrollment. • Adding Hip Hop elements to social contributions transforms the perception of social contributions and promotes participation.	• Even for students with a certain level of curiosity about Hip Hop, it transforms the perception of social contributions. • The polarity between Hip Hop and social contribution, which seemingly have no connection, functions as an appealing factor that appeals to students' desire for enjoyment, enhancing their motivation for content involvement driven by a desire for fulfillment.
[2]	• For the Hip Hop group, Hip Hop is an essential part of life; through Hip Hop, local issues become more relatable and immediate. • Engaging in local problem-solving initiatives can decrease motivation, a negative factor. However, tackling local issues from the perspective of Hip Hop serves as a factor in raising awareness and motivation, thereby influencing the enthusiasm for addressing local problems.	• Adding Hip Hop elements to the class creates a relaxed and enjoyable atmosphere, transforming previously distant local issues into familiar ones. • Adding Hip Hop elements to the class influences the motivation for solving local issues and stimulates a sense of enjoyment discovered in rap production. This stirs up a spirit of challenge toward new experiences and enhances the collaborative motivation (contribution motivation) to improve organizational function during activities related to the class.
[3]	• Before the start of the course, there was a notable lack of understanding of the issues due to low interest and concern about local problems. The seriousness associated with these issues posed a significant barrier to engaging in efforts to solve them. However, incorporating Hip Hop into the discussion transformed local issues into more relatable problems. Hip Hop functioned as a factor driving changes in interest and concern. • As local issues become more relatable, the essence of "enjoyment" inherent in Hip Hop and the allure created by the unrelated polarity of Hip Hop and community problem-solving are influencing factors attributed to Hip Hop.	• Before the start of the course, a lack of understanding about the issues due to low interest and curiosity regarding local problems is evident. However, Hip Hop, a factor in increasing enjoyment, has catalyzed interest and curiosity among Non-Hip Hop groups. • As an influencing factor, Hip Hop catalyzes changes in students' interest and curiosity regarding local issues.
[4]	• Incorporating Hip Hop into the curriculum creates a unique and enjoyable atmosphere distinct from conventional classes, fostering a sense of entertainment not typically found in traditional teaching methods. This fun atmosphere, coupled with the unconventional nature of the class, enhances students' motivation for active engagement in the subject matter, driven by a desire for fulfillment. • The essence of "enjoyment" inherent in Hip Hop serves as an appealing factor for students' "desire for fun," creating differences in motivation based on the presence or absence of Hip Hop elements and contributing to the popularity of classes among students.	• Hip Hop can create a fun atmosphere distinct from regular classes, with the seriousness of addressing local issues. • The enjoyable collaborative atmosphere created by incorporating Hip Hop into the classroom helps build a supportive environment born from positive interpersonal relationships, enhancing collaborative motivation (contribution motivation) and improving organizational functioning. • While peer evaluation of the activities is also at play, differences in motivation due to the presence or absence of Hip Hop elements and the value transformation towards social contribution through Hip Hop not only stir up a spirit of venturing into the unknown but also foster a sense of fulfillment and achievement.

6. Considerations

6-1. Question 1: How did the impression of "social contribution" change when "Hip Hop elements" were added? (How did it affect the motivation to take the course?)

The Hip Hop and Non-Hip Hop groups have shown that adding "Hip Hop elements" to social contribution transforms the perception of social contribution. As mentioned in section three below, before taking the seminar, both groups had a "serious" and "stiff" image of the words "social contribution" and "community issues." However, it can be inferred that engaging in community problem-solving activities (social contribution) "while having fun" through Hip Hop has made community issues more accessible.

Furthermore, it has become apparent that Hip Hop serves as an appealing factor for the "desire for enjoyment" of both groups. William Glasser, the proponent of choice theory, states that there are five basic needs in choice theory, namely "survival," "love/belonging," "power," "freedom," and "enjoyment." Among these, "enjoyment" is the desire to acquire new knowledge and comprises four elements: "humor," "curiosity," "learning/growth," and "creativity" (Glasser, 2021). As evident from this choice theory, Hip Hop stimulates students' "desire for enjoyment," enhances intrinsic motivation, and serves as a factor that pushes forward the decision-making process for course enrollment.

6-2. Question 2: How did the motivation to engage in the initiative change as a result of addressing local issues under the theme of "social contribution through Hip Hop" rather than just "beach cleaning" or "tourism promotion"?

Hip Hop and Non-Hip Hop groups share the aspects where Hip Hop transforms "community issues into familiar problems" and "affects the willingness to solve community issues." However, slight differences were observed in how this transformation and influence occurred. For the Hip Hop group, Hip Hop is considered a "necessary element of life"; hence, there is a nuance that community issues become a part of their daily lives through Hip Hop. Conversely, for the Non-Hip Hop group, the enjoyment of Hip Hop fosters familiarity with community issues, suggesting a difference in the level of "proximity to the issue" for students. As mentioned in the origin of Hip Hop, which is discussed in this paper, Hip Hop culture emerged from a movement to address issues such as gang conflicts and drug proliferation in the devastated neighborhoods of New York. In rap music, some artists perform "conscious rap," addressing social issues, with Common, Talib Kweli, and KRS-ONE being known as representatives of socially conscious rappers. Additionally, many graffiti artworks contain political messages, with graffiti being considered an artistic expression method for social advocacy (KRS-ONE, 2009). In other words, for the Hip Hop group, which has a high affinity with social issues, there is a foundation for perceiving social issues as personal matters, which may contribute to the differences observed between the two groups.

Another point observed in the Non-Hip Hop group but not confirmed in the Hip Hop group is that Hip Hop enhances "the willingness to improve organizational function through cooperative motivation (contribution motivation)." In addition to increased cooperative motivation in Hip Hop, excellent interpersonal relationships among students may also be relevant. In the organizational theory proposed by management scholar Chester Barnard, three elements are mentioned as essential for the formation of an organization: "communication," "cooperative motivation (contribution motivation)," and "common purpose." Among these three elements, "cooperative motivation (contribution motivation)" refers to the desire of organization members to "work together and help each other," emphasizing the importance of building good relationships between members by constantly supporting each other during the formation of the organization (Barnard, 1991). Some student comments indicated that the good interpersonal relationships among the students also contributed to increased motivation. Besides the influence of Hip Hop, it can be inferred that good interpersonal relationships contributed to motivation for engaging in activities.

6-3. Question 3: How did the level of interest and concern regarding the marine litter issue and tourism attractiveness issues in Yamaguchi Prefecture change compared to before the start of the course? Also, do you think Hip Hop influenced this change?

Both groups shared that Hip Hop is a factor in changing the level of interest and concern regarding community issues. One factor influencing this change is the enjoyment generated by Hip Hop. In the Hip Hop group, "enjoyment" is inherent in Hip Hop. In the Non-Hip Hop group, the function of Hip Hop as a factor in increasing enjoyment has become pivotal in changing the level of interest and concern regarding community issues. In the section "2. What is Hip Hop," it was mentioned that the essence of Hip Hop is "peace," "love," "unity," and "having fun." In both groups, the enjoyment created by Hip Hop has softened the rigid image associated with "community issues," thereby altering the level of interest and concern regarding community issues.

6-4. Question 4: How did your motivation towards the course change after taking classes that incorporated Hip Hop elements?

A common point among both groups is that integrating Hip Hop into the curriculum creates a unique and unconventional learning environment, fostering a fun atmosphere. Hip Hop's essence includes the aspect of "enjoyment," as mentioned earlier, the enjoyment (fun atmosphere) created by Hip Hop leads to an improvement in students' intrinsic motivation. Ichikawa (2001) divides learning motivation into two main factors: when the importance of learning content is emphasized, it becomes "content-involvement motivation," and when the importance of learning content is neglected, it becomes "content-separation motivation." Furthermore, he suggests that "content-involvement motivation" involves three orientations: "enrichment," "training," and "practical," while "content-separation motivation" involves three orientations: "relationship," "self-esteem," and "reward" (see Figure 4). As evident from Ichikawa's two-factor model of motivation, the enjoyment generated by classes incorporating Hip Hop corresponds to the enrichment orientation associated with content-involvement motivation.

On the other hand, a characteristic observed in the Non-Hip Hop group, which was

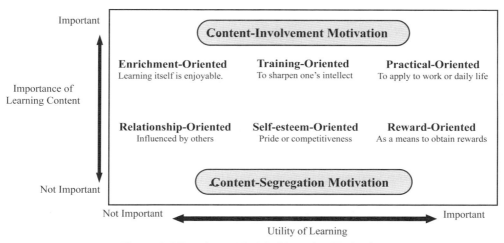

Figure 4: A Two-factor Model of Learning Motivation
(Retouched and Diagramed Based on [Ichikawa, 2001])

not seen in the Hip Hop group, is that besides enhanced motivation influenced by Hip Hop, the positive interpersonal relationships among students contributed to an increased willingness to contribute to seminar activities. This aspect is related to Bernard's organizational theory of "willingness to collaborate (contribution motivation)," as mentioned in the second part. Additionally, it became evident that students in the Non-Hip Hop group were stirred by a spirit of challenge toward the unfamiliar through classes that incorporated Hip Hop, and they experienced a sense of fulfillment and accomplishment.

7. Conclusion

This study has examined how Hip Hop, which appeals to students' interests, has brought about consciousness transformation among students. Additionally, this study has investigated whether there are differences in consciousness transformation between the "Hip Hop group" and the "Non-Hip Hop group." As a result, it became clear that in both groups, the transformation of consciousness regarding "learning" and the transformation of consciousness regarding "community issues" centered around the concepts of "enjoyment of the class" and "the enjoyment of the community activities." And this "enjoyment" was brought by incorporating Hip Hop into the lessons.

<Transformation of consciousness regarding "learning">
- Hip Hop serves as an appealing factor for "the desire for enjoyment," pushing forward the decision-making process regarding course enrollment.
- Classes incorporating Hip Hop create a fun atmosphere, enhancing students' intrinsic motivation.

<Transformation of consciousness regarding "community issues">
Students used to have a "rigid" or "serious" image of terms like "social contribution" and "community issues," but through Hip Hop, students found that by tackling community problem-solving activities (social contribution) in an enjoyable way, these issues became more relatable, and their level of interest and engagement in community problems changed.

The differences in conscious transformation observed between the two groups are as follows.
<Differences in Both Groups>
- The Hip Hop group feels community issues more closely.
- For the Non-Hip Hop group, Hip Hop and good interpersonal relationships have increased their motivation to contribute to class activities.
- Through classes incorporating Hip Hop, there is a stirring spirit of challenge toward the unfamiliar, leading to a sense of fulfillment and achievement.

SL has been shown to bring about various learning outcomes, including improvement in individual abilities such as self-understanding and self-efficacy, enhancement of interpersonal skills, promotion of understanding of learning content, development of critical thinking skills, transformation of perspectives on community issues, and connection with the community as a citizen (Eyler & Giles, 1999). The results of this study also align with the categories of learning outcomes observed in previous research. However, what is noteworthy in this study is that these outcomes were brought about specifically "through Hip Hop." In Japan, examples of educational practices involving Hip Hop are predominantly related to physical education activities involving Hip Hop dance, and they are not based on Hip Hop Based Education (HHBE). Moreover, the author has not encountered any other SL case studies focusing on Hip Hop. Therefore, it is believed that this study has opened up new avenues in HHBE and SL research by demonstrating how student consciousness can be transformed through SL focused on Hip Hop.

On the other hand, while the qualitative analysis in this study was based on six participants selected from the author's practice, quantitative analysis with a larger sample size is also essential. It is desired to conduct quantitative analysis as well to examine further and organize the learning outcomes brought about by SL through Hip Hop. To achieve this, it is planned to continue the practice and conduct continuous questionnaire surveys.

References

Aronson, B. & Laughter, J. (2016). The Theory and Practice of Culturally Relevant Education: A Synthesis of Research Across Content Areas, *Review of Educational Research*, 86(1), 163–206.

Au, K., & Jordan, C. (1981). Teaching Regarding Hawaiian Children: Finding a Culturally Appropriate Solution. In H. Trueba, G. Gutherie, & Au. K (Eds.), *Culture and*

The Bilingual Classroom: Studies in Classroom Ethnography (139–152), Rowley, MA: Newbury.

Baba, T. (2022). Research on Community Engagement Professionals in American Higher Education Institutions—Focusing on Service-Learning Coordinator—. *Aichi University of Education Dissertation*, 1–126.

Barnard, C. I. (1991). *Organization and Management.* Harvard University Press.

Cazden, C., & Leggett, E. (1981). Culturally Responsive Education: Recommendations for Achieving Lau Remedies II. In H. Trueba, G. Gutherie, & Au. K (Eds.), *Culture and The Bilingual Classroom: Studies in Classroom Ethnography* (69–86), Rowley, MA: Newbury.

Central Council for Education. (2005). 『我が国の高等教育の将来像（答申）』. (http://www.mext.go.jp/b_menu/shingi/chukyo/chukyo0/toushin/attach/__icsFiles/afieldfile/2013/05/27/1335580_001.pdf, 2023. 3.15)

Central Council for Education. (2008). 『学士課程教育の構築に向けて（答申）』. (http://www.mext.go.jp/component/b_menu/shingi/toushin/__icsFiles/afieldfile/2008/12/26/1217067_001.pdf, 2023. 3. 15)

Central Council for Education (2012). 『新たな未来を築くための大学教育の質的転換に向けて～生涯学び続け、主体的に考える力を育成する大学へ～（答申）』. (http://www.mext.go.jp/component/b_menu/shingi/toushin/__icsFiles/afieldfile/2012/10/04/1325048_1.pdf, 2023. 3. 15)

Chang, J. (2007). *Can't Stop Won't Stop: A History of the Hip-Hop Generation.* Picador USA.

Condry, I. (2009). *Hip Hop Japan: Rap and The Paths of Cultural Globalization.* Duke University Press.

DIAMOND online. (2021). 『観光で行きたい都道府県ランキング2020【完全版】』. (https://diamond.jp/articles/-/259929?page=3. 2022. 9. 13)

Dover, A. G. (2013). Teaching for Social Justice: From Conceptual Frameworks to Classroom Practices. *Multicultural Perspectives*, 15(1), 3–11.

Emdin, C. (2013). The Rap Cypher, the Battle, and Reality Pedagogy: Developing Communication and Argumentation in Urban Science Education. In Hill, M. L., & Petchauer, E. (Eds.), *Schooling Hip Hop Expanding Hip Hop Based Education Across the Curriculum.* New York, NY: Teachers College Press.

Emdin, C., & Adjapong, E. (2018). *#HipHopEd: The Compilation on Hip Hop Education: Hip Hop As Education, Philosophy, and Practice (Revolutionizing Urban Education: Hip Hop, Pedagogy, and Communities).* New York, NY: Sense Pub.

Eyler, J., & Giles, D, E. (1999). *Where is the Learning in Service-Learning?.* San Francisco, CA: JOSSEY-BASS.

Gibson, H., Canfield, J., & Beamish, A. (2020). Understanding Community Perceptions of Service-Learning. *Journal of Service-Learning in Higher Education*, 11, 5–20.

Glasser, W. (2021). *Choice Theory: A New Psychology Of Personal Freedom.* Harper Perennial.

Hill, M. L. (2009). *Beats, Rhymes, and Classroom Life: Hip Hop Pedagogy and the Politics of Identity.* New York, NY: Teachers College Press.

Ichikawa, S. (2001). 『学ぶ意欲の心理学』. PHP新書.

Inoue, S. (2017). *TOKYO GRAFFITI*, 1, SANTASTIC! ENTERTAINMENT.

Japan Tourism Agency. (2022). 『共通基準による観光入込客統計』. (https://www.mlit.go.jp/kankocho/siryou/toukei/irikomi.html, 2022. 9. 13)

Kinki Nippon Tourist. (2022). 『江田島でエシカル・ツーリズムをはじめよう！』. (https://www.knt.co.jp/tabiplanet/kokunai/221020/, 2023. 6. 11)

Kodama, N. (2018). Teaching Subjects in a Culturally Relevant Way, *Shiga University Departmental Bulletin Paper*. 68, 115–127.

KRS ONE (2009). *The Gospel of Hip Hop: First Instrument*. Brooklyn, NY: powerHouse Books.

Kuramoto, T. (2008). *A study of curriculum management in the USA: From the service-learning perspective* (アメリカにおけるカリキュラムマネジメントの研究——Service-Learningの視点から). Japan: Fukuro Publishing.

Ladson-Billings, G. (1995). Nevertheless, That is Just Good Teaching!: The Case for Culturally Relevant Pedagogy. *Theory Into Practice*, 34(3), 159–165.

Ladson-Billings, G. (2009). *The Dreamkeepers: Successful Teachers of African American Children* (2nd ed.). San Francisco, CA: Jossey-Bass.

Love, B. L. (2015). What is Hip Hop Based Education Doing in Nice Fields Such as Early Childhood and Elementary Education?. *Urban Education*, 50(1), 106–131.

Mohatt, G., & Erickson, F. (1981). Cultural Differences in Teaching Styles in an Odawa School: A Sociolinguistic Approach. In H. Trueba, G. Gutherie, & Au. K (Eds.), *Culture and The Bilingual Classroom: Studies in Classroom Ethnography* (105–119), Rowley, MA: Newbury.

Ministry of Education. (2008). 『中学校学習指導要領解説　保健体育編』. (https://www.mext.go.jp/component/a_menu/education/micro_detail/__icsFiles/afieldfile/2011/01/21/1234912_009.pdf, 2021.4.25)

Ministry of Education. (2013). 『地（知）の拠点整備事業』. (http://www.mext.go.jp/component/a_menu/education/detail/__icsFiles/afieldfile/2014/05/20/1346067_03.pdf, 2023. 3. 15)

Ministry of Education. (2016). 『地（知）の拠点大学による地方創生推進事業（COC+）』. (http://www.mext.go.jp/component/a_menu/education/detail/__icsFiles/afieldfile/2016/10/28/1378661_01_1.pdf, 2023.3.15)

Ministry of the Environment. (2021). 『令和元年度海洋ごみ調査の結果について』. (https://www.env.go.jp/content/900517319.pdf, 2022. 9. 13)

Morrell, E., & Duncan-Andrade, J. M. R. (2002). Promoting Academic Literacy with Urban Youth through Engaging Hip Hop Culture. *The English Journal*, 91(6), 88–92.

O'Connor, C. A. (2016). *A Hip Hop Pedagogy: Effective Teacher Training for the Millennial Generation*. Ubiquitous Press.

Science Council of Japan. (2010). 『大学教育の分野別質保証の在り方について』. (https://www.scj.go.jp/ja/info/kohyo/pdf/kohyo-21-k100-1.pdf, 2023.3.15)

SITE（2020）. 『少年インザフッド 1』. 扶桑社.

Street Dance Association. (2021). 『協会情報』. (https://www.streetdancekyoukai.com/about.html, 2021.4.20)

TABOO 1 (2019). 『イルブロス』. 彩図社.

University Council. (1998). 『21世紀の大学像と今後の改革方策について——競争的環境の中で個性が輝く大学（答申）』. (https://warp.ndl.go.jp/info:ndljp/pid/11293659/www.mext.go.jp/b_menu/shingi/old_chukyo/old_daigaku_index/toushin/1315932.htm, 2023. 3. 15)

Chapter 18

Self-Analysis Sheet Methodology for Teacher Training

Masataka ISOBE, Aichi University of Education
Toshifumi KAWAMURA, Nisshin Nishi Junior High School
Daisuke ITO, Akita Prefectural University

1. Introduction

In November 2016, with the promulgation of the Law on Special Measures for Public Officials in Education (partially amended), each municipality was to formulate "teacher development indicators" (hereinafter from now on from now referred to as "indicators") by specific guidelines provided by the government. Based on these "indicators," the training system will be reviewed. In other words, because training is required in line with the career stages of teacher development, recruitment, and training, establishing a "council" that incorporates the knowledge of universities responsible for teacher development has been a condition for reform discussion. In light of this nationwide trend, the university where the first author works launched the "Aichi University of Education Teacher Training Collaborative Council" in cooperation with the Aichi University of Education Graduate School of Teaching, Aichi Prefectural Board of Education, and Nagoya City Board of Education, and established an estimated project for the six years from 2016 to 2021. The purpose of the budget project is to implement and enhance the training system and training programs to establish the "image of teachers who continue to learn"—promotion of the advancement of in-service teachers by strengthening the collaboration between the Board of Education and the university and has promoted practical research and verification.

Specifically, from the viewpoint of "Team School," we have been promoting verification of various training effects in order to enhance further the more advanced "training for mid-career teachers and administrators" and "training for school board members" programs. Next, as a wide-area type of educational university, we will implement and enhance programs such as "training for mid-career teachers and administrators" and "training for school board members." Finally, we aim to organically upgrade in-service teachers through the satellite concept using bases within the prefecture (education halls, education centers, affiliated schools, etc.) and to reorganize various types of teacher training (for beginning teachers, young teachers, training on specific issues, etc.) to correspond with the "teacher development indicators."

2. The Need for Self-Regulation

According to the deliberations of the Central Council for Education "Toward the Realization of a New Teacher Learning Style for '2021 Japanese School Education'" in November 2021, "Teachers are one of the most familiar figures to children, and their influence on their character development is significant." It can be expected that children will cultivate a desire to continue learning independently when they see teachers who continue to learn independently. The necessity of "optimal individual teacher learning" and "collaborative teacher learning" is also mentioned. Furthermore, in the section on systematic and planned implementation toward specific goals, "appropriate goal setting (future state) and appropriate understanding of the current situation (present state)" are required. In light of the above, teachers need to acquire the ability to adjust themselves (hereinafter referred to as "self-adjustment ability") following the ever-changing times and required educational content.

2-1. Educational practice using self-adjustment sheets

This study aims to develop self-regulation skills, one of the qualities and abilities necessary for teachers who continue to learn independently. Specifically, the "Self-Adjustment Sheet," which was created based on the A Prefecture Teacher Development Indicators, will be used in the in-service education training at the school where the first author works (hereafter referred to as "N Junior High School"). The results of each teacher's learning will be visualized, and whether or not they were able to acquire the qualities and abilities, including the latest knowledge and skills, in line with the times, will be analyzed and verified.

2-2. Research subjects and methods

In this study, 51 teachers at N junior high schools were selected as the research subjects and asked to answer questions on a "Self-Adjustment Sheet." The period of implementation was from May 2022 to December 2022. The "Self-Adjustment Sheet" was created and tabulated using Microsoft Office 365 Forms. The questionnaire consists of 54 questions: 6 main items (A-F), 18 middle items (A-1-F-3), and three questions for each middle item. In addition to the radio-button questions, the questionnaire included a column describing the strengths and weaknesses of each school to which the respondents belonged to get a detailed picture of their situation.

The results of the aggregated responses will be distributed as a "Self-Adjustment Sheet" in in-service education training, and encounters and workshops that can realize "individual optimal teacher learning" and "collaborative teacher learning" will be conducted. In order to visualize the individual results, we show them on a radar chart and have the participants exchange opinions. First, we will conduct an encounter and have the students write their good points on sticky notes. Next, have the students find the teachers who have higher scores than themselves in the items with low scores on their radar chart. For the corresponding item, have them ask the target teacher, "What are you trying to do to improve that item?" In the activity, have them grasp the current

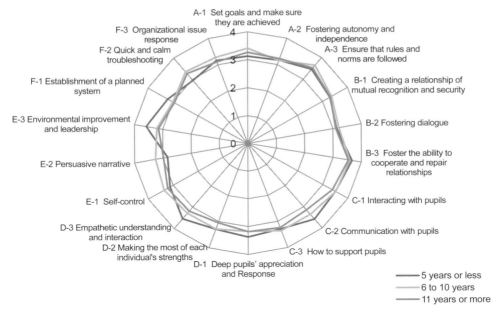

Figure 1: Self-adjustment Sheet Response Results

situation and identify the skills they want to acquire to realize the image they want to achieve. After completing the encounter, have the students think about their strengths and weaknesses and set future issues to address.

2-3. Results and discussion of the study

2-3-1. Qualitative analysis of teacher training using the "Self-Adjustment Sheets"

In the analysis, the teachers' years of experience were divided into three categories based on the County A Teacher Development Index: 5 years or less, 6 to 10 years, and 11 years or more. Figure 1 shows the results of the "Self-Adjustment Sheet" by years of experience.

In the post-training reflections, several comments were found to lead to increased self-confidence, such as, "Even though I thought I was not doing well, others told me otherwise," and "I was honestly happy to hear 'wow' from my junior staff, and it made me want to do my best." Some statements were linked to self-regulation, such as "I was able to understand myself objectively by having my colleagues show me the radar chart" and "I was able to hear many tips, and I would like to use them in the future."

After the training, a questionnaire was administered, asking two questions in a four-question format: (1) "Did you feel the high level of awareness of the teachers around you?" The percentage of positive responses was calculated for the terms "very applicable," "somewhat applicable," "not applicable," and "not applicable at all" and for the questions "not applicable" and "not applicable at all" (Figure 2).

As a result, 85.4% of the teachers answered positively to Question 1) and 87.8% to Question 2). From these results, it can be said that the teachers were able to become aware of their "self," which they were not aware of, by conducting the encounters using the "Self-adjustment Sheet" and were able to grasp the current state of their students. In

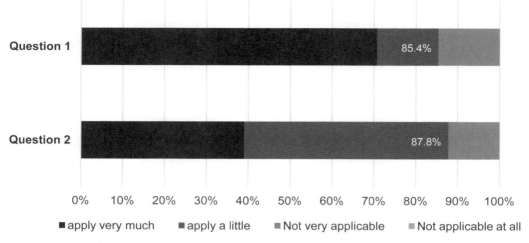

Figure 2: Results of the Post-event Questionnaire

addition, they were able to realize their colleagues' high level of awareness, and it can be inferred that they were able to learn collaboratively, which is essential for the "on-site experience" in the school training.

2-3-2. Quantitative analysis of trends in self-regulation skills of teachers by age

An analysis of variance was conducted on all factors of the "Self-Adjustment Sheet" to see if there were any differences among the categories of years of teaching experience. As a result, significant differences were found for three items: A-1, "setting and achieving goals," B-2, "fostering dialogue skills," and E-2, "persuasive talk" (Table 1).

Multiple comparisons revealed that in A-1 "Setting and achieving goals," the scores of those who had "11 years or more" experience were significantly higher than those who had "5 years or less" experience ($t(28) = -2.64$, $p = .04$). B-2, "Developing dialogue skills," scores were significantly lower for those who had "11 years or more" experience than for those who had "5 years or less" experience ($t(28) = 2.90$, $p = .02$). In E-2, "Persuasive Talking," the scores were significantly higher for those who had "6 to 10 years" than for those who had "5 years" or less ($t(28) = -2.91$, $p = .02$). 28) = -2.91, $p = .02$). Scores were significantly higher for "11 years or more" than for "5 years or less" experience ($t(28) = -2.44$, $p = .04$).

In their post-training reflections, teachers with more years of experience stated that they could adjust themselves sufficiently; for example, "I was able to understand myself objectively" and "It was an excellent opportunity to reflect on myself." Teachers with less than five years of experience also stated that they could build better relationships with children by practicing the tips they learned at the in-service education workshop and that they had learned a lot from the training. Descriptions were found that were able to use self-regulation skills.

The first is that the self-regulation skills acquired by the participants differed according to their age. Second, teachers with less than ten years of teaching experience were

Table 1: Responses to the "Self-Adjustment Sheet":
Means and Results of Analysis of Variance by Years of Experience.

Main items	Main items	Means by years of teaching experience			F value	p-value	
		Less than 5 years	6–10 years	More than 11 years			
A. Foster can accomplish nurture the ability to accomplish	A-1 Set goals and make sure they are achieved	2.98	3.20	3.26	3.48	0.04	*
	A-2 Fostering autonomy and independence	3.13	3.13	3.22	0.52	0.60	
	A-3 Ensure that rules and norms are followed	3.17	3.50	3.43	1.72	0.20	
B. Cultivating a connected mind cultivating a connected mind	B-1 Creating a relationship of mutual recognition and security	3.37	3.44	3.27	0.69	0.51	
	B-2 Fostering dialogue	3.44	3.39	2.96	6.04	0.01	**
	B-3 Foster the ability to cooperate and repair relationships	3.20	3.33	3.50	2.10	0.14	
C. Positive lobbying	C-1 Interacting with pupils	3.37	3.28	3.30	0.12	0.88	
	C-2 Communication with pupils	3.19	3.07	3.18	0.16	0.86	
	C-3 How to support pupils	3.43	3.02	3.12	1.53	0.23	
D. Teaching to make the best use of pupils' appreciation	D-1 Deep pupils' appreciation and Response	3.13	3.35	3.23	0.31	0.73	
	D-2 Making the most of each individual's strengths	2.76	2.93	2.75	0.23	0.79	
	D-3 Empathetic understanding and interaction	3.20	3.13	3.06	0.72	0.49	
E. Autonomous guidance	E-1 Self-control	3.06	3.11	3.18	0.41	0.67	
	E-2 Persuasive narrative	2.65	3.04	2.91	4.57	0.02	*
	E-3 Environmental improvement and leadership	3.30	3.06	3.08	1.32	0.28	
F. Planned and calm response	F-1 Establishment of a planned system	2.85	2.67	2.88	1.85	0.18	
	F-2 Quick and calm troubleshooting	2.94	3.11	3.27	1.91	0.17	
	F-3 Organizational issue response	2.78	3.00	3.02	2.03	0.15	

$* p < .05 ** p < .01$

more influenced by the content of each training course and the opinions of their seniors.

2-4. Summary and future prospects

In this study, teacher training opportunities were set up and continued using the "Self-Adjustment Sheet" as an "indicator" of independent learning. As a result, the issues in each category were found to be different by looking at the values for each year of experience. We believe that in-service training using the "Self-Adjustment Sheet" will improve the quality of education and teacher training, leading to the healthy growth of students. In the future, we aim to utilize the "Sheet" in various settings, such as in-service education in schools, training at various levels, interviews with administrators, and training for beginning teachers and teachers with little or no experience.

In December 2022, two guidelines were issued to realize a "new vision of teacher learning," including the training, recruitment, and training of teachers responsible for "Japanese-style school education in 2022". The second point is to realize "the return of theory and practice" in learning throughout their teaching careers. In other words, it is necessary to put learned theories into practice at school and reflect on one's practice based on the theories.

In light of this, an urgent issue for the future is to increase opportunities to utilize the "Self-Adjustment Sheet" in situations that foster practical knowledge and to accumulate educational practice research that will improve each teacher's qualities and abilities.

3. The Coming of Society 5.0

Our daily lives are rapidly evolving. For example, "robots will enter society" around 2022, "AI will take the place of humans around 2025," and "AI will surpass humans in 2045," etc. Technological innovation progress is full of great expectations.

Thus, it is predicted that the arrival of an era in which advanced artificial intelligence (AI) will make various decisions and that the workings of familiar objects will be optimized via the Internet (the fourth industrial revolution) will drastically change society and our lives.

Simply put, a new society is coming. Amidst mixed expectations and anxiety about the development of technological innovation, the Cabinet Office predicts the arrival of a new society (Society 5.0), the fifth in human history, following the hunting, agrarian, industrial, and information societies of the past.

It represents the realization that evolved artificial intelligence (AI) will drastically change our society and lifestyles, making various decisions for us and streamlining and optimizing work, logistics, information, etc., via the Internet. This is the fourth industrial revolution.

Indeed, the efficiency and automation of work through artificial intelligence will lighten the burden on workers and the elderly and make the world more convenient. In particular, Japan is facing an aging population. Japan's population has been declining since its peak in 2004, and it is expected to decrease to 95 million by 2050, of which 39.6% will be elderly. On the other hand, this also means that existing jobs will disappear. Therefore, there is a growing concern in the general public that "rapid changes in population intelligence will deprive us of our jobs." However, even if such an age should come, students must acquire the universally required qualities and abilities by their developmental stages. In this age of rapid technological innovation and the overflow of information known as "big data," I believe that the following three qualities and abilities will become increasingly important:
(1) The ability to read and understand information
(2) The ability to select and discard information
(3) The ability to diagram information
Reading and comprehending information is listed as one of the essential skills in

the report by the Central Council for Education. Simply put, it is the ability to read and understand information. Reading and comprehending information is increasingly emphasized as a language skill that forms the foundation of all learning.

The ability to select and discard information is the child's ability to separate the information he or she has gathered into similar items or categories. It is also the ability to judge whether the information is necessary to solve and prioritize the problem.

The ability to diagram information refers to the ability to organize necessary information and collect it into charts and diagrams. As adults, we also use presentation software to examine the content of a proposal, summarize the main points, and organize them into bullet points and charts. Children living through the coming age must model a wide variety of information, emphasizing communicating with others while effectively and efficiently utilizing information technology.

Programming education is the education needed to cultivate these three qualities and abilities. On Tuesday, April 19, 2016, Prime Minister Abe proposed at the government's Council on Industrial Competitiveness that programming education be compulsory in elementary and junior high schools. On April 19, the same day as Prime Minister Abe's proposal, the Ministry of Education, Culture, Sports, Science, and Technology launched the "Expert Committee on the Development of Logical Thinking, Creativity, and Problem-Solving Skills and Programming Education at the Elementary School Level." It began discussing the development of qualities and abilities at the elementary school level and the ideal form of programming education. In a summary of the discussions on June 16 of the same year, the following report was presented:

> In order for children to think logically and creatively and find and solve problems while effectively using information technology, it is important for them to understand how computers work, to imagine how they can be used to solve their own problems, to think about how their intended processing can be communicated to computers, and to think about how they can work in the real world via computers. It is important to think about how the intended process can be communicated to the computer and how it can work in the real world via the computer.

This text's two most important points are "understanding how computers work" and "understanding how the intended processing can be communicated to the computer."

"Understanding how computers work" means understanding that valuable machines such as robotic vacuum cleaners and fully automatic washing machines are not magic boxes but computers with all sorts of things built in.

"Understanding how the intended processing can be conveyed to the computer" can be interpreted as understanding that the computer, which has various things built in, is composed of multiple programs (programming).

In other words, for children to think logically and creatively, discover and solve problems, and effectively utilize information technology, they must develop three qualities and abilities while promoting programming education in line with their developmental stages.

Chapter 18
Self-Analysis Sheet Methodology for Teacher Training

A. Practical Skills in Information Utilization	B. Scientific Understanding of Information	C. Attitude to Participate in the Information Society
- Appropriate utilization of information resources based on tasks and objectives. - Proactive collection, evaluation, expression, processing, and creation of necessary information. - Tailored delivery and communication considering the recipient's context.	- Understanding the characteristics of information resources that form the foundation of information utilization. - Understanding basic theories and methods for handling information appropriately, as well as evaluating and improving one's own information utilization.	- Understanding the role of information and information technology in social life and their impact. - Recognizing the necessity of information ethics and responsibility towards information. - Having an attitude to participate in creating a desirable information society.
Example: - Basic operation of ICT, information gathering, organization, and dissemination (such as typing, internet browsing, appropriate utilization of information resources, etc.).	Example: - Programming (understanding the fundamental principles of measurement and control using computers).	Example: - Information ethics (impact on others and society through information dissemination, etc.).

Computational Thinking

Figure 3: Relationship between the Three Information Use Skills and Programming Thinking

3-1. Proposed evaluation criteria table for information use skills

First, the following is a quotation from the commentary of the General Provisions of the Courses of Study for Elementary Schools.

> Let us take a more concrete view of information utilization ability. It includes (among other things) mastery of basic operations of information means and qualities and abilities related to programming thinking, information morality, information security, statistics, etc. (pp.50–51).

The ability to use information consists of the three skills of "practical ability to use information," "scientific understanding of information," and "attitude to participate in the information society." In developing these three abilities, it is necessary to create classes that utilize programming thinking (Figure 3).

Figure 2 is based on a proposal by the Ministry of Education, Culture, Sports, Science and Technology (MEXT), which the author has schematized to show the relationship with programming thinking. Programming education is education to comprehensively acquire the ability to utilize information, which consists of three skills gained through the development of programming thinking. In the "practical ability to use information," the acquisition and use of ICT are enhanced, as are reading, writing, and calculation. For "scientific understanding of information," students must engage in programming. Regarding the "attitude to participate in the information society," information morality should be fostered across subjects such as social studies and moral education.

Therefore, based on the results of various previous studies, we present Table 2, which organizes the goals of the three abilities according to the three pillars of the abilities:

Table 2. Relationship between the three pillars and the qualities and abilities (ability to use information) that form the basis for learning.

Ability to use information. Three Pillars	A. Practical ability to use information	B. Scientific understanding of information	C. Attitude toward participation in the information society
Knowledge and Skills	Use information tools appropriately for the task and purpose (e.g., typing, saving, organizing electronic files, browsing the Internet, sending and receiving e-mail).	The computer is used in our daily lives. Realize that there are steps necessary to instruct the computer to solve a problem (procedures, data, structuring, etc.)	Observe the rules and manners in the information society (understanding and complying with the law). Strive to use information correctly and safely (Wisdom for Safety) Know the basics of information security needed in daily life (information security)
Thinking, judgment, expression, etc.	Independently gather, judge, express, process, and create the necessary information	Logical Thinking Divided into two movements. Symbols ...to a series of activities. ... combine Looking Back	Take responsibility for the information you disseminate and your behavior in the information society (ethics in the information society). Protect yourself from the dangers of the information society and respond to inappropriate information (safety wisdom). Take measures and actions to ensure information security (information security).
Ability to learn, human nature, etc.	Transmit and communicate based on the situation of the recipient.	Cultivate a trial-and-error attitude. Cultivate a sense of humanity that appreciates diversity. Cultivate an attitude of challenge. Cultivate an attitude of cooperation.	Respect your own and others' rights regarding information (ethics in the information society) Control behaviors that are detrimental to safety and health (Wisdom for Safety) Public awareness as a member of the information society (building a public network society)

"knowledge and skills," "ability to think, judge, and express," and "Ability to learn and human nature."

Table 2 shows the final target of the ability to achieve. This arrangement of the relationship between the three pillars and the goals of information useability will be useful when examining the information useability in each school from a cross-curricular perspective.

Next, understanding the goals (evaluation criteria) for the three levels of goals in Table 2, i.e., lower grade, middle grade, and upper grade, makes it easier to consider programming learning appropriate for each grade level. Therefore, based on various previous studies[14-20], the authors created an evaluation criteria table (Tables 3 to 5) for the three skills that constitute information useability. In doing so, we have tried to systematize the goals from the lower to the upper grades in small steps and express them in plain language.

To reach the achievement goals indicated in Table 2's three pillars, one must acquire these goals by stepping up through multiple stages. Tables 3 to 5 show the evaluation criteria for the lower, middle, and upper grades.

In the knowledge and skills section of the evaluation criteria table for practical ability to use information, six small goals related to ICT are listed for each of the two grades.

Table 3: Evaluation Criteria Table for Practical Ability to Use Information

Three Pillars	Target	lower grades of primary school (first, second, and sometimes third grades)	middle grades of primary school (third and fourth grades)	upper grades of primary school (sixth, fifth, and sometimes fourth grades)
Knowledge and Skills	Use the means of information appropriately for the task or purpose (e.g., typing, saving, and organizing electronic files, browsing the Internet, sending and receiving e-mail).	Essential operation of ICT equipment. Essential input, simple drawing with keyboard and mouse, and output to printer and monitor. I am connecting a computer and peripheral devices to capture and print digital camera images to a computer. Basic computer operations (startup, shutdown, saving to file, etc.) Use of the Internet Digital and video cameras take photos and videos, collect images, and record audio for specific purposes. Projection of photos and videos using large presentation devices (electronic blackboards, projectors, etc.)	ICT equipment is operated according to the purpose. Save files using appropriate folders. Draw, move, and transform shapes using a mouse, and create simple digital works of art. Connect the computer to peripheral devices (digital cameras, video cameras, etc.) to store image data appropriately on the computer. Search the Internet, printed materials, and other media that meet your objectives. Use of essential browser functions such as links and favorites Sending and receiving communication tools (e-mail, SNS, etc.) with accurate addresses and titles while understanding network rules and etiquette.	Operate multiple ICT devices according to their purpose. Use of software for collaborative work through digital media (report writing support software) Computers are used to chart various types of data and information. Essential operation of presentation software and editing of images and text Information dissemination through web pages that fully understand the network's rules, etiquette, and characteristics. Appropriate use of search engines (keyword search, similar term search, etc.) Appropriate use of internet communication technologies (Instagram, YouTube, etc.) (browsing and writing)
Thinking, judgment, expression, etc.	Independently gather, judge, express, process, and create necessary information.	Through the operation of ICT equipment and interaction with the media, students collect, judge, and express information of interest on their own or with their teachers.	They find necessary information in media and links prepared by the teacher or in search engines for children and collect, judge, process, and express necessary information by writing down or copying it.	They collect, judge, process, and express information independently by creating relevant media and referring to multiple web pages to find information necessary to solve problems.
Ability to learn, human nature, etc.	Transmit and communicate based on the situation of the recipient.	Students summarize their thoughts in pictures and short sentences and create simple digital works of art to transmit and communicate information accurately.	Information is transmitted and communicated in an easy-to-understand manner using tools appropriate to the audience and situation.	Understands the intentions of the receiver and the situation accurately, and while summarizing multiple opinions and ideas, responds appropriately and transmits and conveys detailed information.

Table 4: Table of Evaluation Criteria for Scientific Understanding of Information

Three Pillars	Target	lower grades of primary school (first, second, and sometimes third grades)	middle grades of primary school (third and fourth grades)	upper grades of primary school (sixth, fifth, and sometimes fourth grades)
Knowledge and Skills	Students will realize that computers are used in everyday life and that procedures are necessary to instruct computers and other devices to solve problems.	Students are aware of the use of computers in every-day life and the procedures (sequential processing, iterative processing, branch processing), and create and modify simple programs using one procedure.	Students know computers' role and impact on society and create and modify programs that appropriately combine each procedure (sequential processing, iterative processing, and branch processing) with data (actual/false values and set data).	Understands that programming is used daily, notices coordinates and random numbers, and creates and modifies programs to meet their objectives.

Thinking, judgment, expression, etc.	Understand the basic concepts of pro-gramming thinking and utilize appropriate program-ming thinking as needed.	Logically advance your thinking.	Make their projections to solve the problem.	Find the necessary relationships among causes and effects and think logically.	Find rules and principles inductively and apply what you have expressed logically to other problems.
		Divide into movements.	Consider large movements (events) into smaller movements (events).	In order to solve a problem, we divide a significant movement (event) into smaller movements (events).	In order to solve a problem, we efficiently divide a signif-icant movement (event) into smaller movements (events).
		Symbol.	Classify similar movements (events) and select the necessary elements (viewpoints) together with others.	Classify similar movements (events), and consider and select the necessary elements (perspectives).	To remove multiple elements (viewpoints) necessary for problem-solv-ing and consider and select the most appropriate element (viewpoint).
		Make it a series of activities.	Think in terms of similarities and relationships within an issue.	Consider how the similari-ties and relationships found can be used in other cases.	Among the similarities and relationships found, extract and consider the similarities and relationships necessary to solve the problem.
		Combination.	Consider various methods and procedures to solve problems.	Consider efficient or effective methods and procedures.	Consider efficient and effective methods and procedures according to the problem.
		Looking back.	Consider the quality of the idea (methods, procedures, etc.).	Consider modifications or improvements to the artistry while incorporating evaluations by others.	Identify problems and issues and find better ideas (methods, procedures, etc.).
Ability to learn, human nature, etc.	Cultivate an attitude of using computer functions to create a better life and society.	Cultivate an attitude of trial and error.	They compare their first idea with the actual situation, notice the difference, and try to correct it without fear of making a mistake, or they try to correct it with their friends or teachers.	The students reflect on the learning process to see if it went as planned initially, notice the causes, and try to correct them independently.	They repeatedly review the learning process to see whether it follows the original plan, record their activities, find areas for improvement, and try to correct them until the end.
		Cultivate a human nature that recognizes diversity.	They are aware of and willing to acknowledge that there are multiple ideas (methods, procedures, etc.) for solving problems.	They respect problem-solv-ing ideas, see the best in each, and try to incorporate appropriate ideas.	They respect problem-solv-ing ideas and try to constructively evaluate and advise on their respective issues and areas for improvement.
		Cultivate an attitude of challenge.	They are trying to reach their goal and finish the job.	They choose complex problems by themselves and try to finish them.	They are trying to tackle the problem of creating new value and disclose their solutions and works to society.
		Cultivate a collaborative attitude.	Listens to his/her friends' opinions and tries to help them.	They willingly ask for their friends' opinions and try collaborating with them.	In creative activities, they value the opinions of friends who differ significantly from their own.

Chapter 18
Self-Analysis Sheet Methodology for Teacher Training

Table 5: Evaluation Criteria Table for Attitude Toward Participation in the Information Society

Three Pillars	Target	lower grades of primary school (first, second, and sometimes third grades)	middle grades of primary school (third and fourth grades)	upper grades of primary school (sixth, fifth, and sometimes fourth grades)
Knowledge and Skills	Comply with the rules and manners in the information society (understanding and complying with the law).	Know and observe the daily rules and manners of handling public information (newspapers, leaflets, magazines, etc.).	Know and observe the rules and manners of information transmission and exchange.	To know and observe the social meaning of acts that violate rules and manners, the social meaning of obeying rules and regulations, and the meaning of contractual acts.
	Strive to use information correctly and safely (wisdom to safety).	Know not to give out contact information to strangers.	Realize that some information is false and know not to divulge personal information to others.	Know how to determine the accuracy of information and not to divulge personal information about themselves or others to third parties.
	Take measures and actions to ensure information security (information security).	Know the promises when quoting from books, magazines, etc.	Consider the impact of information and know how to use sentences and words that consider the feelings and position of the other person.	Know how to protect information from being destroyed or leaked.
Thinking, judgment, expression, etc.	Take responsibility for the information you disseminate and your behavior in the information society (ethics in the information society).	Thinking, judging, and acting to keep promises and rules.	Consider the impact on others, make decisions, and act accordingly.	Consider the impact on others and society, try to make decisions, and act accordingly.
	Protect yourself from the dangers of the information society and respond to inappropriate information (safety wisdom).	Consider using information transmission devices with adults and in an environment where they will not encounter inappropriate information.	When encountering dangerous or inappropriate information, ask for an adult's opinion and consider how to respond appropriately.	Predict and judge dangerous or inappropriate content and information and develop countermeasures.
	Know the basics of information security needed in daily life (information security).	Check the safety of your surroundings and consider the correct way to transmit information to others, depending on the situation.	Understand the importance of authentication and consider how to use it correctly.	Consider how to use the system without unauthorized use or unauthorized access.
Ability to learn, human nature, etc.	Respect your own and others' rights regarding information (ethics in the information society).	Have a heart that values things made by others.	Be mindful of the importance of your information and the information of others.	Know that you and others have rights regarding personal information and respect them.
	Control behaviors detrimental to safety and health (wisdom to safety).	Be prepared to keep the agreed-upon hours of use and commitments to curb behaviors hazardous to safety and health.	Be prepared to set goals for safe living and health and keep their hours of use.	Be prepared to exercise restraint in behaviors that are detrimental to one's health and to refrain from actions that endanger the safety of others.
	As a member of the information society, I have public awareness (building a public network society).	They show interest in using networks in public places and try to use them with their teachers.	They try to use the network to cooperate with their friends.	They are trying to use the network with the awareness that it is for everyday use.

The situations in which ICT is used are systematically described in thinking, judgment, and expression. In the areas of "ability to learn," "human nature," etc., situations in which ICT is used to make presentations (i.e., presentations using materials expressed by ICT) are envisioned.

The knowledge and skills section of the evaluation criteria table for scientific understanding of information indicates the essential elements required for programming. Specifically, in the lower grades, students are expected to understand the essential procedures-related elements (sequential processing, iterative processing, and branch processing). In the middle grades, students are expected to create programs that appropriately combine each procedure with collected data (boolean values and set data). An understanding of coordinates and random numbers is required in the upper grades.

In Thinking, Judgment, and Expression, students gradually ascend the six thinking steps according to the subject and contents to study. For example, check "Logical thinking" in "Thinking, Judgment, and Expression" in the evaluation criteria table for scientific understanding of information.

The lower grades indicate that the level of "making one's predictions to solve a problem" is indicated. Specifically, in a class situation in which students are asked to make predictions in a plant observation scene in a life science class if children are asked to make predictions as hard as they can, it means that "thinking logically" will be activated in their minds.

In the middle school grades, the lesson says, "Find the necessary relationships among causes and effects and think logically." For example, in the 4th grade math class "Perpendicular, Parallel, and Quadrilateral," we will take up a situation in which the children know how to find the area of a triangle but do not know how to find the area of a quadrilateral. In this case, children find the relationship that a quadrilateral is formed from two triangles, and they think that they can solve the problem by using the method for finding the area of a triangle. When we place a lesson that makes children think in this kind of learning situation, their minds work to "think logically."

In the upper grades, the students "find rules and principles inductively and apply what they have expressed logically to other problems." For example, in the 6th-grade science class "Properties of aqueous solutions," in order to organize the characteristics of each aqueous solution, two types of aqueous solutions (hydrochloric acid and carbonated water) that turn red when a blue litmus paper is attached and presented. At this point, rather than immediately teaching the properties of the aqueous solutions, we place importance on having the children think for themselves by having them predict what color the solutions will change to and by having them think about what they can learn from the experimental results and what they would like to investigate further. Children discover that aqueous solutions that change to the same color have something in common, and they try to think about whether the same change occurs in other aqueous solutions. This is an example of children using "logical thinking."

As for the attitude to participate in the information society, the target contents increase with the grade level. For example, in the Knowledge and Skills section, "Endeavor to use the information correctly and safely (wisdom for safety)," in the lower grades, the scope includes not giving out contact information to strangers. In the middle grades, contact information and personal information such as gender and family structure are included in the scope. In the upper grades, students must have the knowledge and skills to protect the personal information of others, such as friends and family members, while considering whether or not the information obtained by the individual is accurate.

Creating lessons and annual teaching plans that consider what subjects and learning contents are necessary to reach the small goals indicated in the individual evaluation criteria tables is essential. Each school is expected to prepare its list of information use skills and teaching plans for each grade, referring to Table 1 and the evaluation criteria tables for information use skills introduced in Tables 2 to 4, and to prepare a system for making information use skills compulsory from the 2020 school year.

References

Central Council for Education. (2021). "Toward the actual transmission of a new form of teacher learning that bears the 'Japanese-style school education of 2021,'" Ministry of Education, Culture, Sports, Science and Technology, 1.

Central Council for Education. (2022). "On the way of training, employment, training of teachers who take charge of '2021 Japanese-style school education', Ministry of Education, Culture, Sports, Science and Technology, 21–27.

Evaluation Criteria for Qualities and Abilities Developed in Programming (Benesse Corporation) (http://benes.se/keyc) (accessed May 6, 2019)

From the Cabinet Office website, "Society 5.0," https://www8.cao.go.jp/cstp/society5_0/index.html

Isobe, M., Omori, Y., Okajima, Y., Kawarada, Y., Ueno, T., Yamazaki, K. & Yamazaki, S. (2019). A comparative study of computing/programming education goals and learning achievement levels at the elementary and secondary education levels in Japan, the United States, and England. *Joetsu University of Education Research Bulletin*, 39(1), 177–191.

Isobe, M., & Ito D. (2017). *Let's Learn by Manga! Active Learning Classroom Building: Classroom Changes, Classroom Power Improvement Project*. Tokyo: Kaneko Shobo

Isobe, M. (2023). Society 5.0: Each evaluation standard table for information useability, annual teaching plan for programming education, and implementation and enhancement of training system and training programs to establish "the image of teachers who continue to learn" (in Japanese), Career Center for Teachers, Aichi University of Education.

Kawamura, T., & Isobe, M. (2023). Creating a group of teacher-teachers who continue to learn independently. Manuscript of a research conference presentation. *Research Report Collection of the Japanese Society for School Improvement*, J-SIRA 2023-1, 85–86

Kawamura, T., Ito D., & Isobe M. (2023). Abstracts of the Japan Society for Educational Technology Fall National Conference (Kyoto Terrsa), 139–140.

Kawamura, T., Tanaka, C., & Isobe, M. (2023). Basic Study of Teacher Training Using

Self-Adjustment Sheets, Research Meeting Presentation Manuscript, JSET2023-3, 347–348

Kojima, H., Takai, K., & Watanabe, H. (2018). Examination of Instructional Content Considering the Qualified Abilities to be Developed in Programming Education in Elementary Schools. *IPSJ Research Report*, 1–12.

Ministry of Education, Culture, Sports, Science and Technology. Model Curriculum for Information Moral Instruction, http://www.mext.go.jp/component/a_menu/education/detail/__icsFiles/afieldfile/2010/09/07/1296869.pdf, 2007

Ministry of Education, Culture, Sports, Science and Technology. Example of Systematic Table of Information Use Ability, (FY2008) Next Generation Education Informatization Promotion Project "Research and Study on Promotion of Information Education" Result Report, http://www.mext.go.jp/a_menu/shotou/zyouhou/detail/1400796.htm

Ministry of Education, Culture, Sports, Science and Technology, Expert Committee on the Development of Logical Thinking, Creativity, Problem-Solving Skills, and Programming Education at the Elementary School Level, http://www.mext.go.jp/b_menu/shingi/chousa/ shotou/122/attach/__icsFiles /afieldfile/2016/05/06/1370404_1.pdf, April 19, 2016

Ministry of Education, Culture, Sports, Science, and Technology. "Programming Education at the Elementary School Level (Summary of Discussion)," Expert Council on Programming Education and the Development of Logical Thinking, Creativity, Problem Solving, and Other Skills at the Elementary School Level. http://www.mext.go.jp/b_menu/shingi/chousa/shotou/122/attach/1372525.html, June 16, 2016.

NTT Learning Systems Corporation, Specific Methods of Efforts for Smooth Implementation of Elementary School Programming Education, FY 2008 Ministry of Education, Culture, Sports, Science and Technology Commissioned Next Generation Education Informatization Promotion Project. "The Purpose of Elementary School Programming Education and the Necessity of Systematic Preparation (1)," https://nttls-edu.jp/mextkenshu2018/programmingseminar/

Omori. Y., & Imade, N. (2016). Tentative Draft on Evaluation Criteria for Systematic Programming Education in Elementary and Secondary Education. *IPSJ Research Report*, 1–9.

Programming education to be compulsory in elementary and junior high schools, Prime Minister Abe proposes [2016/04/19 20:05], https://news.tvasahi.co.jp/news_economy/articles/000073012.html

Shimizu, H. (2016). Free statistical analysis software HAD: Introduction of functions and proposals for use in statistical learning, Education, and research practice Media, Information, and Communication Studies, 1, 59–73.

Takashima, Y. (2018). Research on Systematic Programming Education Curriculum and Support Methods at the Elementary School Stage, Master's Thesis, Joetsu University of Education (unpublished).

Chapter 19

Mentoring and the State of Teacher Training

Takehiro WAKIMOTO, Yokohama National University

1. Overview of This Chapter

This chapter presents an academic review of mentoring research in Japan. Mentoring research in Japan encompasses a variety of forms, including pairs and teams, and is directed toward both students and in-service teachers. This chapter presents an overview of team-based mentoring in school settings for in-service teachers, which involves multiple individuals.

This chapter is structured as follows. It first delves into the unique application of 'mentoring' in Japanese school settings and the emergence of team-based mentoring as necessary. It then describes how team-based mentoring is conducted in Japanese school settings, its current state, and its outcomes. The chapter also explains the effective types of mentoring that contribute to improving school organizations. It will spotlight the case of Yokohama City, where team-based mentoring, initially an institutional initiative, has evolved into a cultural practice among teachers, significantly enhancing teacher retention and student performance. This section will present an overview of the distinctive team-based mentoring for in-service teachers conducted in school settings in Japan.

2. History of Mentoring in Japanese School Settings

In Japan, the relationship in which senior teachers support and learn together with inexperienced teachers naturally exists without being consciously labeled as "mentoring." This relationship is called collegiality and is a characteristic of Japanese teacher culture. Consequently, the term "mentoring" is seldom employed by teachers.

However, in 1989, training for novice teachers was institutionalized, and a system was established where senior teachers formally guided novices as mentors. Novice teachers worked under the guidance of appointed officially senior teachers and received training organized by the board of education to learn the basics of teaching. This system continues today. However, even in this setting, the relationship between novice and senior teachers was rarely referred to as "mentoring."

"Mentoring" was first introduced in Japanese school settings in the 2010s. This phenomenon emerged in response to the growing necessity of deliberately cultivating the professional development of novice educators. The following details are provided.

289

In the past, during the Baby Boom in Japan, the number of children increased significantly, leading to the mass hiring of teachers. As the cohort of teachers hired during this period began to retire in large numbers, a projected shortage of teachers emerged, necessitating another round of mass hiring. Previously, schools had many experienced teachers with a substantial length of service. However, the mass hiring led to a significant increase in inexperienced teachers. Additionally, after the Baby Boom, Japan experienced a decline in birth rates, resulting in decreased demand for schools and prolonged periods of low teacher hiring. This resulted in a low proportion of middle-level teachers. The drastic changes in age composition made it difficult to support inexperienced teachers. Furthermore, Japanese schools have become increasingly busy in recent years. According to international assessments such as TALIS, Japanese teachers work longer hours than teachers in other countries, making it more challenging to provide the informal development that was previously possible.

In light of these circumstances, a necessity emerged for implementing deliberate human resource development initiatives within Japan. Consequently, the concept of mentoring was introduced as a means of addressing this need. Mentoring in Japan was mainly used in business management studies. By incorporating management knowledge, mentoring was applied in teaching. With many inexperienced teachers and increasing busyness, relying on traditional one-on-one relationships for development became difficult. Therefore, team-based mentoring was considered as an alternative approach. For example, in Yokohama City, inexperienced teachers would voluntarily gather to learn from each other after school. The Yokohama City Board of Education proposed mentor teams to build on these initiatives. Mentor teams are "systems in which multiple senior teachers' mentor multiple novice or inexperienced teachers to develop human resources" (Yokohama et al. of Education, 2011). The mentor team initiative has been introduced nationwide, with various names depending on the municipality, and implemented across Japan.

The following sections introduce team-based mentoring in Japan, based on the mentor teams in Yokohama City.

3. Team-Based Mentoring in Japan

Figure 1 illustrates the typical composition of a mentor team. The principal members of the mentor team comprise teachers in their first to fifth year, with teachers in their fifth to tenth year acting as team leaders. The content addressed by mentor teams varies, with the time and timing of implementation being decided according to the circumstances of each school. The relationships between mentors and mentees are flexible but fluid, depending on the theme or content at the time. Both leaders and novices learn together, a characteristic of mentor teams that foster a sense of unity and shared responsibility. This shared responsibility should make educators feel empowered and part of a supportive community. Additionally, management staff, such as principals and vice-principals, and teachers, like head teachers, provide various support to mentor teams. They participate

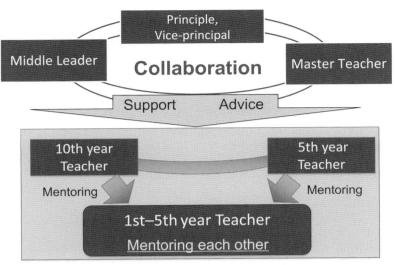

Figure 1: Model of Mentor Team in Yokohama

directly in mentor teams and support the environment to ensure smooth implementation. The circumstances of the school require different strategies to be implemented.

The chapter also introduces a survey conducted by the Yokohama City Board of Education to understand the implementation and effectiveness of mentor teams. In February 2018, the Board surveyed the implementation status of mentor teams in all 513 public schools in Yokohama City. The survey, conducted online and filled out by management or relevant personnel, focused on schools that reported having mentor teams. The analysis of the survey data aimed to understand the types of mentor teams and their perceived effectiveness in school settings.

Figures 2 and 3 illustrate the frequency and duration of activities. Most schools held mentor team activities once a month for 30 to 60 minutes, demonstrating the adaptability of mentor teams to different school schedules. This should reassure educators about the feasibility of implementing mentor teams, even during a busy school schedule. While activities were regularly conducted, some schools adjusted schedules based on school events. In an interview, one school mentioned, "During busy periods with many events, we might skip activities and instead conduct intensive sessions during summer break, planning with consideration for work style reforms," thus indicating efforts to optimize activity frequency and timing.

Figure 4 presents the members involved. Across Yokohama City, 93.8% of teachers with less than five years of experience, 57.7% of teachers with 6 to 10 years of experience, 33.3% of teachers with more than ten years of experience, 23.8% of head teachers, 15.1% of vice-principals, and 13.9% of principals participated. Mentor teams composed solely of teachers with less than five years of experience were present in 49 schools (10.3% of the total), and those composed solely of teachers with 1 to 10 years of experience were established in 43 schools (9.0% of the total). The composition of members varied widely depending on the school's situation. Additionally, Figure 5 illustrates the number of instructors and advisors who were not regular members but participated occasionally.

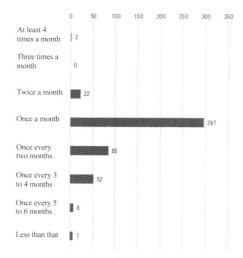

Figure 2: Frequency of Activity

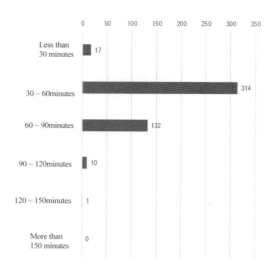

Figure 3: Hours of Activity

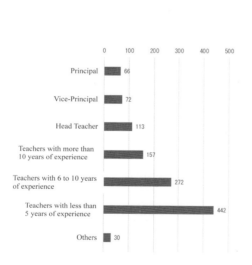

Figure 4: Member

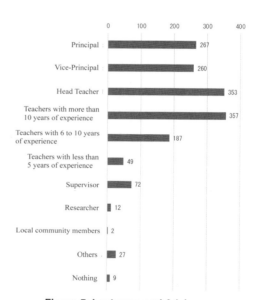

Figure 5: Lecturers and Advisers

The most common participants were teachers with more than ten years of experience, participating in 75.3% of schools as instructors or advisors. Subsequently, head teachers participated in 74.4% of schools. Principals and vice-principals served as instructors or advisors in about 50% of schools. Schools also facilitated connections between mentor teams and external entities such as community members and university affiliates.

Next, Figure 6 illustrates the content of the activities. Everyday activities of mentor teams included "Lesson Study," "Study of teaching materials (Kyozai Kenkyu)," "Student guidance," and "Classroom management," all of which are directly related to daily tasks. These activities were highly needed by inexperienced teachers, with 90.0% of schools incorporating one or more of these contents. Furthermore, 78.7% of schools addressed

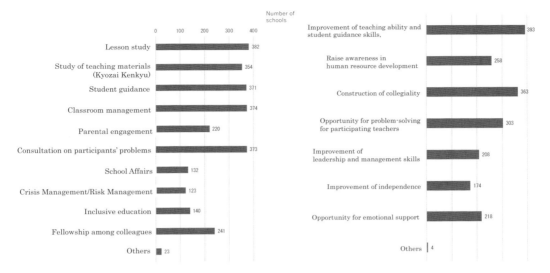

Figure 6: Content of Activities   Figure 7: Outcomes

"Consultation on participants' problems," with seven schools conducting only this activity throughout the year.

Finally, the outcomes depicted in Figure 7 indicate that the most noted outcome of mentor teams was the "improvement of teaching ability and student guidance skills," with 82.9% of schools reporting this. The second most common outcome was "construction of collegiality," at 76.6%. The third was "opportunity for problem-solving for participating teachers," at 63.9%. Approximately 98% of schools reported one or more of the outcomes: "improvement of teaching ability and student guidance skills," "construction of collegiality," and "opportunity for problem-solving for participating teachers." On the other hand, only 46.0% of schools cited "opportunity for emotional support," one of the mentoring objectives, as an outcome.

This indicates that mentor teams are typically conducted monthly, involving various roles such as teachers and management, and are systematically implemented at the entire school level. The content and outcomes are diverse, and schools select and achieve them according to their situation. Up to this point, the survey covering all public schools in Yokohama City was reported to grasp the overall framework of mentor teams. Despite the high diversity, the following research investigates which teams particularly foster the development of novice teachers.

4. Research on Effective Mentor Teams

We have conducted a comprehensive study involving observations, interviews, and questionnaire surveys on mentor teams. Through these methodologies, we examined the characteristics of effective mentor teams. This chapter presents the core analysis conducted to date (Wakimoto et al., 2013).

This analysis examines the elements of mentor teams contributing to problem-solving for novice teachers. Through numerous observations of mentor teams, we hypothesized the following elements contributing to novice teachers' problem-solving:

Hypothesis 1: Sharing experiences of senior teachers during mentor team activities significantly contributes to problem-solving for novice teachers.

Hypothesis 2: Providing opportunities for novice teachers to speak during mentor team activities significantly contributes to problem-solving for novice teachers.

Hypothesis 3: Conducting mentor team activities autonomously significantly contributes to problem-solving for novice teachers.

Concerning Hypothesis 1, acquiring practical knowledge to conduct daily classes better is essential for teachers, and sharing senior teachers' experiences is crucial for novice teachers. Senior teachers' narratives about their past classes and interactions with students serve as valuable references for novice teachers when planning their future classes and managing their classrooms. Furthermore, the format of storytelling plays a critical role. Human thinking styles encompass "categorical thinking" and "narrative thinking." Categorical thinking involves logically analyzing and verifying the correctness of matters, whereas narrative thinking interprets issues within a story framework (Bruner, 1986, 1996). Sharing narratives with others effectively conveys tacit practical knowledge that is difficult to verbalize. Thus, sharing experiences within mentor teams, where various senior teachers share their stories, provides significant opportunities for novice teachers to address their challenges.

Next, regarding Hypothesis 2, mentoring relationships often involve an asymmetrical dynamic where the mentor holds a higher position in terms of status and experience. This dynamic can result in mentors dominating the conversation (Schein, 2009). Consequently, novice teachers may need help to initiate discussions about their challenges. It is essential for senior teachers to first listen to novice teachers, understand their situations, and collaboratively consider solutions. Mentoring teams can effectively address their needs and facilitate problem-solving by enabling novice teachers to speak.

Finally, concerning Hypothesis 3, participants must engage autonomously in mentor team activities. Suppose mentor teams are perceived as mandatory training imposed by the institution, and senior or highly experienced teachers manage their operation. In that case, the activities may be considered burdensome, diminishing their effectiveness. Furthermore, if management dictates the themes, they may not align with the needs of novice teachers.

Additionally, observations of mentor teams revealed that the participation of teachers with more than ten years of experience significantly contributes to problem-solving for novice teachers. Therefore, Hypotheses 2 and 3 also consider the interaction effect. This implies that providing an environment where novice teachers can speak and conduct activities autonomously while involving experienced senior teachers might enhance problem-solving for novice teachers. This interaction effect is also tested.

Table 1: The Analysis Results

	B	Wald	P
a) Comfort in speaking	0.908	29.66	0.000
b) Autonomous activities	0.488	11.17	0.001
c) Senior teachers' experiences	0.963	41.11	0.000
d) Participation of senior teachers with more than ten years of experience	−0.357	2.123	0.145
e) b × d	0.531	2.874	0.090
f) c × d	−0.294	1.085	0.298

Nagelkerke $R^2 = 0.374$

A questionnaire survey was conducted from late November to early December 2011 with novice teachers in public elementary schools in Yokohama City to verify these hypotheses. The survey yielded 266 valid responses, with 261 novice teachers from schools with mentor teams forming the analysis sample. The survey included the following items measured on a five-point Likert scale: independent variables "opportunities to hear senior teachers' success and failure stories" (referred to as "senior teachers' experiences"), "comfort in speaking" (referred to as "comfort in speaking"), and "activities conducted autonomously" (referred to as "autonomous activities"), and the dependent variable "participation led to solving one's problems" (referred to as "problem-solving"). Additionally, the presence of teachers with more than ten years of experience in the mentor team was queried ("participation of senior teachers with more than ten years of experience").

Ordinal logistic regression analysis was conducted with "problem-solving" as the dependent variable and the following independent variables: "senior teachers' experiences," "comfort in speaking," "autonomous activities," and "participation of senior teachers with more than ten years of experience." Interaction terms between "comfort in speaking" and "autonomous activities" with "participation of senior teachers with more than ten years of experience" were also included. The creation of interaction terms followed Cronbach's (1987) method, centering values by subtracting the means to avoid multicollinearity.

The analysis results are shown in Table 1. Significant differences were found for "autonomous activities," "comfort in speaking," and "senior teachers' experiences." No significant differences were found for the "participation of senior teachers with more than ten years of experience." However, significant differences were found between "autonomous activities" and "participation of senior teachers with more than ten years of experience." No significant differences were found between the "ability to speak" and "participation of senior teachers with more than ten years of experience."

Thus, Hypothesis 1, "Sharing senior teachers' experiences during mentor team activities contributes to problem-solving for novice teachers," was supported with a positive significant value. Hypothesis 2, "Providing opportunities for novice teachers to speak during mentor team activities contributes to problem-solving for novice teachers," was also supported with a positive significant value. Hypothesis 3, "Conducting mentor team activities autonomously contributes to problem-solving for novice teachers," was

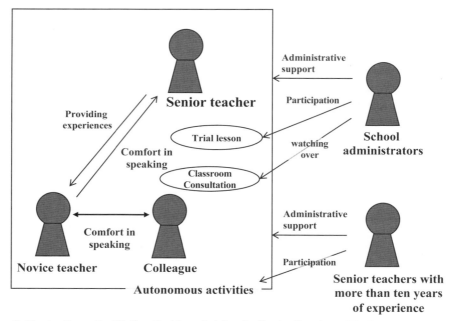

Figure 8: Mentor Team Facilitating Problem-Solving for Novice Teachers (Wakimoto et al., 2015)

supported with considerable positive value. Additionally, the interaction between autonomous activities and the participation of teachers with more than ten years of experience in mentor teams was supported with a positive significant tendency.

Based on these results and analyses concerning management involvement, we summarized effective mentor teams for the growth of novice teachers, as shown in Figure 8. Hypotheses 1 to 3 indicate that sharing senior teachers' experiences, providing opportunities for novice teachers to speak, and conducting activities autonomously are essential for effective mentor teams. Reflecting on experiences is crucial for teacher learning, and comfort in speaking provides a foundation for this reflection. Conducting activities autonomously means following content decided by management or senior teachers and creating mentor teams that meet their own needs based on their experiences, leading to better practices. Senior teachers' experiences allow young teachers to view their experiences from different perspectives and with broader insights, serving as references for future actions.

Regarding management involvement, while novice teachers might be hesitant to speak freely when management is involved in consultation scenarios, management can significantly offer comments and guidance during trial lessons, drawing from their extensive experience and expertise. Thus, careful consideration is needed to determine the appropriate level of involvement.

So far, we have examined effective mentor teams. In Yokohama City, mentor teams have been implemented for over 15 years. Teachers who grew up in mentor teams as mentees now lead and operate the teams as mentors, ensuring generational succession. We analyzed how these initially policy-driven teams have influenced teacher culture by studying the mentors in these teams—the following section reports on these findings.

5. Succession of Mentor Teams

We hypothesized that the experience of being a mentee in mentor teams influences one's actions as a mentor. Specifically, "The experience of being mentored in mentor teams (mentee experience) affects one's actions when becoming a mentor." We tested this hypothesis using data from teachers with six years of experience who have participated in mentor teams in Yokohama City. We divided them into those who have experienced school transfers and those who have not, and we analyzed them using covariance structure analysis.

I. Teachers who have not experienced school transfers
We assumed a model where the experience of mentor team activities during their mentee period (mentee experience) influences their actions as mentors with six years of experience. Considering that mentor team activities impact school professionalism and collegiality, we assumed a model where mentor team activities during the mentee period influence school professionalism and collegiality, promoting mentor actions.

II. Teachers who have experienced school transfers
We assumed a model where past mentor team activities (mentee experiences before school transfers) and the collegiality and professionalism of the current school affect their actions as mentors with six years of experience.

The analysis showed that the models for teachers who have not experienced school transfers (Figures 9 and 10) fit adequately, indicating their validity. Each model is explained below.

(1) Comfort in speaking
First, examining comfort in speaking and past experiences of comfort in speaking in mentor teams significantly influenced mentors' listening and information-providing behaviors. This indicates that novice teachers who experienced comfort in speaking as mentees are likelier to listen to junior teachers and share various experiences as mentors.

(2) Information Provision by Senior Teachers and Autonomous activities
Next, examining information provision by senior teachers and autonomous activities, we can see that these factors in past mentor teams significantly impacted school collegiality and teacher expertise.

(3) Collegiality
Collegiality within the school influences current mentor behaviors, especially promoting listening behaviors. Experience of information provision by senior teachers and participant-led activities in past mentor teams influenced mentor behaviors mediated by school collegiality.

These findings suggest that past mentor team experiences (degree of comfort in

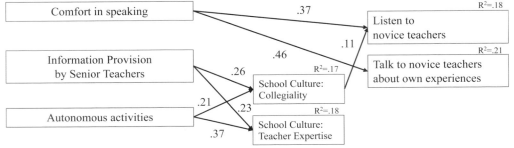

Figure 9: Transition from Mentor to Mentee (No Transfer) (Wakimoto et al., 2015)

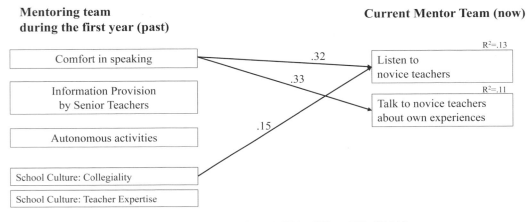

Figure 10: Transition from Mentor to Mentee (with Transfer) (Wakimoto et al., 2015)

speaking, receiving information from senior teachers, and participant-led activities) during the mentee period influence one's actions as a mentor.

For teachers who have experienced school transfers, Figure 10 shows that past comfort in speaking environments significantly influences listening and information-providing behaviors as mentors. This indicates that even when transferred to different schools, mentee experiences are related to mentoring activities in the new school's mentor teams.

In summary, analyzing the relationship between mentee experiences during the first six years of teaching and current mentoring behaviors, it was found that activities contributing to problem-solving for young teachers, such as comfort in speaking environments, participant-led activities, and information provision by senior teachers, lead to mentor behaviors like listening to and providing information to junior teachers. Particularly, mentors who experienced comfort in speaking environments tend to engage in listening and information-providing activities even in new schools after transfers. This indicates that mentoring behaviors are passed on to the next generation, suggesting that meaningful mentoring activities that address young teachers' challenges are crucial for building a supportive culture within schools. Teachers who have experienced such mentoring will likely exhibit similar behaviors when they become mentors, ensuring the continuation of quality mentoring relationships across generations.

6. Conclusion

This chapter introduced team-based mentoring in Japan, highlighting its effectiveness and generational succession. The results indicate that mentor teams, as an institutionalized form of support, aim to replicate the traditional collegiality-based teacher development in Japan within a formal framework. Each school determines the actual operation and content of mentor teams, varying from lesson study, instructional material research, classroom management, and consultations on student-related concerns, reflecting each school's circumstances.

While cautious involvement by education boards is necessary to avoid overstepping into school collegiality ("contrived collegiality" as termed by Hargreaves, 1994), mentor teams are autonomously decided by schools and members, with education boards providing support for their implementation. Given the changes in age structure and increasing business in Japan, spontaneous collegial activities have become problematic. Therefore, creating an institutional framework supported by the education board allows for autonomous mentoring activities, promoting the growth of young teachers. Ultimately, this framework could enhance collegiality throughout the school and contribute to building a Professional Learning Community (PLC).

From ongoing interviews, it was noted that schools effectively running mentor teams often show seamless integration between mentor team activities and other interactions among teachers. Initially, activities may start within the mentor team framework, but as mentor teams progress effectively, interactions and practices among teachers naturally occur beyond the framework.

This chapter is based on the following works and papers previously written by the authors:

Takehiro Wakimoto, Daisuke Choshi, Jun Nakahara (2015). *The Science of Teachers' Learning* (教師の学びを科学する). Japan: Kitaohji Shobo.

Takehiro Wakimoto, Daisuke Choshi, Yasutomo Sanui, Jun Nakahara (2013). A Study on The Effect of Organizational Mentoring Methods for Young Teacher: Focusing on the elementary school teacher. *Aoyama Information Science*, 41(1), 4–13.

Takatoshi Yanagisawa, Takehiro Wakimoto (2021). A Study on the Current Status and Methods of Team-Based Mentoring—From the survey analysis on the implementation status of mentor team in Yokohama City in FY2018. *Journal of Education Design*, 12(1), 225–234.

References

Bruner, J. (1986). *Actual Minds, Possible Worlds*. Cambridge, MA: Harvard University Press.

Bruner, J. (1996). *The Culture of Education*. Cambridge, MA: Harvard University Press.

Schein, H. E. (2009). *Helping: How to Offer, Give, and Receive Help*. Berrett-Koehler Pub.

Cronbach, L. J. (1987). Statistical tests for moderator variables: Flaws in recently proposed analyses. *Psychological Bulletin*, 102(3), 414–417.

Chapter 20

Reforms and Issues in Developing School Administrators through Administrative Training in Japan
—As a Fundamental Condition for School Curriculum and Organizational Development—

Atsuko HOMMA, Doctoral program student, Hyogo University of Teacher Education
Yasuki OHNO, Hyogo University of Teacher Education

1. Introduction

Since the late 1990s, Japan has undergone school reforms that have applied a new public management framework. These reforms include deregulating school education, especially the curriculum, delegating authority to local educational administrative bodies and schools, and strengthening administrative responsibility and/or accountability. Under these reforms, administrators (leaders) at the school level are expected to contribute to developing school visions and curricula suited to the conditions of school districts and students. Accordingly, the need to cultivate school administrators with such capabilities has been recognized.

Japanese school organizations have long been composed of three layers: principal, vice principal, and teachers. Those with ample work experience as teachers (planning and coordinating school curriculum and student guidance, etc.) are appointed vice principals and principals through selection by administrative agencies. In addition, in the case of Japanese public schools, prefectural and ordinance-designated city boards of education (and their affiliated educational centers) have historically played a significant role in the official formation of competence from teachers to vice principals and principals. However, the quality and systematicity have been insufficient.

In the school reforms mentioned above, the 2007 amending act of the School Education Act led to the stratification of school organizations (creating new positions such as senior vice principal and senior teacher). In addition, the 2016 amending act of the Law concerning Special Regulations for Educational Public Service Personnel stipulated that prefectural and designated city boards of education must develop and implement "indicators" for teacher training (descriptions of the competencies that should be acquired for each job level and career stage) and "training plans" based on these indicators. These reforms are expected to improve the system for developing the competencies of Japanese school administrators. However, as reforms are still ongoing, the current state of their functioning needs to be examined.

This chapter focuses on the training of school administrators, which is an essential condition for school curriculum development and organizational development. It begins by examining the historical context and current trends of training for school administrators led by Japan's educational administration, then considers the content and issues of new training for prefectures and designated cities through teacher training indicators and training plans following the 2016 law amendment (We also mention reforms of teacher training in collaboration with teachers' colleges.) and discusses future issues for training school administrators in Japan.

2. Framework and Trends in School Administrators Training in Japan

2-1. Basic framework for school administrators training in Japan

Except for a short period after World War II, Japan did not have a professional licensure or qualification system for school administrators (principals, etc.). As per laws and regulations, only individuals holding a teacher's certificate and having a certain period of work experience in education can be appointed as school administrators. Therefore, the position of the school administrator is envisioned as an extension of the schoolteacher's career.[1] The regulation requires high school administrators to obtain the specialized certificate (on completing a master's degree); however, this regulation is not currently being applied. Consequently, there has been little development in graduate school training for school administrators in Japan.

Traditionally in Japan, the training of public school administrators has been considered a process of "securing and training the next generation of school administrator candidates," "selecting school administrators," and "training current school administrators" (National Institute for Educational Policy Research 2014). The main actors in this process are the prefectural / designated city boards of education (and the education centers that serve as their affiliated organizations) , which recruit and select school administrators and teachers. At the lower secondary school and elementary school levels, municipality boards of education (which establish these schools and have the authority to supervise the performance of the staff) may also provide supplementary training[2], and a national-level organization (e.g., the former National Education Center, currently known as the National Institute for School Teachers and Staff Development (NITS)) also includes training for core school administrators in cooperation with the prefectural and municipal boards of education. On the other hand, it can be pointed out that the certain degree of school administrator training in Japan is "informal/OJT-style" training, in which school administrators at each school hand down the critical points of organizational management to mid-career teachers through daily school duties.

As mentioned above, the training of school administrators in Japan is characterized by local boards of education mainly carrying out formal training for experienced teachers. This training framework is in harmony with past educational administration norms, where standards and regulations for the curriculum (and controls schools by the boards of education) were relatively strong. However, since the end of the last century, school management reforms have been emphasizing the development of school curricula and school organizations in a way that fosters the holistic development of students. Simultaneously, the current situation regarding the training of school administrators, which differs significantly from international trends, is recognized as an essential issue in Japan.

2-2. Current trends in school administrators training led by boards of education
2-2-1. Brief history of school administrator training after WWII
In Japan, in-service training was mainly provided by the National Educational Association before World War II. After the war, as drastic educational reforms progressed, training programs led by the former Ministry of Education (MOE) and local boards of education were started as workshops to simultaneously convey the national educational policy. Their role increased with the establishment of highly centralized local educational and teacher administration systems throughout the 1950s.

For principals (after the abolition of the licensing and training system that existed for a short period from 1948 to 1952), the MOE introduced central training for principals and supervisors in 1960. Simultaneously, training programs hosted by the boards of education also began in some prefectures. Such boards-of-education-led school management training programs were subsequently developed with a variety of programs (in terms of the number of days and training contents) for different positions and new and current employees under the global trends in "curriculum development in schools" and school organization reform introducing the vice principal and the position of head teacher (Shunin). However, until the mid-1990s, training opportunities led by the board of education (BOE) were reported to have been limited in duration, particularly for mid-career teachers such as head teachers, and hence, lacking systematicity or continuity (Yaosaka, 1998). Moreover, the other issues are listed about the contents (focused on legal interpretation and administrative tasks) and implemental method (concurrent lecture style) of the training sessions from the viewpoint of developing school administrators who can oversee autonomous organizational management (Kitagami, 2004; Owaki, 2007). On the other hand, in Japanese schools, there is a well-established norm that senior staff imparts on-the-job training to juniors, which gives the principal the image of a "teachers' teacher" (Shinohara, 2003).

2-2-2. Political / practical trends in school administrators training in the 2000s and 2010s
In the mid-1990s, driven by the economic and social changes, school reform discussions at the central government level began focusing on developing children's competencies. Accordingly, New Public Management-style school reforms focused on expanding the discretion of local authorities and schools and increasing management autonomy. Since the 2000s, these reforms have placed new expectations on school administrators, especially principals, to assume new roles ("managerial" abilities). Meanwhile, Japan has seen a mass retirement of teachers hired during the second baby boom, raising concerns

about a quantitative shortage of teachers and school administrators. Without any system of qualification for school administrators, these trends have strengthened the training of school administrators led by local boards of education.[3]

In 1998, the MOE revised the national curriculum standards (course of study) in response to administrative reforms that increased schools' discretion, such as stipulating the period for integrated study to elementary and lower secondary schools, and the revision of a ministerial ordinance in 2000 to strengthen the management authority of school principals. The Ministry of Education, Culture, Sports, Science, and Technology (MEXT, reorganized in 2001) established a task force within the ministry in the early 2000s, and in 2004, the MEXT published a curriculum model for training (fundamental theories and thinking tools for school organization management) to help school administrators build their management vision and develop their abilities to develop school organizations (MEXT 2004). This model curriculum was disseminated to core local leaders through training programs run by independent administrative institutions under the ministry's jurisdiction. As a result, since the late 2000s, practical training contents related to school organizational management has been incorporated into school administrator training organized by prefectural boards of education and education centers, and it has also been adopted into the training contents for mid-career teachers (e.g., senior teachers and head teachers). This trend created momentum for content- and continuity-based reform of administrator and candidate training.

This trend intensified in the 2010s and 2020s. In its 2015 political report, the Central Council for Education of the MEXT proposed the establishment of "development indicators (at prefectural / designated city level)" of the abilities expected to be demonstrated by public school principals and teachers at each level of job experience[4] and the "comprehensive plan of training opportunities and content based on the indicators (mainly at the prefectural / designated city / core cities boards of education)." These two proposals were institutionalized by the amendment of the Law concerning Special Regulations for Educational Public Service Personnel in 2016. In addition, several legal amendments have significantly modified the teacher training system in each prefectural / designated city BOEs. Attempts are being made to align the content of school administrator training with the set ability indicators or to establish a systematization of training before appointment as vice principal or principal (which may include mid-career teachers) and after appointment (initial / experienced). In summary, in Japan, present school administrator training places a certain emphasis on the curriculum/organizational development, and attempts are being made to enhance both the contents and systematization. On the other hand, there are differences between prefectures, how they respond to the 2016 legal amendments (indicators and training plan formulation) and the need to reduce overtime work for school administrators and teachers leads to streamlining administrative training nationwide. Thus, further examination of the actual situation, effectiveness, and issues of administrative training for school administrators in Japan is necessary.

In the following section, we will examine several boards of education (prefectural / designated cities) in Japan, analyze the conditions for setting indicators, and plan administrative training opportunities before and after appointments with school administrators. In addition, the achievements and issues in terms of both the contents and systematization should be considered.

3. Current Conditions and Issues of School Administrator Training by Prefectural and Designated City Boards of Education

3-1. Research design and prior literature

In this section, we will look at the current state of administrator training provided by prefectural and designated city boards of education (BOEs secretariat/education center), taking municipalities A(APBE) through D(DCBE) as examples. The focus is on the relationship between the development indicators (from now on "indicators") for principals and school administrator training. School administrator training includes pre- and post-appointment training for principals and vice principals and leadership training[5] for senior teachers and middle-level staff to develop school administrators. Municipalities A through D are all located in western Japan (Kansai and Chugoku regions). These municipalities were chosen because a wide range of publicly available information allows us to obtain the data necessary for analysis. In addition, we thought we could grasp nationwide trends by taking municipalities A through D, which have significantly different population sizes.

Research on training for school administrators in Japan has been ongoing since the early 2000s, with the development of professional standards for principals by academic societies (JASEA 2009) and the exploration of the possibility of a graduate school training system (Ojima, 2004; Shinohara, 2017). However, research on the content and process of school administrator training by government agencies has not necessarily been active. Regarding the actual state of teacher/principal indicators and plans of training (school administrator training), which have become major national-level reforms, qualitative analysis of the contents of teacher/principal indicators established in various regions since 2017 and examination of changes in training plans have been conducted (NITS 2019, 2020, Ushiwata and Ushiwata 2022). These studies clarified the elements necessary in local governments (trust building, human resource development, organizational management) and similar principal images (two-axis classification of education-management and centralization-decentralization) through text mining of principal indicators. They also find that awareness of the link between principal training and indicators is increasing among prefectural and designated city boards of education. On the other hand, analysis of the link between school administrator training and related indicators and the actual systematization has not yet progressed sufficiently.

3-2. Perspectives and methodology

In this chapter, we attempted to analyze the indicators and training plans set by each BOE based on the following three perspectives.

a) To what extent do the indicators set by each BOE correspond to the school

administrator training provided by the BOE (relevance of indicators and training)?
b) To what extent is the training for positions other than principals related to the principal training (systematic nature of training)?
c) To what extent is collaboration with universities and graduate schools prevalent (collaboration and utilization with multiple institutions)?

For perspective a), to confirm the correspondence between the indicators and training content, we selected one element of an indicator that best matched the content of each session of various administrator training programs listed in the training plan of each BOE and examined to what extent it was covered in the entire training. Even if the training contents was related to other elements, we limited it to the most closely related ones. If the corresponding element was not determined (not applicable), it was recorded as having no corresponding perspective.

Regarding perspective b), to confirm the systematic nature of each administrator training course, we checked the degree to which each was related to each indicator. In cases where multiple training courses were related, we compared the contents of those courses to confirm their relevance.

Regarding perspective c), we examined whether university-sponsored courses or NITS's e-learning materials were accredited as attending the prefecture's regular training. Cases wherein university professors were invited to be training instructors were deemed temporary relationships and therefore excluded.

3-3. Findings from case studies

3-3-1. Case 1: A Prefectural Board of Education (APBE)

APBE set 15 indicator items from 15 elements (there are also items related to qualifications) for the principal indicators.[6] It is not easy to find clear correspondence between the contents of training planned and implemented by the prefectural board of education and each indicator item. The training plan shows indicators related to the training contents. However, it only lists broad criteria that collectively include 3 to 4 indicator items (elements) and does not clearly show which indicator item corresponds to each training content.

APBE revised its principal indicators after the 2022 revision of the MEXT Minister's guidelines on indicator formulation. In line with the revised indicators, "facilitation" and "assessment" were added to the training for new principals.

The APBE training plan emphasizes training for newly appointed principals and vice principals (5.5 days per year for each). These two training courses correspond to 10 of the 15 indicator items. During the COVID-19 pandemic, APBE proactively introduced online training (mostly synchronous style) like the other prefectures, but face-to-face training still continues in both trainings.

Meanwhile, APBE also conducts training courses for mid-career teachers. There are two types of training, totaling four days. In both cases, participants are teachers who are candidates for the vice principal (those who have passed the selection process and are listed on the appointment list) and need a recommendation from the municipal BOEs.

Table 1: Relevance of Training / Indicators for School Administrators (APBE)

elements=indicator items[15]:

1. strong educational philosophy
2. building a school management vision
3. assessment on the school environment
4. facilitation to enhance teaching capacity
5. Judgment and decision-making ability/leadership
6. school crisis management
7. promoting lesson improvement
8. career education
9. support for students with special needs
10. utilization of ICT, information and educational data
11. responding to individual student issues
12. building trust with faculty and staff
13. health management and mental health care for faculty and staff
14. appropriate staff evaluation and human resource development
15. building a system for collaboration and cooperation among faculty and staff

APBE categories of training	training duration (days)	face to face	online synchronous	on-demand	other type	1	2	3	4	5	6	7	8	9	10	11	12	13	14	15
principal/all	0.5		0.5												○				○	
principal/2nd years	0.5		0.5																○	
principal/newly appointed	5.5	3.5	1		1	○	○	○	○	○	○								●	
principal/voluntary (optional)	0.5×9	0.5*	4+0.5*					●	●	●	●			●		●			○	
senior vice principal	0.5		0.5																	
senior vice principal/newly appointed	0.5		0.5				○				○			○		○		○	○	
vice principal/2nd years	0.5		0.5																○	
vice principal/newly appointed	5.5	3.5	1		1	○	○													
senior teacher/newly appointed	0.5		0.5							○										
teacher (school level leader)	2	1	1				○		○	○									○	
teacher (middle leader)	2	1	1				○		○	○									○	

*Choose in-person or online

Chapter 20

Reforms and Issues in Developing School Administrators through Administrative Training in Japan
—As a Fundamental Condition for School Curriculum and Organizational Development—

The training contents include basic knowledge as a manager, school administration, building trust with the community, school organization management, human resource development, and leadership, all of which overlap with themes in other managerial training courses.

Under a partnership agreement, APBE has established collaborative courses offered by the local university that are available to teachers in the prefecture. However, training for school administrators does not fall under this category, and the educational administration authorities provide all training for school administrators on an original basis.

3-3-2. Case 2: B Prefectural Board of Education (BPBE)

BPBE has formulated separate indicators (each consisting of 6 elements, and 17 indicator items) for principals and senior vice principals, vice principals, senior teachers, advanced-skill teachers, and others. Its training plan is distinctive in that the training for each position is comprehensive. Those who will attend training before being appointed vice principals are designated as those who have passed the selection (those on the appointment list) and are not selected based on the principal's recommendation. The plan for each training shows the correspondence with the indicators at the beginnings. In addition to training content, its objectives are described in the training plan, clarifying the relationship between the qualities and abilities described in the indicator items and the comprehensive training content.

As mentioned earlier, BPBE places importance on linking the training content to the indicator items. However, the specific training content is diverse, and in many cases, about three topics are handled in a short period.

Regarding the number of training days, as with APBE, the training duration for newly appointed principals (3 days) and vice principals (2 days) is relatively long. The training that precedes the appointment of principals covers five of the six elements. Because BPBE's indicator items are classified into only six elements, one element contains many indicator items. This results in a plan structure that clearly shows the correspondence between the training content and the indicator elements.

Another feature of BPBE is that "human rights education training" is incorporated into the training for school administrators and others. This shows that human rights education is a critical educational issue for the BPBE. In addition, "personnel evaluator/trainer training" is scheduled for two half-day sessions at each level: new senior vice principals/vice principals, new principals, and principals.

3-3-3. Case 3: C Prefectural Board of Education (CPBE)

CPBE has formulated separate indicators for principals, senior vice principals and vice principals, which are classified into eight elements, each containing between one and three items. In the training plan, mid-career teachers (Middle Leaders) training is the most critical training duration and lasts for 4.5 days. Next, the training duration is long for new vice principals (3 days) and new principals (2 days), and it can be seen that higher positions have shorter training duration. Mid-career teachers training covers a wide range of content. Two of the five sessions are on-demand training, and one is online.

Table 2: Relevance of Training / Indicators for School Administrators (BPBE)

BPBE categories of training	training duration (days)	duration (in detail)				elements[6] / indicator items[17]					
						1(3)	2(3)	3(3)	4(3)	5(3)	6(2)
		face to face	online synchronous	on-demand	other type	perspective of management	administration and operation on organization	personnel management and human resources development	crisis and safety management	public relations	school business and finance
principal	2	1*		1+1*			○	○			
principal/newly appointed	3	2		1		○	○	○	○	○	
vice principal	1.5	1*		0.5+1*			○	○			
vice principal/newly appointed	2	1		1		○	○	○	○	○	
principal/appointment list	0.5	0.5				○	○				
vice principal/appointment list	0.5	0.5				○	○				
senior teacher/newly appointed	1	0.5		0.5		○	○	○		○	
advanced-skill teachers/newly appointed	1	1				○	○				

*In-person or on-demand depending on years of experience

Twenty-three types of "problem-solving ability development training" are frequently used in training for school administrators (including mid-career teachers training) and are treated as optional training for comprehensive training and as optional training for a broader range of targets.

In the CPBE training plan, two to three training courses correspond to each of the eight indicator elements. The 2023 revised indicators based on the 2022 revision of the Minister's guidelines will add "facilitation" and "assessment" similar to APBE, and training on these themes will be implemented in the training for new principals. Additionally, the CPBE has set some indicator items that are expected to improve as the principal's years of experience increase (although no corresponding training could be confirmed).

The Faculty and Staff Division of the Board of Education secretariat oversees the formulation of CPBE indicators. The diagram of training shows that training for school administrators provided by the secretariat's department includes "crisis management training," "human rights education training for principals," "focused briefing sessions on school education," and "training for vice principals in school affairs management." However, little information is available about the actual training content provided by

Table 3: Relevance of Training / Indicators for School Administrators (CPBE)

CPBE categories of training	training duration (days)	duration (in detail)				elements[8] / indicator items[16]							
		face to face	online synchronous	on-demand	other type	1(3) building and sharing a vision	2(2) respect for human rights	3(2) crisis management and response	4(3) human resources development	5(2) creating a comfortable working environment	6(1) informatization of education	7(2) external partnerships/collaboration	8(1) creating a safe school
principal													
principal/newly appointed	2	1		1		○		○	○			○	○
principal (human rights)	details unknown												
vice principal (school duties)	details unknown												
developing problem-solving skills (voluntary/optional)*	0.25×17 0.5×6	0.5×4	0.5×2	0.25×17		●	●	●	●	●	●	●	●
vice principal/2nd years (required/optional)	0.25–0.5	select one course from "developing problem-solving skills"											
vice principal/newly appointed	3	1	1	1		○		○	○	○		○	○
senior teacher/2nd years	0.25–0.5	select one course from "developing problem-solving skills"											
senior teacher/newly appointed	1.25	0.5		0.75		○				○			
teacher (middle leader)	4.5	2	0.5	2			○			○	○	○	

*Ten of these are courses offered by partner universities

departments other than the Prefectural Education Center. In addition, the content of the vice principal's training is unclear from the publicly available materials.

3-3-4. Case 4: D City Board of Education (DCBE)

DCBE has formulated school administrator indicators for principal, senior vice principal and vice principal positions by adding a comprehensive overall indicator to 11 elements (21 items).

In the case of DCBE, the training plan includes limited types of pre-appointment (for school administrators) training. Since the three-day training for school administrators is "administrative explanations", the actual training for DCBE school administrators in line with the indicators is considered one day for new senior teachers, 3.5 days for new vice principals, 3.5 days for new principals, and 1.5 days for principals. DCBE extensively

Table 4: Relevance of Training / Indicators for School Administrators (DCBE)

DCBE categories of training	training duration (days)	face to face	online synchronous	on-demand	other type	1(3) sense of mission and responsibility	2(2) self-professional development	3(2) sense of human rights	4(2) leadership	5(1) identifying issues and setting a vision	6(2) enhancing and promoting school education activities	7(1) informatization of education	8(2) organizational and environmental development	9(2) human resources development	10(2) external partnerships	11(2) crisis management
principal	1.5		0.5	1					○		○	○				
principal/newly appointed	3.5	0.5	1	0.5	0.5	○			○	○		○		○	○	○
school administrator	1		1												○	○
school administrator (voluntary/optional)	0.5×2		0.5	0.5											●	●
school administrator (required/optional)	details unknown *Can be used for collaborative courses offered by universities															
vice principal/newly appointed	3.5	1	0.5	1.5	0.5	○		○					○	○		○
senior teacher/newly appointed	1	1				○										

uses online synchronous and on-demand training opportunities, and group/face-to-face training is limited to 2.5 days: 0.5 days for new principals, one day for new vice principals, and one day for new senior teachers. Although these training courses cover the 11 indicator elements that the quality of the training may be undermined by the limited number of days and the fact that a large proportion of the training is on-demand training. DCBE's indicators emphasize (in the overall description) that "assessment" and "facilitation skills" are necessary skills for principals. However, it was impossible to discern whether these are covered adequately in administrator training.

The city's Education Center is responsible for the majority of DCBE training. However, even in cases where another department is in charge, the department responsible is added to the training plan. The Education Center is the department responsible for formulating the indicators.

DCBE introduces university collaborative courses as training and says this can be used as one class in the mandatory elective for administrator positions. However, these collaborative courses are aimed at all teaching staff, and no university collaborative courses were identified as administrator training.

3-4. Consideration

Although the above four cases differ in terms of the number of elements/items of indicators, contents/descriptions, and training duration, the training contents for each position covers almost all the indicator elements (at least the perspective level). It was inferred that the correspondence between indicators and training in the BOEs is generally high. It was shown that the perspectives of indicators that do not have directly corresponding training are also treated as related contents in each training.

In each case, the indicator items or elements corresponding to each training content were shown to participants in the training plans and guides, and it can be seen that both the training planners and instructors are aware of the qualities and abilities represented by the indicators. It was also confirmed that APBE and CPBE are reorganizing their training contents for new principals in line with the revision of indicators accompanying the 2022 revision of the Minister's guidelines.

The summary of the details of the current indicators and training plans for school administrators in the four case studies is as follows. First, concerning the consistency between the indicators and the training contents, although the indicators indicate the qualities and abilities that should be developed, there were some cases wherein the training content did not match the indicators that were subsequently formulated, or the purpose was unclear because it applied to everything. It is unclear whether this is due to the difficulty of simply reducing the indicators to match specific training content, inadequate training duration, or other factors. One possible reason is that the indicators and training contents are formulated by different departments (the indicators were formulated by the Faculty and Staff Department for APBE and CPBE, the High School Department for BPBE, and the Education Center for DCBE).

Next, in terms of training continuity/systematicity, it was confirmed that the weight of training for new principals was generally considerable in each case. On the other hand, in all cases, training for mid-career teachers was conducted before the appointment of vice principals, and there was a tendency to develop candidates for the school administrator position from an early stage. Regarding the training content, some programs, such as "school organization management" and "leadership," were repeated from mid-career to principal training. Some of these, such as APBE, aimed to systematically organize and enhance the principal training content. However, the number of training days was limited in all cases, so it cannot be said that systematic training was set for each indicator item. Instead, even in training related to items such as "school organization management," contents of "school administration" and "school crisis management" were also added, and the contents were sometimes diffused. In addition, there were cases such as APBE and CPBE where the majority of training for principals and vice principals was elective or voluntary (these are considered controversial in terms of the continuity and autonomy of the training).

Regarding collaboration with universities, the case studies in this chapter show that there are cases where participation in university-sponsored courses is recognized as attending regular training, which can be seen as one of the momentum of the proactive development of the people involver's abilities based on the indicators for school administrators. On the other hand, apart from the temporary cooperation of university professors as lecturers, there appears to be little progress in administrative agencies' efforts.

3-5. Further examination of changes in school administrator training before and after the institutionalization of "indicators" (Case 5)

To examine how the school administrator training provided by the BOE has changed before and after the established indicators, we attempted to compare administrator training in a designated city (E City Board of Education: ECBE) in 2006 and 2019.[7] Following the method described in 3-2 above, we reviewed the training guides for both years in the city and confirmed the relationship between the contents of the administrator training for each year and the elements (10) of the city's principal indicators as of 2019 (established in 2018).

We found significant differences in the installation of pre-appointment training, the total number of days, and the training contents. Pre-appointment training for each position, which did not exist in 2006, was implemented in 2019. The total number of days was 24 in 2006, and 19 in 2019, which is a decrease of 5 days. In 2006, the number of in-service training days for principals (8 days) and vice principals (7 days) was exceptionally high. However, in 2019, 11 types of administrator training lasted for 1-3 days each, indicating a structured and evenly distributed training schedule.

Furthermore, 7 of the ten elements of the school administrator indicators corresponded to training in 2006, regarding the relationship between the indicators and training contents. Meanwhile, in 2019, training was set to correspond to all ten elements. Although the training plan covers each competency item, the depth of each training course is unclear. Concerning this, the training in 2006 was structured to emphasize school and garden management, especially school organizational management, for both vice principals and principals. However, in 2019, the degree of emphasis regarding the number of days and systematicity weakened.

4. Conclusion: Achievements and Issues of School Administrator Training

This chapter examined how school administrator training led by Japan's local educational administrative bodies has changed in recent years in line with policy trends that favor school-based management and curriculum management. Although the analysis presented in this chapter is limited in terms of data collection, the achievements and shortcomings concerning the changes in training for school administrators in prefectures and designated cities following the 2016 amendment of laws related to formulating teacher/principal indicators and the training plan can be explained as follows.

4-1. Achievements

In each case, the training was planned to correspond to the elements of the indicators,

Table 5: Changes in Training before and after the Institutionalization of Indicators

Elements (2019 indicators):
1. compliance with laws and regulations
2. respect for human rights
3. self-improvement
4. school management
5. crisis and safety management
6. promote schools that are open to communities
7. operation of organization
8. service management/discipline
9. guidances, advices for teachers and staff
10. human resource development/staff evaluation

2006 SY

ECBE categories of training	training duration (days) (24)	1	2	3	4	5	6	7	8	9	10
principal	8		○		○			○		○	
principal/2nd years	2		○		○						
principal/newly appointed	3	○			○						
principal/pre-service											
school administrators	7						○				○
vice principal	2		○		○					○	○
vice principal/2nd years	2	○	○		○						
vice principal/newly appointed											
vice principal/pre-service											
senior teacher											
senior teacher/newly appointed											

2019 SY

ECBE categories of training	training duration (days) (19)	1	2	3	4	5	6	7	8	9	10
principal	2		●	●			●	●		●	● ○
principal/2nd years	1					○					
principal/newly appointed	2	○			○						
principal/pre-service	1				○						
school administrators	3									○	
vice principal	2		○		○						
vice principal/2nd years	1		○		○						
vice principal/newly appointed	3	○			○	○		○			
vice principal/pre-service	1								○		
senior teacher	2									○	
senior teacher/newly appointed	1	○							○	○	

and training purpose was clarified to participants by showing them the training content and the related indicator items/elements for each session. Although the training hours tend to be reduced as the other pressure of "work style reform" cannot be ignored, a series of training covers almost all of the indicators. In addition, it is now more necessary to clarify the qualities and abilities required of principals after the Minister's guidelines has been revised in 2022. This has encouraged improvements in school administrator training and is thought to have made the relationship between indicators and training more conscious.

In addition, although each case has specific differences, administrator training is systematized (strengthening in continuity) by structuring training in line with indicators from the mid-career period. The overall number of hours for school administrator training is on the decline. At the same time, in all regions, relatively many days are allocated to training for new and vice principals, and emphasis is placed on it. The training method has also remained relatively face-to-face. As the skills required of principals have evolved and become more complex, it appears that while both training courses are being retained as much as possible, efforts are being made to systematize the management training by distributing it among all other training programs.

4-2. Issues

First, looking at each case, it is found that some training is unrelated to the indicator items/elements. Although the aim is to build a training system based on indicators, some training content still exists as administrator training without meeting the requirements. In Japan, administrator training may be carried out by other secretariat departments and the Education Center, which is responsible for it. Moreover, the department in charge of making indicators is often the Faculty and Staff Department, and the Education Center, the training implementation institution, often has limited involvement. These are thought to affect the relationship between indicators and training.

Second, the school administrator training target is expanded, and training is aimed at starting from the mid-career period. Although this is seen as a positive trend in systematic training based on the indicators, the number of hours for each training course is short, and the content tends to be thin. Due to another factor, the pressure of "work style reform," it is currently impossible to allocate more time for administrative training. Gradual continuing training may solve this problem, but there is another challenge to note: as the total number of hours of training conducted by the entire organization is decreasing, the content covered in the training is expanding. Although it is possible to complete a full range of training courses to develop the qualities and abilities required for management positions as required by the indicators, it is becoming difficult to focus on contemporary issues in a focused manner. There are cases where three training courses are completed in half a day (approximately three hours), and it is surmised that covering the indicators is prioritized over enriching the content. To deal with this issue, training opportunities are being expanded by offering elective trainings covering a wide range of themes.

Third, in this chapter, we also examined the role of collaboration between universities and the BOEs in the advancement of training. In Japan, collaboration between educational administrative agencies and universities has been actively promoted since the late 2000s as part of teacher education reform implemented through teacher training, recruitment, and in-service training (Ohno, 2024). As a result, in the 2010s, pioneering developments have been reported, such as the joint development of new vice principal training / pre-service training programs for vice principals that are rich in both length and content, utilizing the human and intellectual resources of universities (in some cases, the program is recognized as a graduate school credit). However, in this case study, although some boards of education recognized participation in university-provided courses as participation in regular training, no significant changes were observed overall. In conclusion, the systematization and advancement of training mediated by university collaboration remains a project for the future.

* * *

Regarding the training for school administrators provided by Japan's educational administration agencies, there has been progress in linking the competencies prescribed by the indicators with the training content and establishing systematicity throughout careers. However, issues can also be highlighted regarding the inadequacies of training duration and content (particularly the need to align the training more with the target competencies). In this chapter, we showed that there is a need to address issues in the setting of indicators at the BOEs level, and refine the systematicity and level of the training content, toward to promote curriculum management at the school level, develop competencies of school leaders. To this end, it is also necessary to improve efforts in areas such as collaborations between universities and the BOEs (in terms of resource constraints), and the system-level reforms being introduced by the central government (qualifications and training systems for school administrators).

Notes

1) Originally, the basic qualifications required for the position of principal were a teaching license and either five years of work experience in education or ten years of work experience in a school. But a legal amendment made in 2000 made it possible for all public and private schools to appoint private citizens with no work experience as principal. In a sense, Japan is in a conflict, emphasizing the ability and training of school administrators with no public qualification or license system (Shinohara, 2017).
2) For training of teachers and school administrators conducted by these administrative agencies, the local governments generally bear the costs, and the recipients do not pay any fees.
3) At the present in Japan there is no graduate school-level training system for school administrators. However, the introduction of professional schools for teacher education (professional degree) in 2008 was a symbolic turning point. Proposals have been made to develop the capabilities of teacher leaders, including school administrators, at the master level and to enhance administrative training for school administrators

through collaboration between universities (above professional schools) and boards of education/education centers (Ojima, 2004). Collaborative development of training programs is underway in some regions.

4) Indicators for teachers/school administrators are formulated by prefectural / designated city boards of education with the authority to appoint teachers. Indicators are to be formulated by a council consisting mainly of representatives from the BOE and teacher training universities, considering the guidelines set by the minister of MEXT. The specific content of the indicators for school administrators is displayed in two dimensions: "Abilities expected to be demonstrated ([broader criteria/] elements/ indicator items)" and "Career stage (principal/vice principal [/senior teachers etc.])." Indicators for teachers are displayed in two dimensions: "Ability items expected to be demonstrated" and "Experience stage (training/just after joining/middle-aged/ veteran, etc.)."

5) To date, many boards of education have begun offering training specifically for developing leadership and management skills for senior teachers and other late or mid-career teachers (excluding the statutory training for teachers approximately after ten years of experience). However, it is not required by law.

6) The school administrator's indicators of APBE are designed to show only the content corresponding to the principal position. In addition, the perspectives and items are formulated as a pair, and the 15 perspectives = items are organized into four major categories. In this case study comparison, we focused on the part of perspective = items.

7) The position of chief teacher was institutionalized nationwide in 2007. However, City E (ECBE) had already introduced an equivalent position, and there is no difference in the rank between the two points in time.

References

Japanese Association for the Study of Educational Administration. (2009). Professional Standards for Principal: Desired Principal Image and Competences (2009 edition) (校長の専門職基準［2009年版］), http://jasea.jp/wp-content/uploads/2016/12/2009_kijun.pdf

Kitagami, M. (2004). Current status and improvement trends of training in prefectures. In Ojima, H. (eds), *Qualification and Training System of the principal and the Role of Graduate Schools* (校長の資格・養成と大学院の役割), *Toshindo*, 67–77.

Ministry of Education, Culture, Sports, Science and Technology. (2004). *Training on School Organization Management—Model Curriculum* (学校組織マネジメント研修—これからの校長・教頭等のために［モデル・カリキュラム］).

National Institute for Educational Policy Research. (2014). *Research Report on the Current Training of School Administrators and the Possibility of Utilizing Graduate Schools* (学校管理職の現状と今後の大学院活用の可能性に関する調査報告書).

National Institute for School Teachers and Staff Development. (2019). *Functions and Utilization of Teacher/Principal Development Indicators* (育成指標の機能と活用).

National Institute for School Teachers and Staff Development. (2020). *Current Status and Issues of School Administrator Training based on Development Indicators* (育成指標に基づく管理職研修の現状と課題).

Ohno, Y. (2024). In-service Training Function of the Japanese Professional Schools for Teacher Education. *Bulletin of School Administration* (Otsuka Society for the Study of School Administration), 49, 27–38.

Ojima, H. (eds). (2004). *Qualification and Training System of the Principal and the Role of Graduate Schools* (校長の資格・養成と大学院の役割). Toshindo.

Owaki, Y. (2007). Creating school leadership education in graduate schools. In Ojima, H. (eds) *School management Reform in the Turning Point of History* (時代の転換と学校経営改革). Gakubunsha.

Shinohara, K. (2003). *Postmodern Educational Reform and the States* (ポストモダンの教育改革と国家). Kyouiku-kaihatsu Press.

Shinohara, K. (2017). *Training School Administrators Overseas* (世界の学校管理職養成). Jidaisha.

Ushiwata, J., Ushiwata, R. (2022). *Reexamination of Standards Policy in Teacher Education* (教師教育におけるスタンダード政策の再検討). Toshindo.

Yaosaka, O. (1998). Current Status and Issues of School Management-related Training for Head and Mid-career Teachers at Education Centers. *Education Law Quarterly*, 115, Eidel Inc., 43–51.

Final Chapter

The Future of Research: School-Based Curriculum Management and Lesson Study for Teacher Education

Tetsuo KURAMOTO, Shizuoka University of Art and Culture
Mam CHANSEAN, National Institute of Education/Cambodia
Masataka ISOBE, Aichi University of Education

Abstract

The significant purpose is firstly to promote theoretical and practical developmental research of School-Based Curriculum Study and Lesson Study (1st, 2nd, and 3rd circles) through a collaborative effort between the World Association of Lesson Studies (WALS) and The Japanese Society for Curriculum Studies (JSCS). This collaboration ensures that international teacher training is developed using the research results and effectiveness verification is conducted. Importantly, this is done with the active participation of the educators, making them feel valued and integral to this solution-oriented project.

Finally, in a powerful collaboration with WALS and JSCS, including the National Institute of Education (NIE) of Cambodia, this developmental research project will establish an international network for research in related fields and enhance global teacher training. This emphasis on international cooperation and the global impact of the research will make educators feel connected and part of a larger, global community.

1. The Future Research Vision: School-Based Curriculum Study & Lesson Study (1st Circle, 2nd Circle, 3rd Circle)

Figure 1 shows the significance and necessity of The Collaborative Research Project between WALS and JSCS, highlighting the overall structure (Phase 1–Phase 4).

First, it was created by the academic collaboration between WALS and JSCS. Phase 1 (Plan) needs to embody theoretical and practical development research of School-Based CS & LS (1st circle, 2nd circle, 3rd circle). This practical approach will engage the educators and make them feel involved in the project, knowing that the research they are contributing to will directly impact their teaching practices.

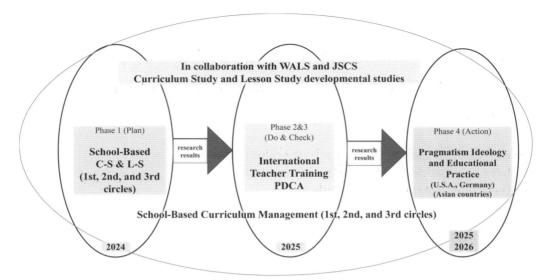

Figure 1: Structure of the Curriculum Study and Lesson Study in Collaboration with WALS

Second, in Phase 2 (Do), while utilizing the research results of Phase 1 (Plan), the need arises to develop and implement international teacher training and verify the training effectiveness in Phase 3 (Check). In this case, primary teacher training will be conducted by directly visiting overseas research institutes or combining indirect instruction (online) as necessary. In Phase 3 (Check), the project will conduct a theoretical research study while verifying quantitatively and qualitatively using local teachers' and students' learning outcomes, specific skills, and knowledge that students acquire as a result of the teacher training programs.

Third, in Phase 4 (Action), the project aims to provide a theoretical synthesis of the interface between academic CS and practicum teaching lesson research. It will achieve these goals by incorporating practical findings from adequately verifying teacher training programs. Additionally, it will specifically focus on the educational philosophy and practice of pragmatism, aiming to overcome the 'dichotomy of curriculum research'—the perceived separation between theoretical CS and practical teaching research. This dichotomy is a significant challenge in the field, and by juxtaposing it with the relevant theories, the project offers an original perspective. In doing so, it is necessary to focus on the 'educational philosophy and practice of pragmatism (in the U.S. and Asian countries)' and compare them with the relevant theory in Japan, for example, from the perspective of overlooking the 'dichotomy of CS,' the state of civic education theory with proactive citizenship and democratic citizens, and it will compare them with Japanese theory.

In summary, as shown in Figure 1, this developmental research through academic collaboration between WALS (Lewis, 2002a; 2002b; Lewis et al., 1998; Kim & Yoshida et al., 2021) and JSCS will lead to the forming of an international research network in related fields. This emphasis on international cooperation will make educators feel connected and part of a global community. As elucidated above, the ultimate significance of this research lies in the potential to establish a 'cornerstone (a model case) of

Table 1: International Teacher Training Development at National Institute of Education (NIE of Cambodia, 2024 March 17th)

Keywords: Teachers as Lifelong Learners, Teacher development Index, Teacher Training Program

8:00–9:25 Lecture 1	Recess	9:40–11:00 Lecture 2	13:00–14:25 Lecture 3	Recess	14:40–16:00 Lecture 4
Kuramoto & Mam Chansean		Isobe & Mam Chansean	Kuramoto & Mam Chansean		Kuramoto & Mam Chansean
Leadership Lecture & Workshop (Q&A)		ICT & Modan Education (Q&A)	School-Based Curriculum Management Lecture & Workshop (Q&A)		Ph.D.& Ed.D. from Action Research Perspective (Q&A)

a collaborative network of international contributions in pedagogy (educational methodology, curriculum studies, teacher education). It could revolutionize how the study approaches and understands pedagogy, inspiring innovation and progress in teaching practices worldwide.

In particular, the International Teacher Training Development for Phase 2 (Do) and Phase 3 (Check) have already been implemented as a precedent case. This significant milestone was achieved through the collaborative efforts of Mam Chansean (Ed.D.), Deputy Head of the Planning and Management Department and chief of the International Relations Unit of the National Institute of Education (NIE of Cambodia), and our international partners. This project was conducted at NIE of Cambodia in March 2024. 137 Participants included graduate, master's, and doctoral students. Their current jobs include lecturing at universities, teaching at general education schools, and administrators in the Ministry of Education, Youth and Sport of Cambodia. They learn at NIE of Cambodia on Saturday and Sunday, and they work in their institutions on weekdays.

As shown in Table 1, the program was executed according to the following content and schedule (Kuramoto et al.).

The survey and analysis regarding the project consisted of a free answer questionnaire on lectures and exercises, with open-ended responses sought. Implementing and verifying this training program revealed that the international teacher training aims have mainly been achieved.

Additionally, in Phase 3 (Check), the project will conduct a theoretical research study while verifying quantitatively and qualitatively using local teachers' and students' learning outcomes, specific skills, and knowledge that students acquire as a result of the teacher training programs. The future phases of research hold great promise, offering the potential for further understanding and improvement in international teacher training. This ongoing commitment to research and development should inspire hope and confidence in the future of international teacher education.

2. Future Research Purpose No.1: School-Based Curriculum Management and Knowledge Management

To elaborate on The Future Research Vision: School-Based Curriculum Management (1st circle, 2nd circle, 3rd circle) and Knowledge Management, it is beneficial to consider the input and output theory, which contains input, black box, and output (Piggot et al., 2015; Russell, 2014). The SECI model, a knowledge creation theory developed by Nonaka and Takeuchi in 1995, and Knowledge Leadership for school organizations indicate the importance of teachers' professional development and student achievements (Cheng, 2019). The SECI model, which stands for Socialization, Externalization, Combination, and Internalization, is a framework for understanding the knowledge-creation process within an organization. It is particularly relevant to school-based curriculum management as it emphasizes the importance of socialization and collaboration in knowledge creation, which are critical aspects of effective teaching and learning.

Correspondingly, SBCM, with Knowledge Management's fundamental managerial aspects from the SECI model and knowledge leadership for school organizations (Nonaka,1991; Nonaka et al., 1995, 2006, 2008, 2009.), is divided into three factors. These three factors consist of 1) input factors (e.g., curriculum philosophy, educational goals, school mission, vision, and strategy); 2) black box factors (e.g., lesson study/SECI model, individual teacher, teacher's team, school theory, knowledge leadership, school culture/ Ba, and teacher's assets); and 3) output factors (e.g., student's academic achievement and personal growth, the enhancement of teachers' professional skills, parents, and community involvement) (Kuramoto, 2024a; Kuramoto et al., 2014, 2021). The details of the functional structure of SBCM with lesson study, from the perspective of input and output theory of the SECI model and knowledge leadership for school organization, are shown in Figure 2.

First, the most fundamental and initial school management strategies include input factors such as SBCM and Knowledge Management, curriculum philosophy, educational goals, and school mission/vision. It is essential to establish a PDCA cycle for SBCM and Knowledge Management; the school's common educational goal and content should be established primarily by managing its organizational performance. Developing SBCM and Knowledge Management is necessary to create strategic teaching and curriculum. Finally, improving the quality of curriculum philosophy and others should be accomplished for students and teachers within a school year.

Second, for black box factors of SBCM and Knowledge Management, in particular, the knowledge leadership for school organization, which promotes the teachers' knowledge and skills, consists of:

1. Creation and activation of Ba and the school culture/system.
2. Promotion of the lesson study with the SECI process.
3. Establishment of teachers' knowledge vision and development of knowledge assets.

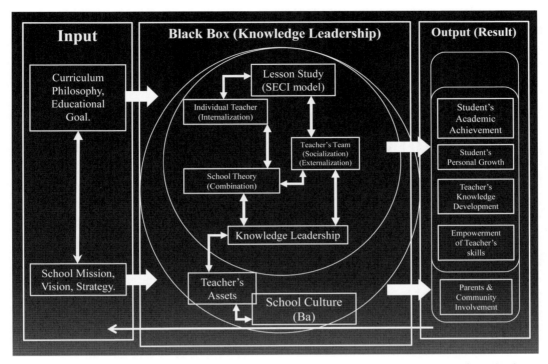

Figure 2: Input and Output Theory of SECI Model and Knowledge Leadership for School Organization (Kuramoto, 2024, p.51)

For example, internal collaboration can be understood through the school culture/system and creating Ba of knowledge leadership. Individual teachers' volition and motivation significantly affect outcomes because combined explicit knowledge is reinterpreted and internalized by teachers to recreate tacit knowledge. It has been discussed whether this issue should be addressed with individual teachers or if systematic support should be provided. Considering that the SECI model suggests spiral development (Nonaka et al., 1995), it is recommended that lesson studies be performed in a successive system with several sessions per year. The lesson study process would respond to the SECI model process in four steps. The lesson study counterpart of the SECI model socialization involves producing a teaching plan and participation in pre-class discussions. The SECI model externalization is a workshop for a research class in which other teachers participate and observe. The SECI model combination is constructing school improvement through a post-lesson discussion (Dudley, 2012, 2016). The SECI model internalization reaches this unique realization by reflecting on the study of school improvement. These examples demonstrate how the SECI model can be applied in school-based curriculum management to promote knowledge creation and sharing among teachers, leading to improved student learning outcomes.

Third, the output factors of SBCM and Knowledge Management are related to school improvement theory. For school improvement, there are the general elements of organizational problem-solving, school culture formation, independent and autonomous school organization, and open cooperativity in school systems (Japanese Association for the Study of Educational Administration, JASEA, 2009). Therefore, parents and community involvement are ultimately the most critical issues in school-based curriculum management, with lesson study perspectives regarding students' academic achievement/personal growth, enhancing teachers' professional skills, and knowledge development.

3. The Future Research Purpose No.2: Empowering Educators and Administrators: Managing School-Based Curriculum and Lesson Study to Cultivate Intellectual Capital

The Ministry of Economics and Industry Japan has recommended the idea of Intellectual Capital, IC, to small and medium-sized companies since the 2010s. This recommendation is not limited to the business sector but also holds significant implications for the education sector. According to the Ministry of Economics and Industry (METI), intellectual property is the value of unique information that may provide the knowledge, skills, business training, or competitive advantage of a company or its employees. Intellectual capital is considered an asset broadly defined as collecting all information resources (METI 2018). Maintaining the companies' intellectual capital management (see Figure 3) to produce sustainable benefits must be recognized and evaluated by stakeholders. Therefore, companies must open management strategies and information regarding tacit intellectual assets and explicit intellectual properties (Khavand & Khavandkar, 2013; Serenko & Bontis, 2017; Cheng, 2022). The potential benefits of this management are vast and promising.

Intellectual assets are a company's hidden organizational assets, such as human resources, technologies, organizational capacities, customer network, and brand/reputation. They are necessary competitive traits that must be improved for the organization's benefit (Urasaki, 2005).

These concepts differ from intellectual properties comprising explicit knowledge and strategies, such as industrial licenses and knowledge. As mentioned above, the extensive concepts are based on the assets of companies' strengths.

Consequently, *management strategies* combining tacit intellectual assets and explicating intellectual properties are defined as intellectual capital management for companies METI recommends.

IC generally consists of three factors: human capital, structural capital, and relational capital. The concept summary is as follows. Through lesson study, this study reconsiders intellectual capital in school organizations from an SBCM perspective (Wiig & Karl, 1997; Kuramoto, 2022; Aichi University of Education, 2022).

1. Human capital in schools

Human capital refers to the teaching staff's collective knowledge, skills, know-how, and proficiency in schools. Human capital integrates individual teachers and school organizations to solve problems and manage explicit intellectual property. It also considers how successfully the school organization uses a teacher's human resources.

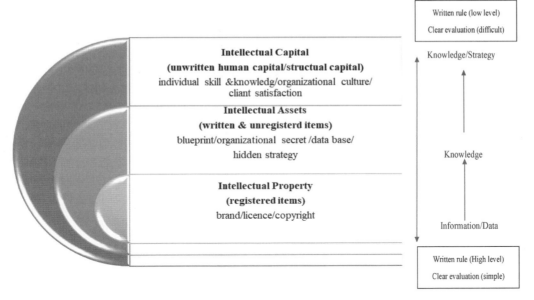

Figure 3: Company Management of Intellectual Capital (Kuramoto adapted from Urasaki, 2005, p.117)

2. Structural capital in schools

Structural capital includes the school's organizational philosophies and systems for managing the school organization's proficiencies. This could involve the allocation of resources, the design of the curriculum, and the implementation of teaching methodologies. School structural capital consists of assigned individual roles within the system, technologies, procedures, and curriculum to perform better qualitative teaching.

3. Relational capital in schools

It comprises supply and demand relationships with schools, which parents, the community, and educational administrations value. The relationship with them, separate from human and structural capital, shows fundamental importance to the organization's value in improving school organizational quality.

4. Conclusion: School-Based Curriculum Management and Teacher Training by Using Intellectual Capital: Empowering Educators and Policymakers

The IC refers to tacit knowledge and the company's system, which are hidden organizational assets such as human resources, technologies, organizational capacities, network with customers, and the company's brand/reputation, which are necessary competitive abilities to improve the organization (Urasaki, 2005, p. 117). IC comprises explicit knowledge and strategies such as industrial licenses and expertise. As mentioned above, these extensive concepts are based on the company's strengths. Consequently, *management*

Table 2: Teacher Training Index from the Perspective of School-Based Curriculum Management (SBCM) & Intellectual Capital (IC), Isobe & Kuramoto, 2024.

<Objectives> Equip teachers with knowledge and skills for appropriate school management and promotion of characteristic teaching activities and train teachers to be the core of individual schools and communities as "a teacher with continuous learning."

<Contents> Goal for training "teachers who can continue learning" and improve overall independent abilities for solutions and management, coping systematically with problems and difficulties that individual schools confront

constant improvement in quality and specialty through stages of education, employment, and training

Quality and specialty	Stage I — Education and Employment: To start working, a teacher should possess the essential attitude of continuous learning and meet the employment requirements of the Board of Education.	Stage II — Starting Rank to Several Years Experience: This stage requires a teacher to have the essential attitude of a teacher and to become a class teacher with comprehensive capabilities.	Stage III — Ten-Year Training Course: At this stage, the focus is on acquiring teaching specialties and expanding practical abilities.	Stage IV — At this stage, teachers should aim to heighten their specialty as school team members or middle leaders, deepen cooperation and collaboration, and exert propulsive force.	Stage V — Playing a broader role in the school and community. 1. veteran teachers	Stage V — 2. managerial position
Sense of mission	as a public service teacher, I am deeply committed to my sense of mission, which drives compliance with laws.					
Human relationship	having a deep understanding of human growth and a keen sense of human rights and building a trusting relationship with infants, school children, teachers, parents and guardians, and communities					
Pedagogical Love	concerning communities and having great pride as a teacher, showing pedagogical love to infants and young school students					
Teaching of subjects-fields	an attitude of self-improvement of specialized knowledge in subjects and fields, including moral education, special activities, and integrated study, and the capability of independent learning					
Well-educated	knowing how to cope with social changes and wide-ranging cultural education with broad perspectives					
Understanding of contents of specialized subjects	capable of preparation of teaching plans and models based on teaching plans and performance of class teaching	capable of preparation and performance of teaching plans based on the guidelines for the course of study, considering teaching procedures	capable of setting up and the appropriate performance of learning plans by guidelines for the course of research and the management plans and teaching policies of the school	capable of conducting appropriate examinations, modification, and improvement of teaching plans with overall perceptions on various learning problems of the subject depending on schools and grades	ability to perform and contrive class teaching and supporting and advising, regarding teaching classes, to teachers in the school for the improvement in various issues in overall school teaching and also in a specialty subject	guiding teachers in school for the improvement in-class teaching to further promote specialty and to reduce overall school problems
Comprehension of actual states and setting up goals (Plan 1)	capable of understanding meanings and necessities of conducting studies on learning materials that meet students' needs for understanding	capable of conducting appropriate examinations on learning materials to achieve teaching goals	capable of reconstructing learning materials and tools to adjust to actual situations of school children and to correct teaching plan procedures	capable of learning specialized knowledge regarding teaching plans and utilizing that knowledge to enhance teaching material study	ability to provide support and advice based on their specialized knowledge to improve teaching materials and tools	supervising the improvement of teaching materials and tools based on their specialized knowledge
Preparation of teaching plan and assessment plan (Plan 2)	not only learning fundamental skills regarding contents, guidance, and assessments of the guidelines for the course of study but also understanding the forms of teaching plans	deeply understanding teaching units (theme) and materials, and being able to prepare teaching unit (theme) plans with clear goals	not only relating goals to teaching contents and assessments but also being able to prepare teaching models with clear plans and methods for assessment	ability to set up an overall plan for each teaching unit (theme) focusing on the development and learning level of school children	ability to support and advise, not only clarifying meanings of teaching plan preparation based on individual school teaching policies but also understanding various issues of teaching in individual schools to improve teaching plans	guiding not only with clarifying the meaning of preparation of teaching plans based on individual school policies but also with comprehension of problems in individual school teaching and for the improvement of teaching plans
Perceptions of teaching skills and forms (Plan 3)	learning and acquiring skills of how to talk, write on a blackboard, and how to approach to students	learning and acquiring skills of approach (asking questions, instructions, and explanations)	capable of writing on blackboards, focusing students' flow of understanding and thinking	able to develop a teaching lesson according to the development and learning level of schoolchildren	not only comprehension of the actual states of individual teachers regarding their class teaching but also their ability to give appropriate support and advice to them for the improvement of class teaching	playing a role not only in comprehension of the actual states of individual teachers but also in guidance to them for the improvement of class teaching
Guidance and assessment during class (Do)	understanding the meaning of classroom lessons for school children to acquire scholarly ability	capable of asking a question which can elicit diverse opinions from students	capable of asking proper questions with a deep understanding of the thinking flow of students	capable of performing a model workshop class in/outside the school	Ability to appropriately evaluate each teacher's class lessons and to promote teachers' motivation by giving them support and advice.	Play a role in appropriately evaluating class lessons that each teacher performs and motivating teachers with instructions.
Check and Action	able to understand the importance of preparation in evaluation criteria based on goals	able to prepare evaluation criteria based on goals	able to reexamine skills and goals that teachers want students to acquire and reconstruct evaluation criteria and teaching contents	able to improve class teaching on their own through observing multiple teachers' classroom lessons	able to set up concrete schemes regarding in-school systems for the improvement of class lessons	Play a role in presenting and conducting concrete schemes regarding in-school systems to improve class lessons.

Quality of teachers

Human Capital (Curriculum & Lesson Study)

Ability of teaching, guidance, & counseling) (1st circle/SBCM)

Capital category	Skill	Level 1	Level 2	Level 3	Level 4	Level 5	Level 6
Human Capital (Guidance & Counseling)	Student guidance	able to understand the importance of respecting the individual characteristics and personalities of students through meeting a diverse variety of children	able to provide flexible and appropriate measures, understanding diverse children through teaching practice and experiences of volunteer activities	aiming to understand that individual students act independently and can correspond with them by student guidance policies systematically	able to provide systematic and deliberate guidelines for students to understand a diverse variety of children	able to provide teachers with support and advice, including preventive measures, along with the construction of a promotion system in enhanced cooperation with related institutions	playing a role in establishing promotion systems in enhanced collaboration with related institutions and providing guidance to teachers, including preventive measures
Human Capital (Guidance & Counseling)	Student Counceling	capability to actively talk to children, learning how to provide appropriate actions with consideration to concerns of surrounding situations	understanding of the importance of attentive listening and being able to provide proper support based on the educational needs of students	grasping situations regarding the class, grade, and measures, being able to actively consult with coworkers, senior and managerial persons, and providing proper support	understanding of students with consideration of guardians' thoughts and family background, being capable of instructing students to have mutual understanding between students	Able to provide teachers with appropriate and concrete support and advice, where individual teachers are involved with school children on all fronts in/outside school	Provide appropriate guidance for individual teachers to act appropriately and engage with school children on all fronts in and outside school.
Structural Capital (School Management)	Human resources development and leadership	understanding of the importance of continuous learning, attentively listening to other's advice, and making efforts to improve themselves	able to consult and share points of uncertainty and troubles	able to enhance practical skills through consulting and sharing points of uncertainty and troubles	able to promote environmental improvement through mutual support, sharing problems and troubles, and supporting each other	able to consider the importance of training human resources and being able to improve the environment for effective development in human resources, focusing on the experience of individual teachers	playing a role in promoting effective development in human resources, with consideration of the importance of human resources development, according to individual teachers' experiences and characteristics
Structural Capital (School Management)	Cooperation as a team with co-workers	able to work collaboratively in various groups	able to work collaboratively as a member of an organization through teaching practice and volunteer activities	listening to coworkers, senior and managerial persons with modesty, and being capable of actively participating in the organization	capable of promoting a teacher group, which has the same direction for the goal, as a head teacher of a grade or a division	able to understand individual teachers' roles and capacities, promote collaborative organization, and prepare policies for schools, families, community organizations, and collaborative organizations	Understanding individual teachers' roles and capacities, promoting collaborative systems, and establishing measures for systems that collaborate with families, communities, and related organizations
Structural Capital (School Management)	Risk management and safety management	able to learn basic knowledge regarding school security and risk avoidance	able to learn the necessary knowledge for risk management and safety management	able to adopt appropriate measures for risk management and safety management for the class	able to plan and conduct training sessions regarding risk management and safety management of the school	able to establish a cooperative system with schools, families, communities, and various related organizations regarding risk management and safety management in the school and to determine and conduct appropriate countermeasures in an emergency, comprehending the management system	Play a role in establishing cooperative systems with schools, families, communities, and various related organizations regarding risk management and safety management in the school and to determine and conduct appropriate countermeasures in an emergency, comprehending the management system, and deal with the aftermath.
Structural Capital (School Management)	Taking advantage of resources (human, things, events, information, time, and funds)	capacity to find a countermeasure for troubles when they are involved in a diverse variety of problem-solving while they are university students	having a complete understanding of necessary resources for solutions to class problems, learning how to take advantage of methods with resources	when solving problems in a class or a grade, being capable of finding necessary resources and taking advantage of various resources in/outside school, such as different types of schools and communities	determining adequate resources for problems overall school and teaching activities and utilizing them	able to effectively use available resources they have in/outside school to promote systems and to provide appropriate support and advice to other teachers	They should play a role in effectively utilizing available resources in and outside school, promote systems, and provide appropriate guidance to other teachers.
Relational Capital (School Management)	Cooperation and collaboration with parents, gradians, and institutions outside school (establishment of communities with the school as the core)	understanding the importance of cooperation and collaboration with parents and guardians and other organizations	understanding the necessity to build a harmonious relationship with parents and guardians and other organizations, providing information to them	able to build harmonious relationships with parents and guardians and communities based on cooperation and collaboration	able to prevent and solve problematic behaviors through cooperation and collaboration with various related organizations	able to establish networks to achieve cooperation and partnership with parents and guardians, communities, and various associated organizations	Play a role in enhancing the system by establishing a cooperative and collaborative network.
Relational Capital (School Management)	Team School: System correspondence toward problems of education at present (Information and Communication Technology, ICT, career education, human rights, social integration, Education for Sustainable Development, ESD)	able to actively learn essential knowledge and understanding of problems in education at present	able to make efforts to exert support and guidance for children regarding issues in education at present	able to have appropriate knowledge and understanding as an organization, to a certain level, regarding issues in education at present	able to plan, prepare, and conduct training sessions and report meetings regarding present educational issues	able to make continuous efforts to gain the latest information regarding present educational problems and to enforce systematic correspondence with the school	always being cautious about the latest information to enforce systematic correspondence with the school regarding the issues in education at present

Management skills (2nd and 3rd circles/SBCM)

strategies that combine tacit intellectual assets and explicit intellectual properties are defined as IC management, which METI recommends.

Conversely, the IC comprises human, structural, and relational capital, and organizing the "Table 2. Teacher Training Index from the Perspective of School-Based Curriculum Management (SBCM) & Intellectual Capital (IC), Isobe & Kuramoto, 2024." is significant (Cheng, 2022; Kuramoto, 2022; Aichi University of Education, 2022). The objectives of the Index are to equip teachers with knowledge and skills for appropriate school management and to promote characteristic teaching activities. They aim to train teachers to be the core of individual schools and communities, embodying teachers with continuous learning. The contents aim to set goals for training teachers who can continue learning and enhance overall independent abilities for problem-solving and management. This involves systematically addressing problems and difficulties that individual schools face.

Teacher Training with IC, a professional development process involving teachers working collaboratively to plan, observe, and critique lessons and other school activities, is a crucial component of SBCM. This study presents an innovative research agenda that analyzes the concepts of school intellectual capital from the perspective of SBCM. Our research team posits that using SBCM, lesson study (a professional development process where teachers collaboratively plan, observe, and critique lessons to improve their teaching techniques), knowledge management, and other ideas can significantly enhance teaching quality and teacher training in schools, strengthening the overall intellectual capital. The potential of this framework to strengthen overall intellectual capital in schools is significant, instilling a sense of potential for growth and development in educators. The argument is that by developing the leadership competencies of principals and managers to conduct lesson study, teacher professional abilities could be enhanced and become crucial human capital in schools. Operating the PDCA lesson study cycle for knowledge creation of SECI model percent is a structural capital. If external experts participate in conducting LS of the schools, the relational capital will be developed through external experts.

As discussed regarding the Teacher Training Index, the IC management also possibly provides an analytical lens to Japan's new national curriculum implementation standards that came into force in 2020, which introduced intellectual capital concepts to schools. For instance, raising the standards of teachers' professional ability is a way to enhance human capital in schools; streamlining the PDCA cycle of lesson study for knowledge creation is to develop structural and relationship capital among teachers.

Conversely, LS is much more powerful than external support in enhancing SBCM's teaching abilities. However, external school support enhances the LS for teacher learning (Kuramoto et al.,2012a; 2012b). This finding supports the MEXT policy to provide external resources for schools to apply Lesson Study to enhance teacher abilities for curriculum implementation. Interestingly, the finding shows that an external teacher training program is less effective than using a Lesson Study to enhance teacher learning. Therefore, lesson study for SBCM could enhance teaching knowledge and address the curriculum implementation gap, providing a reliable solution to a significant educational challenge. The results also indicate that knowledge internalization, the process of incorporating new knowledge into the existing knowledge structure of an individual or organization, plays a critical role in developing structural capital to provide learning by following a routine for developing human capital for the school.

Applying SBCM with LS and the SECI model as a guiding process could improve educational vision and teaching ability (Cheng & Kuramoto, WALS webinar, Lesson Study: A Knowledge Management Perspective, 2019). The Ministry of Education, Culture, Sports, Science, and Technology (MEXT) should require teachers to develop individual educational abilities through lesson studies as part of SBCM and improve teaching methods and learning assessments. The teacher should observe social changes and improve teaching through training for 21st-century skills. Indeed, SBCM policies can strengthen schools' overall intellectual capital, paving the way for a brighter future in education. By developing the leadership competence of principals and managers of LS, teachers' professional abilities can be enhanced and become crucial human capital in schools. Restructuring SBCM with LS and IC for teachers' knowledge creation increases structural and relational capital among internal and external agents (Kuramoto, 2022). It would be beneficial to manage the curriculum with LS and formulate effective annual teaching plans, course hours, and weekly schedules that comply with the national curriculum guidelines for effective school management.

Beyond our research argument for teacher education and training, one suggestion regarding the future development of SBCM with LS is a new theoretical framework based on the relationship between School Management and IC (Wiig, 1997; Serenko,2017). This new theoretical framework can open up exciting avenues for future research in BCM with LS and IC, sparking the educators' interest and curiosity.

Footnote

International research on School-Based Curriculum Management (SBCM) was developed for this book publication based on the International Scientific Research Program (20KK0050) of SBCM and Lesson Study for Teaching Training.

References

Aichi University of Education, Graduate School of Education, The Career Center for Teaching. (2022). Final report on enhancing training systems and programs for establishing lifelong learning teachers (学び続ける教員像の確立に向けた研修体制・研修プログラムの実施充実最終報告書).

Cheng, E. C. K., & Kuramoto, T. (2019). World Association of Lesson Studies webinar: Lesson study: A knowledge management perspective. Retrieved from https://www.walsnet.org/blog/2019/10/28/lesson-study-a-knowledge-management-perspective/

Cheng, E. C. K. (2019). *Successful transposition of lesson study: A knowledge management perspective*. Springer.

Cheng, E. C. K. (2022). *Managing school intellectual capital for strategic development:*

Lessons from Asia and Europe. Routledge.

Dudley, P. (2012). Lesson study development in England: From school networks to national policy. *International Journal for Lesson and Learning Studies*, 1(1), 85–100.

Dudley, P. (2016). *Lesson study: Professional learning for our time.* Routledge Research in Education.

Fernandez, C., & Yoshida, M. (2004). *Lesson study: A Japanese approach to improving mathematics teaching-learning.* Lawrence Erlbaum Associates.

Japanese Association for the Study of Educational Administration. (2009). Professional standards for principal: Desired principal image and competencies, 2009 edition. Retrieved from http://jasea.jp/wp-content/uploads/2016/12/e-teigen2012.6.pdf

Khavand Kar, J., & Khavandkar, E. (2013). *Intellectual capital: Management, development, and measurement models* (3rd ed.). Ministry of Science, Research and Technology Press.

Kim, J., Yoshida, N., Iwata, S., & Kawaguchi, H. (Eds.). (2021). *Lesson study-based teacher education: The potential of the Japanese approach in global settings.* Routledge.

Kuramoto, T. (2008). *A study of curriculum management in the USA: From the service-learning perspective* (アメリカにおけるカリキュラムマネジメントの研究——Service-Learningの視点から). Japan: Fukuro Publishing.

Kuramoto, T., & Shi, H. (2012a). Action research of lesson study in Japan: From the view of students' achievement and teachers' professional development. *Journal of the Faculty of Culture and Education, Saga University*, 17(1), 119–132.

Kuramoto, T., & Shi, H. (2012b). Summary of lesson study and curriculum management in Japan. *Journal of the Faculty of Culture and Education*, Saga University, 17(1), 133–147.

Kuramoto, T., & Associates. (2014). *Lesson study & curriculum management in Japan: Focusing on action research.* Fukuro Publishing.

Kuramoto, T., & Associates. (2021). *Lesson study & curriculum management in Japan: Focusing on action research.* Fukuro Publishing.

Kuramoto, T. (2022). Developing intellectual capital in Japanese schools through lesson study: A perspective from curriculum management. In E. C. K. Cheng (Ed.), *Managing school intellectual capital for strategic development: Lessons from Asia and Europe* (pp.69–79). Routledge.

Kuramoto, T. (2024). *School-based curriculum management: Teacher education and lesson study perspective.* Fukuro Publishing.

Lewis, C., & Tsuchida, I. (1998). A lesson is like a swiftly flowing river: Research lessons and the improvement of Japanese Education. *American Educator*, Winter, 14–17, 50.

Lewis, C. (2002a). *Lesson study: A handbook of teacher-led instructional improvement.* Research for Better Schools.

Lewis, C. (2002b). Does lesson study have a future in the United States? *Nagoya Journal of Education and Human Development*, 1(1), 1–23.

Lewis, C. (2024). Japanese curriculum study: Can it leverage change around the world? *Curriculum Studies*, 33, 99–108.

Ministry of Economy, Trade, and Industry (METI). Retrieved from https://www.meti.

go.jp/policy/intellectual_assets/

Ministry of Education, Culture, Sports, Science, and Technology in Japan (MEXT). (2016). The Central Council for Education, a working group on Higher Education, and a teacher training committee regarding improving teachers' quality and ability in charge of school education. Retrieved from https://www.mext.go.jp/b_menu/shingi/chukyo/chukyo3/

Nonaka, I. (1991). The knowledge-creating company. *Harvard Business Review*, 69(6), 96–104.

Nonaka, I., & Takeuchi, H. (1995). *The knowledge-creating company*. Oxford University Press.

Nonaka, I., Krogh, G., & Ichijo, K. (2000). *Enabling knowledge creation: How to unlock the mystery of tacit knowledge and release the power of innovation*. Oxford University Press.

Nonaka, I., & Krogh, G. (2009). Tacit knowledge and knowledge conversion: Controversy and advancement in organizational knowledge creation theory. *Organization Science*, 20(3), 635–652.

Nonaka, I., & Hirata, T. (2008). *Managing flow: A process theory of the knowledge-based firm*. Palgrave Macmillan.

Nonaka, I., & Ichijo, K. (2006). *Knowledge creation and management: New challenges for managers*. Oxford University Press.

Nonaka, I., & Nishiguchi, T. (2001). *Knowledge emergence: Social, technical, and evolutionary dimensions of knowledge creation*. Oxford University Press.

Piggot, I. E., & Rowe, W. (2015). Conceptualizing indicator domains for evaluating action research. *Lesley Educational Action Research*, 23(4), 545–566.

Russell, V. (2014). A closer look at the output hypothesis: The effect of pushed output on noticing and inductive learning of the Spanish future tense. *Foreign Language Annals*, 47(1), 25–47.

Serenko, A., & Bontis, N. (2017). Global ranking of knowledge management and intellectual capital academic journals. *Journal of Knowledge Management*, 21(3), 675–692.

Urasaki, N. (2005). The measurement of intellectual capital from the OECD project (知的資本の測定と報告――OECDの取り組み). *Journal of Business and Economy Japan*, 51(3), 111–133.

Wiig, K. M. (1997). Integrating intellectual capital and knowledge management. *Long Range Planning*, 30(3), 399–405.

Contributors

Foreword	Mohammad Reza SARKAR ARANI, Nagoya University
Introduction	Tetsuo KURAMOTO, Shizuoka University of Art and Culture
Part 1. Illuminating International Research of Curriculum Study and Lesson Study for Teaching Training Development	
Chapter 1	Tetsuo KURAMOTO, Shizuoka University of Art and Culture
Chapter 2	Tetsuo KURAMOTO, Shizuoka University of Art and Culture
Chapter 3	Eric C. K. CHENG, Yew Chung College of Early Childhood Education, Hong Kong/China
Chapter 4	Bruce LANDER, Matsuyama University
Chapter 5	Tavilya AKIMOVA, Center of Excellence, NIS, Kazakhstan
Chapter 6	Anthony RYAN, Nanzan University
Chapter 7	Jack RYAN, Shizuoka University of Art and Culture
Part 2: Insights of Lesson Study in Teacher Education and Curriculum Development—Showcasing in the Context of Digital Transformation in Vietnam	
Chapter 8	Thanh-Nga NGUYEN, Ho Chi Minh City University of Education, Vietnam Hoai-Nam NGUYEN, Hanoi National University of Education, Vietnam Thanh-Trung TA, Ho Chi Minh City University of Education, Vietnam Viet-Hai PHUNG, The University of Da Nang - University of Science and Education, Vietnam Thuy-Quynh LE-THI, Ho Chi Minh City University of Education, Vietnam
Chapter 9	Nam-Phuong NGUYEN, Hanoi National University of Education, Vietnam Van-Tu NGUYEN, Northeast Normal University, China Quoc-Khanh MAI, Hanoi National University of Education, Vietnam Trung-Kien PHAN, Hanoi Metropolitan University, Vietnam
Chapter 10	Dinh Chien TRAN, Hung Vuong University, Vietnam Nam-Phuong NGUYEN, Hanoi National University of Education, Vietnam
Chapter 11	Duc Giang NGUYEN, Hanoi National University of Education, Vietnam Thi Phuong NGUYEN, Vietnam National University, Vietnam Van Hai TA, National Academy of Educational Management, Vietnam Minh-Yen NGUYEN, Scholar Vietnam Education System, Vietnam
Part 3: School-Based Curriculum Management from the Perspective of Lesson Study and Teacher Education in Japan	
Chapter 12	Kaoru HORIUCHI and Sachiko NAKANISHI, Yokohama National University
Chapter 13	Tomoko TAMURA, Osaka Kyoiku University
Chapter 14	Toshiya CHICHIBU, National Institute of Education
Chapter 15	Kiyotaka SAKAI, University of Teacher Education Fukuoka
Chapter 16	Yuya AKATSUKA, Sagami Women's University
Chapter 17	Takeshi BABA, Baiko Gakuin University

Chapter 18	Masataka ISOBE, Aichi University of Education Toshifumi KAWAMURA, Nisshin Nishi Junior High School Daisuke ITO, Akita Prefectural University
Chapter 19	Takehiro WAKIMOTO, Yokohama National University
Chapter 20	Atsuko HOMMA, Doctoral program student, Hyogo University of Teacher Education Yasuki OHNO, Hyogo University of Teacher Education
Final Chapter	Tetsuo KURAMOTO, Shizuoka University of Art and Culture Mam CHANSEAN, National Institute of Education/Cambodia Masataka ISOBE, Aichi University of Education

Editor: Tetsuo Kuramoto (Professor/Ph.D., Japan)

Professor Tetsuo Kuramoto's expertise in teacher education encompasses school management and leadership, curriculum, and teaching methods. His research interests are equally diverse, ranging from curriculum development/management, classroom research, knowledge management/leadership, service learning, and Ed.D. programs. His primary research focuses on the conceptual structure of lesson study, school-based curriculum management, and the educational effects of action research, demonstrating his broad knowledge and expertise in the field.

His significant professional experience includes serving as a chief professor at Yokohama National University, Aichi University of Education, and Saga National University in the master's and doctoral courses of the teacher training program. He has also held significant leadership roles, such as a council of the Japan Association of Professional Schools for Teacher Education (JAPTE), the Japan Society for Curriculum Studies (JSCS), and the Japan Association of American Educational Studies (JAAES), which underscore his influence and authority in education.

He has actively contributed to the National Institute for Educational Policy Research (NITS) and prefectural boards of education and education centers. He has also served as the national evaluation committee chair for the Teacher Master's Program at the Ministry of Education (MEXT). In addition, he has served as an examiner for overseas doctoral Ed.D. programs and is often invited to give lectures and take part in projects overseas.

Academic Publication

1) Tetsuo Kuramoto. (2024). *School-Based Curriculum Management—Teacher Education and Lesson Study Perspective—*, Japan: Fukuro Publishing, 1–233, ISBN: 9784861869044

2) Tetsuo Kuramoto & Associates. (2021). *Lesson Study and Curriculum Management in Japan —Focusing on Action Research—*, Second edition (electronic book, Discover 21), 1–270, ISBN: 9784861868375

3) Tetsuo Kuramoto. (2008). *A study of curriculum management in the USA: From the service-learning perspective* (アメリカにおけるカリキュラムマネジメントの研究—Service-Learningの視点から), Japan: Fukuro Publishing, 1–345, ISBN: 9784861863332

**School-Based Curriculum Management and Lesson Study
for Teacher Education**

2025年3月20日　初版発行

著作者　倉本哲男/Tetsuo Kuramoto　ⓒ 2025

発行所　丸善プラネット株式会社
　　〒101-0051　東京都千代田区神田神保町二丁目17番
　　電話（03）3512-8516
　　https://maruzenplanet.hondana.jp
発売所　丸善出版株式会社
　　〒101-0051　東京都千代田区神田神保町二丁目17番
　　電話（03）3512-3256
　　https://www.maruzen-publishing.co.jp

組版　　株式会社オメガ・コミュニケーションズ
印刷・製本　富士美術印刷株式会社

ISBN　978-4-86345-579-5　C 3037